# Belsen

In April and May 1945, Belsen concentration camp was liberated and entered Western consciousness for the first time through unprecedented and disturbing images. Tens of thousands lost their lives in the months before liberation. *Belsen: The liberation of a concentration camp* by Joanne Reilly examines British responses to the liberation of Belsen and its importance as a landmark in British history and ideas about the Holocaust.

*Belsen: The liberation of a concentration camp* re-evaluates the place of Belsen in the 'Final Solution' and distinguishes it from other concentration camps. The author includes survivor testimony and sources to show both the liberation experience and the politics of the immediate postwar world. The chaos of Germany in general was reflected in Belsen a hundred-fold. When the camp was liberated, the inmates, Jews, Poles, political prisoners and a small number of Sinti and Romany prisoners, were found dying of typhus, exhaustion, and mostly from hunger.

By examining Belsen's particular place in the Holocaust, as well as Anglo-Jewish and popular responses in the media, the author provides the context for Western reactions to concentration camps and analyses descriptions of Britain's part in the Second World War. She argues that Belsen played a key part in postwar perceptions of Nazism, becoming a symbol of the righteousness of the British war effort and even a justification of 'saturation' bombing of German cities. She also discusses distortions in the representations of Belsen and misconceptions about its purpose.

**Joanne Reilly** is Education and Outreach Officer at the Wiener Library.

# Belsen

The liberation of a concentration camp

Joanne Reilly

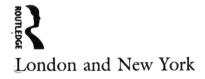

London and New York

First published 1998
by Routledge
11 New Fetter Lane, London EC4P 4EE

Simultaneously published in the USA and Canada
by Routledge
29 West 35th Street, New York, NY 10001

Typeset in Galliard by
BC Typesetting, Bristol

Printed and bound in Great Britain by
Mackays of Chatham plc, Chatham, Kent

*British Library Cataloguing in Publication Data*
A catalogue record for this book is available from the British Library

*Library of Congress Cataloging in Publication Data*
Reilly, Joanne
    Belsen: the liberation of a concentration camp/Joanne Reilly.
        p.      cm.
    Includes bibliographical references and index.
    1. Bergen-Belsen (Concentration camp).  2. World War, 1939–1945-
-Concentration camps–Liberation–Germany.  3. Holocaust, Jewish
(1939–1945)–Public opinion.  4. Public opinion–Great Britain.
5. Great Britain–Ethnic relations.  I. Title.
    D805.A1Z85  1998                                        97-20026

ISBN 0–415–13827–2

# Contents

# Acknowledgements

I gratefully acknowledge the valuable help provided by the following institutions and their staff: Bergen-Belsen Memorial Centre, Germany; British Library National Sound Archive, London; Colindale Newspaper Library, London; Contemporary Medical Archives Centre, Wellcome Institute, London; Central Zionist Archive, Jerusalem; Greater London Record Office; Imperial War Museum, London (and especially Paul Kemp for his kind assistance); Institute of Historical Research, University of London; Keele Photographic Library, University of Keele; Manchester Jewish Museum (in particular, Bill Williams); Mass-Observation Archive, University of Sussex; Parkes Library and the University of Southampton Archives (with special thanks to Jenny Ruthven, Chris Woolgar and the archive staff); Public Record Office, London; Wiener Library, London; Yad Vashem, Jerusalem.

The funding for the research on which this book is based (1990–93) was provided by the University of Southampton Archive Studentship Scheme, of which I was the first recipient. This type of doctoral funding scheme, linked to an archive collection rather than a raft of teaching commitments, is a rarity, today even more than then, and I feel privileged to have benefited from it. In addition, I would like to gratefully acknowledge a monetary prize awarded by the Richard Newitt Fund, University of Southampton, which allowed me to visit archives in Israel, and a further grant given by the Holocaust Education Trust, London which funded me through the final stages of writing the original thesis. Thanks also to the judging panels of the Wellington Prize at Southampton University and the Fraenkel Prize in Contemporary History for recognising my work as worthy of merit in 1995. To receive one prize was a surprise, to say the least, to receive two prizes in one year was a real honour.

Several people have read the manuscript in its various forms and I would like to thank Geoffrey Alderman, David Cesarani, Adrian Harvey, John Oldfield and Tony Kushner for their invaluable comments and suggestions for improvement. Thanks also must go to Jenny Overton as copy-editor, for her exceptional contribution to the final text, and indeed, to all the staff who have worked on the book at Routledge for their patience in seeing it through to the end.

I have never had any desire or ambition to publish a book, let alone one on such a subject as this, and I cannot answer easily inevitable enquiries as to how it has come about. I am, however, able to point to four influential people, without whose inspiration and encouragement it could not have happened. First, Martin Brownlee, the type of teacher that all schools deserve to employ, a teacher whose energy and innovation gave me a passion for the discipline of history that will never leave me. Second, Colin Richmond, whose recent early retirement from Keele University is a loss to all future students, who will miss the benefits of his refreshing unconventionality and belief in challenging education. It was he, an expert in medieval history, who offered a second-year university course on the Holocaust when so few other British university lecturers thought it imperative and he who taught the subject so absorbingly that I was encouraged to study further. Third, to Tony Kushner, who was a superb doctoral supervisor to an insecure novice researcher and who remains a good friend. More than generous with his time, he provided expert help and encouraging comments at all the right moments. I will always remember and appreciate the unequivocal confidence he held in my ability to complete a doctoral project. Finally, I owe my greatest debt to Adrian Harvey who has supported me in innumerable ways during the long process of producing this monograph. Only he will share my relief when the doctoral thesis is tangibly a book – a book to be placed on a shelf, inconspicuous in our lives, thought of only occasionally.

With love, and as a small token of my thanks for all they have given to me, this book is dedicated to my parents and to John.

# Abbreviations

| | |
|---|---|
| AJA | Anglo-Jewish Association |
| AJDC | American Joint Distribution Committee |
| ASY | Adath Sheerith Yisrael |
| BLA | British Liberation Army |
| BOD | Board of Deputies |
| CBF | Central British Fund |
| CCG | Control Commission for Germany |
| CJC | Central Jewish Committee (of the Liberated Jews in the British zone) |
| CJG | Committee for Jews in Germany |
| CRREC | Chief Rabbi's Religious Emergency Council |
| DP | Displaced Person/s |
| Gestapo | Geheime Staatspolizei (secret police) |
| HMG | His Majesty's Government |
| IRO | International Refugees Organisation |
| IWM | Imperial War Museum |
| JCRA | Jewish Committee for Relief Abroad |
| JRC | Jewish Relief Committee |
| JRU | Jewish Relief Units |
| JTA | Jewish Telegraphic Agency |
| MO | Mass-Observation |
| NSDAP | National Socialist German Workers Party |
| PW and DP | Prisoners of War and Displaced Persons Division |
| QA | nurse from QAIMNS |
| QAIMNS | Queen Alexandra's Imperial Military Nursing Service |
| SA | Sturm Abteilung (storm-troops unit) |
| SAS | Special Air Service |
| SHAEF | Strategic Headquarters Allied Expeditionary Force |
| SS | Schutzstaffel (Nazi elite corps) |
| UN | United Nations |
| UNRRA | United Nations Relief and Rehabilitation Administration |
| VE | Victory in Europe |
| WJC | World Jewish Congress |
| WVHA | Economic Administration of the SS, Main Office |

# Introduction

Bergen-Belsen was the first concentration camp after Buchenwald to be liberated by the Western Allies and the only intact major camp to be liberated by the British Army. In April and May 1945 the British people were exposed to an unrivalled amount of information on the German concentration camps; Belsen, in particular, entered British consciousness for the first time through the unprecedented and disturbing images of the newly liberated camp. At no time in the previous four years had the press given to the extermination centres in Poland anything approaching the coverage and comment as they now gave to the camps exposed in Germany. Belsen, along with Buchenwald, dominated conversation and the newspaper letter pages. Wireless broadcasts, newspaper reports and newsreels triggered a wave of genuine shock and marked horror across the whole country. Many have never forgotten the feelings evoked in them on seeing the newsreel footage of Belsen for the first time.

For the past fifty years the liberation of Belsen and the disclosure of the evil of the Nazi regime have remained an important landmark in the collective memory of British society, passed from the postwar generation to the next, both of the war in general and the horrors of Nazism in particular. A new British national identity was forged during the Second World War, that of a small but united, and inherently good, nation standing alone against the evil which had overtaken the Continent. Only Britain, of the belligerent European nations, resisted capitulation and collaboration. And it was the British who marched triumphantly through northern Europe liberating the oppressed people they found there. How fitting, continues the myth, that a British unit should have liberated a Nazi camp that was to expose the worst excesses of the Nazi regime. The liberation of Bergen-Belsen was in keeping with this perceived national identity and mission and reinforced the division between good and evil as represented by victor and conquered. Belsen is 'our' camp and has become a symbol of the righteousness of the British war effort.

Yet, this account of Britain's part in the Second World War is distorted. Belsen – that is, what Belsen represented – both aided in the distortion and was a victim of it. The scenes of barbarity relayed from Belsen shocked the world. They also presented Britain with a convenient and unquestionable reason for having fought the war. The lone and valiant effort had been vindicated.

Furthermore, as the evil nature of Nazism was patently apparent, 'so the good-
ness of the Allies could be assumed'. The less glorious aspects of the British war
effort were easily laid aside (and many are yet to be fully investigated). One, the
'saturation' bombing of German cities, has even been absolved in the light of
Belsen.[1]

The fact that Belsen, a camp with an unusually high percentage of Jewish
survivors, was held up as the vindication of the whole war is ironic. The British
government strenuously resisted particularising the Jewish plight and any notion
that it might be fighting a 'Jews' war'.[2] The Jewish character of Belsen was not
highlighted in April 1945; the experience of the camps was universalised. Along
with the liberation of Paris and of Berlin, the liberation of Belsen came to represent the restoration of freedom to Europe and all her citizens. For the liberators,
the liberation was remembered as an enduring and disturbing and collective
British experience. And as far as they were concerned, they encountered and
largely overcame in Belsen not a particularly Jewish tragedy but a human one.
Since the war, and with the gradual realisation of the full implications of the
Nazis' racial policies, Belsen has been integrated into a popular if distorted
British view of the 'Final Solution'. The impact of the liberation of the German
concentration camps, and the impact of the realities of the 'Final Solution' with
its 6 million dead, did not strike British society simultaneously. The latter only
really followed after the Nuremberg War Crimes Tribunal (November 1945–
October 1946) and is still ongoing. As a consequence, the British have had a
false idea about the history of the Belsen camp. The scenes remembered from
the Belsen newsreels filmed in 1945 have been merged with 'facts' since learned
about the 'Final Solution'. Thus, to the postwar generation Belsen has become
synonymous with the extermination centres, with gas chambers, and only then
with the Jewish tragedy.

The confusion of Belsen with extermination camps like Treblinka and
Birkenau has been pervasive even in contemporary Britain. In colourful, popular
books and encyclopedias relating to the war the myth of Belsen is reinforced. In
the *Encyclopedia of World War II*, reprinted in London in 1990, the subject of
the Holocaust receives nineteen lines. An extract runs thus:

> After the outbreak of World War II the Nazis began to set up concentration
> camps in occupied countries and to set up the campaign against the Jews. . . .
> After the Wannsee Conference (January 1942) it was decided to implement
> the 'Final Solution', the killing of all the Jews, and special extermination
> camps were built at Auschwitz, Sobibor, Belsen, Chelmno, Treblinka and
> other places. These camps were run by the SS and had mass gassing instal-
> lations and body disposal furnaces.[3]

The editor's claim to be concerned with facts is cast into doubt by this passage.
It should be stated here that Belsen was not in an occupied country, it was not
an extermination camp comparable with Treblinka and it did not have a mass
gassing installation. It might be argued that such confusion arises partly from
the attempt to deal with such an immense subject as the Holocaust in a very

general overview of all aspects of the Second World War. Indeed, arguments about whether, in such cases, the Holocaust should be included tokenistically or left out altogether are ongoing.[4] Nevertheless, the point remains that when such inaccuracies find their way into print, they serve no useful purpose so far as Holocaust education is concerned.

The Belsen myth is not only fostered in popular writing. The British academic establishment has also been at fault in presenting the history of Belsen in an erroneous light. In 1992, *The Times Higher Education Supplement*, the major newspaper for university educationalists in Britain, illustrated a review article – of two books dealing with Nazi Germany – with the now infamous image linked with the Auschwitz-Birkenau camp: three sets of railway tracks in the foreground of the picture converge at a long single-storey building and pass under a central archway, with a guard tower overhead, out of the camp. This was the 'ramp' where thousands of prisoners were unloaded from the trains from all over Europe. In *The Times Higher* article the caption under the picture read: 'The gates of hell: the entrance to Belsen concentration camp'. A similar mistake printed in the *Observer* carried with it a certain irony. In reviewing a book which attempted 'to challenge head-on the revisionist lie that the gas chambers were a figment of the Jewish imagination', Richard Overy (or the editor) tells the reader: 'Much of the evidence [in the book under review] comes from the experiments with gassing long before the formal extermination camps – Treblinka, Sobibor, Belsen, Birkenau – were constructed.' Here again, Belsen is included in a list of extermination centres which were specifically constructed and installed with gassing installations in 1942 in order to implement the 'Final Solution'. As we shall see, Belsen was not built until 1943 and then, it was for a very specific purpose which actually defied the extermination policy.[5]

It may seem extraneous to highlight these seemingly minor misunderstandings. Belsen, after all, was a part of the Nazi concentration camp system, and could be described as a death camp in view of the thousands of people who lost their lives there. On the contrary, it is argued here, the fact that such mistakes happen is indicative of the relationship between British society and the Holocaust. It is important that we get the details correct not only from the point of view of the history of the Belsen camp, but also for a more consequential reason: to protect against the danger of Holocaust denial. If it is commonly believed that the Belsen camp held gas chambers in which hundreds of thousands of people were murdered when in fact it did not, then the manner in which such information could be used by an individual attempting to prove the 'Final Solution' as fictitious, is obvious.

Historians who have taken an interest in British attitudes to the Holocaust during the war have posited that the present lack of understanding in British society has its roots in wartime attitudes.[6] Britain's lack of proximity to the implementation of the 'Final Solution' in Europe, it has been argued, is not an explanation for the inability of the British public during the war to grasp and believe exactly what was happening to the Jews of Europe and the true nature of Nazi anti-semitism. In the early 1940s the British press printed

accurate details about the 'Final Solution' and British society had the opportunity to assimilate reliable information on the extermination, almost as it
happened. Yet, whether because the information was psychologically incomprehensible or dismissed as exaggerated propaganda, it has been argued that the
British perception of the Nazis' atrocities remained confined to the image of
the concentration camps of the 1930s until after the end of the war. Thus
when the British gave consideration to Nazi atrocities, they thought not of
the specially constructed gassing installations of Treblinka and Birkenau and
thus the systematic extermination of the Jewish people, but rather of the
camps such as Dachau and Buchenwald which were constructed in the 1930s
for the purpose of detaining in the main, but not exclusively, political prisoners
and dissenting voices in the Nazi state. This enduring perception, at the popular
level, has simply not received the critical censure it deserved in Britain over the
past fifty years.

It should be stressed that the number of British historians working on the
study of the Holocaust has always been very few and the number working on
British links with the Holocaust even smaller. The implementation of the
'Final Solution' was carried out a long way from British soil and British citizens
are not commonly associated with it. Perhaps this is the reason British historians
have shied away from the subject. Certainly, over the past three decades they
seem to have been happy to leave research to their colleagues abroad in America,
Israel and Germany as somehow more their territory; it is not, as George Steiner
put it, 'our patch'.[7] Furthermore, the neglect of the subject at an academic level
has been reflected in British society as a whole, in the level of general knowledge
and awareness about the Holocaust and, until recently, in the shamefully poor
treatment of the subject in schools and even more so universities in Britain.
Non-British historians of the Holocaust, meanwhile, have tended to refer to
Britain only in terms of the lack of a rescue operation executed by the British
government.

One of the first attempts to examine the relationship between Britain and the
Holocaust was Andrew Sharf's *The British Press and the Jews under Nazi Rule*.
Sponsored by the Institute of Race Relations in London and published in
1964, this book offered a critical perspective on the policy of the British government towards the rescue of European Jewry. Yet Sharf was based in Israel,
attached to the Yad Vashem Institute. British historians chose not to take up
the debate on the Holocaust and presented no further research on the subject
until the 1970s. Several studies on British responses to the Holocaust have
appeared in the last twenty years or so. Initially, research work was concerned
with the political and diplomatic response of the British government to the refugee crisis and the issue of rescue during the Nazi era. The work by A.J. Sherman
and Bernard Wasserstein opened the debate in the 1970s, examining the pre-war
years and the war years respectively. In 1981 Martin Gilbert's book *Auschwitz
and the Allies* examined the British and American responses together, and
more recently Louise London has provided a new perspective on British immigration control during the Holocaust period. Tony Kushner's *The Holocaust*

*and the Liberal Imagination* (1994) complements these political studies by providing us with a social and cultural history of the Nazi era, the Holocaust and the period beyond. Looking at popular as well as governmental reactions to the Holocaust in Britain (and America), this work seeks to depart from the purely top-down approach common in the previous historiography.[8]

Kushner has not been alone in his appreciation of the fact that we cannot hope to understand responses to the Holocaust without reference to popular opinion, to the work of interest groups and to the experience of the individuals concerned, the refugees and survivors. The last decade has seen a burgeoning of interest in the critical study of the Anglo-Jewish community and, in particular, Richard Bolchover's book *British Jewry and the Holocaust* (1993) examines the Anglo-Jewish response to the catastrophe. This theme has also been developed by Geoffrey Alderman in his *Modern British Jewry* (1992). On the experience of refugees and survivors two works have predominated, that by Marion Berghahn on German-Jewish refugees from the Third Reich and another by Anton Gill which investigated the impact of the Holocaust on the life of the survivors, the way in which they have come to terms with their memories and the reaction they met from the societies in which they tried to rebuild their lives.[9] The universal nature of the implications of the Holocaust for twentieth-century culture and society should mean that British academics are not precluded from studying the subject. It is not necessary for scholars to justify an interest in the Holocaust by finding a British 'link' – the concentration camp on Alderney or the British prisoners in Auschwitz, for example, although such studies do need to be researched. Nevertheless, this book, *Belsen: the Liberation of a Concentration Camp*, is based on an important connection. Belsen was liberated by the British in 1945 and it was largely British soldiers and British reporters who transmitted the descriptions and impressions of the camp to the British people and the world beyond. These images had a profound effect on the British and have dominated the way in which many British people have considered the Holocaust, from 1945 to the present day. One purpose of the book is to unravel the myth and memory surrounding the camp and show the detailed history of Britain and Belsen (which continued to exist as a Displaced Persons' camp from 1945 to 1950).

This study thus forms part of a growing body of historical work on British responses to the Holocaust. The research presented here contributes to all three historiographical approaches outlined above – using political and grassroot sources in addition to survivor testimony – and examines both the liberation experience and the politics of the immediate postwar world through the prism of the Bergen-Belsen camp. If the study of British responses to the Holocaust in general has been relatively neglected, this is even more true of the liberation period and the last few months of the war as a whole. Yehuda Bauer in an article on the death marches in the final stages of the war has commented on the lack of detailed research in this area.[10] Surprisingly few historians have treated the final days of the death camps in any detail and until recently the subject of liberation has been largely ignored by scholars. With the growing recognition of the importance of eye-witness testimony to the history of the period, however (together with the realisation that, fifty years on, the time needed to collect this testimony is running out), there has been greater emphasis on interviewing men and women who were in any way connected with the camps.

In America, this has included the liberators. In 1985 Robert Abzug published his book *Inside the Vicious Heart* which sought to describe the experience of GIs and other American witnesses involved in (and deeply affected by) the liberation of the German camps. He was able to draw on a number of oral history collections in America which included liberator testimony. In 1981 the United States Holocaust Memorial Council organised a conference to bring the liberators – military and medical personnel and war correspondents – together with the liberated in order to share their experiences. The proceedings from the conference were published in 1987.[11]

The first researched work on the liberation period came in 1990 in the rather disappointing form of Professor Jon Bridgman's book *The End of the Holocaust*. A short, poorly referenced monograph, it forms an introduction to the subject but succeeds in indicating the gaps in the historiography rather than trying to fill them. This book too originated from an American university. In Britain, what limited interest there has been in the liberation period has rather surprisingly been generated by the Imperial War Museum, renowned for its *lack* of emphasis on the Holocaust rather than as a leader in the field. In fact, the establishment at the museum, in 1991, of a new permanent exhibition on the relief of Belsen marked an attempt to incorporate material on the Holocaust into the collection for the first time. The various archive departments in the museum now have a substantial collection of documents, testimony and film which deal with the liberation of Belsen. To coincide with the opening of the exhibition a book of eye-witness accounts was published.[12] In 1995 the fiftieth anniversary commemorations of the liberation of the camps generated some further interest in the process of liberation.[13]

Yet, the liberation experience, and particularly that of the British liberators, remains a neglected area in historical research. Military historians of the Second World War have not viewed the liberation of the Nazi camps as particularly significant against the decisive military manoeuvres which led to VE day. Historians of the Holocaust have recognised the importance of the liberators' accounts in finally convincing the world of the Nazis' crimes, but generally have not felt it necessary to examine the impact of this testimony further. The research presented in this book on the British liberation of Belsen attempts to assess the impact of the ordeal on the individuals concerned but also to question whether the experience brought them and, on a wider scale, British society, nearer to an understanding of the Jewish tragedy.

The book not only examines the period of relief work in Belsen but concentrates also on the rehabilitation of Jewish Displaced Persons who established a community in Belsen whilst the political controversy over the future of Palestine unfolded. The subject of the Jewish DP communities in Europe after the war is another area that has been dominated by American and Israeli researchers. At the same time they have tended to concentrate their studies on the American zone of occupation in postwar Germany. It is true that the largest Jewish community was to be found in the American zone but this does not explain the complete lack of attention afforded to the significant communities in Belsen and elsewhere in the British zone.[14] Indeed, as we shall see, a study of the Belsen Jewish community, living as they did under the control of the very government that held their future in its hands, adds an essential dimension to the history of the period.

Before moving on to examine the postwar links between Britain and Belsen in detail, it is crucial first to understand the development of the concentration camp system. The concentration camps played a pivotal role in the National Socialist system of government from its inception; these camps, and later the extermination camps, constituted the extreme of the 'new order' which the National Socialists had devised for Europe.[15] Thus we now turn to a brief summary of the events which preceded the implementation of the 'Final Solution' and provide a history of the role of the Belsen camp in the Nazi regime.

# I

What follows – a general outline of the development of the camp system in the Third Reich – is by no means an exhaustive narrative; the review is intended as no more than a brief introduction to the subject in order to place the establishment and role of the Bergen-Belsen concentration camp in its historical context.[16]

The major domestic aim of Nazism was the creation of a new and unified national community – *Volksgemeinschaft* – based on Teutonic myth and the methodology of nineteenth-century race theory. Nazi ideology sought to rid German society of its perceived impurities and thus persecuted those who did not conform with the new ideal: of Aryan race, 'genetically healthy', 'socially efficient' and politically and ideologically reliable. These people, of the same 'Blood, Race and Soil', would together restore Germany to greatness. Ideological enemies and those classed as 'asocials' (including, for example, communists, trade unionists and Jehovah's Witnesses) were regarded as a threat to the purity of the *Volk* and in need of political re-education by means of a period in a detention centre or concentration camp. Some groups, in particular Jews, Gypsies, Slavs and Blacks, it was claimed, were fundamentally inferior and beyond re-education. Jews and (as they were often linked together with communism by the Nazis) Jewish Bolshevism were portrayed in vicious Nazi propaganda as the root of all evil.[17]

In order to facilitate their political programme the Nazis required machinery far removed from the bureaucracy and judiciary inherited from the Weimar Republic. Thus, immediately upon the proclamation of Hitler as *Reichskanzler* (State Chancellor) in 1933, a series of decrees effectively gave legal authorization to arbitrary and unlimited detention. In particular, the Law for the Protection of the People and the State, 28 February 1933, served as a base for 'protective custody', a term adapted to meet the requirements of the Nazi regime. Initially, members of the German Communist Party, the Social Democrats and trade unionists, as the most vocal political opposition to the Nazis, suffered most as a result of the decrees. By the end of 1933 there were almost 30,000 people in 'protective custody', many the victims of unofficial or so-called 'wild' arrests initiated and controlled by the SS (*Schutzstaffel*), or Nazi elite corps, the Gestapo (*Geheime Staatspolizei*), or secret police, and the SA (*Sturm Abteilung*), or storm-troops unit, the brown-shirted armed wing of the National Socialist German Workers Party (NSDAP). In March 1933 the Enabling Act allowed Hitler to pass laws without the consent of Parliament. Henceforth, the formation of new political parties and the existence of trade unions became illegal.[18]

In effect the 1933 promulgations laid the ground for the establishment of the first concentration camps. The growth of the camp system was linked inextricably with the consolidation and stabilisation of the executive within the National Socialist regime. The realisation came very early that the individual or the organisation who exercised authority through the camp system would also command a considerable amount of power within the state. Thus in 1933 many rival camps were established independently by the SA and the SS throughout Germany. In the interest of cost-cutting and exercising a more effective control over the many scattered detention centres, consolidation (and hence, a power struggle) was inevitable. Eventually, prisoners in protective custody were concentrated into a small number of camps, the largest of which was Dachau, located near Munich in Bavaria and established under the authority of Himmler, the police president, in March 1933. By summer 1934, Himmler, then chief of police in the German states, had gained control of all of these camps. The SS, having liquidated many of the SA leaders, were revealed as an integral element of the Nazi state. They strengthened their own position within the German police network, and gained official recognition for the newly reorganised concentration camps. Furthermore, the original rationale of the camps – to provide 'political education' – was disposed of and instead the prisoners were subject to torture and hard labour.[19]

As the 1930s progressed and further restrictive legislation was passed, the range of persons liable to imprisonment in the concentration camps increased. In the years preceding the outbreak of war, 165,000 people were interned and in 1939 the six major camps in the Reich – Dachau, Sachsenhausen, Mauthausen, Flössenburg, Buchenwald and Ravensbrück (the camp for women) – held over 21,000 internees.[20] From 1936 the camps were linked with Germany's rearmament and military preparations, and new camps were located with a view to using forced labour in huge construction projects. Prior to 1938, in addition to political prisoners, these camps also held Jehovah's Witnesses, homosexuals, criminals, the 'work-shy' and some Jews.

Anti-semitism was an important facet of Nazi propaganda throughout the 1930s and 400 anti-Jewish laws were passed by the Third Reich.[21] Throughout the decade the civil and human rights of the German Jewish population (or at least those arbitrarily defined as such in the racial laws) were systematically eroded. In 1935 the Nuremberg Laws deprived German Jews of their citizenship and proclaimed marriage and sexual relations between Jews and Aryans illegal. Jews lost their right to vote, were removed from schools, universities and certain professions and in 1938 were dispossessed of any business interests. After the outbreak of the war the position of Jewish people within German society deteriorated further. After a series of legal measures, for example, it became illegal for a Jew to own a radio or a telephone and all were forced to wear a prominent yellow star of David on their clothing.

The year 1938 proved to be a watershed in the treatment of the Jewish population. In March the *Anschluss*, the occupation of Austria, brought a further 185,000 Jews into the Third Reich; they were subject to the German anti-Jewish laws immediately. On the night of 9–10 November, following the murder of a German embassy official in Paris by a Jewish student, the Gestapo ordered that reprisals be taken against the German Jewish community. In a night of extreme violence across Germany known as *Kristallnacht* ('Crystal Night'), synagogues were burned, Jewish shops and houses destroyed and many individuals killed.[22] An estimated 31,000 Jews were placed in concentration camps following the pogrom. Many were subsequently released but only on agreeing to emigrate, leaving any assets behind; 1,000 are thought to have lost their lives. For the first time, Jewish prisoners became a significant percentage of those incarcerated in the camps. What is more, they were imprisoned for no other reason than being Jewish. The violence and ferocity of *Kristallnacht* shocked the German population in a way previous anti-Jewish action had not. Yet following the outrage, the position of the Jew in German society became only further eroded as thousands were forced to leave the country. Those Jews who remained in Germany at the outbreak of war undoubtedly faced an uncertain future. None, however, could have been prepared for what was to come.

Following less than two years of total war, the National Socialist regime was in a position by 1941 to begin the systematic murder of the Jewish population in Europe.[23] In Poland the Jewish population had already been subjected to tremendous deprivation. Those who were not killed were forced to move into overcrowded ghettos where rations were at starvation levels. They were joined by Jews from Germany, Austria and Czechoslovakia; thousands of people died from disease and malnutrition.[24] In 1941 the Soviet Union was invaded and the pattern set in Poland was repeated. The murder in the Soviet Union, however, was on a much larger scale. *Einsatzgruppen*, or killing squads, preceded the *Wehrmacht* (Germany's conventional armed forces) into Russia and the Baltic states, shooting more than 1 million Jews in under three months.[25] Nevertheless, this method of extermination was thought to be inefficient and another solution to the 'Jewish problem' was sought.

Hence, the 'Final Solution' – the planned extermination of the remaining Jewish people in Europe in specially built death camps – emerged as a policy. Gassing installations were built at Chelmno, Belzec, Sobibor, Treblinka – camps acting solely as killing centres – and also at Majdanek and Auschwitz, where there were also 'conventional' concentration camps but on a massive and more brutal scale, on the same site.[26] The Jews in the Polish ghettos and large numbers from the communities in western Europe were transported in their millions to these centres and murdered.

When discussing the instruments of Nazi repression it is possible to talk of a concentration camp system, however *ad hoc* the development of that system was. This might seem to imply that there was a archetypal camp which set the pattern for the rest. In reality, it is very difficult to compare the camps in such a simplistic way. The war effort demanded a massive increase in the number of people who were herded into the camps. Additional labour camps and transit camps were established in the occupied territories by the local SS and police leaders, often independently of the existing camp network. There were hundreds of Nazi camps, sub-camps and factories employing slave labour and one was rarely exactly the same as another. This remained the case even after February 1942 when the organisation of all the various camps was finally consolidated and centralised under the SS Economic Administration Main Office (WVHA), headed by SS General Pohl. The regime and the conditions faced by the prisoners could vary enormously. Moreover, camps did not remain static but developed and changed as the National Socialist regime required. Initially, the Auschwitz camp, for example, served as a prison for dissident Poles. Theresienstadt, in Czechoslovakia, was established as a 'model' camp in order to mislead the International Red Cross and public opinion as to the reality of conditions in Nazi camps in general. In fact, conditions were much worse than the façade suggested and thousands of people were transported from there to Auschwitz-Birkenau.[27]

There were also transit camps, of which Westerbork in the Netherlands is an example. Here, the Dutch Jewish population was collected together before being transported to the 'east', the euphemism for the death camps. Of all the camps, labour and prison camps were the most prevalent, such as that at Mittelbau-Dora in Germany, a satellite of Buchenwald. In these camps the type of work, the conditions and the regime could vary from one to the next but they served the same end: to gain the maximum reward in terms of human labour for the minimum economic expenditure. The real costs were paid in ineffable human suffering. The roles of a camp could be conflicting, as best exemplified in Auschwitz. As the German war machine came under increasing pressure, the need for forced labour in order to increase productivity became greater. At the same time, however, the machinery of the 'Final Solution' demanded more victims. In Auschwitz, then, when the train loads of Jews arrived, selections were made on the platform: the children, the aged and those unfit for work were sent immediately to the gas chambers; those who were relatively fit and healthy were allowed a temporary reprieve, instead to be worked to death for the benefit of the German war machine. The concentration camps, those other than the extermination camps, invariably had in common cruelty and torture, punishingly hard work and starvation rations. Nevertheless, it would be very difficult to define the 'typical' camp.

In a report dated 15 August 1944, the WVHA stated that the number of concentration camp inmates was 524,286 (compared with 224,000 a year earlier and despite terrific mortality rates).[28] This figure continued to increase. German troops were retreating on all fronts and fervent attempts were made to accelerate arms production. More workers were forcibly recruited and employed in underground factories. Furthermore, in the last months of the war thousands of prisoners, in order that they did not fall into Russian hands, were marched from the camps in the east towards concentration camps in Germany.

Before the enemy approached, Himmler had ordered that the 'Operation Reinhard' killing centres, their job complete, be dismantled and no trace left. Killing had stopped first in Chelmno in March 1943 (although it was resumed temporarily in June and July) and the camp was liquidated in January 1945. Treblinka, Sobibor and Belzec were destroyed in the autumn of 1943. During the latter part of 1944 only one camp was still operating at full capacity: Auschwitz. On 25 November, Himmler ordered the dismantling of the killing stations there too, and on 17 January 1945, he ordered a full-scale evacuation of those prisoners still remaining. When the Russians reached the camp on 27 January 1945, they found only 2,000 inmates, the majority Jews and most too ill to move; the SS guard had fled, having failed to destroy all traces of the camp. Camps within German territory were evacuated in the face of advancing Soviet troops. In February, Gross Rosen in Silesia was evacuated and the prisoners moved further west to Buchenwald. Forced marches of prisoners also left Sachsenhausen and Ravensbrück.[29]

The threat of Russian arrival, then, did not result in the emancipation of thousands of prisoners, but rather precipitated the death marches of the winter of 1944–5. Prisoners were moved in their thousands on long marches lasting several days or weeks in freezing conditions and without adequate clothing or food. Those who collapsed were shot or left to die where they lay. Many were loaded on to trains but their lot was hardly easier. People were packed tightly, often into open cattle cars with no sanitary provision, and taken on long journeys constantly threatened by Allied bombing raids. Helmut Krausnick estimates that at least a third of the more than 700,000 concentration camp inmates recorded in January 1945, lost their lives on the death marches and in the catastrophically overcrowded reception camps in the months before the end of the war.[30]

## II

Bergen-Belsen was one such reception camp, situated north of Celle, near Hanover in north-west Germany. Belsen is a camp which, for people around the world, and perhaps nowhere more so than in Britain, provided the most vivid visual images to encapsulate Nazi barbarity. The camp was liberated by the British on 15 April 1945. In contrast to the extermination centres in the east, which when liberated by the Russians were all but deserted, Belsen held an estimated 60,000 emaciated and dangerously ill people crowded together in frightful conditions. The overwhelming ignominy revealed by the liberation of Belsen was fixed in the public consciousness when countless photographs and reports detailing the horror of the place were relayed to the outside world.

Few historians writing on Belsen have failed to point out the irony of the fact that following two years' existence as a relatively lenient camp for privileged prisoners it should have become in April 1945 the most representative example of the evils of the National Socialist regime. Eberhard Kolb, writer on the wartime history of Belsen, believes it is only an apparent paradox, however, and advocates that the development of Belsen from a detention camp into the 'inferno' where thousands lost their lives in 1945, was not inadvertent but reveals something of the mentality behind the concentration camp system. In his work, Kolb seeks to show that the Bergen-Belsen camp was firmly integrated into the Nazi system of oppression.[31] In fact, at no point in the camp's history could conditions have been described as satisfactory; at best, life in Belsen was relatively endurable, at worst it was totally insufferable. The evolution of the camp perhaps merely illustrates that Bergen-Belsen was typical in its untypicalness.

Nevertheless, Belsen from its inception did hold a particularly unique position in the camp system. It was established, unlike any other camp, in order to house a special group of Jewish prisoners who, it was envisaged, might be utilised in a diplomatic exchange plan. During 1941 and 1942 negotiations took place between the British and German governments which resulted in the exchange of Palestinian nationals, trapped in Europe by the onset of hostilities, for a number of German citizens, primarily a group of Templars, an orthodox Lutheran sect, who years before the war had made their home in Palestine but now wanted to return to Germany. Two successful exchanges were executed in Istanbul with the help of the British Legation in Switzerland and the Jewish Agency in Palestine, the first in December 1941 and the second eleven months later. The precedent was set. In 1942 officials in the German Foreign Office arrived at the idea that further exchanges might be possible, particularly of notable Jews held in Europe. With Himmler's consent, an agreement was reached between the Foreign Office and the SS that 30,000 Jews would be held back from the transports and detained in order that they might be exchanged for German citizens who had been interned by Britain or the United States. Their selection was based on one of three main criteria: those with important connections abroad; those whose fate was of enough concern to outsiders that they could be used to put political or economic pressure on the Allies; and prominent figures in public service.[32]

Himmler ordered the construction of a special camp in order to house these 'exchange Jews' (*Austauschjuden*). The WVHA located a suitable site near Hanover. Attached to a Soviet prisoner-of-war camp, the area given over to the WVHA had been neglected and, during the summer of 1943, 500 slave labourers were brought in to rebuild the camp. They continued to be accommodated in what was named the Prison Camp (*Häftlingslager*), the first of several sub-camps eventually established. Here the prisoners lived in terrible conditions and endured hard labour.[33] The name Bergen-Belsen appeared officially for the first time in a circular in April 1943 and it was initially designated a 'civilian internment camp'. This decision was hastily revised, however, on realising that all civilian internment camps, under the terms of the Geneva Convention, were subject to visits from the international committees. Hence, as Raul Hilberg so sardonically notes, while Belsen by Nazi standards began as a model camp, nevertheless, it could ill afford an inspection by a foreign government.[34]

The first 'exchange Jews' – 2,500 Poles – arrived in Bergen-Belsen in two transports in July 1943 and were housed in isolation in the so-called Special Camp (*Sonderlager*). A year later all except 350 had been deported to Auschwitz. As future arrivals at the camp were to discover, the future in Belsen was no more certain than in any other camp. Many of those sent to their death had held Latin American papers – often simply a letter from a foreign consul guaranteeing citizenship rather than an actual passport. A large number of these papers were probably of dubious quality. The sale of forged documents became a lucrative business in Europe and Gestapo agents were known to be involved; certainly, an important traffic in Honduran and Paraguayan papers was uncovered in Switzerland. Often even those people who were legally entitled to these papers were forced to pay huge amounts of money to unscrupulous consular representatives who saw an opportunity to make money for themselves.[35]

Those Poles who remained in the Belsen camp held *bona fide* documents. In the summer of 1943 they were joined by 367 Spanish Jews and 74 Greek Jews, all brought from Salonika. Though living in Greece, the 367 were Spanish nationals and as such were placed in a new sub-camp, the Neutral Camp (*Neutralenlager*). They were later joined by other small transports of Spanish, Portuguese, Argentinian and Turkish Jews. Conditions here were reasonably good and the prisoners were not subjected to hard labour. In February 1944 the Spanish Jews from Salonika left Belsen for Spain and eventually reached Palestine.[36]

The Greek Jews, meanwhile, were placed in a large section of the camp which became known as the Star Camp (*Sternlager*). Many of these Jews received the dubious honour of becoming camp Kapos and aided the SS in supervising the arrival of future transports to the camp. From the early months of 1944, they were joined by a large number of Dutch 'exchange Jews' deported from the transit camp at Westerbork. The vast majority of Jews at Westerbork, from July 1942 onwards, were sent directly to Auschwitz or Sobibor to be killed. For a small number, however, deportation to the East was deferred. Various government agencies insisted that certain groups be exempted so that, for example, a large number of diamond-cutters were held back from the transports on the order of the Armaments Office of the *Wehrmacht*. Other groups, those who held proof of their status as alien citizens (of a country not under German occupation), or an important connection to an enemy state, together with those people on the so-called 'South America Lists' or the 'Palestine Lists', also gained a temporary reprieve from the transports to Poland.[37]

This latter group were prominent Zionists or people with relatives in Palestine. In late 1942 and 1943 both the Jewish Agency in Palestine and the Jewish Council in Amsterdam were independently compiling lists of prominent Jews known still to be in the Netherlands. Once a name came on file every effort would be made to forward some form of documentation to that individual in the hope that it might save the person from the transports. In Palestine, people with relatives in the Netherlands were becoming increasingly worried for their safety and put pressure on the Jewish Agency to act. The agency entered into complex negotiations with the British authorities in Palestine but as the issue of immigration certificates was limited by strict quotas imposed by the Mandate, this avenue was very restricted. Indeed, at this time the British authorities were concerned with negotiations over another list of actual Palestinian citizens who had been trapped in Europe at the onset of war. As a second-best solution, then, the Jewish Agency agreed to form a register of the Dutch Jews who were known to it and issue documentation to that effect which could be forwarded to Europe and act at least as some form of protection. Copies of the lists were sent to the International Red Cross in Geneva and to the British Colonial Office in London. In addition, as often as possible the Jewish Agency would issue any available immigration certificates to those who were eligible and known to be still alive. Meanwhile, separate lists (although there was sometimes some overlap) were produced by the Jewish Council in Amsterdam, recording individuals in the Netherlands with Palestinian connections. If the Jewish Council was satisfied with the credentials of applicants, they would be issued with 'A' letters (after the leader of the Jewish Council) and their names entered on the provisional Palestine exchange register. All of the names were submitted to the Swiss Legation in Berlin, which was conducting negotiations with the authorities concerned.[38]

By July 1943 there were 1,200 people on the deferment list in Westerbork by virtue of the Palestine exchange scheme alone. Hannah Pick-Goslar's family, for example, had been able to buy Paraguayan citizenship through an uncle in Switzerland (she was required to learn the name of the capital city in case she was asked) but in addition, her father, as leader of Mizrachi in the Netherlands, and the rest of the family were eligible for the 'Palestine Lists'. The 'exchange Jews' continued to live from day to day in Westerbork; by no means was immunity from deportation guaranteed and some people were indeed sent east regardless of any papers they might have. Only in November 1943 were any of the people held back from the transports informed that they should prepare to leave for Bergen-Belsen camp, at that time largely an unknown entity in Westerbork. In fact, the journey was postponed until January 1944 by which time many had lost faith in the belief that an exchange plan would ever be realised. Nevertheless, the first of eight transports left Westerbork on 11 January and by September a total of 3,670 people had been transferred to the Star Camp in Belsen. Thus, the number of exchange prisoners in the Star Camp rose in seven months from under 400 on 1 January 1944 to over 4,000 on 31 July.[39]

A great many of the 'exchange Jews' arrived in family groups and although men and women in the Star Camp were segregated at night, they were allowed to mix during the day.[40] Work was mandatory in this camp. The prisoners were divided into work parties, the largest of which was the shoe 'commando'. Here the labourers were required to take apart thousands of old pairs of shoes and boots which had been delivered to Belsen from all over Germany as part of a winter relief collection. The reusable leather was to be salvaged and sorted. Men, women and children worked for long hours in filthy conditions, constantly supervised by abusive SS guards. Imprisonment and the withholding of food rations were the punishments for not meeting work quotas. Other commandos were assigned to cutting wood, kitchen or office work, gardening, bricklaying and carpentry, and sorting luggage and personal property as it arrived in the camp. Some jobs were sought after more than others. Those who tended the camp pigsty, for example, were not only able to supplement their own rations with pigswill but, more importantly, they were able to exchange it for other goods. Naturally, kitchen workers were in the best position to steal extra food. On the other hand, the most gruesome task in the camp was undoubtedly that allocated to Arnold Keller and Hans Horowitz. These young men lived and worked in complete isolation and secrecy in a small building separated from the rest of the camp. This was the crematorium. They were required to burn the bodies of the prisoners who died in the camp, having first removed the gold teeth, fillings and anything else of 'value'. In return they received superior rations.[41]

The Star Camp was also known as the 'Albala Camp', after the Greek Jewish elder, Jacques Albala. He headed the Jewish Council which was formed in April 1944 and was invested with the right by the camp authorities to impose punishments on his fellow prisoners. The other council members were drawn from the Greek and Dutch communities. There was even a Jewish court with an appointed judge and lawyer who sentenced prisoners to periods of detention in a cellar for such misdemeanours as stealing.[42]

During the first half of 1944 life was bearable but very basic. Food consisted mainly of coffee, soup, bread and margarine and the staple food, turnip. Hunger was always a problem. Sanitary conditions were primitive and there was no privacy. One section of the camp was converted into a hospital area by the prisoners but in reality there were very few medicaments available and the level of care which could be effectively administered was restricted. Cultural activities were pursued as much as was practicable. Prisoners tried to teach the children formal lessons and more general lectures and discussions were organised. On Fridays they sang Hebrew songs and an effort was made to celebrate the festivals. Life was hard but for the majority faith in the exchange plan provided the strength to go on.[43]

After the Star Camp, another sub-camp was formed in Belsen. Following the military takeover in Hungary in the summer of 1944, the Hungarian Camp (*Ungarnlager*) was established and in July 1,683 Hungarian Jews were brought in. They were treated reasonably well and were not required to work. These people were in fact pawns in complicated negotiations which were taking place between Himmler and Jewish organisations in the later stages of the war; the plan was to attempt to trade these few Jewish lives for money and goods.[44]

Despite the original intentions of the German Foreign Office and the immense bureaucracy involved in implementing the scheme, the actual number of 'exchange Jews' held in Belsen who gained their freedom through genuine exchange was only 358. On 12 July 1944, 222 people from Belsen, together with a smaller number from the Vittel camp in France, reached Palestine in an exchange negotiated between the British and German governments. This was only a small number of the 'exchange Jews' in Belsen; it might have been more had the British been able to locate more German citizens who were suitable for exchange than was ultimately the case. In another exchange, 136 people holding South and Central American papers were taken from Belsen to safety in Switzerland in January 1945.[45] Meanwhile, the majority who were not chosen for exchange began to lose hope. The Belsen exchange camp continued to function yet, during 1944, the site as a whole changed quite dramatically, both in terms of its role and its appearance.

The WVHA office, under Pohl, decided that the Belsen camp was being under-utilised. In March 1944 the Prison Section of Belsen was designated as a reception camp for the sick prisoners from other labour camps and factories under WVHA control. The name given to this sub-camp – a recuperation camp (*Erholungslager*) – proved to be a euphemism. When the first transport of 1,000 men with tuberculosis arrived from Dora in March 1944, no attempt was made to restore them to health. They were placed in empty barracks without blankets, mattresses or hot food and received no medical attention. The high mortality rate in this 'recuperation' camp reflected the conditions.

The evacuation of camps in the east and the movement of thousands of prisoners inside German territory, placed an enormous pressure on the existing concentration camps. The German war machine could no longer afford the existence of a detention centre and Bergen-Belsen was gradually transformed into a concentration camp proper. As we have seen, the conditions in some parts of the camp were very harsh and even the Jews who were there to be exchanged did not live a particularly privileged life. Nevertheless, in 1944 conditions became even worse and the state of *all* the prisoners in Belsen deteriorated, not through hard labour as in many other camps but through neglect. In a matter of months the camp developed into the charnel house we so associate with the liberation of the concentration camps. In the summer of 1944 the camp was expanded with the creation of a women's transit camp. In effect, this was an area of land adjacent to the Star Camp where female forced labourers, transported from camps further east, lived in tents before moving on to the next factory. In the autumn other large transports of women arrived from Auschwitz-Birkenau. As newly erected barracks in the Star Camp were not yet ready, these women, too, were housed in tented accommodation. There were no sanitary arrangements and the sawdust intended to act as mattresses simply soaked into the mud. The tents were no protection from the rain or icy winds and one night a storm ripped them away. The women were then moved into a section of the Star Camp, although a barbed wire fence prevented them from mixing with the other prisoners.[46]

Naturally, along with the prisoners evacuated from Poland, the SS personnel who had administered the death camps were also relocated. Thus, the changing character of Bergen-Belsen was sealed with the arrival in December 1944 of a new commandant, SS Captain Josef Kramer, previously in a position of command at the Auschwitz-Birkenau complex. He and the staff who accompanied him imposed a strict and vicious regime on the camp as a whole. By this time conditions in Bergen-Belsen had deteriorated greatly so that hunger and illness preoccupied the majority of prisoners. The onset of winter only worsened the situation. A punishing twice-daily roll call, where the prisoners had to gather to be counted in often atrocious weather conditions, could last for hours and took many lives. Disease became rife in the camp and eventually it became normal to see dead bodies piling up. Typhus spread like 'a forest fire' in such conditions. In the words of an internee doctor, even the sick bay, 'louse-infected from top to bottom, was a breeding place for typhus and for all our efforts it was impossible to check it'. Other prisoners, apart from the doctors, attempted to help those who became too ill to fend for themselves. Janny Brandes-Brilleslijper joined a cell of Hungarian women who met secretly in the corpse pits knowing the SS would never look for them there. Each woman was assigned a job in the barracks looking after the ill and performing rudimentary operations. They conspired to exploit every opportunity to gain access to extra food rations and medicines.[47]

Belsen held 15,257 prisoners on Kramer's arrival. This number multiplied rapidly, however, as more and more evacuation transports rolled into Bergen railway station, carrying weak and starving prisoners. Prisoners were brought from all over Germany following chaotic routes often targeted by Allied bombing raids. In March Mr Abisch endured a typical journey from Dora to Belsen, with little food and no water, which lasted eight days in a cattle truck covered with tarpaulin. Paul Trepman was one member of a party taken to Belsen from a secret munitions plant in the Harz mountains in March 1945. For six days he and 4,000 others, with no food or room for movement, were hauled along a route which should have taken seven hours. Other prisoners were rounded up in Hanover and Hamburg, where they had been clearing bomb sites or working in factories, and literally dumped in Belsen.[48]

The perimeters of the camp were physically expanded – to encompass a former POW hospital area and the land formerly occupied by the women's tents – yet Belsen could still not accommodate all the new arrivals. Conditions worsened further to an appalling degree. By 31 March 1945 there were 44,060 prisoners in Belsen, yet in that month alone it is thought that over 18,000 people died. An estimated 35,000 people lost their lives in the first four and a half months of 1945, before liberation. Included among them was Anne Frank who died in February, probably of typhus.[49]

The chaos of Germany in general was reflected in Belsen a hundred-fold. Transports of weary and emaciated prisoners arrived at the camp with their SS guards and were turned away. Others were accepted. In the weeks preceding the liberation various transports of prisoners were evacuated to and from the camp, on balance increasing the population. It is thought that 7,000 people were on three trains which left (it is presumed) for Theresienstadt in April. Many of those who left were replaced by prisoners marched on foot from Neuengamme camp, evacuated in the face of advancing British troops. Likewise the Americans were closing in on the area around the Mittelbau-Dora complex and many of the prisoners evacuated from there – over 25,000 – descended on Belsen. These thousands could not possibly have been accommodated in the main camp and were taken to the barracks of a Panzer training school just over a mile away.[50]

When the British liberated Bergen-Belsen on 15 April they found a camp rife with typhus containing over 60,000 emaciated prisoners of all nationalities. Among them were many Jews, Poles and political prisoners and a smaller number of Sinti and Romany prisoners. In the words of one internee, although fewer people died in Bergen-Belsen than in Birkenau, death was more visible: 'In Birkenau entire groups would simply disappear. . . . In Bergen-Belsen . . . you died slowly, from illness, exhaustion, cold, most of them from hunger. . . . In Bergen-Belsen you stared death in the face at every moment.'[51]

## III

This book examines the liberation of Bergen-Belsen from several differing perspectives. The impact that the experience and recollection of this event have had on British society and its view of the Holocaust is a major theme. Chapter 1 deals with the period of the military and medical liberation of Belsen, the initial relief effort and the impact of the experience on the soldiers and medical staff, male and female. The second chapter examines British popular responses to the liberation, the manner in which society received the information on the camps and the way in which this information was interpreted.

In the second half of the book, the scope is broadened beyond the spring of 1945 to a survey of the postwar years and the issues surrounding the lives of the Jewish Displaced Persons in the British zone. Chapter 3 outlines the development of the Displaced Persons' (DPs) camp which was established after the war near Belsen and housed many survivors awaiting transfer from Germany to a new life. Further, this chapter examines British state responses to the liberation of the Jewish DPs and, in particular, focuses on the tensions which existed between the British authorities and the Jews in Belsen, against the background of both the Palestine issue and the early developments in the Cold War. In the penultimate chapter the reaction of the Anglo-Jewish community to the liberation of Belsen is critically examined. Following on from Chapter 3, this discussion also highlights the differing approaches of the various sections of Anglo-Jewish political and religious opinion to the problem of the Jewish DPs in Europe. Finally, in Chapter 5, the theme of liberation is examined once again, this time from the viewpoint of the survivors. The first half of the chapter questions the commonly held notion of the liberation as a period of unqualified rejoicing in the light of survivor testimony, while the second section outlines the growth of community life in the Belsen DP camp. This final chapter, moreover, provides a critique of the Zionist hegemony model which currently dominates the historiography of the Jewish DPs in the postwar period.

# 1 The military and medical liberation

*Until Belsen*[1]

We thought we had seen it all.

Our cheeks bloomed like peaches,
Bright eyes, Quick light movement.
Flashes of scarlet, snow white caps,

We thought we had seen it all.

The London Blitz, bombs, fires, headless corpses,
Screaming children: Yankee Doodle Dandy!

We thought we had seen it all.

Scabies, Lice, and Impetigo, T.B., Polio
And unmentionable V.D.

We thought we had seen it all.

Then France.
Day followed night then another day
Of mangled broken boys.
Irish, Welsh and Scots
Jerries, Poles and French –
They cried in many tongues as needles long and sharp advanced.
Their blood ran cold and so they died.

We thought we had seen it all.

Our souls shrank deep and deeper still,
Until with nowhere else to go, soft hearts
Hardened and cocooned themselves.
Laughter broke like glass over fields and orchards
And from tent to tent.
We tried; we really tried, but some of them died.

We thought we had seen it all.

Until Belsen

There are no words to speak.
We hid within our souls, deep and silent.
We clung together trying to understand,
The smell pervaded the mind and the sights and sounds
Reached those souls buried deep within and for so long
Encased in rock.
Bitter, scalding tears melted the rock
Our hearts were broken.

We had seen it all.

Thus in 1945 did Joy Trindles, a nursing sister with 29th British General Hospital, attempt to encapsulate her war experience and the overarching impact of witnessing the horrors of Bergen-Belsen. The poem acts as a fitting introduction to this first chapter which explores the liberation of Belsen from the viewpoint of those who liberated the camp; the reactions which it provoked in them and the impact of the experience on their lives. Many of the Belsen liberators had experienced the full horrors of war and yet not a single individual was prepared for what they were to encounter at Belsen in April 1945. For numerous men and women the part they played in the relief of the camp proved to be the central milestone, not only of the war, but also of their lives as a whole.

In part, this chapter is concerned with what were some of the earliest contributions to the large body of Holocaust literature which exists today, and yet which have been largely ignored by scholars of the Holocaust: the reports, letters, diaries and memoirs of the Allied liberators which constitute some of the first elementary attempts by those who did not personally experience the Holocaust to articulate a coherent response to the horror that faced them. Joy Trindles ventured a response to her feelings through the medium of poetry and she is successful in depicting the marked contrast between her own terrible experience of war and the even greater barbarity that was the reality of Belsen. What Trindles does not attempt, however, is a description of the actual horror of the place. For that 'there are no words to speak'. When faced with the scale of the atrocity and in dealing with the onus of sheer incomprehension Trindles simply could not find the language. She is not alone in facing such a barrier. In his article on British Holocaust poetry, Jon Harris has highlighted the truism that absolute horrors transcend linguistic description. He points to the fact that the majority of poets themselves feel that they have failed to deal adequately with the tragedy they have attempted to address.[2] The question of the limitation of language, particularly in relation to Holocaust literature, is one which has been the focus of much scholarly attention. As Lawrence Langer has noted, 'The challenge of writing about the Holocaust is stylistic as well as historical – not only to tell what one knows, but also to find an idiom and image for what one envisions'.[3] This simple sentence disguises an almost impossible endeavour; there is fierce academic debate on the question in the artistic sphere of whether this has been achieved, will ever be possible or, indeed, should even be attempted.[4] Diarists, poets and novelists of the Holocaust, survivors and non-survivors, have had fifty years to struggle with the challenge but few are recognised as having triumphed over the intrinsic difficulties and restraints presented by artistic form and language in representing the Holocaust. If after fifty years of articulation the vocabulary with which to convey the essence of the Holocaust experience still eludes the majority of humankind, it is hardly surprising to find that the liberators of the camps encountered tremendous difficulty in locating an appropriate vocabulary to describe the previously unimaginable and incomparable atrocity which they suddenly encountered. Nevertheless, as important eye-witnesses in an era before mass television ownership, they were forced by necessity to find words for what they saw. These words, the substance of army reports, private letters and newspaper articles, informed the world about the concentration camps. The liberators came from a world outside the camps and had to communicate what they experienced in words that would be understood and assimilated by that world.[5] The language and analogies used by them were predictable and inappropriate in describing the camps. Yet no matter how unsuitable we might recognise them to be with regard to our present understanding of the Holocaust, those words set the precedent for future generations to follow. Indeed, we are still largely using the same vocabulary.

Yet, literary analysis, with its strengths and limitations, is not this chapter's sole concern. As James Young states, 'contemporary theory and its often all-consuming vocabulary can obscure as much as it seeks to illuminate'.[6] The chapter presents an historical narrative of the military liberation and subsequent relief of Bergen-Belsen. The manner in which the camp was liberated is briefly examined and there follows a discussion of the huge task faced by the British personnel and their responses to it. In the first phase of the liberation period, the military, in addition to adjusting to their new role and circumstances, were concerned primarily with the practical matters of establishing food and water supplies to the camp and burying the dead. The second phase and the beginnings of the rehabilitation process began with the arrival of the main body of medical staff and a reorganisation of the camp.

From the end of April and throughout May, Camp I was evacuated and on 21 May, it was burned down. Hospitals were set up, volunteer helpers flown in and a routine of orderliness established. In this period – from approximately two weeks after the liberation until the summer months – several changes in the running and character of the camp can be identified. The units involved in the original takeover of the camp were replaced. Distinct improvements were visible around the camp and the internees, gradually increasing in strength and morale, were able to communicate better their needs and also what had been their experience under the Nazi regime. The experience of the British personnel working in the camp was thus different from that of the original liberators. They had far more personal contact with the internees than had their predecessors and were able to offer individuals tangible help. Great problems still faced the liberators, however, and this chapter will seek to identify these problems and establish to what extent they were dealt with.

In this second phase women began to feature more prominently in the camp. A decision was taken by the military authorities that women should not be admitted into Camp I, the 'horror camp', and so in the first week the few women working in Belsen were employed in preparing the hospital areas. After the first phase, new medical teams brought more women into the camp. The history of the liberation of Belsen, as it has so far developed, is essentially one written by men. The major images associated with the liberation are those from Camp I and thus we see only British 'Tommies' – men in military uniform – on the scene. We might be forgiven for thinking that women played little part in the relief of Belsen. This view would be largely backed up by a review of the literature, including the memoirs and letters, which came out of the camp after the liberation. The vast majority of documents are written by men and, it will be argued here, give a distorted view of the role played by women. The material, written from a solely male viewpoint, is inherently biased but, by the same token, gives a valuable insight into the view the army took of both its own women personnel and the female internees. Thus, finally in this chapter, the roles of men and women in Belsen will be examined in the light of work on gender issues, redressing in some part the current imbalances in the historiography.

## I

In what was an unusual development, the Belsen camp was officially surrendered to the British on 12 April 1945 as part of a local cease-fire. The decision to relinquish the camp to the Allies gives an indication of the turmoil experienced at all levels of German authority in the later stages of the war. Hitler believed until the very end that the elimination of 'World Jewry' was a goal of such importance that it should take precedence over everything else; if the Reich was to be destroyed, then its enemies in the concentration camps should not have the satisfaction of emerging from the ruins as 'triumphant conquerors'.[7] By the spring of 1945, as is clear from the Bergen-Belsen truce, an increasing number of people around him, and a great many of the troops on the ground, refused to follow his fanaticism.[8]

The exact circumstances leading up to the surrender of the Belsen camp are difficult to establish and the subject of some historical debate.[9] In the early months of 1945, Himmler had been persuaded to take part in secret negotiations with the Red Cross and the neutral countries in order to salvage all he could from the increasing chaos in the camps. With the knowledge that there had been an outbreak of typhus in Bergen-Belsen, Kurt Becher, an aide to Himmler, visited the camp on 10 April 1945. The Allies were quickly approaching the Belsen camp and it was clear to the German command in the area that they could not afford to move the inmates away from the front and so expose German troops to the threat of disease. On the recommendation of Becher, Himmler gave the order that the Bergen-Belsen camp should not be evacuated or destroyed as had been the fate of other camps in previous months, but instead be handed over intact to the advancing British.[10]

On 12 April, Colonel Schmidt, a German emissary, came through the British lines to declare the presence of a concentration camp at Belsen. Later that day, an agreement was reached between the Chief of Staff, 1st Parachute Army, Military Commandant Bergen and the Chief of Staff, British VIII Army Corps. The Germans agreed to neutralise a zone of 8 kilometres by 6 kilometres around the camp and erect 'Danger – Typhus' notices and white flags at all road entrances to the area. *Wehrmacht* troops were to be allowed to return to German lines, while the Hungarian troops guarding the camp were to be placed at the disposal of the British forces. The SS administrative personnel were to stay at their posts. They were compelled by the truce agreement to hand over the records of the camp inmates, although in fact the majority had already been destroyed on orders from Berlin.[11] Indicative of the low morale of the German Army was a letter to the Commander of the Allied troops, Bergen, from Oberst Harries, Commander of the *Wehrmacht* in Belsen, asking that they not be returned to the front line:

> A great part of these soldiers ist [*sic*] not able to take the difficulties of war and to fight at [the] front. Some of them have their home here or their families living in this area as fugitives. Therefore, we ask to give your permission that these soldiers leave the German army because they are only a burden to the [A]llied troops on marching to the German lines.[12]

Clearly, in the face of defeat, Himmler did not stand alone in his defiance of the Führer.

Having landed in Normandy in June 1944, the 2nd British Army, deployed between the 1st Canadian and the 9th US Armies, crossed the Rhine in March 1945. Under General Dempsey, 2nd Army pushed north-eastward towards Lübeck and the Baltic coast, and VIII Corps, on the right flank, crossed the River Weser in early April.[13] On 13 April, Lt-Col. Taylor, commander of 63rd Anti-Tank Regiment, Royal Artillery, received written instructions from the Brigadier General Staff, VIII Corps that he was to assume control of the area around Belsen as given in the agreement with the *Wehrmacht*.[14] On 13 and 14 April, the British forces were heavily engaged in forcing a crossing of the River Aller at Winsen and Walle and the liberation of the camp was delayed for forty-eight hours.[15]

In his famous book, *Belsen Uncovered*, Derrick Sington attributes to himself the unenviable appellation of the first British officer into Belsen, under the command of Taylor.[16] Certainly there are other contenders in the quest for the credit.[17] Survivor testimony makes reference to there being other British troops in the camp before the main liberating body arrived. Paul Kemp, writing on the liberation, suggests that 29th Armoured Brigade, involved in fierce fighting around Bergen, were the first British troops to come across the Belsen camp. Led by Brigadier Roscoe Harvey, they arrived at the camp on the morning of 15 April. Harvey, probably unaware of the truce, was unable to stop at the camp but did send in a tank and a few men to look briefly and report on what they found.[18] Moreover, it is possible that Intelligence and the SAS reached the camp before Sington.[19]

It was not until the afternoon of 15 April that the leading elements of Taylor's regiment, No. 249 (Oxfordshire Yeomanry) Battery, commanded by Major Barnett, penetrated the neutral zone and 63rd Anti-Tank Regiment became the official 'liberators' of Bergen-Belsen. Taylor ordered Sington, at that time commanding No. 14 Amplifying Unit, and two other NCOs, who between them could speak five European languages, to proceed into the camp in a loud-speaker van. They were to broadcast a message from the Corps Commander advising the internees that although they were liberated no one would be able to leave the camp for the time being because of the danger of spreading typhus.[20]

From the outset it was clear that this was not just another operation like so many others executed in camps and villages during the campaign through northern Europe. On entering the Belsen camp the liberating soldiers had to adjust to a new and strange realm of experience which shattered all previous norms. Sington was shocked by his reception when he entered the camp for the first time but then shock was to be the liberators' reaction to everything in Belsen. 'I had tried to visualize the interior of a concentration camp', wrote Sington, 'but I had not imagined it like this. Nor had I imagined the strange simian throng, who crowded the barbed wire fences, surrounding the compounds, with their shaven heads and their obscene striped penitentiary suits.' The welcome could scarcely have been more different from the one they were used to:

> We had experienced gratitude and welcome in France, Belgium and Holland. We had been surrounded in Paris, embraced and thanked. In a Flemish village our truck had been loaded with tomatoes and ripe pears, and jugs of cool beer had been handed to us by joyful people.
>
> But the half-credulous cheers of these almost lost men, of these clowns in their terrible motley, . . . impelled a stronger emotion, and I had to fight back my tears.[21]

Others reacted with less restraint. One survivor remembers seeing British officers and soldiers weep at the sight which unfolded before their eyes: 'Even the most hardened warriors were crying, vomiting and cursing at this never-imagined depth of human depravity.'[22]

On the first day in the camp, Lt-Col. Taylor interviewed the Camp Commandant, Oberst Harries, who declared that the SS, led by Josef Kramer, was solely responsible for and had complete control of the camp. Kramer himself was interrogated and the same night placed under close arrest.[23] In the intervening time, the main body of troops since detailed for the operation in Belsen had reached the camp. Brigadier Glyn Hughes, Deputy Director of Medical Services 2nd Army, had also arrived and a dispatch rider had been sent to Corps Headquarters with an urgent request for food, water and medical aid.[24]

Immediately after his interview with Kramer, Taylor, together with Glyn Hughes, made his first reconnaissance into Camp I proper. Taylor described in a report his first impressions:

> As we walked down the main roadway of the camp, we were cheered by the internees, and for the first time we saw their condition. A great number of them were little more than living skeletons with haggered [*sic*], yellowish faces. Most of the men wore a striped flannel gown, or any other garment they had managed to acquire. Many of them were without shoes and wore only socks and stockings. There were men and women lying in heaps on both sides of the track. Others were walking slowly and aimlessly about – a vacant expression on their faces.[25]

Camp I, the main camp, was in a hopeless situation when the British arrived. Approximately 40,000 people were housed in the five compounds, suffering from extreme malnutrition, typhus and other virulent diseases.[26] An estimated 10,000 corpses, mostly naked and in an advanced state of decomposition, lay around the camp, on the main roadway, inside and outside the huts. Throughout the weeks prior to the liberation, the death rate had reached an alarming pace, so that the removal of bodies had become a serious technical problem for the camp administration. The camp crematorium could take only three bodies at any one time, and so the camp authorities resorted to burning the bodies in hugh piles interspersed with wood and doused in petrol. Internees later testified that the stench of burning flesh had been overpowering. Eberhard Kolb records in his work on Belsen:

> By the end of March this method of disposal had to be discontinued because the forestry administration prohibited the use of wood for this purpose, and the officers of the [nearby] army training ground were annoyed by the disgusting stench which filled the air for miles around.[27]

For two long weeks then bodies were left to decompose where they fell. Only when it became clear that the British were soon to take over the camp, was any effort made to remove the corpses. The work fell to the remaining prisoners. Barely able to walk themselves they were forced to drag the corpses to the newly dug mass graves in remote parts of the camp.[28] 'We started work at sunrise and were up quite a long time before that', testified a former prisoner, Harold de Druillenec, at the Belsen trial in September 1945. 'We got no food before we started and worked 'til about 8 o'clock in the evening. In those five days or so I spent on this burial work neither a spot of food nor a drop of water passed my lips.'[29]

By mid-April, the death rate in the camp averaged 500 per day. Bodies examined by British medical staff indicated that death had taken place anything up to a period of three weeks beforehand and there was evidence that cannibalism had been a practice in the later stages of German control. The living, all famine-stricken, wandered aimlessly through the camp or lay in filthy huts. Discarded rags and human filth of every sort were evident all over the camp. Excreta-laden dust blew everywhere and constituted a serious medical threat, not only to the internees, but also to the liberators attempting to relieve the situation.[30]

When asked at the Belsen trial what was the general state of nutrition in the camp, Glyn Hughes answered simply, 'Extreme emaciation and complete malnutrition of all those who had been there for any length of time.'[31] All the prisoners had been without food for over three days before the liberation; drinking water and electricity supplies had failed days earlier. During the fortnight prior to his arrival, Glyn Hughes estimated that the prisoners had been receiving only 400 calories a day in the form of bread and a thin stew. During the final four days, the bread supply failed completely and one bowl of stew with no calorific value was provided. Those too weak to fend for themselves got nothing at all.[32]

Overcrowding could scarcely have been more acute. Huts intended for sixty housed ten times that amount. Double and three-tier bunks were in use and often three or four internees, some corpses, lay in one bunk. Many lay on the floor. The smaller of the women's compounds, which contained the majority of the typhus cases, had no bunks and little bedding. The few blankets available were in a filthy state. Glyn Hughes in his testimony described the sanitation in the camp:

> most of the internees were suffering from some form of gastro-enteritis and they were too weak to leave the hut. The lavatories in the hut had long been out of use. In the women's compound, there was a deep trench with a pole over it but no screening or form of privacy at all. Those who were strong enough could get into the compound: others performed their natural action from where they were. The compounds were absolutely one mass of human excreta. In the huts themselves, the floors were covered, and the people in the top bunks who could not get out just poured it onto the bunks below.[33]

A mile from Camp I was the newly created smaller Camp II in the Panzer Training School. The barracks consisted of many two- to four-storeyed buildings set around large barrack squares. Some of these were occupied by 15,000 internees, all male, the majority Russians and Poles. Conditions here were poor but at least the prisoners, though grossly overcrowded, were housed in well-built accommodation. There was no typhus in this camp but many internees were ill and all were severely undernourished.[34]

In the first forty-eight hours of British occupation resources and manpower were obviously inadequate to deal with the situation in hand. The lack of food and water overshadowed everything else. By 16 April, however, rations, water carts and coal had reached Belsen and 63rd Anti-Tank Regiment did what it could to distribute them. On 17 April No. 224 Military Government Detachment arrived and took control of Camps I and II under the military commander. On the same day the urgently requested medical units reached the camp.[35]

The logistics of the relief operation was difficult enough but in addition the conditions in the camp were so monstrous as to turn even the most simple practical tasks into a terrible ordeal. The food problem was not so much one of supply, but to provide rapidly the right food to the thousands of starving people of which over one quarter were physically incapable of either serving themselves or digesting the food that could be provided in the first few days.[36] Initially, many of the British soldiers, overcome by pity for the people around them, shared out what food they had. One contemporary witness noted, 'We gave a bar of chocolate to be divided between three women and they did not have sufficient strength between them to break it into three portions. The biscuits we gave them were fought over and wolfed.'[37] Unfortunately the internees simply could not take such rich food and eating it invariably made their condition worse or caused fatalities. The food lorries which reached the camp the morning following the arrival of the British troops carried dried milk powder, rye flour, oatmeal, sugar and salt, together with tinned meat and vegetable rations. Thus, the first official meal of the internees also turned out to be overly rich and, tragically, a number of deaths from overeating followed this original distribution.[38]

The distribution of food to the internees was an immense undertaking. Distribution parties were organised but it was a physical impossibility to provide enough feeders in the early stages owing to the large numbers involved. It was not until a couple of weeks later, when more voluntary help had arrived at the camp, that it could be said with any certainty that all internees received regular and sufficient food. Until then the weakest in the huts often remained hungry.

After the initial emergency convoy from 8th Army Stores, most food and supplies used in the camp were of German origin. On 16 April Major Berney of 817 Military Government Detachment, who was now responsible for general administration in Camp I, was asked to find the nearest food store. To the disgust of the soldiers, a well-stocked German supply depot was discovered adjacent to the Panzer Training School which contained many tons of potatoes, tinned meat, dried milk, sugar, cocoa, grains and other foodstuffs which had they been distributed weeks earlier might have saved countless lives.[39] Next to this store was also a bakery capable of producing 40,000 three-pound loaves per day. Three kilometres from Belsen at Bergen was a dairy with a daily production capacity of large amounts of milk, butter and cheese, with two small slaughter houses adjacent. Steps to organise these two installations were taken by 912 Military Government Detachment and the first deliveries of milk, butter and cheese to the camp were effected by 25 April.[40] Military Government also organised the requisitioning of foodstuffs from the villages and towns around Belsen to supplement the camp stores.[41]

An emergency water supply was provided to the camp by a convoy of water carts which arrived with the food lorries on 16 April. This was supplemented and later replaced by the pumping of water to the camp using civilian fire engines from Celle. The normal water supply to the camp was badly damaged and no clean drinking water had been available.[42] One eye-witness reported: 'Dotted about the camp were numerous cess-pools where women washed in the nude and washed clothes. Until our forces supplied water this was also their drinking water.'[43] Such scenes became commonplace but the soldiers remained horrified. Indeed, how else could one react if like Lt-Col. Gonin one witnessed a 'woman standing stark naked washing herself with some issue soap in water from a tank in which the remains of a child floated'?[44]

The soldiers were constantly surrounded and preoccupied with the dead and the dying, all the time painfully aware that they were powerless to help so many of the people when faced with the long-term effects of starvation and disease. For Derrick Sington, 'the sight of the dying was even more heart-rending than that of the dead'. He was particularly struck by the '*Muselmanns*' (*sic*). These were people who had lost all hope and were usually to be seen lying prostrate about the camp, their life slowly draining away. 'To have attempted to save these men,' wrote Sington, 'to have tried to feed them one by one, even to ask their names, would have necessitated at least ten times the relief workers that were actually present at Belsen in those first few days.'[45] Ultimately, the liberators felt utter despair at their inability 'to rescue character and personal destiny' from the mass of emaciated figures.[46]

With an estimated death rate in Camp I of 300 to 400 each day it was not until 28 April – over two weeks after the British had arrived – that Camp I was considered to be clear of corpses. Moreover, the liberators could not even comfort themselves with the thought that the victims were receiving a fitting burial. Perhaps of all the photographs and reels of film that came out of Belsen in those first few weeks, one of the most striking images was that of a British soldier bulldozing bodies unceremoniously into a mass grave. According to an official report, this happened only on two occasions. Two of the huge piles of bodies to be buried had become very decomposed. Blankets could not be spared and without blankets the bodies could not be handled. As the only solution, pits were dug alongside the bodies and they were then pushed in by the bulldozer. A combined service was held by the various Chaplains when each pit was finished and a notice board was erected stating the approximate or actual numbers of dead and the date when the pit was closed. During this time, no attempt had been made to identify the bodies. Once the need for mass burials was gone, trench graves were dug for subsequent burials. Bodies were placed alongside one another, and the grave was closed daily, a peg being put at the head giving number, name (if available) and nationality of each body.[47]

The work undertaken by the men in Camp I was harrowing to say the least. The soldiers, doctors and journalists who arrived early at the camp were horrified, literally nauseated, at the filth, the stench and the degradation in the camp. Their experiences in Belsen had a deep and lasting effect on the rest of their lives. The extent to which the British personnel were prepared for what they were to encounter, and the difficulties they faced in coping with the realities which faced them in Belsen, are the themes explored in the next section.

## II

The liberators of Belsen entered, in the words of one former prisoner, 'probably the foulest and vilest spot that ever soiled the surface of this earth'.[48] Few of the soldiers entering the camp had been briefed for what they were to confront. None had any true knowledge of Belsen and even the officers were expecting to find another prisoner-of-war camp like the many they had already liberated on their journey through northern Europe.[49] In fact, they unknowingly entered a different world when they drove into Belsen, a world with a code of moral values completely distinct from that to which they were accustomed. In Primo Levi's experience of Auschwitz as a prisoner 'the moment of entry into the camp was the starting point of a different series of thoughts, those near and sharp, continually confirmed by present experience'. Further:

Day by day everyone felt his strength vanish, his desire to live melt away, his mind grow dim; and Normandy and Russia were so far away . . . hunger and desolation so concrete, and all the rest so unreal, that it did not seem possible that there could really exist any other world or time other than our world of mud and our sterile and stagnant time, whose end we were by now incapable of imagining.[50]

What was simply reality for Levi, and so too for the people in Belsen, was beyond the imagination of the British troops, and usually this was reflected in their responses to everyday Belsen situations. The men were initially and continually shocked to see women in states of undress or to see individuals squatting down to excrete or urinate in the open, quite unconcerned about 'normal decencies'.[51] The magnitude of the problems in the camp, however, allowed little time for such thinking as Sington was soon to realise. One day he saw four women squatting in a compound urinating. 'That took me by surprise', he wrote. 'But the little shock of astonishment was succeeded by a greater one for just behind these women lay a tangle of legs and arms and buttocks with here and there a tousled head of hair . . . [that] was the last time I was to be surprised by the sight of dead bodies.'[52]

Many of the soldiers involved in the liberation were younger than Sington and relatively inexperienced, although, in fact, age and experience seem to have mattered little in preparing individuals for the scenes in Belsen. Glyn Hughes, an experienced soldier and long serving officer, testified, 'I have been a doctor for thirty years and have seen all the horrors of war, but I have never seen anything to touch it.'[53] Norman Turgel, an Anglo-Jewish officer in Intelligence, wrote much later: 'As a young soldier who had witnessed the killing of soldiers and animals on many occasions, I found this a shocking experience. I had seen my share of battle casualties . . . I remember the sight of shell-shocked soldiers . . . returning from the battle lines. But to see thousands of innocent people in a camp . . . being starved to death, murdered . . . was beyond belief.'[54]

If even eye-witnesses could use the term 'beyond belief' then the difficulties in persuading civilians of the truth of the atrocities were obvious. Here, the army photographers and film units were to play a crucial role. On 17 April people from the No. 5 Army Film and Photographic Unit arrived at Belsen to record the conditions in the camp and expected business as usual. Sgt William Lawrie, a film cameraman, recalled that the prisoners were totally apathetic about their liberation: 'They sat about, very little movement. Some of them were too far gone to move. There was absolutely no way we could ask them to rehearse a piece for us.'[55] This seemingly callous remark, however, sums up the challenge posed by the Belsen camp. It was completely unique in the experience of these servicemen, it was simply not just another job to which they could apply usual routines. Many of the photographers were extremely uncomfortable with their task, feeling voyeuristic.[56] George Rodgers, the late world-renowned photographer, nevertheless vowed not to take photographs during wartime again following his harrowing experience of composing shots amidst the horror in Belsen.[57] Belsen had a penetrating effect on Rodgers's life. The same was true of Mervyn Peake. The novelist and war artist who, throughout the war, wrote to his wife describing his war experiences, wrote nothing of his visit to Belsen; the shock it seems 'was too great for comment'. Yet the camp was to have a more profound effect on him than the rest of his wartime experiences put together. It seemed to his wife 'as if he had lost during that month in Germany, his confidence in life itself'. Peake sketched people in Belsen while they died, but, according to his biographer, felt deeply shamed by his actions, by his intrusion on 'something too terrible and too sacred to be the subject of public curiosity'.[58] He explored these feelings later in his writings. In particular, he was burdened by the image of a dying girl he had sketched in Belsen. In his poem 'The Consumptive: Belsen 1945' he questioned his own capacity for compassion:

> If seeing her an hour before her last
> Weak cough into all blackness I could yet
> Be held by chalk-white walls, and by the great
> Ash coloured bed,
> And the pillows hardly creased
> By the tapping of her little cough-jerked head –
> If such can be a painter's ecstasy
> (Her limbs like pipes, her head a china skull)
> Then where is mercy?[59]

Today even the most graphic of the photographs and films shot by the British Army are relatively well known. In 1945, very few were released for the public to see, for they were felt to be too distressing. Those that were shown were shocking enough, but, particularly in the first crucial weeks after the liberation, it was in fact the written word which was most often employed to convey the horror of Belsen. Those who were involved in the liberation were very keen that the British public should know what had happened in the camp. A public voice among these people was Richard Dimbleby who made one of the most unforgettable broadcasts of his career from Belsen. For the first time in his life he broke down when recording a despatch but was adamant that he must attempt to relay every detail of what he saw, even if people did not believe him. Indeed when the report reached the BBC in London they were disbelieving and hesitated about transmitting it before it had been verified by newspaper reports. Dimbleby, enraged, insisted and the broadcast eventually went out in abbreviated form.[60] Other witnesses penned letters home or maintained personal diaries but struggled to describe adequately what they saw. According to Glyn Hughes the conditions in the camp were 'really indescribable' while a Sergeant Midgley could literally find 'no words' to describe the atrocity.[61] In her testimony a survivor of Belsen expounds on the difficulties faced by those attempting to articulate the reality of the camp: 'Belsen . . . can never be described, because every language lacks the suitable words to depict its horror. It cannot be imagined because even the most pathological mind balks at such a picture.' She in fact finds herself dependent on analogy:

> While in Auschwitz I believed that it was the site of ultimate horror, a place which made Dante's Inferno appear a musical comedy. . . . When I arrived in Belsen-Bergen [*sic*] . . . I discovered that Auschwitz was no more than Purgatory. Hell was enclosed between the barbed wire fences of Belsen-Bergen.[62]

In the same way, seeking a means by which to express their feelings and emotions, some liberators turned to metaphor, making comparisons between Belsen and Dante's Inferno or comparing the internees to animals.[63] Alvin H. Rosenfeld has posited with reference to Holocaust literature in general, that when 'lost in a place whose dimensions we cannot easily recognise, let alone acknowledge as our own [that is, the position of the liberators in Bergen-Belsen], we strive for orientation through intimacy with the common and familiar things in the world'. Initially, these analogies may seem to suffice but ultimately under scrutiny they reveal their inadequacy. Those chosen by many of the liberators in their testimonies are clearly unsuitable when applied to the concentration camps. The victims in Belsen should not be likened to Dante's damned. Such a comparison leads us to accept that the Jews and the other scapegoats of the Nazi regime were somehow deserving of the condemnation and ceaseless torment to which they were subjected. It is clearly objectionable to imply that like Dante's damned, who suffered as a result of their sins, the internees in Belsen had earned their fate. Langer makes this point in an essay he calls 'Language as Refuge' and goes on: 'When we use words to make us feel better, we cannot expect them simultaneously to help us *see* better.'[64] Similarly then, the prisoners in Belsen were not, as Colonel Treagear commented in a report, 'degraded to the standards of animals'.[65] The internees did not act like animals but like human beings who had been systematically starved, persecuted, exhausted and denied all access to medicines, sanitary facilities or privacy. In the words of a survivor, reacting against the common descriptions of the liberators:

> The Jews weren't dehumanized, they felt pain when they saw bodies burned alive . . . so when they told that they found us dehumanized and in heaps and begging for bread that is really not true because they were begging for sanity . . . but they were not begging, they just saw they were being liberated and wanted to be taking notice [*sic*].[66]

Indeed, it was the very fact that both the victims and the perpetrators were so human which makes the Holocaust so horrific – and so difficult to confront. One does, however, have a great deal of sympathy with the soldiers attempting to describe the horror of Belsen. In the same way that the perpetrators, in order that they could kill on a massive scale, attempted to alienate their victims from themselves by stripping them of their civilising qualities, the only way the liberators could deal with the survivors was to view them as other to themselves; only by creating this distance were they able to cope with the tasks at hand.[67] The liberators were faced with a situation that mocks our vocabulary.

The inappropriateness of certain images used to describe the camp only highlights the difficulties of attempting to find words of comparison for such incomparable atrocity. Ultimately, however, one must agree with Rosenfeld's premise
that 'There are no metaphors for Auschwitz, just as Auschwitz is not a metaphor
for anything else'.[68] If we do accept this then we must be prepared to take on
board Langer's thoughts:

> Now literary critics can consider the possibility of writers on the Holocaust
> altering our perception of moral reality rather than trying to adapt the fact
> of extermination to ideas of suffering and heroism that have governed
> man's secular or religious fate throughout the Judeo-Christian era.[69]

The inability to deal with the horror around them led many of the liberators to
externalise it in an expressed hatred of the Germans.[70] Much of the anger at what
they saw in the camp they directed into a loathing of the SS and the German
people. One brigadier would never 'forgive the Race, who produced men capable of such cold blooded misery and death to the thousands who were driven
into Belsen'.[71] While Lt-Col. Gonin believed

> that it is a sacred debt we owe to the hundreds of thousands who have died, or
> who are about to die, as a result of the concentration camps of Germany that
> the true character of the Germans is never forgotten by civilised people.[72]

Thus, the inability of the liberators to understand what they saw in human terms,
also led them to demonise the German as 'other' and inhuman.

As we shall see in the next chapter, a significant number of people in Britain
saw the reports from Belsen as just more wartime anti-German propaganda.
One RAF officer, Squadron Leader Lyons, had received a letter from home
remarking on the fact that many people in England regarded the publicity
given to Belsen and Buchenwald as exaggeration. When the opportunity then
arose to visit Belsen for a day, he took it and was shocked by what he saw. Writing
home to his wife he commented, 'If in five years time, I hear people saying that
Belsen, etc., were so much propaganda, I shall be in a position to argue with
conviction.'[73] The extensive press reporting, together with letters written
home by British troops, encouraged by the army, generally helped to dispel
doubts in Britain that the German atrocities had been exaggerated. In many letters on Belsen, the writers recorded the conditions accurately; others took upon
themselves the role of propagandists, exaggerating the horror that already
existed. The news of Belsen spread to troops stationed all over the vicinity.
Representatives from the various units were sent as visitors with the task of
reporting back to their colleagues. That many rumours and embellished tales
were circulating is clear from some of the letters that were produced. One correspondent pressed upon the reader to '[r]emember that for three years the
camp had no water . . . and no sanitary arrangements whatsoever. Outside the
huts . . . there had lain until a few days ago the accumulation of three years
excreta and rotting flesh of those who had walked out of the hut and died.'
One of the more ludicrous accounts claimed that two million people had died

at Belsen since it opened in 1933, that is, from the beginning of the Nazi regime.[74] Such exaggerated news, though not widespread, in the short term only served to jeopardise the authenticity of the factual reports. In the long term, perhaps, it served to foster the 'Belsen myth': that Belsen was a camp with a gas chamber and on a par with Birkenau.[75]

The publicity surrounding the liberation did not succeed in establishing fully the role that the Belsen camp had played in the Nazi scheme of genocide. It might be expected that, through their first-hand experience of the camp, and with spending weeks alongside people who constituted the remnants of European Jewry (and had in many cases experienced the death camps), the British personnel might have gained a fuller understanding of the 'Final Solution'. Yet, with limited prior conception of the Holocaust and faced with the horrors of Belsen, the liberators might have been forgiven for thinking that in fact *Belsen* represented the limits of Nazi barbarity. They could hardly believe or describe what they saw in Belsen; how then could they conceive of *extermination camps*?

To what extent the soldiers who went into Belsen had a knowledge of the Holocaust is difficult to judge. Certainly some would have had access to British newspapers, which began reporting the 'Final Solution' as early as 1942, either because they were based in Britain, or because newspapers were sent to them in the field. In the sources examined for this chapter, however, few references are made to the extermination camps and it seems the troops made little or no distinction between the extermination camps and a concentration camp such as Belsen. More Jewish internees were liberated from Belsen than any other camp, yet many commentators failed to recognise the fact. For example, an official 113th Light Ambulance publication on the story of Belsen made no specific reference to the Jews.[76] When soldiers did comment on the number of Jews in the camp they rarely seemed to make any direct connection between their presence in the camp and the Holocaust.

The language barrier did not help in the soldiers' understanding of the situation. Some had a little German or French and a few prisoners had some English. But in the chaotic first weeks after the liberation many internees were too ill to speak and the soldiers too busy to listen. Military units, therefore, could be moved on after a week or two in Belsen without really acquiring a true picture of what the internees had experienced in the years before their liberation. The soldiers took with them the horrific memories of Belsen but not necessarily a better understanding of the Holocaust.

## III

While the army combatant forces were working in the camp restoring water and food supplies and burying the dead, the medical units and voluntary agencies who arrived in the camp in the first few weeks were busy establishing hospitals in the former Panzer Training School.[77] A large hospital area, based around eleven barrack squares, was established to provide accommodation for almost

7,400 patients. The German occupants of a well-equipped military hospital were evacuated to Sandbostel on 4 May and the 'Roundhouse', formerly used for recreation purposes, was equipped with beds and brought into use.[78] By 19 May, 14,000 had been admitted to the various hospitals from Camp I. This figure would have been much greater had it been possible to hospitalise every-body in need. As it was, a decision was made to admit only those who were thought to have a reasonable chance of survival but who were not fit enough to fetch their own food.[79]

The huts in Camp I were destroyed as they were emptied and on 21 May the last one was ceremoniously burned down. Meanwhile, every week a new unit or group of relief workers arrived in Belsen and was directed towards the newly created smaller camps and hospital area.[80] It became apparent very early that the medical units faced a problem of great clinical and logistical complexity, exacerbated by the mental state of the patients and the lack of interpreters of European languages.

Even weeks after the liberation, the number of workers in the camp remained hopelessly inadequate. Criticisms were made at the time, and have been made subsequently, that not enough British personnel were directed to Belsen in those crucial early weeks and that more lives could have been saved.[81] The 32nd British Casualty Clearing Station – nine doctors, eight army nurses, under Senior Sister Higginbotham, MBE, and a transport unit – with sufficient medical equipment for giving treatment to only 200 wounded, were faced with a task so enormous and problematic as to make it seem impossible. Morale was low from the very beginning. Four Psychological Warfare teams could have been fully employed in Camp I alone. Initially only one team was available to deal with thousands of mentally scarred prisoners but even this was removed for 'operational reasons' before the evacuation of Camp I got under way.[82]

It cannot be denied that the British authorities in Germany were slow to react to a desperate situation and made some unfortunate decisions relating to the camp. As early as 13 April, the day that the truce with the Germans was called and two days before the liberation of the camp, 8 Corps War Diary recorded what was then known about Belsen. Taylor-Bradford noted that the camp contained approximately 60,000 prisoners and that 'disease was a considerable problem'. It was considered that the area 'should be kept as free of troops as pos-sible'.[83] It is clear that the British were still largely ignorant of what awaited them in Belsen; the extraordinary decision to instruct the first British troops into the camp to uphold the authority of the armed German and Hungarian camp guard is evidence enough. The main concern of the British at this stage was to prevent the spread of disease to British troops and to ensure that no prisoners escaped, and with heavy fighting in the area continuing this was an understandable con-cern. Yet it might have been assumed that the army would have *at this stage* alerted medical units at the rear to be prepared to deal quickly with a large camp where serious diseases, including typhus, were known to be present. In fact, it was only when the shocking truth of Belsen was revealed to the 63rd Anti-Tank Regiment that medical units were sent for.

The situation in Belsen was a confused one from the very beginning and remained so in the weeks to follow. Obviously, no policy had been drawn up by the military authorities for dealing with the liberation of a concentration camp and the officers on the ground had to form their own working policy from day to day. Units detailed to work in the camp were frequently moved from one area of the camp to another causing breakdowns in the chain of command. The frustration of Major W.H. Miles is clearly evident in a report in which he was forced to admit that the work of his detachment had been an attempt to co-ordinate without authority; his task was made only more difficult by the high turnover in superior officers. Miles was one of the few officers openly critical of the way the operation was handled. The fighting units, who had liberated Belsen, viewed the camp as falling under their command, while Miles believed it was essentially a Military Government problem and should have been handled by that branch with other backup when requested. Such lack of co-ordination, in addition to all the other problems involved in bringing relief to Belsen, did not help in the primary task of saving lives. Indeed, Miles went further and noted that had Military Government had sole authority over decisions relating to the evacuation of Camp I, the process would have been 'accelerated with a consequent saving of life'.[84] Similar comments were made by Patrick Gordon Walker who visited Belsen in April to record material for the BBC. He criticised the lack of emergency medical supplies and planning and also the fact that there no single officer of sufficient seniority in the camp to take the initiative and make high-level decisions.[85]

Decisions affecting the Belsen camp were made without consulting the people on the ground. The evacuation of the village of Bergen is a case in point. The area was evacuated, presumably by Military Government headquarters, at short notice and put to use as an ex-prisoner-of-war reception centre. Since, however, 10 Garrison was not informed of the plan, it lost the services of local labour whose specialist knowledge of the Panzer Training School had proved invaluable in repairing the water and electricity supplies. A 10 Garrison report estimated that the action delayed the reinstallation of some services by three days.[86]

These criticisms must be qualified to some extent. The demands on the medical services in Germany in April 1945 were great. In addition to fighting commitments they had to deal with the large numbers of DPs and German wounded who filled the hospitals in the line of advance. In a wartime situation it was unrealistic to expect totally adequate numbers of nursing staff to be available to meet an emergency. In Belsen, even with a ratio of one nurse to every ten patients, over 5,000 nurses would have been required, not to mention the staff needed to administer and maintain the camp. Further, the discovery of Belsen was a unique event for the British Army of the Rhine. Along the line of advance, the British had liberated numerous prisoner-of-war camps in France, the Netherlands and Germany, where the prisoners, though often in a poor state of health, were protected under the Geneva Convention and more often than not had been in receipt of Red Cross parcels. For those expecting to find similar conditions in a concentration camp, Belsen, as we have seen, was a tremendous shock. The men on the ground had to think on their feet and learn by their mistakes. In recognition of the latter, 8 Corps produced some 'Notes on taking over a Concentration Camp', to cover the first forty-eight hours after a camp was uncovered. Based on their experiences at Belsen Camp, the notes were presumably to aid other units who found themselves in a similar situation. They offered information on what a unit might expect – 'It is most important to realize the general conditions which will probably reign in a German concentration camp' – as well as advice on equipment needs and, for example, instructions on how to organise the kitchens.[87] Obviously, the exceptional difficulties encountered in Belsen prompted the writing of these notes. There was a desire to ensure that the same mistakes be avoided if another concentration camp was uncovered.[88]

Although we can find fault with the way in which the British authorities handled the running of the camp at a higher level, very little criticism can be levelled at the many individuals who worked in the camp day after day, often on their own initiative. It is to these individuals that thousands of Belsen survivors owe their lives. In spite of the depression induced by the miserable conditions in the camp, they worked long hours tackling 'with vigour, problems never met with before'.[89] A notable individual in the camp from the very beginning of the British occupation was the Reverend Leslie Hardman, among the first of the Jewish liberators and a man who worked tirelessly for the internees during his initial six-week stay. He was greatly affected by the condition in which he found the people and was particularly distressed by the high daily death toll. Hardman worked in Camp I, personally visiting the barracks to offer comfort, and was often discouraged by the bureaucracy and delay seemingly involved in the relief operation. His own willingness to work long hours led him to criticise his officers for not clearing Camp I more quickly.[90]

The evacuation of the main camp was under way by 21 April and continued at a steady pace over the ensuing weeks. There were three main stages in the supervision of the patients in Camp I. The first was care *in situ*, or at least such care as could be given in the appalling conditions inside the huts. In the second stage patients were taken by 11th Light Field Ambulance from Camp I to a place known as the 'Human Laundry'. Here, in a sterilised barrack block in Camp II, German nursing sisters waited to wash and wrap the patients in clean blankets. Stage three involved taking the internees to the hospital blocks or, if they were classed as 'fit', to Camp III or IV to await repatriation.[91]

The demanding job of providing care inside the barracks, before evacuation, was undertaken by a group of ninety-seven medical students who had been flown in directly from the London teaching hospitals. In their final year, most in their early twenties and all male, they had in fact answered a call for volunteers to work in the Netherlands and Belgium amongst the starving and war-stricken there. Before leaving Britain, however, they were told they were to be diverted to Bergen-Belsen. The students, 'plucked from their comfortable existence' into a 'morass of human degradation', arrived at the camp in the first days of May and remained for the whole month, working under the direction of Dr Meikeljohn of the United Nations Relief and Rehabilitation Administration (UNRRA).[92]

The medical students formed an interesting and unique group within the camp, being relatively early arrivals, and from a civilian background. As students in London, they were exempt from conscription but they had seen many friends of the same age go to war and some had felt guilt at not themselves going off to fight.[93] When given the opportunity to carry out relief work in the Netherlands, they jumped at the chance to participate in the exciting Allied victory and to experience life in war-torn Europe. In fact they were diverted to Belsen but not until the story of the liberation of the camp had broken back home. Most who had seen the newspapers and newsreels before departure agreed these reports were not comparable with the real thing and did not, in fact, prepare them for what they were to encounter: the bleakness of the camp, the shocking conditions inside the huts, the apathy of their patients and the all-pervasive smell: 'As a medical student . . . you're not really of the sort of age group where you take these things too seriously and so [Belsen] was really quite a . . . surprise to me. I didn't really expect things to be so awful.'[94] For most, Belsen was a maturing experience, one which shattered previous illusions of war as an exciting game[95] and brought home reality sharply. They were neither prepared for what they encountered nor given any time to adjust. On the evening of their arrival they were briefed by Dr Meikeljohn and the next morning driven to the main camp. Each student was given a task; most were to supervise a hut, others the dispensary and the cookhouses. Thus began an exhausting ten-hour daily routine.

The kitchens had been re-established during April, ensuring a regular food supply, but very little could be done for those still inside the huts who were too ill to move. For them the quality of life was little different under British control. In the second half of April there was more food in the camp, but, as before, the ill and weak saw this food only if they had friends or relatives fit enough to collect it. A 10 Garrison report paid special credit to those whose duty took them inside the huts where conditions were 'so unpleasant that it required a definite physical effort to make oneself go inside and then to overcome the nausea the conditions induced'.[96] In fact, throughout the remaining life time of Camp I, the only people, with few exceptions, to work in the huts on a regular basis were the medical students and the Hungarian guard: 'nobody else ever came in'.[97] They perhaps came the closest to experiencing what daily life was like for the most seriously ill internees in Bergen-Belsen. The Hungarian guards (who had remained in the camp as part of the original truce) were placed at the disposal of the medical students and put to work fetching water and sweeping floors. One body of students together with Hungarian help managed to clear and disinfect several huts within Camp I and thus created a makeshift hospital area where 1,200 of the most sick were cared for pending their removal. They were nursed by the students and by volunteers from among the more active internees.[98] It seems impossible that one medical student could make any great impact on the lives of 500 starving, diseased patients, particularly as the only medicaments available were bandages, aspirin and a little opium. For the first time in months, however, the internees received food, clean water and human kindness, vital to any recuperation they might make. These ninety-eight volunteers were a pitifully inadequate solution to the problem: nevertheless, by their individual efforts, in combination with the increasing cleanliness of the camp and the evacuation policy in operation, the students helped to cut down the death rate considerably.[99]

Undoubtedly, the most pressing task of the medical students was to give everyone some food. On his first day Michael Hargrave managed to give each of his 240 patients one cup of an Ovaltine/Horlicks/cocoa mixture, two cups of glucose solution, one square of chocolate and one biscuit. He could do little more.[100] Most of the students seemed to agree that although they did make an impression on the situation, their *medical knowledge* was not a great asset in the task at hand:

> I don't think any of my knowledge as a medical student, apart from opening the odd abscess, was really of any use . . . if somebody had pneumonia, you couldn't do anything about it, there was no point in diagnosing it. . . . And if you gave a pill to anybody you had to give a pill to the next one too because . . . they thought . . . you were showing favouritism![101]

The students aided the medical officers in making agonising decisions as to which of the sick and dying patients were to be taken first to the hospital areas. Many of the decisions were undoubtedly arbitrary and based on incomplete diagnoses; the truth was of course that all the patients required hospital treatment. Each patient also needed individual attention, impossible under the circumstances, but the students tried to boost morale in as many simple ways as they could. Thus, if one pulse was felt, then inevitably several arms would be outstretched and the student would spend the next five minutes feeling pulses and nodding reassuringly.[102] Primitive operations were performed in the huts, as described in a typical diary entry from Michael Hargrave:

> Opened a breast abscess with a razor blade heated in a flame and then cooled in alcohol. Made quick 2″ incision and then backed with Marine gauze – no anaesthetic and patient must have been in great agony – did not yell. Opened boil on forearm in similar way.[103]

The students coped remarkably well, the urgency of the situation enabling them to adjust to their bizarre surroundings and endure the unpleasant conditions. The comparatively young age of the volunteers may have aided them in coming to terms with their task. When talking of their Belsen experience many years later, some of the men believed that they had been more resilient, somehow better able to cope in their youth. In the words of Dr D.C. Bradford:

> I think that being young as we were – I was about twenty-three . . . – one could stand it more . . . I think if one had to face it now and realise that these people who were in this terrible state were human beings . . . I don't

think one could have borne it . . . it was I think that we were young and much more flexible and could take it in those days.[104]

The sheer *scale* of the horror itself acted almost as a perverse coping mechanism, a phenomenon often associated with great human tragedy. John Dixey describes the powerful impression of bodies being bulldozed into open graves. His insights are reflected in the recounted experiences of others:

It wasn't as totally horrifying as you might reasonably expect it to be because it was on such an enormous scale. . . . If it had been several hundred bodies one might have been desperately upset and affected by it mentally and psychologically, at any rate. But no it was on such a huge scale it was rather like trying to count the stars. There were thousands and thousands of dead bodies and you couldn't really consider them to be your aunt or your mother or your brother or your father because there was just too many and they were being bulldozed into graves.[105]

It seems, as this diary entry indicates, that one quickly became accustomed to distress in Belsen:

Two brothers and sister – refused to be separated. One died and sister refused to let go – kissing/embracing him – had to separate her forcibly when they came to bring him. However, one sees so much of this sort of thing that it didn't upset me very much.[106]

In reality, the camp workers had very little time to dwell on their day-to-day experiences. During their month in Belsen, the medical students probably worked physically harder than they ever had before and any spare time was largely spent eating and sleeping or writing letters and diaries.

Other methods of helping medical staff endure life at Belsen were employed. Alcohol, intended to be a morale booster, was in plentiful supply. Because of their arduous work, each student had a double rum ration every night with their evening meal and nearby RAF units would often take some men to their messes for a good meal and some entertainment. In the words of one student, 'we needed that type of thing to give us a feeling maybe that we were still in the world of the sane'.[107] Entertainment came to Belsen quite frequently in the form of theatre and cinema. A theatre company performing George Bernard Shaw's *Arms and the Man* in Hamburg came into the camp to play with a cast including Ralph Richardson, Laurence Olivier and Margaret Readman.[108] Cigarettes were issued to each student by the Red Cross and they received bottles of wine from the local RAF units. In the evenings they tended to eat and write letters or go for a walk. Later a dart-board and a wireless were acquired for the mess, and a gramophone with 100 dance records. On their days off, some hitch-hiked around the German countryside viewing German life and the destruction of cities like Hanover and Hamburg. There was even a form of night-club, the 'Coconut Grove', set up by Captain Winterbotham. Free drinks were provided and a British Army band played for dancing. There was just enough room for twenty-five men and twenty-five women and each night a different unit was given twenty-five double tickets.[109] Captain Winterbotham, anaesthetist to the 32 Casualty Clearing Station, was one of the best-known Belsen personalities. He and his enterprises were often the most heartening things in Belsen. These included 'Harrods', from where thousands of sets of new clothing and footwear were distributed; a hair-dressing establishment with Hungarian staff; and a place where wirelesses and bicycles were serviced.[110]

In an interview, one of the volunteers denies having been emotionally affected by his time in Belsen; rather, his 'method of survival' was to develop more of an interest in the diseases than the people.[111] Certainly, from the medical point of view, Belsen gave a unique opportunity to study medical conditions rarely seen in modern life:

> [O]ne saw pathology there, the like of which one will never see again . . . it was so gross it just wasn't true. You read the text books where they gave you lovely pictures of what a thing should look like, a particular problem, a disease, an ulcer, you name it, there you were seeing it in real life and from that point of view it was quite incredible.[112]

Specialist medical staff were flown in to offer expert advice and carry out medical research in the Belsen camp. Dr Robert Collis, a child psychologist, worked in the children's block and based a book on the subject.[113] Dr Janet Vaughan was part of a small team sent to Belsen at the end of April by the Medical Research Council to test the relative value of hydrolysates, skimmed milk and serum in the treatment of starvation. Specialist treatments were also introduced. A so-called Bengal Famine Mixture, previously used to treat starvation cases in Asia during the war, was imported into Belsen in great quantities. Though the mixture was found to be too sweet for the majority of Belsen patients (who, as East Europeans, preferred 'sour'-tasting foods) it was, nevertheless, successful and the patients were encouraged to take it as medicine. On 21 April, Major Davis of the USA Typhus Commission arrived in Belsen and was assigned responsibility for the creation and command of a Typhus Control unit whose primary duty was preventative. In a short time all the internees had been deloused and every person in the vicinity of Belsen was dusted with DDT. As the evacuation of Camp I was completed, the medical students joined the other medical teams in Camp II and continued their work in the hospitals, with each as his own porter, anaesthetist and surgeon, until their departure on 27 May. The ex-German military hospital was by far the most advanced of the hospital areas with excellent facilities including X-ray equipment, a dispensary and sterilising machines[114] but elsewhere such luxuries were scarce and the wards were fairly primitive. Conditions were, however, less chaotic and more conducive to examination and treatment, in spite of the persistent problems of the lack of workers, the shortage of medicines and the language barrier.[115] Most of the medical students mention the problem of language in their diaries and testimonies; very few seemed to manage a full conversation with the internees. Thus, the students were unable to learn a great deal about their patients' pasts. The name of Auschwitz was mentioned and some of the students gathered that it was a terrible place, but stories were incomplete and the extent to which they understood the facts about the 'Final Solution' at this stage is questionable.[116]

An initial inability to relate to the survivors as 'normal' human beings is a common thread which runs through many of the British testimonies. This in itself was perhaps a coping mechanism. The internees were dying in large numbers every day and if one were to survive the situation it surely helped to distance oneself from them. Few of the witnesses refer to patients as individuals, rather, they are seen as a mass, almost like a herd of animals, one indistinguishable from another.[117] In common with the other workers in the camp, the medical students had not been prepared for work inside a concentration camp. They lacked the medical experience to appreciate and understand fully the psychological problems of the internees and found it difficult to relate to them. One student, having witnessed some of the internees taking out their frustrations by destroying areas of the camp, admitted, 'Somehow I cannot bring myself to like the internees as they are making such an infernal mess of the camp . . . and they still live by the law of the clutching hand.'[118]

In the early stages, many of the workers in the camp did not wholeheartedly believe in their task, some thinking it would be impossible to make an impression on the death rate and that, even if they did, the survivors would never make a full recovery. It was assumed that many of the internees would be incapable of integrating into normal society and of leading a normal life. Major R.J. Phillips, Advisor in Psychiatry to 2nd Army, admitted that on the first of his three visits to Belsen camp, he had thought it impossible to believe that people who had been so badly treated could ever recover.[119] One of the medical students considered that his time would be wasted in treating one of his patients 'because even if she survives she will never be a useful member of the community'.[120] This was exactly the attitude of which Leslie Hardman despaired. He believed that with sufficient care and concern from the relief workers the majority of the internees would make a full recovery. Hardman did have a valuable advantage in the knowledge of Yiddish which enabled him to talk to a large proportion of the internees. Language, so often a barrier to communication in Belsen, enabled Hardman to relate to the internees and recognise their problems in a way other relief workers were unable to do.[121]

The British medical personnel believed that the major psychological problem amongst the internees manifested itself as a 'loss of normal moral standards and sense of responsibility for the welfare of others'. This was considered to be directly related to the degree of undernourishment suffered by the patient. It was discovered that the 'recovery of normal behaviour ran parallel with improvement in bodily health and was often surprisingly rapid'. Indeed, after a few days in hospital 'all except the more seriously ill began to regain their self-respect. Girls were doing their hair and men asking for razors.'[122] As conditions in the camp improved and the patients slowly regained their strength they also began to reassert their individual personalities. They behaved more conventionally and the medical workers were gradually able to relate to them as normal patients, individuals worthy of respect. Morale amongst the staff rose considerably when there were noticeable improvements in the condition of the patients. For Dr Bradford, 12 May 1945 was a day to celebrate; his diary entry reads simply, 'Nobody died today!'[123] During May the medics began to see their hard work producing results as people showed signs of recovery. In the hospital in Camp II, Michael Hargrave had given one girl a blood transfusion and it was with satisfaction that he noted her improved condition in his diary: 'I think she's one girl that we have quite definitely saved from dying as in the hut at one stage we had labelled her status gravis and now she is asking for chocolates and cigarettes.'[124]

## IV

Thus far this study has failed to give mention to a group amongst the liberators who, though they did not witness the conditions in Camp I and take a direct part in its evacuation, nevertheless played a crucial role in the relief of the Belsen internees. This final section examines the contribution made by women to the history of the liberation of Belsen and the way in which their role was perceived in the camp in general. 'Whatever the present status of women in the battle for sexual equality might be', writes Eric Taylor, author of *Women Who Went To War*, diplomatically, 'they have certainly proved what they can do under the most trying and terrifying conditions in two world wars.'[125] In recent years a significant body of academic work has been undertaken in order to document women's participation in the war effort, yet, crucially, women remain absent from the core history of the Second World War (included, if at all, as a tokenistic addendum). In the field women inevitably had to prove themselves able to do a job better than many men and had to work doubly hard to be noticed and to be taken seriously. By the end of the Second World War there were nearly half a million women in the forces. Many were exposed to considerable dangers but perhaps none more than the nurses in the combat zones – the Queen Alexandra's Imperial Military Nursing Service (QAIMNS or 'QA's). They were crucial to the war effort and in 1943 were granted wartime commissions and wore the insignia of military rank (although they had the rank of an officer, they did not receive an officer's salary). Yet no matter how their presence was appreciated by the individuals they nursed or by colleagues on the ground, their perceived role in the general scheme of the war was summed up neatly at a briefing conference given by General Montgomery: 'The most important people in the Army are the Nursing Sisters and the Padres – the sisters because they tell the men they matter to us – and the Padres because they tell the men they matter to God – and it is the men who matter.'[126] In Belsen the army nursing staff mattered to the relief operation; nowhere more than in the concentration camps of Germany did women establish their ability to equal their male colleagues.

In her book, *Women Workers in the First World War*, Gail Brayburn demonstrates skilfully the remarkable consistency of male attitudes towards women's work, even in the exceptional time of war.[127] Her study concentrates on women on the home front and refutes the commonly held view that the demand for women's labour during the First World War led to a fundamental change in opinions on women's position and role in society. Brayburn argues that

> women's work, and men's attitude towards women, should not be seen in iso-
> lation. The four years of war cannot be separated from the rest of history, and
> women's work cannot be detached from the broader issues concerning work
> roles [and] sexual stereotyping.[128]

Penny Summerfield explores similar issues in relation to the Second World War and challenges the standard interpretation, advocated, for example, by Arthur Marwick, of the role of the war in the social history of women. In the spheres Summerfield examined in her work, namely domestic work and paid employment on the home front, she found that in spite of 'the challenge and expectation of change' during the war, there was in fact a considerable amount of continuity with 'pre-war attitudes and practices' towards women.[129] The same consistency of male attitudes towards women's work, it is argued here, can be identified in this study. It might be imagined that under extreme circumstances such as Belsen presented, traditional gender roles would have broken down, that the tremendous urgency of the situation, the lack of personnel, the shock, the determination, would in some way have led to a blurring of the customary male/female ascribed functions. Conversely, the crisis situation and the disorientation thus induced might equally have led to a reinforcing of subconscious (gendered) behaviour patterns. In fact, traditional roles were maintained in the relief of Belsen – if not further entrenched. In such a military environment, where power was resolutely in male hands, the demarcation of established work roles and sexual stereotyping was firm.

Among feminists, such as Kate Millett, 'feminine' and 'masculine' have long represented social constructs. Within patriarchy a series of 'feminine' characteristics has developed – passivity, subservience, virtue and modesty, for example – while the 'masculine' is characterised by aggression, intelligence, efficacy and bravery. Failure to conform leads to one's being labelled unnatural. This socialisation has a second strand, what Millett terms the sex role: 'In terms of activity, sex role assigns domestic service and attendance upon infants to the female, the rest of human achievement, interest and ambition to the male.'[130]

It was ruled by army officials that the conditions in Camp I were so terrible that women should not be permitted entry at all.[131] This decision reflects the paternalism of the time and was clearly motivated by a desire to protect the sensibilities of the women who could not (and should not have to) withstand such horror. The imperative towards protection was probably nowhere stronger in British society than amongst the class that produced army officers. For whatever reason, it seems that a senior nursing sister with vast experience, not least that of participating in the battles across Normandy and the Netherlands, was in some way deemed less suitable to work in the camp than a 21-year-old man not yet out of university.[132] It was probable that the majority of women working in Belsen were extremely grateful not to have to work inside Camp I. Yet one cannot escape the feeling that the reason for totally excluding them was not only to do with offending sensibilities but also with the expectations of the female capacity to cope professionally with the situation.

In Belsen, after the liberation, the woman's role, whether internee or personnel, was as cleaner and carer, and occasional dance partner. When Camp I was evacuated, the very first to be moved were women who were fit and 'suitable for employment in the laundry and cookhouses' in Camp II. Internee 'seamstresses' were put to work on producing hundreds of standard Belsen nightgowns for the sick.[133] Similarly, when Hardman wanted to use SS guards to scrub out several huts in Camp I, he chose six female guards. These women, however, were taken away after a few days by a superior officer who believed it most undignified for an officer and a gentleman to make women work.[134] There was, however, a differentiation made between the different groups of women in Belsen by the male majority of liberators.

Modern feminist analysis and the 'tools' of socialisation can offer some interesting insights into the position of women in Belsen. Under patriarchy women can be classified into two camps, broadly the 'good' and the 'wicked', the extremes of Madonna and Whore. The 'good', portrayed as representatives of a higher or purer nature, can be venerated using the symbolism surrounding angelic, virginal and Mother of God figures. They manifest qualities of order and harmony, purity, virtue, chastity, decency and modesty. Conversely, women vilified by patriarchy, who are symbolised by darkness and represented as the Whore of Babylon figure, are inherently sinful, immodest, indecent, promiscuous and seek to contaminate society with their wickedness. The latter are detestable and open to abuse, the former in need of protection.[135] These twin concepts (though perhaps not in the extreme forms outlined above) can be applied to Belsen when examining male responses to the different groups of women in the camp.

A variant on the mother figure is represented by the British female relief workers. Respected and virtuous, these women have to be protected from the real horrors of the camp by the British officers. Thus, they were not allowed into Camp I, were prevented from doing night duty in the hospital and most definitely must not drive the death cart which collected the bodies of those who had died in the hospital area. At the other extreme were the female SS guards. These women held a fascination for the liberators and the press, who focused on their brutality as a real indicator of the baseness of the Nazi regime. Those of the women who were middle-aged, stocky and heavily built, however, were largely dismissed. The real fascination was with those women who were young and more conventionally attractive, and particularly with one individual, Irma Grese. This young, blonde-haired, attractive woman was highlighted by the media and suitably vilified. Grese fits the classic Whore model. She hides her true nature, her wickedness, under a veil of beauty and strives to allure and seduce the men around her.[136]

The third and largest group of women in Belsen, the internee women, in general do not fit either category. These women on the whole were seen as the antithesis of the feminine ideal; they had been stripped of their femininity and thus became dehumanised. It has already been noted how the liberators working in Camp I found it difficult to relate to the internees in a human way. This proclivity was further heightened in the case of the women, who through starvation had become, to a certain extent, amorphous and ungendered. A revealing illustrative comment on the relationship between the male liberator and the female liberated is that made by one of the medical students. Working daily in one of the female barracks, he recorded: 'The stench of these filthy emaciated bodies has long ceased to bother me, and they have long ceased to have any sense of feminine decency or modesty.'[137] This is a two-part statement. In the first half we have a comment on the awful condition of the internees and the way in which the student has come to terms with the situation. In the second part of the sentence we are told that these emaciated bodies are women and, more crucially, the writer's view on how a woman should look – decent and modest. What the student is in fact telling us is that he does not recognise these internees as women because they do not conform to his view of how women should be. The second statement follows directly from the first: that the stench has ceased to bother him *because* the women had long ceased to have a sense of feminine modesty and decency. The male liberators faced a double difficulty in relating to the female internees. Their humanity should have been defined as such through certain feminine signifiers but with these missing, the men did not, indeed could not, recognise them as women. To have identified with the internees and accepted them as being like themselves would have made the liberators' experience totally unbearable. They were forced to distance themselves in order to cope. Leslie Hardman was one who could not show detachment. Whilst, on one hand, his close relationship with the internees allowed him to see past the physical appearance and reach the humanity (and the Jewishness) of the survivors, he was perhaps to be more greatly affected by his experience.[138]

Some internee women, the least emaciated at the time of liberation, were viewed sexually by the men working in the camp and the male power and superiority were thereby reinforced. As the weeks passed, more and more women, recovering in health, joined this category. 'Men move freely among naked women', commented one male visitor to the camp. 'It goes without saying', said an orderly, 'that they would like to screw some of them. Their figures are tempting.' The visitor reassures us that 'once committed to their tasks, the gunners soon learned to view their charges with medical objectivity'.[139] There is little question, however, that some exploitation took place (by liberators and other internees), particularly as in many cases the threat of pregnancy was removed by the absence of menstruation. Indeed, the women were often keen to rediscover or to begin to re-display their feminine characteristics in order to make themselves attractive to the men around them.[140]

Returning to the relief effort and the role of the women relief workers, the majority who arrived in the first week of liberation found themselves working in improvised hospital blocks in the nearby *Wehrmacht* Panzer School. They had virtually no equipment. The staff of ex-internees, few of whom could speak English, all needed feeding and much rest. Of the nurses of 32 Casualty Clearing Station, one QA was put in charge of the large dining block and kitchen and made responsible for the catering, while the other seven sisters supervised the cleaning and preparation of wards in the main barrack building. They were joined by a party from the Friends Relief Society (RS 100), teams from the Red Cross and a Girl Guide team.[141] A large percentage of these voluntary workers were women and were detailed to help improvise the hospital barracks and distribute food and clothing. The women of the British Red Cross under the leadership of Sisters Silver-Jones and Beardwell, were sent to the hospital to take care of the first 600 patients admitted.[142]

The conditions in the Belsen hospitals were gruelling. The medical staff were faced with a range of illness from typhus and tuberculosis to gangrene and various forms of skin disease. The majority of patients – probably 80 per cent – were suffering from diarrhoea and most were confined to their beds. There was a marked shortage of even the most basic equipment, including bed pans. Needless to say the hospital rarely approached the exacting sterile standards usually demanded by the medical profession. Indeed, when the time came for the medical students to hand over their duties to the newly arrived British nurses, the latter were often horrified at the conditions on the wards and had to adjust quickly. It was a great cause of resentment to the medical students that these people who had not seen the conditions in Camp I a month ago, and the striking improvements made since, could walk in and criticise the hospital so freely.[143]

The high death rate in the hospital continued to cause dismay and one of the most dreadful tasks the nurses had to face every morning was to identify and remove the night's fatalities. People would climb out of bed during the night and their bodies be discovered the next morning in all kinds of grotesque positions. It reminded one nurse of the terrible childhood stories told to her of the Black Death in the Middle Ages and the cries of 'Bring Out Your Dead!'[144] There remained an acute shortage of staff. A hospital block of 150 beds was supervised by one army sister and there was just one doctor to each square of five blocks. Typical staffing levels for one block would be: one QA nurse; two medical students; a couple of internee nurses (usually Polish or Russian) to do day duty; German nurses to cover the night shift; and some Hungarian soldiers to clean the wards. It had been hoped that the internee staff would be able to work in the wards unsupervised but this proved impossible. They were simply apathetic or spent much of their time trying to scrounge food, sometimes from the patients; they too had been through the camp system and often had the same mental scars as their patients. The German nurses tended to be professional and motivated and so gained the respect of their British colleagues. Their presence also helped break down language barriers and they were of particular value in explaining the use and dosage of the German drugs. The scarcity of British nursing staff meant that the authorities gave little thought to any negative feelings the patients might have to being treated by a German. Some patients displayed their resentment by openly humiliating the nurses. In one incident a group of Russian women stole the nurses' uniforms and managed to shave some of their heads whilst they were sleeping.[145]

In the words of Annig Pfirter, a member of the Red Cross, life in the hospital centre was quite different from anything anyone had ever experienced:

> It seemed to us sometimes that we were living on another planet; we had in fact to forget all our habits, our ideas as to tidiness, cleanliness, moral considerations and human dignity in order to try to comprehend our patients' psychological and mental state.[146]

This was never easy. On one occasion documented by Pfirter, a nurse asked a patient to state her name, nationality and place of birth. The woman managed only to pull up the sleeve of her nightgown and stammered, 'Me . . . no name – only number – no country, just a Jewess, do you understand? I am only a dog. . . . How I wish I were like you – a human being.' Naturally such pitiful words left the nurse shaken – 'the unfortunate woman's eyes seemed to reflect the multitude of nameless people who could no longer believe they were human beings'. The language barrier was a hindrance everywhere but particularly when a patient needed to tell her story and explain her traumatic experiences. Somehow the nursing staff managed to understand: 'the past came back so vividly that we were able, from their gestures and the expressions on their faces, to understand what they were trying to tell us.'[147] At this stage of the relief effort when conditions were a little less chaotic and a basic routine had been established, the British personnel had more time to spend talking to the internees on an individual basis. It is probable that the women amongst the internees found it easier to talk to other women. Eva Kahn-Minden worked as a nurse in the maternity unit in Belsen. She was given a gold locket by one of the new mothers who told her: 'I want you to have it because you have listened to me when I unburdened myself for the first time about the worst period of my life. Since that talk, I feel free and am now happy to be going home with my baby.'[148]

The internees' preoccupation with food overrode all other interests and hoarding was common. The nurses would find slices of bread and meat under a patient's pillow, sacks of stolen potatoes under their beds, and, once, even half of a small calf![149] As the patients regained their strength they often became restless and impatient and difficult to manage. Many felt indignant at the restrictions the hospital imposed and took to wandering about at night, stealing food and raiding locked stores. The camp became so unsafe at night that the QAs were forbidden to do night duty.[150]

Not all the wards were so dispiriting. The children's blocks were said to be the happiest in the camp for, although many were still poorly, many also were beginning to recover. Happily, the younger children were laughing and smiling and seemed to show none of the terror symptoms so evident in the adults in Belsen. For similar reasons, Eva Kahn-Minden felt lucky to have started her work in the maternity ward. There at least the internees began to show signs of caring again.[151]

In a similar situation to that in the Belsen hospitals, several miles away in another camp, the QAs of 10 Casualty Clearing Station coped well with an arduous daily regime. In a detailed army report, written by Lt-Col. F.S. Fiddes (on the liberation of Sandbostel camp by British troops) a special mention is given to the work of the nursing sisters. The camp, previously known to the British as a prisoner-of-war camp holding 15,000 prisoners, had in recent weeks seen the influx of 8,000 political prisoners – all male and all in a severe state of malnutrition and disease. The nurses played a vital role in the relief of the camp and this report, whilst giving them credit, also gives a valuable insight into how their position was viewed by male colleagues. Fiddes concedes that the 'main burden of organising and directing the nursing and general management of the patients' fell upon the women and that the 'fearlessness' with which they nursed serious cases of typhus and TB was 'impressive'. Criticism, however, was made of their 'indulgence in the prerogative of criticism and free comment', which is consistent with the pervasive male view of women. The QAs at Sandbostel eventually received admiration from their male colleagues. First, however, they had to disprove the expectation that they would collapse within a week working under such sordid conditions – as the report says, 'this was an essentially masculine belief to which the sisters themselves had never subscribed'. The efforts of just nine British sisters and a number of recruited German nursing staff resulted in a transformation of an improvised hospital area which allowed the patients to be taken out of the overcrowded huts.[152]

The report of the liberation of Sandbostel is quite unusual in highlighting the role played by women at all. Women are integrated so rarely in official wartime documentation. As a consequence the depiction of women in war is often quite removed from reality. Marion Korzak, reviewing a 1970s exhibition, 'Women At War – A Celebration' in the Imperial War Museum (IWM), directed her criticism at the fact that the depiction of women in the contemporary propaganda posters – 'Smiling faces, jaunty girls, uniformed, spruce, brave nurses' – was rarely challenged in the exhibits chosen. Patronising praise was given in the exhibition and the word 'sacrifice' glibly used but the actual results of women's war effort did not emerge.[153] Certainly, in the plethora of documentary material in the IWM on the liberation of Belsen, at the time of writing, there are only three contributions from women. This may be because women did not write about their experiences. Many of the longer testimonies and diaries written about the camp are those by the medical students for whom Belsen was a singular wartime experience outside London. They were young and held a unique position within the camp and perhaps felt more inclined to record the episode on paper. The nursing staff, on the other hand, were continuing their work in Belsen. The location was new and conditions were the worst they had ever seen; nevertheless, there was some sense of continuity in their routine and perhaps for this reason they did not feel the necessity to write down their thoughts. This may be a partial explanation. It is difficult, however, to believe that it is the sole reason why a dearth of women's testimony exists in the public domain.

The involvement in the Belsen relief operation of so many women received very little acknowledgement from the predominantly male official report and dispatch writers. Furthermore, in contemporary literature describing the operation in Bergen-Belsen recurrent mention is made of admirable work by the medical students, the research teams, the civilian workers and the combatant troops but no mention is made of the army nursing sisters. Obvious resentment of this fact and a sense of duty to her female colleagues prompted Hilda Roberts to write a letter to the *British Medical Journal* reminding the medical profession of the demanding role fulfilled by the women in the QAs. It is perhaps fitting to end this section with her observations. Describing the conditions under which they worked she reminds us that the army sisters 'showed a willingness and initiative that deserves the highest praise' and that they too 'came to Belsen immediately following a hectic and gruelling time dealing with casualties of the Rhine crossing, and at the end of nearly a year's service with the BLA [British Liberation Army]'.[154]

## V

The documentary evidence and testimony provided by the liberators of the concentration camps, both male and female, is an important part of the documentary evidence of the Holocaust. This chapter has examined the liberation of Belsen and the responses invoked in the liberators. These unsuspecting soldiers, journalists and nurses were the first to attempt to articulate what we now glibly call 'man's inhumanity to man'. The liberators, so close to the events, were not able to face up fully to the realities that confronted them and struggled to describe a scene completely beyond the imagination. Fifty years on we continue to sympathise with them. We too, despite the historical distance, still struggle to fathom the meaning of Bergen-Belsen and search for suitable words.

Furthermore, the liberation of Belsen is an important part of modern British history. When the British Army publicised the scenes in Belsen it introduced British society to the Holocaust in ways that could not be easily doubted or ignored. How Belsen Camp was presented to the British people has affected the way in which Belsen has become synonymous with the 'Final Solution' in Britain. Chapter 2 examines the processes through which the British people received information on the liberation of Belsen and how, in turn, they interpreted it.

# 2   British popular responses

This chapter will examine British government, press and public responses to the liberation of the German concentration camps. Buchenwald, the first camp to be liberated, was reached by the Americans on 11 April 1945 and, after a succession of other camps, Mauthausen was the last to be freed on 8 May. During April, and in the months to follow, the British people were exposed to an unprecedented amount of information on the camps. Wireless broadcasts, newspaper reports, newsreels and, to a lesser extent, letters or conversations with friends or family in the forces, all revealed the true horror of Nazi Germany and induced a wave of shock and outrage across the country. Few escaped the images from the concentration camps and, for the majority of the population, these revelations constituted the first conclusive proof of wartime Nazi atrocities. Yet, from as early as 1942 the British press had kept the public informed about the advancement of the 'Final Solution' – the Nazi attempt to annihilate Europe's Jewish population. This chapter builds on and, indeed, presents further evidence in support of the hypothesis presented by several Holocaust scholars, most recently Tony Kushner: that, during the war years, the vast majority of the British public did not comprehend the true nature of the Nazi offensive against so-called 'inferior races'.[1] Further, it will challenge the assumption that such comprehension came with the liberation of the German camps in 1945.

A great many of the people liberated in the concentration camps were the survivors of what we today term the Holocaust. In particular, it is the extent to which the British people grasped this truth at the time which concerns us here. We might expect that the British involvement in, and the widespread coverage by the media of, the liberation of a camp where thousands of the survivors of the 'Final Solution' were incarcerated, might have imbued large sections of British society with a widespread understanding of the nature of Nazi wartime policies against the Jews. As we shall see, however, this was not generally the case.

In his work on British perceptions of the 'Final Solution' during the war, Kushner has stressed the importance of understanding

> that when the news of the Final Solution reached Britain in the summer of
> 1942 it would be received by the state, public and Jewish community in a

specific light. Past considerations of atrocities, attitudes towards Jews and the general state of the war would be as important as the news itself.[2]

The same is true of the liberation of the western camps in 1945. Reactions and responses to the liberations were usually based on predetermined and often unsophisticated ideas and judgements about the camps based on knowledge acquired *before* the war. Such judgements often ignored the facts and implications of the 'Final Solution' which had been implemented subsequently. Consequently, the specific Jewish aspect of the suffering in Belsen was not assimilated. Research on British responses to the 'Final Solution' has shown that even when the Nazi extermination programme was confronted during the war, it was not generally related and emphasised as a Jewish plight. It has been argued that the existence of a dominant liberal discourse in British society was largely responsible for shaping British attitudes towards the Holocaust.[3] This liberal doctrine, while not condoning the persecution of the Jewish minority, could explain anti-semitism only in terms of Jewish exclusivity or difference and thus tended to put the blame on the Jews themselves. Traditional rationalisations, however, could not justify the extreme nature of Nazi anti-semitism as it was revealed during the war. Thus, the common response, from the government and the public, was 'to ignore evidence to the contrary, or, less frequently, to suggest that stories of persecution were subject to Jewish exaggeration'.[4] Throughout the war, government officials continually rejected the idea that the Jewish persecution in Europe was in any way unique. To do otherwise would also have been illiberal. During the war and, as we shall see in the next chapter, the postwar period, the British state refused to highlight specific cases of Jewish victimisation as, it was argued, this would be to use Nazi tactics: that is, to treat the Jews differently from the rest of the population. Thus, British policy was always to refer to victims of Nazi persecution according to their European nationality rather than with reference to their religious or cultural background. Wartime campaigners who lobbied for effective rescue measures to be implemented on behalf of European Jewry were met with consistent opposition from government officials who insisted on the universal approach; the most appropriate way to save Jewish lives was to concentrate resources fully on the long-term aim of winning the war.

Against this background then, it should be no surprise to discover that the Jews were largely missing from the camp revelations in April 1945. Moreover, at that stage in the war, it was even more unlikely that their presence would be emphasised: the political agenda in Britain at the end of the war, it will be argued here, demanded that the existence of Belsen and other camps be regarded within universal terms of reference. Responses to the liberation of the camps, and the evidence of Nazi atrocities exposed there, show that the reports were interpreted in ways that were relevant to the British concerns at the time. Needless to say, at the end of the war British concerns were not generally with Europe's Jewish population.

The foremost response to the camp revelations was understandably emotional as the public attempted to come to terms with the horrific images that confronted them. Thus, on one level, the camps were viewed in terms of their universal significance for mankind. Subsequently, the existence of the camps was incorporated into debates which were already taking place in Britain. In the months after the Normandy landings, and particularly in 1945, the government, press and public, certain of victory, were absorbed in discussions on the end of the war, the nature of the peace settlement and the extent to which the German people should be punished. The timing of the liberations and the level of suffering they uncovered determined that the camps inevitably influenced these discussions; indeed, the bulk of responses generated by Belsen and the other camps were applied directly to these issues. Thus, to cite one example, the revelations conveniently provided the government, in the absence of any stated war aims, with the perfect justification for having fought the war (rather ironically in fact, having fought the whole of the campaign attempting to play down the Nazi atrocities against the Jews, in 1945 they gratefully exploited the conditions in Belsen, a camp where at least half of the internees were Jewish, as vindication for having fought the war). By the same token the camps usefully helped to salve any guilt or shame that might have existed on the British side for their less commendable actions of the war – the bombing of German civilians, for example. Thus a preoccupation with these debates and the usefulness of the camp revelations to them, prevented British society on the whole from grasping the significance of Belsen in terms of the Holocaust. Finally, a third response was encouraged by party politics. Although Bergen-Belsen was a new name to the general public in 1945, the other camps liberated in the same period, and, in particular, Buchenwald and Dachau, were names familiar from the 1930s. As we know, before the war these camps had been built to confine the political opponents of the Nazi Party; in particular, socialists and trade unionists. In Britain, fellow liberals and left-wingers had campaigned against Nazi policy and tried to publicise the conditions which existed in the concentration camps. They also criticised the appeasement stance of the Conservative government, which did not openly speak out against these camps. In 1945, when the name of Buchenwald hit the headlines again and the terrible conditions found there were exposed, it seemed the cause of the left had been finally substantiated. Mindful of an approaching general election, and with the dreadful images from the camps as a backdrop, left-wing politicians lost no time in reminding the public of Conservative policies in the 1930s and what they had led to. Thus, partisan commentators used the camps to score political points. This served to ensure that Belsen was identified with the pre-war image of Nazi concentration camps and once again the full implication of its liberation remained obscured.

Before we can examine the responses to the liberation of the western camps in 1945 in more depth, it is important first to establish what was already known about them in Britain before and during the war. Andrew Sharf in his *The British Press and the Jews under Nazi Rule* presents us with a useful survey of press opinion for the whole of the Nazi period.[5] Throughout the 1930s the British press followed events closely and were 'fully alive to the violent aspect of anti-semitism in Germany' from its beginnings.[6] Information on the day-to-day persecution of the Jews was relatively easily available to foreign correspondents, and the *Manchester Guardian* in particular gave it serious attention. National Socialist Germany did not openly publicise its concentration camps, yet a significant number of articles appeared throughout the British press revealing the existence of the camps and the treatment of the prisoners therein. Nevertheless, the extreme measures of Nazi internal policy did not fully come to light until the *Kristallnacht* pogrom of November 1938. Until this time, the main actions against the Jews had been economic and social; the camp population consisted, on the whole, of political opponents to the Nazi regime – the communists, trade unionists and the 'work-shy'. The extreme violence of the pogrom, the rounding up of Jews and the resultant rise in the camp population, secured a great deal of attention in the British press.[7] The immediate shock may have been short-lived[8] but the names of Dachau and Buchenwald in particular, as the most notorious of the German camps, were fixed in the public mind. Indeed, throughout the 1930s, liberals and those on the political left in Britain had campaigned on behalf of their comrades in Germany and the name Dachau especially represented to them everything that was abhorrent in Nazism.

## I

Before the war began, the only organised inquiry into Nazi brutalities was that concerned with the treatment of the political opposition in Germany made by the British left.[9] Throughout the 1930s, the cornerstone of British foreign policy was appeasement. The government, therefore, was reluctant to give emphasis to the press reports of the concentration camps. Once war was declared, however, the Foreign Office published a White Paper on German atrocities. Issued in October 1939 and compiled from consular reports, the 36-page document recorded details of the floggings, tortures and hard labour that were regularly inflicted on political prisoners in Germany.[10] The government, however, keen to avoid giving credence to the 'Jews' War' accusation, did not present the Nazi anti-semitic outrages as particularly significant.[11] In press circles the White Paper was generally welcomed, although mainly because it authenticated what the newspapers had already reported rather than because it said anything new.[12] None the less, its release was deemed to have been a failure by the Foreign Office, serving only to alienate many members of the public who believed the Paper to be a propaganda stunt.[13] The public, it was deemed, linked the White Paper to similar tales of atrocity, which had emanated from official sources, about the German regime during the First World War. Such stories had circulated widely but after the war were proved to be false. The 1939 White Paper, then, was viewed by some sections of the public as in the same vein of government propaganda designed to alienate any pro-German opinion. The question of whether the British public believed the atrocity stories about

the German concentration camps in the 1930s or not is an important consideration but it is of secondary importance as far as we are concerned in this chapter.
The crucial factor to bear in mind is that even those people who chose not to
believe the reports, were forced, nevertheless, to give thought to the subject
and, for a short time at least, they had their minds focused on the names and
existence of camps such as Buchenwald. As we shall see, this was a significant
element in shaping British responses to the liberation of the concentration
camps in 1945.

The third year of the war, 1941, witnessed the implementation of the 'Final
Solution' to the 'Jewish Problem' in Europe. According to Sharf, 'It is a remarkable fact that . . . a great deal of information about Jews in German-occupied
territory did appear in the British Press during the whole of the war'.[14] Reliable
information from a range of sources was available on exterminations and gas
chambers in Britain by the end of 1942. As early as January 1942, the *Daily
Herald* reported that Poles, in large numbers, were being transported to
Oswiecim (Auschwitz) concentration camp in cattle trucks, where they were
the victims of much cruelty.[15] *The Times* and the *Sunday Times* carried a similar
story five months later.[16] Reports became more widespread in the summer of
1942. For the first time in June the *Daily Telegraph* published reports, based
on information from the Polish *Bund*, which made it clear that the Jews were
actually being exterminated in Poland as part of a Nazi plan. The Chelmno
camp and the use of gas vans were highlighted in the first report and in the
second, under the headline, 'More than a Million Jews Killed in Europe', the
deportations of the Jews in western Europe were detailed.[17] Following a press
conference on 29 June, at which Dr Schwarzbart of the Polish National Council
further outlined the fact of the gassings in Europe, the majority of newspapers
carried the story.[18] These reports were confirmed in August 1942 in a telegram
sent to London and Washington by Gerhard Riegner, representative of the
World Jewish Congress in Switzerland.[19] As further disturbing reports reached
the 'free world' pressure increased for the Allies to make some form of condemnatory statement. The newspapers in Britain, and particularly the *Manchester
Guardian*, continued to carry details on the death camps as they emerged,
culminating in a series of reports during the winter of 1942–3. Finally, on
17 December 1942, a Declaration by the Allies gave official sanction to the
reports that the Jews of Europe were being systematically exterminated.[20] As
it transpired this was to be the peak of reporting on the 'Final Solution'; over
the following two years interest in and press coverage of the events in Poland
were to decline. According to Harold Nicolson, MP, writing in 1943, 'the
press was bored with atrocity stories'.[21] Nevertheless, some news did get
through. In November 1943 the *Sunday Times* reported that a large concentration camp had opened up in Lublin, in addition to that at Majdanek, where gas
chambers had been installed to carry out mass murders and the average life of a
prisoner was seven to eight weeks.[22] The following June, several papers again
highlighted the gassing of Jews at Oswiecim, one paper labelling the camp
'where hundreds of thousands of Jews have perished' as 'notorious'. In July

and August 1944 the plight of the Hungarian Jews and the liberation of the Majdanek camp, respectively, were featured, although certainly not so prominently as might now be expected, given the critical nature of the events.[23]

Scholars writing subsequently on the Allied knowledge of the Holocaust – such as Walter Laqueur and Martin Gilbert in the 1980s[24] – have agreed with Sharf that information on the 'Final Solution' was widely available in Britain by 1942, but that the information was never widely accepted or understood. Laqueur insists that psychological barriers prevented the full comprehension of the unprecedented Nazi crimes, both at government and public levels: 'Barbaric fanaticism was unacceptable to people thinking on pragmatic lines, who believed that slave labour rather than annihilation was the fate of the Jews in Europe. The evil nature of Nazism was beyond their comprehension.'[25]

More recently, Tony Kushner has taken the debate on British perceptions of the 'Final Solution' during the Second World War a stage further, using social history to complement analysis based on press and government records.[26] He maintains that, while psychological factors were important in forming the attitudes of the British public to the news of the Jewish plight, they did not work in isolation, but operated in an ideological and cultural framework which we must also understand. In Britain, Kushner argues, the existence of a commanding monocultural liberal ideology 'led to a total failure of imagination . . . with regard to the Final Solution'.[27] The reluctance of the government to identify the specific Jewish plight and the inability of people to grasp the true nature of Nazi anti-semitism (implicated not in pogroms but in a far more sinister and systematic programme of mass killing) helped ensure that the majority of the British population had little or no idea of the enormity of the impact of Nazi racist policy on the Jews of Europe during the war.

Understanding did not follow the liberation of the camps in 1945 despite the tremendous effect of the findings on the public. If, as Laqueur affirms with reference to the difficulties the public faced in assimilating the scale of the Jewish massacre, 'Big figures become statistics, and statistics have no psychological impact',[28] the opposite is true of photographs and moving pictures. In the spring of 1945 the British press was awash with images of the concentration camps. There can be no doubt they made a great psychological impact on almost everyone who saw them. The question, however, of whether these images brought the British people any nearer to an understanding of the Holocaust, in a way that the newspaper reports of the massacres had not, is debatable and will form the basis of the discussion below. It is necessary first to examine the ways in which the British public was informed of the camps.

## II

Buchenwald was the first of the western camps to be liberated. On the evening of Sunday 15 April 1945, the BBC broadcast the account by Ed Murrow, an American journalist following the US 3rd Army, of his visit to Buchenwald on 12 April, the day after its liberation. Murrow was known in Britain to be 'a man of great integrity' which perhaps gave added validity to his descriptions of the terrible scenes he witnessed.[29] The next day, on 16 April, the British newspapers took up the story, some, like the *Evening Standard*, quoting the broadcast in full, 'lest the British people ever forget this greatest Nazi crime against humanity'.[30] Over the weeks that followed there was hardly a newspaper or magazine which did not carry pictures of one or more of the concentration camps. Buchenwald continued to feature in the newspapers but Sunday 15 April had seen the liberation of Belsen; those papers who had correspondents on the scene quickly were able to print reports on 18 April, although the majority came out on or after 19 April.[31]

The stories were profiled prominently by the daily papers for a number of issues, particularly by those with correspondents on the spot who sent back powerful eye-witness accounts. *The Times*, for two weeks after the liberation of Belsen, gave some mention to the camps every day. The Buchenwald reports, which came first and detailed the numbers of 'opponents of Hitlerism' who had died in this 'camp of death and misery', were rivalled by the death of Roosevelt on 13 April. Five days later, while the paper reported on page 3 that the citizens of Weimar had been forced to view Buchenwald, including the crematorium with two piles of emaciated dead just outside, the leading article on page 4 dealt with the service in memory of Roosevelt held at St Paul's Cathedral. The next day, 19 April, the first report on Belsen received a more prominent position on page 4, detailing as it did 'the most horrible, frightful place' the eye-witness who provided the story had ever seen. Many other papers used the same story to introduce their readers to the Belsen camp.[32] Across the board all the papers attempted the same end, to present the reports in a way in which left the reader in no doubt as to their authenticity.

Thus, in the first week of reporting, the stories were rarely allowed to stand on their own. Editors, conscious of the difficulties the public would face in accepting the camp reports and wary of the dangers of distressing readers to the point of alienation, often felt it necessary to preface the stories with a rationalisation for their decision to print them. Thus, under the headline 'Torture Camps: This Is the Evidence' the *Daily Mail* stressed that the article to follow was 'a factual account of German atrocities prepared from reports to the Editor by Daily Mail on-the-spot war reporters. . . . It is presented without the intention of harrowing readers' feelings or revolting their sensibilities. But it is presented without apology.' The *Evening Standard*, often slightly ahead in printing the stories, maintained that the focus and motivation behind printing the articles was to record and document on paper these important eye-witness accounts 'lest the British people ever forget this greatest crime against humanity'. On 18 April the sensationalist headline 'I Was a Prisoner in Buchenwald' was preceded by the admonition in bold type: 'Lest We Forget: Here for the record, is the direct evidence of a British officer out from the worst of the Nazi concentration camps.' The *Daily Sketch* believed it necessary to introduce its story on Belsen with the comment 'Hitherto the world found it hard to believe atrocity stories. Now British and American correspondents are seeing for themselves the full extent of German crimes against humanity.' Naturally, the correspondents, themselves extremely shocked by what they had seen, were determined that the British public should not be spared their stories. The *Sunday Times* reporter R.W. Thompson stressed this point:

> We few who have had the opportunity to view this atrocity against mankind have the right to demand your attention.
>
> There are perhaps three to four hundred of us, war correspondents perhaps 20, the rest soldiers, and our words, our honour must suffice that this terrible deed against the human spirit may be known to the world.[33]

The fact that the most horrific conditions found by the Western Allies were in a camp hitherto unheard of, made the task of the journalists presenting the story slightly more difficult. As we have seen, it was considered that descriptions of Belsen were perhaps more than the British people could absorb and endure. The BBC was not even prepared to trust its own correspondents. It has already been noted that when Richard Dimbleby sent his dispatch with haste to the BBC in London, they waited until press sources had confirmed the story before they broadcast it.[34] Looking at the first newspaper reports, one can determine that particular attention was given to authenticating the accounts. The difficult task of the journalists was to describe what they saw in words which did justice to the horror but did not threaten the integrity of the reports. A *Times* article of 19 April, based on a statement made from 2nd Army Headquarters, serves to illustrate the point:

> General Dempsey's senior medical officer, a brigadier, said here today that the Belsen concentration camp, near Bremen, with its thousands of typhus, typhoid and tuberculosis cases was 'the most horrible, frightful place' he had ever seen. . . .
>
> 'The prison doctors tell me that cannibalism is going on', the brigadier said. 'There was no flesh on the bodies. The liver, kidneys and heart were knifed out.'

The report, from Reuter, places a stress on the fact that the information given is based on the account of a high-ranking British officer who was an *eye-witness* at the Belsen camp. Brigadier Glyn Hughes is indirectly quoted throughout the article until the reporter has to deal with the allegation that cannibalism had been a practice in Belsen. This horrific fact, exactly the stuff of 'atrocity' propaganda and bound to meet with some scepticism from *Times* readers, was placed in direct quotation marks. The journalist thus distanced himself from the allegation and stressed that the seemingly inconceivable report is from an official and reliable source. Readers were then directed to page 6 of the newspaper where they would find pictures of the camps which 'confirmed' the published accounts of German brutality. Similarly, the *Daily Mail* was keen to emphasise that the 'factual account of the German atrocities' given in the issue of 19 April, was prepared by 'on-the-spot reporters'.[35] Such factual reporting did help in the acceptance of the camp reports. So, too, did the obvious emotion of the correspondents writing direct from the scene. One of the most moving accounts of Camp I in Belsen came from Ronald Monson writing for the *Evening Standard*. He poignantly describes one enduring image of Belsen:

> The indignity of death above ground – the bared teeth, the revealed frame that should be sacred, and once was sacred to some loved one, the piled bodies in their ghastly greyness, the pitiable little thing with claws instead of a hand was a baby, still within the protecting grasp of an emaciated bone that was once a mother's arm – all on the Nazi death heap.

Monson, too, was determined that readers would not doubt the truth of his words: 'I have been close to the wake of armies for eight years now, in Spain, China and over most of this war's battlefields . . . but . . . believe me when I tell you that what I saw this day was worse than anything I have ever seen anywhere.'[36]

Unlike previous atrocity stories reported during the war, reports were given prominence and not hidden away off the main news pages. We must bear in mind that this was a time when many national dailies and provisional papers were limited to four pages because of paper rationing. Secondly, with the Allies advancing towards Berlin, this was a very crucial point in the general progress of the war. Yet, many columns were found for the camp reports and headlines often appeared in large bold typeface in order to seize the attention of the reader.

The newspapers often fastened their stories on the reputation of their regular and trusted war correspondents. The *News Chronicle* readers followed the unfolding of the Belsen liberation story through the accounts of Colin Wills. On 18 April a general report by Wills was published, detailing the fact that 60,000 starving prisoners were now in the control of the Allies. The following day the camp disclosures received greater attention. Readers were presented with 'Belsen Camp: the Full Terrible Story' written by Wills following an actual visit to the camp: 'The worst horrors I described in yesterday's dispatch are far exceeded by what I have seen since.' In the same issue Wills offered a new angle on the story which continued to fascinate the press over the ensuing weeks: 'The Kind of Women Who Staffed Concentration Camps'.[37] Indeed, in much of the coverage of the camps, particularly in the popular papers, there was a discernible duality of purpose in the reporting. While the need to inform the readership was clearly evident, so too was a tendency towards sensationalism and the need to provide a certain amount of titillation from the camp material.

The newspapers presented the camp stories in a way fitting to their general editorial policy. Thus while reports in *The Times* and the *Manchester Guardian* were generally quite restrained and factual, the *Evening Standard*, as we have seen, was more prone to sensationalist headlines. Few chose a style as graphic as the *Daily Worker* which, incidentally, also managed to impose a crude 'class' analysis on the story. Under the banner 'The Black Hole of Belsen – the most terrible story yet to come out of Hitler's Germany', the paper promised its readers:

> It tells of the dead lying rotting in piles and in the gutters and the drains; of typhus, typhoid and tuberculosis sweeping through the camp unchecked; and of luxurious German barracks for SS officers only a few yards away from this charnel house.[38]

All the reports, however, revealed the same difficulties which had faced the soldiers, in trying to describe the camps adequately. Ed Murrow told listeners of the BBC, 'For most of it I have no words.' A Reuter correspondent insisted that to tell the whole story of the camps would 'offend public morality'. Ronald Monson for the *Evening Standard* asserted in the same vein: 'Because of the niceties of language, because none should be offended unnecessarily, it is hard for me to tell you what you should know.' The horror of Belsen was said to be 'impossible to exaggerate or describe'.[39] As we have noted in Chapter 1, a common recourse for eye-witnesses was to construct comparisons with images which might be familiar with the reader. As is clear from the following example, taken from a report on Belsen by John D'arcy-Dawson, such analogies add little to the reader's understanding: 'We came to the first enclosure and the wire gates swung open to let us into the first approach to hell, not the hell of burning death but the cold hell of purgatory.' It is only when the reporters attempt to describe the camp that we gain a stronger perspective. The people in Belsen seemed to D'arcy-Dawson 'caricatures of humanity [with] their eyes sunk deep in their heads, their faces black with dirt, their rags hanging around legs thin as a wrist'. With one sentence he ably constructs a powerful impression of the camp.[40]

That editors were aware of the difficulties in presenting such horrific accounts in a manner acceptable to their readership is clear from the way in which they handled photographic evidence. Although the press had been covering the war for over five years, the public had never been confronted with the actual realities of fighting, that is, images of killing and bloodshed.[41] There was little precedent for showing the kind of horrific images made available by Supreme Allied Head-quarters.

Nevertheless, pictorial evidence was considered crucial in the campaign to prove the reports of atrocity were true, and photographs were chosen and used carefully. Readers of *The Times* were directed to the more discreet back page on 19 April for three pictures of the conditions in Buchenwald, Ohrdruf and Nordhausen camps.[42] The more popular papers were a little less cautious. The *Daily Mail* published a photograph of an open burial trench at Nordhausen on the same day and others followed suit. This was true of the *Daily Herald* in particular. Although its editorial comment was confined to the dual drives of the Allies to Berlin and the Labour Party to potential electoral victory, camp reports featured prominently on its front page together with photographs.[43] Neverthe-less, editors shied away from printing the worst images available to them as these were simply too terrible. The dilemma was faced most directly by the picture weeklies, papers like the *Illustrated London News* and *Picture Post*, which covered the war and daily news largely through the medium of photographs and artists' impressions. The solution of the *Post* was not to cover the liberations at all. The first mention of the camps came in the 5 May issue when an article, admittedly featuring pictures from Nordhausen, dealt with the issue of how the German people tolerated the camps. Similarly, the *Illustrated London News* did not cover the camps in the first issue after their disclosure but held back until 28 April. Then the editor considered the pictures from the camps to be so shocking as to warrant being placed in a four-page detachable pull-out.[44]

The Jewish press had, not surprisingly, been very well informed about the Nazi extermination policies against the Jews, although it was not always so keen to stress the specific Jewish aspect of the atrocities.[45] On 9 February 1945 the *Jewish Chronicle* reported that the Oswiecim camp had been liberated a week earlier and that the first investigations put even those at Majdanek in the shade: 'It is estimated that over 1,500,000 victims were done to death at Oswiecim, and hundreds of thousands of them were Jews.' On 13 April the same paper reported evidence that 3.2 million Polish Jews alone had been slaughtered by the Nazis.[46] In the light of such reports then, the *Chronicle* did not greet the concentration camp revelations with as much shock and surprise as the majority of the British press. In an editorial of 27 April the paper asked incisively: 'Why have we had to wait till now for this widespread revulsion?' The editor, Ivan Greenberg, earnestly disparaged those who had dismissed the previous mountain of evidence as 'Jewish atrocity stories': 'It is not long since Majdanek, scene of atrocities infinitely more gruesome even than those of Belsen and Buchenwald, was practically ignored by the leading newspapers.'[47] Indeed, many people in Britain at this time would not have recognised the name of Majdanek or Auschwitz.

At no time in the past three years had the press given to the extermination centres in Poland anything approaching the coverage and comment they now gave to the German concentration camps. The publicity triggered a wave of genuine shock and marked horror across the whole country. For a time the concentration camps formed the major topic of conversation in shops, in offices and on trains and trams everywhere.[48] Newspaper editors were inundated with correspondence. A measure of the impact of the reports on the British people is that for a number of days they proved to be of more interest than the general war news – a rare thing in a war-weary Britain following eagerly the Allied advance towards Berlin.[49] Every news broadcast seemed to bring worse tidings. On 19 April, the BBC broadcast Richard Dimbleby's moving account of his visit to Belsen. Initial reactions were largely unvarying: 'After listening to a description of one of the camps a deathly, grim silence falls: nobody can give expression to what they are feeling, horror, pity, anger, amazement and helplessness – I think they all feel the same.'[50] The newspaper reports undoubtedly had a marked bearing on people but they did not match the wireless broadcasts for immediacy; to be able to hear the emotion in the voice of the reporters as they described the scenes before them made a deep and lasting impression.

Pictures of the camps, some hitherto unpublished by the newspapers, were placed on public display. The first exhibition of photographs opened on

24 April at the offices of the *Daily Express* in Regent Street. Admission was free and the exhibition, which included enlarged pictures of Buchenwald, Belsen and Nordhausen, was open daily from 10 a.m. until 7 p.m., including Sundays.[51] Towards the end of April, the Ministry of Information allocated an extra allowance of film stock to the newsreel companies so that they were able to include full scenes of the conditions in the concentration camps in the next week's editions.[52] The newsreels, which contained footage from several of the camps, but particularly Belsen, began showing around the country in the week beginning 30 April. Ordinarily, each issue of a newsreel was shown for three days but in this case, the showing was extended to a week.[53] Frequent visits to the cinema were a regular part of British life; in 1945 an average of 30 million tickets were sold per week so that the camp footage reached a large audience.[54] Indeed, by 1 May all box office records had been broken in the London news theatres.[55]

The newsreel audiences were spared the most horrific scenes from the camps and some people even commented that the films were not as bad as they had imagined.[56] The explicitness of the newsreel, in general, tended to depend on the newsreel companies; Gaumont-British, for example, had a reputation for producing direct, hard-hitting films. The newsreels were supposed to be shown in all cinemas across the country, although the cinema owners did not always approve and sometimes refused to show the films. At a Manchester cinema the Buchenwald film was taken off when in one morning performance, one hundred people left the auditorium just as it was about to be shown. The manager obviously saw this as indicative of the public's disapproval of this type of film and was not prepared to risk his takings by continuing its showing.[57] In fact, most people did approve of the showing of the camp newsreels although not always necessarily the way they were presented. The cinemas often showed only a shortened version of the film (too short to be properly convincing) and insisted on presenting it, rather distastefully, as part of a programme including Walt Disney shorts and blatant propaganda films, the latter then casting doubt on the authenticity of the concentration camp material. One woman, having visited a London newsreel cinema, was sickened at the way the camp film had been shown: 'I think it's ridiculous, handling the public in this kid glove way. They should show the whole thing, and nothing else, in special programmes at all the newsreel cinemas, and they shouldn't mix it up with Donald Duck or any light relief at all. The majority of people are neither squeamish nor sadistic, and they can stand the full truth. And the deeper the impression the better. People *must* stop saying about horrors "It's just propaganda".'[58]

Remarkably, like the general public, the government, too, seemed to have been genuinely shocked by the camp revelations. On the ground, the Allied advance was directed by Strategic Headquarters Allied Expeditionary Force (SHAEF) and General Eisenhower, the Supreme Allied Commander. Nevertheless, Churchill was surprisingly out of touch as far as the camps were concerned. Furthermore, the Members in both Houses of Parliament relied on press and wireless reports in the same way as the general public. On 6 April the American 4th Armoured Division liberated Ohrdruf, one of Buchenwald's 136 auxiliary camps, where they found over 3,000 corpses. The next day, units of the 7 Corps of the American 1st Army, entered another such camp at Nordhausen. It was not until 18 April, however, that Eisenhower telephoned Churchill for the first time about the entry of his troops into these camps.[59] Photographs of Belsen had reached the presses before Churchill had received on 19 April (very limited) information on further camp discoveries. On that same day, the Prime Minister addressed the House of Commons:

> No words can express the horror which is felt by His Majesty's Government and their principal Allies at the proofs of these frightful crimes now daily coming into view. . . .
>
> I have this morning received an informal message from General Eisenhower saying that the new discoveries, particularly at Weimar, far surpass anything previously exposed.[60]

In the light of the liberation of Belsen and the press coverage already given to the camps, Churchill's statement was already out of date. Placing that aside, however, the announcement that the conditions at Buchenwald far surpassed anything previously exposed, was quite remarkable, coming, as it did, from the leader of a government which just over two years earlier had made a statement on behalf of the Allies acknowledging the Nazi extermination policy, and from a man who had, at least by July 1944, 'learned the full extent of the mass murder of the Jews at Auschwitz'.[61] This detail received no comment from his biographer. On 20 April, Churchill telegraphed his wife who was in the Caucasus: 'Here we are all shocked by the most horrible revelations of German cruelty in the concentration camps.'[62]

General Eisenhower suggested to Churchill that he might arrange for a party of MPs and journalists to visit SHAEF Headquarters at once, where arrangements would be made to send them forward to the scenes of the atrocities. Eisenhower was keen that the camps be inspected at first hand by a respected group of civilians who could confirm that the situation had not been exaggerated. He was concerned that an American delegation would 'be too late to see the full horrors, whereas an English delegation, being so much closer, could get there in time'.[63] Churchill agreed to the general's request and when volunteers for the trip were asked for in the House, fifty MPs put forward their names. As a further measure, the Prime Minister arranged that photographs of the camps be circulated around the House. An all-party delegation, chosen by the Whips, of nine men and one woman left for the Continent on 20 April. The arrangements had been hurried and although it had originally been thought that the MPs would see several of the camps,[64] in the event a limited timetable allowed a visit to Buchenwald only. Nevertheless, the report that resulted from the trip – drafted by Tom Driberg, MP, widely publicised by the press and published as a White Paper – was successful in the first of its aims, to give further credibility to the 'atrocity stories'. The White Paper's second objective was to make it impossible for 'some German order of the future to maintain that these prison camps were in fact a myth'.[65] Of the White Paper 80,000 copies were sold and 30,000 supplied in free distribution.[66] There were calls from politicians, press and public for more delegations ('trained observers', doctors and church representatives were a few suggestions) to visit the camps and complement the lay-person's findings.[67] V.H. Galbraith, of the Institute of Historical Research, wrote to *The Times* that further eye-witness accounts were desirable: 'The last word on these matters will lie with the historian and the historian is justly sceptical of the "atrocities".'[68] The advice was prudent. Despite the mountain of evidence corroborating the facts of the Nazi racial policy, the legacy of scepticism is still much in evidence over fifty years after the events.

## III

The press, public and government reactions to the liberations in the spring of 1945 make it perfectly clear that there had been little acknowledgement or credence given to the reports on the 'Final Solution' during the war. British society had viewed them as 'atrocity stories', perhaps having some truth, but largely exaggerated for propaganda purposes. Many people, and indeed the government, were always mindful of the widespread propaganda campaigns which had abounded during the First World War. Western allegations of German atrocities, such as the use in soap factories of Allied corpses, were endorsed by reputable writers but found subsequently to be untrue. Thus in the Second World War, 'the general inclination was to disbelieve . . . [any atrocity story], frequently with reference to "lessons" from the First World War: no one wanted to be misled for the second time within one generation.'[69] Clearly, there was an implicit assumption in the actions of those whose task it was to bring the news of the camps to the public in 1945: that their audience would be difficult to convince. Had there been a widespread acceptance of the scale of operations in the Polish extermination centres, then the impact made by the western camps would not have been quite so shocking. As it was, comparisons were rarely drawn between the barbarity of the concentration camps and that which had already been exposed in the Polish camps. In the minds of British ministers in 1945, Buchenwald exceeded 'all example or indeed imagination' and Belsen was 'the acme of atrocity'.[70]

In general, the efforts of eye-witnesses and those in the media to ensure the reports of the camps were not classed as atrocity propaganda, were largely successful and the majority of people did accept them as true. The evidence seemed irrefutable. The horrific photographs reproduced in the majority of newspapers and shown on the newsreels, the eye-witness accounts by respected western *Allied* journalists and military personnel, and the on-the-spot reports by well-known broadcasters, together convinced the populace that the horrific conditions in the camps were real. Moreover, in later weeks the reports were reinforced when people began to receive letters from close friends and relatives who had seen the concentration camps and firsthand accounts from eye-witnesses who returned from Europe.[71] The army had been taken by surprise at the terrible conditions in the camps.[72] A sense of genuine outrage persuaded the military to do their utmost to ensure that the news from the camps was not viewed at home as distasteful propaganda. In particular, officers encouraged their forces, although such encouragement was usually unnecessary, to write letters home and confirm the press reports of the camps as true.

The descriptions and images of the camps shocked the army, the politicians and the British public as a whole because they were all forced to *confront* them. Here was evidence in abundance, from reliable sources, which could not be ignored. Walter Laqueur draws the distinction between 'knowing' and 'believing' facts that are difficult to accept, as a means of explaining the inability of the public to assimilate information on the 'Final Solution' as it was imple-mented.[73] He suggests that no matter how much information is given to an indi-vidual, if that information is unacceptable, for whatever reason, then the individual will reject it. We can take this simple point further and also recognise the distinction between 'knowing' or 'believing' and 'understanding'. We may have been acquainted with a set of facts, we might even believe them to be true, but for those facts to be palpable, that is, for us to be able to *relate* to them, to understand them and be able to empathise, is a different matter. The pictures from the concentration camps helped British people to relate facts to feelings, and to give the facts a context. Earlier in the war, the reports from the east seemed so far away because Europe, geographically close, was symboli-cally as well as literally lost when conquered by the Axis. In 1941 the details of Operation Barbarossa were probably remote to many ordinary people who were more relieved that the persistent bombing campaign of the previous year was over for the time being. Most general interest in trends in the war was turned on the North Africa or Atlantic campaigns where the British at least had a direct influence. As the Allied armies closed in on Greater Germany in 1944 and 1945, then Europe became psychologically closer to home. The liberation of the camps in 1945 came as part of the Normandy campaign, which was fol-lowed closely and with great interest by the British public. Further, when the camps in Germany were liberated, the names, to a certain extent, were familiar; these were not the strange-sounding Polish names associated with earlier atrocity reports, which were difficult to pronounce. The accounts reached the British public from sources they recognised, names and personalities they knew. On 18 April 1945, Mass-Observation (MO) organised a pre-peace news question-naire in which a cross-sample of the population was interviewed. The answers to the question 'Do you think the atrocity stories are true?' are very interesting, particularly when compared with the answers to the same question four months earlier:

*Table 1* Comparison of percentages of population believing atrocity stories surrounding the Nazi regime, December 1944/April 1945

| Response | % on 18 Apr. 1945 | % on 1 Dec. 1944 |
| --- | --- | --- |
| True | 81 | 37 |
| Partly | 16 | 29 |
| False | 3 | 11 |
| No opinion | 0 | 23 |

*Source:* Mass-Observation pre-peace questionnaire, 18 April 1945

We can see that the great majority of the people who were asked in 1945 believed the 'atrocity stories' to be true and not a single respondent was uncertain enough to give no opinion. In 1944, however, it is evident that a great many people were unsure about the 'atrocity stories'. The shift was undoubtedly in part due to the widespread coverage the camps had received in 1945 so that more people felt able to express an opinion. According to at least one interviewee, however, 'seeing the pictures' made a great difference.[74]

The fact that Buchenwald was the first of the major western camps to be liberated also contributed to the readiness of the British people to accept the reports. As we have seen, together with Dachau, it was a name well known to a great many people in Britain. The camp had not been at the forefront of too many minds during the war, but when people were reminded of the name in 1945, images of the pre-war period were triggered once again: the reports of torture, floggings and hangings outlined in the government White Paper of 1939 were recollected.[75] Newspapers reprinted and recalled their pre-war reports on Buchenwald and Dachau and reminded readers that the camp horrors 'were common immediately after the coming to power of Hitler'.[76] For those on the political left, in particular, the name Buchenwald brought to mind the reality and horror of the fascist dictatorship which incarcerated any of its own nationals who dared voice dissent. Further, when Dachau was liberated at the end of April, the *Daily Telegraph* carried the story heralding Dachau as the 'most notorious of all Nazi concentration camps'.[77] The overdue liberation of this camp had been awaited with trepidation by some who expected the conditions to rival still further anything that had been thus far uncovered by the Allies.[78] It is important to note here that no significant amount of information had reached Britain about the movement of German prisoners from camps in the east to those in the west, or that the death camps in Poland were in any way connected to the concentration camps in Germany. Thus, the public had no reason to believe that the make-up of the population or the function of Buchenwald had changed in the past eight (or in the case of Dachau, twelve) years.

Belsen, however, was not a name familiar to many in Britain. The history of the camp has been outlined elsewhere and suffice it to say here that Belsen had not existed as a concentration camp in the 1930s and had not received any press coverage in Britain until its liberation. *The Times* mentioned the camp for the first time on 14 April in view of its unique status in the war as the only area subject to a truce in the fighting between the British and the German forces. At this stage, few details were available to *The Times* except that the British were to take guard of a 'prison camp' which was known to contain 60,000 prisoners 'both criminals and anti-Nazis'. Thus, the Belsen camp was immediately assumed to be of a similar type to the 1930s concentration camps.[79]

It must not be assumed that everybody believed the 'atrocity stories'. Memories of the First World War British propaganda stories about the German 'Hun' did linger. These memories, combined with the shocking nature of the new reports and the rumours that the war was to end soon, led some people to be sceptical. One MO diarist admitted finding it difficult to keep an open mind on the horrors disclosed in the newspapers:

> I have not forgotten the recent controversy over the last war atrocity stories, and to me they have always smacked of propaganda – the Germans are our enemies, therefore we must hate the Germans, so additional evidence must be given us to whip up this hatred. . . . Cruelty has obviously been one of the trade marks of Nazism ever since 1933. . . . It is hard to believe, however, that this mass cruelty has been perpetrated on so many thousands of victims.[80]

Others were hard and fast in their scepticism and nothing would convince them of the truth in the reports from the camp. Sydney Silverman, MP, having recently returned from his visit to the Buchenwald camp, received a letter from a man who regarded the whole story as a fake. The writer explained in some detail how he believed the photographs of the MPs had been superimposed on the film.[81] Such extreme reservations were not typical. The number of doubters, however, was not insignificant. More often than not their misgivings stemmed from the fact that they were misinformed or confused about the nature of the camps in question.

The war situation was one in which anxieties were high and rumours rife. Personal experience often counted for a great deal although, as in the case of one man in Yorkshire, it could lead to confusion. He disbelieved all the 'atrocity stories' simply on the evidence that two friends of his had returned from France, having been interned by the Germans, and had 'nothing to grumble about'.[82] In fact, a significant minority of people were not entirely clear what constituted a concentration camp. Many believed the atrocity stories referred to the internment or prisoner-of-war camps under the control of the Germans.[83] Some linked the stories in the newspapers to the British prisoners of war, freed from Europe, whom they saw arriving back into London.[84] Parochial concerns tended to figure highly in the minds of the reporters and the readers of the war news. Those people who were already worried about relatives in German prisoner-of-war camps, only became more anxious when reading about Buchenwald and Belsen. Aneurin Bevan, MP, speaking in the House of Commons, recognised that such confusion was causing anxiety to the civilian population. He asked the Prime Minister to make it clear that British and American prisoners of war were not generally confined in those camps linked with the atrocities.[85] It is possible to see how this kind of confusion could arise for the uninformed reader, if one examines some of the reporting in the newspapers. In the *Illustrated London News* of 28 April, for example, the capture of Fallingbostel (with the subsequent release of thousands of British prisoners from Stalag 11B) and the reluctance of the German population to acknowledge the Belsen 'torture' camp, were reported in a single small paragraph. No attempt was made to distinguish between the nature of the two camps mentioned.[86] Further, when one of a very small number of British prisoners in the concentration camps was identified by a journalist, the case was inevitably highlighted in the news-papers, to give added authority to the reports. Thus, for instance, on 18 April the *Evening Standard* printed the account of Lt Christopher Burney, a Com-mando officer, under the sensationalist headline, 'I Was a Prisoner in Buchen-wald', appealing to parochial considerations.[87]

The majority of the public, in fact, were able to draw the distinction between a concentration camp and a Stalag and did trust in the reports emanating from the former. One MO diarist, a vicar, noted that the revelations had impressed and changed the outlook of many people: 'They realize that these are hard facts and not just atrocity propaganda, and for once they feel that something should be done about it.[88]

What action should be taken in the light of these atrocities, that is, what fate should befall the German population who let them happen, was a subject that occupied a great many British minds in 1945. Indeed, as we shall see, one of the major debates in Britain after the liberation of the camps concerned German guilt. According to Ian McLaine, in his study of the Ministry of Information in the Second World War, the ministry had expended a great deal of time and energy over the preceding five years in persuading the public as to what their attitude towards the enemy should be. Initially, in 1939, with the spirit of appeasement still strong, and with the hope still alive that the National Socialist Party would be ousted from power, the ministry was keen to exonerate the German people from blame for the Nazi crimes. As the war moved closer to home, however, the Policy Committee at the Ministry agreed that the separation of the German people from Nazism should be avoided; Nazism was to be por-trayed as but the latest and most virulent manifestation of the inherent wickedness of the German race.[89] A Psychological Warfare Executive Central Directive, dated 21 October 1943, stated, 'Always emphasize that these [cases of terror, persecution and tyranny] are being committed in the name of the whole German people.'[90] The conviction of Brendan Bracken, Minister of Infor-mation, to maintain the links between the Nazi crimes and the German people, was evident as late as April 1945 when he answered questions in the House on the concentration camps:

> if the German people did not endorse the conduct of the German people whom they put in power, then the German people must remember that they have to accept the consequences of their government. . . . In this war the Germans have shown themselves to be good at organising fighting, and let me warn the House that they will be equally good in organising whining.[91]

A lesson Churchill had drawn from the First World War and one he was resolved to put into practice in the Second, was that the government should not be drawn into declaring peace aims. This attitude had caused the Ministry of Information great problems in depicting an image of postwar Europe. Without any declared peace objectives to work towards, they continued to insist on the inherent wickedness of the enemy in the last years of the war; for the ministry then, the camp discoveries made by the Allied armies in Europe actually seemed to prove their long-held convictions.

In September 1944, the Cabinet formally agreed to the first phase of a policy of 're-education' for the German people.[92] As Nicholas Pronay explains, they 'were not to be treated as if they themselves had been the victims . . . of Hitler or the Nazis. . . . Instead they were to be treated as the race which needed its spirit of "militarism" broken once and for all.'[93] The British people themselves needed to be persuaded of the need for such an unprecedented policy. In the newsreels, during the winter of 1944–5, the psychology of the German nation was incessantly portrayed as one of a culpable people with an innate compulsion to war. Popular stereotypes and existing attitudes were mobilised in support of this policy, so that it appeared a logical extension of public opinion. How far did the propaganda about the German nation affect the public's reaction to the concentration camps?

Certainly, the immediate reaction of one section of the British population on seeing the pictures and newsreels, was to advocate that 'the German people' deserved no less harsh a treatment than they had dispensed to others. Feelings ran high and spur-of-the-moment remarks such as 'Death is too good for them' and 'Kill the lot of 'em' were commonly heard. One woman, when asked her views on how the German people should be re-educated, replied, 'I don't suggest re-educating them – I suggest exterminating them!'[94] Such instantaneous verbal responses should not be taken as an indicator of the feeling in the country as a whole. A great many people, however, having given time and thought to the subject, still proclaimed the necessity for drastic action against the German population. J. Gordon in a letter to the *Sunday Express* admitted to being 'a complete and fervent advocate of the utter extermination of [the German] nation'.[95] An MO diarist in Birmingham proclaimed that 'the German nation should be wiped out of civilisation, for they are not fit to belong to it' and another advocated that 'our men should use flame throwers on every [German] town and village they come to and wipe them *all* out'.[96] One diarist thought that only Germans under 25 years of age should be placed in the 'leathal chamber' (*sic*) whilst another woman stated that it was the children that should be taken out of Germany while the adults were exterminated. Other comments were only marginally more lenient. Although it was the view of Hyde C. Burton, a Commander in the Royal Navy, that the only decent German was a dead one, he realised it was 'outside the realm of possibility to exterminate them all' and proposed, instead, that every German within the Reich, 'other than those who have suffered under Hitler', should be rendered sterile.[97] These strong opinions and rash calls for drastic reprisals were reminiscent of those expressed during the intense bombing of Britain by the Germans in 1940. According to a Home Intelligence report at that time, large numbers of people felt 'that no peace can ever be considered which does not ensure that Germany will *never* again be able to declare war on England. . . . Many . . . want to exterminate, or at least ostracise, the whole German race.'[98] That such feelings were evoked in 1945 is a measure of the direct and shocking impact of the camp liberations. Precedent showed, however, that such feelings tended to abate quickly once the emergency was over.

Retributive feelings towards the German population as a whole were extended to include German prisoners of war in Britain, and, to give an indication of the level of ignorance of certain sectors of British society, even to those Germans who were refugees in Britain. Many Britons thought that German prisoners of war should be made to see the pictures of the concentration camps and indeed they were. By the summer the film of the concentration camps had been seen by 202,404 prisoners in 136 camps in Britain and Northern Ireland.[99] There were those who advocated that German prisoners should be punished further. The only solution in the words of one man interviewed in Hampstead, was to 'castrate every prisoner of war before he's released'.[100] A shop assistant in London was heard to say, 'After seeing that muddle-up of all those bodies in the paper I hate all Germans – even the ones over here.'[101] In a letter to *The Times* of 27 April, J.H. Gebhardt wrote, in despair, of a factory in Birmingham; the workers there had been so shocked by the revelations of the German atrocities that they protested against the employment by the firm of refugee workers of German origin.[102] The crucial fact that these refugees had travelled to Britain precisely to escape the concentration camps and had, more likely than not, lost members of their families in those same camps, had evidently escaped them.

Extreme and reactionary viewpoints were heard all over the country during the months of April and May. Many were disturbing in their voracity and, to the modern reader, have more than a touch of irony. The more enraged comments usually came from those who took the view championed by the Ministry of Information that the Germans were a barbaric race, the only race who could have been capable of such crimes. Most people advocated punishment along the lines of an 'eye for an eye' but naturally did not draw any parallels between their own outbursts and the behaviour of the National Socialists. In effect these people advocated that the Germans, members of a nation perceived through caricatures, deserved to die *en masse* because they were German. The parallels with the Nazis' distorted portrayal of the Jews during the 1930s and 1940s are clear: the Germans were as 'barbaric' as the Jews were 'insidious'. Ironically, such comments as those voiced in Britain after the disclosures from the camps serve only to strengthen the conviction that 'if the Germans can do these things others can'.[103] Few people made this connection. One exception was a 30-year-old woman, interviewed outside the *Daily Express* exhibition:

I'm afraid it didn't make me feel anti-German; it made me feel anti-humanity. Would the same have happened here, I wonder, if we'd had the same government? I've heard some violent anti-Semitic talk which makes me think it would. I feel it's the fault of humanity at large, not the Germans in particular.[104]

The MO archive provides us with evidence that there was a notable amount of ignorance and prejudice surrounding the perception of Jews in Britain at 1945. According to George Orwell, anti-semitism was a neurosis which lay very deep in 1940s Britain.[105] In an office discussion in Cheshire an old clerk argued that instead of torturing and killing the Jews, he thought the Germans could have passed laws, curtailing Jewish business. The man himself showed his prejudice, for the implication in his statement was that the Jewish businesses were too powerful, but also his ignorance of the Nazi legislation against the Jews in the 1930s. The clerk was strongly opposed, although sadly only by those colleagues whose prejudicial ideas were stronger: 'You can't pass laws against people in power. The Jews have the banks and the industries. You *couldn't* just make laws.'[106] In September 1945, at the time the Belsen trial was making headlines, a young woman from Stanmore in Middlesex made the following diary entry:

> Notice that a lot of fuss and rumpus is being made about the Jews again. I wonder if it is all true, or merely what Douglas Reed says 'Because of the organised state of Jewry, we always know if 20 Jews suffer, but not if thousands of non-Jews do'. If only one *knew* what was true. I am a little suspicious.
>
> The play [broadcast on the wireless] was quite good. Why are blustering thick-headed fathers in plays always North-Country?[107]

The answer lies, surely, with ignorance and prejudice, of which Douglas Reed was a practised and evil exponent.

The British wartime propaganda machine showed results. One woman, for example, who believed that when the armistice was signed the Allies should go on bombing for a fortnight, commented that her view might be barbaric 'but they are a barbaric race, and understand such actions'.[108] But its impact was not total. A civil servant writing for MO noted, 'My reaction (which I feel is a common one) is to determine that I *won't* be persuaded to hate Germans on the mass.'[109] In a second entry she observed:

> In all the bulletins and commentaries now they keep emphasising the hardness of the fighting still ahead, and the horrors of the prison camps. I don't doubt for a moment that it is all true but it annoys me because of the deliberate intention to make us think a certain way. . . . Our official propagandists are almost as crude as their German opposite numbers at times.[110]

Some people believed such a hate campaign was futile and would only hamper the peace negotiations. 'To me it seems worse than useless to try to start "the peace" with this outlook', remarked one Mass Observer, 'as it is only fermenting worse trouble to come.'[111] The subject of re-education was mentioned frequently at this time. The public and MPs were keen that as many of the German people as possible should be forced to see the camps or at least the films of the atrocities.[112] The village of Burgsteinfurt in Germany was labelled the 'Village of Hate' by the British military press when two young girls laughed having been shown the atrocity film. They were forced to see the film a second time.[113] Lord Denham, speaking in the House, wanted as many Germans as possible to be filled with remorse, for with remorse came repentance, and with repentance the chance that the German nation could be re-educated and regenerated. For the most part the public were in agreement with the policy of re-education. A young woman writing for MO in Winchester believed it was imperative to read about the atrocities so that one could understand the problems faced by Britain after the war – Nazism must be eradicated and the Germans re-educated. Another diarist noted that the camp revelations indicated the Germans were not fit to govern themselves. 'It seems to me that Germany should be occupied for many years to come.'[114] The outrage generated by the camps indeed helped give sanction to future governments who were to implement this policy.

A further debate largely fuelled by the liberations was that concerning German guilt. In June 1945 a Ministry of Information Directive insisted that '[t]he moral responsibility for these crimes should be laid wholly and solely on the German nation'.[115] Laying aside the fact that scholars now accept that other nations were culpable during the Holocaust, contemporary interpretation of such statements caused a considerable amount of public discussion. The debate was largely generated by prominent figures, some on the left, who were usually unconventional figures or outsiders in society. They reacted against the type of rhetorical statements about the German people quoted above, and instead urged the British to remember exactly those who had suffered under Hitler. Among them was the New Zealand cartoonist David Low whose well-known cartoon 'Not All Guilty' was published in the *Evening Standard* on 19 April 1945.[116] Low tried to remind those whose passionate denunciation embraced all Germans indiscriminately that many German nationals had in fact died in the camps for their opposition to Hitler. In a long article in *Picture Post* Bertrand Russell put forward the intellectual grounds on which the German people should not be condemned as a whole and Victor Gollancz, in his 3*d* specially published pamphlet entitled *What Buchenwald Really Means*, maintained that the evidence from the camps proved that the Germans could not be collectively guilty.[117] These individuals, and others who added voice to their claims, well remembered the fight to expose the German concentration camps in the 1930s. At every opportunity they reminded the public that the concentration camps, such as Dachau and Buchenwald, were pre-war and aimed at political enemies of the dictatorship: 'One must rub that in to counter this stupid and terrible anti-German business.'[118] There is no doubt that this issue needed to be addressed. The government's anti-German propaganda throughout the war had coloured the public's view to a certain extent and the outrage felt at the revelations from the concentration camps, as we have seen, had served only to strengthen the perceived link between the German population as a whole and notions of evil. The fundamental point that some German nationals had suffered in the camps needed to be understood if there was to be any widespread understanding of the Nazi regime. Naturally, such knowledge would have been crucial in gaining a perception of the nature of the Holocaust and in particular the 'Final Solution'. Obviously, if the British public was not prepared to accept that the Nazi state had used its power to crush political and ideological opponents – German anti-Nazis, German Jews, German Gypsies – then the mental leap needed to accept the widespread deportation and extermination of the Jewish people from all over Europe was a mighty one, to say the least. In this post-liberation dialectic, however, members of the public were not ready for such mental leaps and the truth was that those leading the debate showed little interest in this end.

After the liberation of the concentration camps there was very little public acknowledgement or comprehension concerning the extermination camps in Poland or the role that the camps on German territory had fulfilled in the latter stages of the war. This can be partly explained by the fact that even those who knew the facts about the 'Final Solution' well were not concerned wholly in emphasising them in this period. The response of Eleanor Rathbone, an Independent MP on the centre-left of British politics, to the liberation of the camps in 1945 is a case in point. Rathbone had been a critic of the existence of concentration camps before the war and of the British government of the time. As a member of the National Committee for Rescue from Nazi Terror, she had also been one of the relatively few people in Britain to grasp the enormity of what was happening to the Jews of Europe during the war. No one in Britain, with the exception perhaps of Victor Gollancz with whom she worked closely, campaigned more tirelessly and with such self-sacrifice on the behalf of the European Jewish community as Rathbone. In 1945 not surprisingly she joined the public debate on the subject of the concentration camps. On 22 May 1945, Rathbone wrote to the editor of the *Manchester Guardian*:

> it is evident that the ignorant part of the public, and some people who should know better, are misinterpreting the lessons of Buchenwald by assuming that the ghastly horrors found there and in other concentration camps are proofs of the wickedness of the whole German nation. Actually . . . their significance is just the opposite. They add to a long chain of proofs of the formidable and widespread character of the opposition inside Germany, to Hitlerism.[119]

This was a valuable argument and one which needed to be stressed to help counter the anti-German view. Continually placing the emphasis on 'political' prisoners and on the pre-war period, however, meant that the opportunity was lost to illuminate the plight of the racial victims of the Nazis, and especially the Jews, after the war.

One would hardly guess the Holocaust had taken place at all from an examination of the responses to the liberation of the concentration camps. The British – both public and politicians – had little idea that in the chaos that was Europe in 1944–5 great changes had taken place in the camps. It was assumed, wrongly, that the same conditions that were alleged to have been present in the camps in the 1930s were those uncovered in 1945. Thus, in an MO questionnaire of April 1945, a third of the sample claimed to have realised how horrible the camps were before hearing the liberators' reports.[120] The public saw the revelations as vindicating the 'atrocity stories' they had heard and disbelieved previously. For example, the rather distasteful exhibition of waxworks which had been shown in London throughout 1944 displaying 'Horrors of the Concentration Camps' and 'real Nazi tortures', would now have been viewed as indicative of the crimes the Nazis had committed during the war.[121] Furthermore, the press in its reporting on the camps perpetuated the idea that the conditions in the camps were little changed since the 1930s. Thus, *The Times* on 28 April thought it worth noting that the horrors described in the MPs' report on Buchenwald 'owed nothing to war time conditions, but were common immediately after the coming to power of Hitler'.[122] This is partly true of Buchenwald but in Belsen, for example, conditions had everything to do with war conditions.

To understand why the debate on the German 'atrocities' almost seemed to go back into the 1930s it may be useful to look at the contemporary political situation in Britain. As we have seen, during the 1930s, the left had been critical not only of the concentration camp system in Germany but also of the Conservative politicians in Britain who had refused to acknowledge them. In April and May 1945 the Labour Party was ready to take every opportunity to discredit the Conservatives and, although it was no less outraged by the disclosures than was the rest of the population, the news from the concentration camps played fortuitously into its hands. Here was an emotive issue which had affected the whole of public opinion and over which criticism of the Conservatives could easily be made. Thus, E. Hough from Rainhill wrote to the editor of the *Manchester Guardian*:

> Now that we have irrefutable proof . . . it is interesting and instructive to recall, the attitude of much of the press . . . of many Conservative MPs and of a good section of the deluded public in the earliest days of the Nazi regime towards the accounts of the atrocities which did filter through.
>
> Such accounts were dismissed as mere propaganda put forward by Socialists or Jews, or alternatively, if the atrocities were admitted – well, it was only those 'wicked Socialists' or 'despicable Jews' who were being ill treated.[123]

Provoked by the response of many on the right and in large part by the British establishment (who proclaimed that in view of the evidence from the concentration camps they were correct in stating that in effect all Germans were Nazis), left-wing and liberal thinkers reacted angrily. These people continued to refer the public mind back to the evidence of the 1930s, reminding British society that many *Germans* had been the victims of the Nazis. In the House of Commons, MPs seized every opportunity to mock their Conservative colleagues. Sir Thomas Moore, MP, who had supported the Nationalist Socialists in the 1930s, was taunted by J. McGovern and Sydney Silverman when on 18 April he proclaimed that the Germans were collectively responsible for the misery they had inflicted on the world. On another occasion in the House, Silverman used the MPs' visit to Buchenwald to score political points. The newsreel footage of the delegation, he complained, had been presented to the public in such a way as to associate the delegation with the views of two interviewees – Lord Vansittart and Congresswoman Claire Booth Luce. Silverman objected on the grounds that 'the whole purpose of the visit was to establish, in an objective fashion and without propaganda or political purpose of any kind, the accuracy or otherwise of the allegations'. He strongly objected to the 'collective German guilt' attitude presented by the interviewees.[124]

The Socialist press attacked the opposition on 1930s issues, to the point of being self-congratulatory about its role, and used the evidence of the 1945 liberations as ammunition. On 22 April the *Reynolds News* carried an editorial under the headline 'The Death Camps':

> Readers of *Reynolds News* and the few Socialist and Liberal papers which have never ceased to attack and expose Fascism will be least of all surprised by the terrible stories of the last few days. There were death camps in Nazi Germany as bad as any now exposed in every one of the years from 1933 onwards. When your eye flinches from the pictures now appearing in the Press . . . do not forget the powerful men in this country, many still holding positions of political authority who played their part in making Hitler possible.[125]

A similar tone was evident in a *Tribune* editorial published two days earlier. The paper criticised those newspapers which had covered Ed Murrow's broadcast from Buchenwald but had made no mention 'of the most outstanding fact about Buchenwald', that it was a camp for 'the martyrs of anti-Fascism'. The editorial continued:

> Is our Press so gagged as that of Hitler's Germany that no one dares to mention these facts? Has it become so pervaded with that spirit of despicable Jingoist hypocrisy that even the fearful discovery of Buchenwald serves but as yet another peg for the monotonous reiteration of the tale that all Germans are equally guilty?[126]

There were many communists held in the Buchenwald camp at the time of the liberation, some had been there for many years, but there were also a significant number of survivors of the extermination centres in Poland. This fact by-passed the majority of commentators.

An understanding of the Holocaust and of the 'Final Solution' came very gradually to Britain. In the immediate wake of the liberations, the specific plight of the Jews was mentioned infrequently in the newspaper reports and the connection between the concentration camps and the extermination centres was not clearly established. These links, however, were not entirely absent. As early as 16 April the *Manchester Guardian*, in a report on Buchenwald, mentioned the Jewish victims specifically in relation to gas experiments and reported that, according to prisoners, the outstanding place of extermination in the world was Auschwitz where Jewish Polish and Russian men, women and children had been liquidated.[127] The report resulting from the MPs' delegation to Buchenwald served to highlight this fact further. Incidentally, the *Manchester Guardian* was one of the few newspapers to realise the significance of the inclusion of Sydney Silverman, MP, in the delegation: 'It is supremely fitting that a Jew should be on the delegation and should stand . . . in the newly liberated camps, the tombs of so many Jews.' Indicative of the government's policy not to emphasise the Jewish plight as unique, was that Silverman was not among the first to be chosen for the task. More likely than not, it never occurred to the selectors that it would be appropriate to have a representative of the Jewish Community visit the camps, and so it was only when Mr Sloan, MP, was taken ill that Silverman was given the opportunity to travel to Europe. During the visit, only Silverman specifically sought out Jewish internees in the camp so that he could hear their story.[128]

Well over half of the population of Belsen, on liberation, were Jewish. It is not a factor which featured heavily in any of the newspaper reports concerning the camp. One might suggest, however, that this was less because the fact was not recognised, and more because it was thought to be insignificant. The extreme, sickening and offensive conditions overpowered the journalists and they were able to identify only figures reduced to a level of uniform baseness. They barely recognised the survivors as human beings and to many, the question of race or religion of the victims probably seemed wholly irrelevant. As we shall see in the next chapter, neither the British Army nor, subsequently, the British zonal authorities were keen to stress the Jewish aspect of the Nazi atrocities. A few newspapers did go further than others in highlighting the links between the camps in Poland and Germany. On 22 April, the *News of the World* recounted a statement made by a Polish prisoner who explained that both Josef Kramer, the commandant of Belsen, and a number of the prisoners had originally been in Auschwitz where whole transports were regularly placed in the gas chambers (neither the witness nor the transports are identified as Jewish in the report although it was mentioned that experiments were carried out on Jewish girls).[129] On 24 April, the *Daily Mail* printed the text of a broadcast made in Belsen by Patrick Gordon Walker for Radio Luxembourg. Walker's report showed particular insight:

> There were large numbers of girls in the camp, mostly Jews from Auschwitz. . . . Over and over again I was told the same story. The parades at which people were picked out arbitrarily for the gas chambers and the crematorium, where many were burnt alive.[130]

*The Times*, on VE day, presented the findings of an investigation into the Auschwitz camp made by Soviet experts which was to be published in *Pravda*. Four million (an over-estimate for Auschwitz alone) were said to have perished but there was no mention made of specifically Jewish deaths. The *Manchester Guardian* was the only newspaper in the period immediately following the liberation of the western camps to refer expressly and accurately to the collective fate of the Jews. An editorial on 26 April 1945 made the first call for a more generous immigration policy and the creation of a Jewish state in Palestine in the light of the persecution the Jews had suffered. The piece reminded the readership that the Nazis had not broken all of their promises; Hitler had almost succeeded in annihilating the Jewish race in Europe and of the 6 million Jews in Europe outside Russia, only 200,000 were thought to have escaped.[131] Such facts were still to be assimilated by a great many people in Britain and it would take more than one editorial in an individual newspaper to alter the situation. Furthermore, even this editorial did not equate the 'Final Solution' in any way with the camps recently liberated in Germany.

The more graphic reports that had reached Britain during the war on the extermination centres and the progress of the 'Final Solution' made a significant impact on only a minority of people. Mrs O., from Glasgow and a foreign correspondent by profession, had been extremely distressed by the reports in August 1944 of the gas chambers in 'Lublin'.[132] She, like the editor of the *Jewish Chronicle*, believed that the news from the concentration camps, when compared with previous reports from Poland during the war, was less notable (although these, too, caused her to lose sleep). As we have seen, most people disagreed. A remarkable *Times* editorial of 20 April commented, 'Terrible things have been told, during and before the war, of the cruelties perpetrated in the political concentration camps . . . among them Majdanek stands out, in eastern Europe.' Nevertheless, it could then go on to contend that the new revelations from camps such as Buchenwald and Belsen 'show indeed that the slow horrors of torture [and] starvation . . . are more foul than the worst that has been told or suspected'.[133] To debate which gross method – starvation or gassing – is the worst way to die is both macabre and pointless, and besides, this is not in question here. *The Times* article is further evidence that the British people were unable to grasp or understand at this stage what the Nazis had accomplished during the war years. The concentration camps had not been *established* to murder anyone deliberately and the conditions uncovered in 1945 were not representative of the conditions that had prevailed in the years previously. The British public, however, did not grasp this, nor the fact that there *had* actually been six other camps established solely for the purpose of extermination. The brutality of the methods used in the concentration camps, as confirmed in the photographs, was as much as the public could take; people could not comprehend that there could exist anything more sinister. A diary entry from Mrs O., detailing a conversation with two friends ('both intelligent women'), illustrates the extent of unawareness about the Holocaust:

> I said, what I have thought over the weekend, 'Last August when the reports of Lublin were issued there was no public stir. Why should there be this stir over Buchenwald, which to me is less horrible?' (My own judgement is that last August people did not believe that Lublin was true, they thought it was propaganda, whereas this time they accept the reports. Probably that is because it is our own forces which are up against the present horrors.) But Miss [M] and Miss [S], whom I had to remind of the details of Lublin, said they thought that was less horrible. If people are gassed they don't

suffer. Some of the people at Buchenwald have been there twelve years. And they are Germans too, their own folk.[134]

A widespread comprehension of the Holocaust in Britain did not follow the liberation of the concentration camps. It was only when the war was over, when the investigative process into the camps had begun and the major war crimes trials had taken place, that the public really started to grasp the implications of the extreme Nazi anti-semitic policies. The progress of the Belsen trial, begun in September 1945 and conducted over four weeks, was followed closely by the British press and the main testimonies were reported in detail. Even here, however, the prosecuting counsel Colonel Backhouse, who 'piled horror upon horror', was reticent about the extent of the Nazi crimes, 'he spoke of thousands, *probably* millions, having been deliberately exterminated' (my italics). Major Winwood, defence counsel for Kramer, caused a stir with his astonishingly prejudiced statement that the concentration camps had contained 'the dregs of the ghettos'. In the whole proceedings, the word Jew was mentioned only a small number of times.[135] Even at this trial, where the majority of the defendants were sentenced for crimes perpetrated at Auschwitz and Belsen, and the link between the two camps was inextricably made, the uniquely Jewish aspect of both was sidetracked. Similarly, in the official film of the atrocities, authorised by the British government and compiled by Sidney Bernstein from the footage shot by the liberating armies, there are remarkably few references to Jews.[136]

## IV

Despite the detailed reports on the implementation of the 'Final Solution' which reached Britain during the war, the very scale and nature of the killing meant that the reports were not fully assimilated by the British public. The liberation of the western camps in 1945, moreover, did not promote an understanding of specific Jewish suffering nor the true nature of Nazi racial policy. The images presented to the public made a profound impact and convinced all but a small minority of their truth. Nevertheless, the debate surrounding the revelations made it *more*, not less, difficult for the British to grasp the nature of the Holocaust.

The insistence on universalising the atrocities not only had an important impact in the short term, as will be demonstrated in the next chapter, on the way in which the Jewish Displaced Persons resident in the British zone of occupation were treated after the war, but also in the long term on general British attitudes to the Holocaust and Holocaust education.[137]

# 3   Belsen Displaced Persons' Camp: British state responses

The previous chapters have been concerned with the period immediately follow-ing the liberation of Bergen-Belsen. In this chapter, and those to follow, the focus of the book will be broadened to survey the position of the Belsen Jewish camp in the years between 1945 and 1950, when the last of the displaced persons (DPs) were evacuated from the area.[1] The following chapter appraises the response of the Anglo-Jewish community to the liberation of Belsen and Chapter 5 examines the experiences of the survivors in Belsen.

As previously noted, the main camp of the Belsen complex was evacuated and burned down a little over a month after the British Army moved in. The inter-nees were moved to smaller camps at the *Wehrmacht* barracks, a mile or so down the road. This new site, named Höhne by the British authorities after a nearby German village, eventually became a centre for Jewish displaced persons. Against a background of the demilitarisation and denazification of Germany, the eco-nomic difficulties of the whole of Europe, the 'Cold War' and, most crucially, the political struggle for Palestine, this chapter will examine the developments in the often tense relationship between the British authorities and the Jewish community of Belsen. The approach will be broadly chronological, looking first at the establishment of the early Jewish administration in Belsen and also at the way in which the British perceived the Jewish DP problem in 1945. The chapter will then trace the developments in British policy before and beyond the establishment of Israel in 1948: the divergence from the American authorities in Germany; the response to the increased pressure from Jewish terrorism and illegal immigration to Palestine; and the way in which British-Jewish tensions manifested themselves in the Belsen camp. Before proceeding it is necessary first and briefly to outline the conditions that existed in the British zone of Germany at the end of the war and the scale of the DP problem.

German defeat was complete by May 1945. On 20 April 1945, with the Third Reich falling around him, Hitler took his own life. His proclaimed successor, Admiral Doenitz, was never recognised by the Allies and his attempts to negoti-ate a peace settlement were dismissed. As had been decided in 1943, only uncon-ditional surrender was acceptable and in the end, on 7 May at Rheims, it fell to General Jodl to sign the peace. The Third Reich had been destroyed but so too had much of Germany itself; the army, the economy and all political authority were in complete disorder. Dominion passed into the hands of the four occupying powers and Military Government was imposed on Germany as was agreed first at Yalta in February 1945 and then at Potsdam in July. The occupation zones were not intended to divide Germany. Each zone was governed internally by the respective commander-in-chief and on matters affecting Germany as a whole the four would meet in Berlin as the Control Commission for Germany (CCG), the supreme authority. The long-term task of the Control Commission – never completed – was to draw up a peace treaty for acceptance by a future German government. In the short term, the objectives of disarmament, denazification and the reconstruction of democratic politics were pursued, with the aim of ensuring uniformity across all four zones.[2]

Allied unity was short-lived. With the onset of growing mutual mistrust, hopes of jointly administering a unified Germany faded. The postwar events which set the pattern for the 'Cold War' are well documented and do not require repeating here. By 1946, the Soviet zone was following diverging economic policies from the three Western zones. In June, free movement between the zones was halted and 1947 saw the economic fusion of the British and American zones, with the French joining later. In spring 1948 the Control Commission met for the last time.[3]

Politically, the Western Allies had been encouraging the formation of parties devoted to democratic principles. Local elections were held from 1946 onwards in the Western zones, with the Social Democrats initially emerging as the strongest party. In September 1949, however, shortly after the establishment of the German Federal Republic, it was the Christian Democratic Union which emerged with the largest proportion of the vote. Its leader Konrad Adenauer became the first Federal Chancellor.[4]

The provinces of North Rhineland-Westphalia, Lower Saxony, Schleswig-Holstein and the city of Hamburg formed the British zone of Germany. The British Army of the Rhine, its headquarters at Lübbecke, was led by General Montgomery. He also represented Britain on the Control Commission. For administrative purposes the zone was divided into three corps districts – Hanover (30 Corps), Westphalia (1 Corps) and Schleswig-Holstein (8 Corps). The social and economic infrastructure of Germany had been devastated by the war: in the British zone in May 1945, only 650 out of 8,000 miles of railway track were open to traffic; the roads were badly damaged; and the Rhine and the canals were almost all out of use. Iron, steel and coal production had been severely affected by the bombing and in addition there were very few young and middle-aged Germans immediately available to work in industry. Finally, in the British zone, 22 per cent of the housing stock was destroyed and a further 35 per cent was damaged, a higher proportion than in any other zone.[5] The Military Government was faced with a difficult task in making the zone economically viable. In the words of Brian Horrocks, then commander of the Hanover Corps District: 'Having spent the last six years doing our best to destroy the German Reich, almost overnight we had to go into reverse gear and start building her up again. This required a considerable mental switch.'[6]

An important humanitarian problem in the postwar period was that presented by the millions of displaced persons and refugees in Europe. The majority of these people were deportees, forced labourers, the survivors of concentration camps, ex-prisoners of war, members of the armed forces previously under German command, or stateless persons. An estimated 13 million people were cared for or repatriated by the Allies up to September 1945.[7] In the British zone, at the time of capitulation, there were 2 million displaced persons and a similar number of prisoners of war; a colossal problem for which the military was only partly prepared.[8] During the war, plans had been laid to the effect that immediately following the cessation of hostilities, responsibility for the DPs would pass to UNRRA, established in November 1943. By mid-1944 a Displaced Persons Branch had been set up at SHAEF and as the Allies advanced, new assembly centres were established on the major transport routes to deal with the ensuing 'crescendo of refugees'.[9] From these centres the DPs were either repatriated directly to their home country or moved to alternative camps housing other DPs of the same nationality. In addition to the Red Cross and other voluntary agency relief teams, there were some 322 UNRRA teams in the field by the end of June 1945. This number fell considerably short of those initially requested by Eisenhower, and in some histories UNRRA has been criticised for lacking realism and motivation in preparing for the postwar relief work.[10] Nevertheless, by 11 August 1945, 136 teams were working in the British zone.

The bulk of the Western European DPs were repatriated very quickly to their former homes in the absence of any serious political complications. In July 1945 *The Times* reported that already the Allies had repatriated 3.2 million people to western Europe and the USSR.[11] Over 200,000 Soviet nationals alone had been returned by September but eastward repatriation in general raised political and logistical problems and was often a protracted process.[12] The Yalta agreement had made provision for the repatriation of Soviet nationals. In consequence, and despite the assurance in May 1946 of John Hynd, Chancellor of the Duchy of Lancaster, that 'we have, of course, refused to consider any question of forcible repatriation of all except war criminals', many people were repatriated to Eastern Europe against their wishes.[13] In the summer of 1945, exchange points were established on the British/Russian zonal border. SHAEF transports carried the Russian DPs, formerly in Western hands, over to the Eastern zone and returned with West European DPs.[14] A 2nd Army report for the week ending 12 May 1945 stated (immediately before there was to be a territorial change between the British and Russian zones), 'It is the intention to stock up the 18 Corps area to the maximum with Russians before the territory is handed over.'[15]

The repatriation of the Polish DPs, and also the Yugoslavs and the Czechs, was held up by shortages in transport but also by the fact that, for political reasons, many of these people did not want to return. Often they had reason to fear for their lives under the newly established political regimes and, in fact, many of those who did return, later reappeared in the West illegally. Some groups, including Poles, those from the Baltic states and many Jews, refused to be repatriated at all, preferring for the time being to remain stateless in DP camps in the West. On 20 June 1945 a special category of DPs, 'non-repatriables', was introduced by the Allies to encompass these people.[16] The Belsen camp became one of the centres in which non-repatriables were accommodated.

The first premise of the Allied repatriation policy had been the belief that all liberated peoples in Europe desired to return home. The slow realisation that this was not the case for many forced the military to review their policies. The DPs would need to be accommodated for a much longer period than had been at first anticipated. In May 1946, 40,000 people still remained in the British zone and became known as the 'hardcore' cases.

# I

A significant number of those 40,000 DPs formed the Belsen Jewish community and it is to these people that we now return. It has already been noted that the original Belsen camp, on liberation, held many Jews. As repatriations proceeded through 1945, the camp took on an even greater Jewish identity. The history of Belsen in the five years after the war is the history of this Jewish remnant, the community they established and the difficulties they encountered. It is also in large part the history of the British postwar policy on Palestine before the creation of Israel. Although the British attempted to keep the Jewish DP issue and the Palestine issue completely separate, they inevitably became intertwined in Belsen.

On a cautionary note, it must be stated that all figures relating to the number of Jews liberated from the concentration camps should be treated as estimates, not least because it was a keynote Allied policy after the war to regard Jewish DPs as nationals of their home country. Thus, many may have been lost in the statistics. M.J. Proudfoot, in 1957, estimated that there were 66,000 Jewish survivors of the camps.[17] Later work has proved this to be an under-estimate and Yehuda Bauer puts the figure at 200,000 (100,000 after the legacy of diseases from the camps had taken its toll). Bauer acknowledges that more research is needed on the last months of the war and his figures remain uncorroborated.[18] In Belsen approximately 60,000 people were liberated. Once again it is difficult to know exactly how many of the survivors were Jewish but it is estimated they formed at least half of the camp population.[19] Certainly, more Jews were liberated in Belsen than in any other Western camp.

In accordance with the policy outlined above, the Western nationals were speedily repatriated from Belsen. As early as 19 April, 3,000 Westerners from Camp II, in the *Wehrmacht* barracks, were available for repatriation.[20] Most people at this stage were evacuated to a secondary assembly centre before being transferred home. In May 1945 there were twenty-eight such centres in the British zone, including, for example, that at Celle where four camps housed 10,000 people.[21] On 2 May, 4,000 Russians were taken from Camp II to nearby Falling-bostel where many of their compatriots were housed already. Throughout May and June thousands of French, Dutch, Belgians, Italians, Yugoslavs and Czechs were moved to various designated Displaced Persons' camps including Wetzendorf, Celle, Bergen and even Buchenwald.[22] Some of the 17,000 people repatriated by 21 May were undoubtedly Jews. Certainly, it is known that a number of German Jews were given passes to go home during May. Similarly, the high death toll in the camp after the war – the army had recorded 12,453 deaths by 15 May 1945 – must have included many Jews.[23]

Nevertheless, a substantial number of Jewish DPs remained in Belsen and in the summer of 1945 a large section of the Belsen DP camp took on a Jewish identity. Indeed, by September 1945 the great majority of internees were Jews of Polish origin. There were a number of Jews of other nationalities and also a contingent of non-Jewish Poles; the latter lived in a separate section of the DP camp. Contemporary estimates place the number of Jews in Belsen in the second half of 1945 at between 10,000 and 12,000 and thus the camp accommodated the largest Jewish community in the British zone.

## II

When one recalls the opinion of many British observers of the 'horror camp' at Belsen to the effect that the survivors would never again make useful members of society, the emergence in 1945 of a thriving Jewish community in the DP camp must have seemed remarkable. In Israel today, the name Bergen-Belsen is not only a symbol of horror and despair but conversely one of Jewish rehabilitation and resilience, a place where the Jewish remnant organised themselves socially and politically to fight British authority for the recognition of their rights as Jews – and for the right to live in Palestine.

Political activity within the Jewish community began almost immediately after the liberation. Many of the internees, after years of suffering debasement and degradation under the Nazis, and contrary to expectations, were eager to exert their new freedom and independence. An incident in which several internees were shot dead by Hungarian guards over a few potatoes, happening as it did *after the liberation*, was incomprehensible for the survivors. The deaths, however, also caused anger, acting as a 'signal to organise'.[24] Just days after the shootings a group of survivors met in Block 88 of Camp I and immediately elected a committee to represent the interests of the Jewish internees. Displaying remarkable determination these representatives, from different class and cultural backgrounds, and united only by their recent experiences, set out to take control again of their own lives, encourage physical and spiritual rehabilitation, search for their surviving relatives and, last but not least, win for themselves political representation *as Jews*.

The chair of the first temporary Belsen Jewish Committee was Josef (Yossel) Rosensaft, a 34-year-old Polish Jew and a survivor of Auschwitz. A few months later he became the unofficial representative of all the Jews in the British zone when the Central Committee of Liberated Jews was formed. Alex Easterman, then of the British Section of the World Jewish Congress, described him as 'a man small in stature, but massive in intelligence, with a remarkable capacity for leadership and organisation'. Further, he had 'a fearless courage to assert and defend the rights and freedoms of his people, to the bewilderment and often the dismay of the authorities'.[25] The name Rosensaft remains a symbolic expression of the rejuvenation of the Jewish Remnant after the war. Of the nine other members of the committee five were doctors, including Hadassa Bimko who took charge of the Belsen health department and later married Rosensaft.[26]

The work of this first committee and those that followed brought them into direct conflict with all levels of British authority, from local Military Government to the Foreign Office in London. With the help of contacts forged with Jewish representatives and organisations in Palestine, Britain and America, they were to fight their liberators every step of the way in order to see the establishment of a Jewish state in Palestine.

When the committee was established, naturally issues of food, health and hygiene were immediate concerns. An early political decision, however, set the pattern of events for the next five years. The majority of the Jewish people in Belsen were determined not to return to their countries of origin. They had nothing to go back to. Families and whole communities had been totally destroyed, the roots of Ashkenasi culture decimated and yet still anti-semitism had not abated. The surviving Jews refused to return to what they perceived as a hostile graveyard. Instead, they turned their hopes for the future towards other parts of the world, predominantly Palestine.[27] How many survivors, at this stage, were actively pro-Zionist is difficult to determine; there was an early awareness, however, that Palestine was one of the few places where Jewish settlement on a large scale was a *realistic* possibility. This question is further examined in Chapter 5.

The first dispute with the British came soon after the liberation, following a decision by the military to 'repatriate' a proportion of the camp internees by moving them to other assembly centres in the British zone. The intention was to transform part of the military barracks into a one-nationality camp and to transfer the internees of other nations either to national camps or to the Stateless Camp at Lingen. This was in keeping with the policy to group the DPs, including the Jews, according to their pre-war nationality rather than on racial or religious grounds. The move would also take pressure off the hospital facilities in Belsen and improve the administrative situation; '[t]he present babel of tongues and international discord in Belsen does not assist administration', noted one report.[28] The Jewish Committee vetted the new camps. In May almost 3,000 people were taken to a centre in Celle, including several of the original members of the first committee.[29]

Similar evacuations to Lingen and the camp at Diepholtz, situated on the German border with the Netherlands, were more strongly contested. As a consequence of their refusal to be repatriated, the Polish Jews were informed that they were to be sent to the Lingen camp instead. They were, however, reluctant to be classified as stateless, with the uncertainty that such a classification entailed with regard to their future. The senior Jewish chaplain for the British zone, Rabbi Isaac Levy, backed the army's position but with an ulterior motive.

Following the Jewish Agency line, he felt sure that if a large number of stateless Jews could be concentrated in one camp, it would strengthen the case for opening the gates of Palestine. He exerted pressure on his fellow Jewish chaplains to persuade the internees of the advantages of the move. The logic of moving the relatively fit internees in order that the sick in Belsen could receive better care was of further appeal.[30] Yet, the internees feared leaving the relative security of Belsen and, even at such an early stage, the camp leaders, intuitively believed it was in their political interests to keep the community together in one place. Tension in the camp increased when a number of DPs were warned menacingly by a Polish liaison officer: either they went to Lingen voluntarily or they would be forced with bayonets.[31]

It was clear to the Jewish Committee that a thousand people would be moved no matter what their protestations. A plan was devised, therefore, to protect, as far as possible, the interests of those who were to be transferred. A thousand people would go but all under false names. If conditions at Lingen were worse than in Belsen, then the DPs would be able to return without detection and resume their own identities.[32] More importantly they would not lose their entitlement to Belsen rations. As far as the committee was concerned, the deception proved necessary. On 24 May, 1,117 Polish Jews left Belsen accompanied by a Reverend Richards and Jane Leverson, the first Jewish welfare worker to reach the camp. Negative reports of the new camp came back before the second convoy had left.[33]

Lingen camp was not vacant as they had been led to believe but already housed 5,000 Russians and Poles. The accommodation offered to the Jewish DPs was old and decrepit, without light or running water. Moreover, the authorities in charge of administering the camp had not been informed of their coming. They arrived in the dark, confused and distressed. In the long term the Lingen camp was made more bearable and a camp committee was established.[34] Meanwhile, however, a number of DPs returned to Belsen. Josef Rosensaft demanded that the military authorities cancel their plans to evacuate internees to Lingen and refused to allow the second transport to leave. The Jewish Committee won the fight but not without penalty. Because of the committee's decision to ignore British orders, Rosensaft, as the chair, was put on trial before a military tribunal. He was eventually acquitted and continued in his post as unofficial camp leader.[35]

In the event, the committee leaders had been correct not to follow the advice of the Jewish Agency and, arguably, in terms of the history of the Jewish DPs in the British zone, that early decision was the most crucial they ever made. The Jewish Agency did procure a convergence of Jewish DPs in the British zone but it was at Belsen rather than Lingen or Hanover, as Levy had suggested. As a bargaining tool in negotiations over emigration to Palestine it went one better. Belsen was a name that registered with world public opinion in a way that Lingen did not.

The run-in with British authority did not persuade Rosensaft and the other committee members that they ought to give up their fight for representation.

Indeed, the victory over the Lingen affair only gave encouragement to the DPs. They had proved that they could influence the authorities and win for themselves the right to decide their own future. The most difficult battle, however, had yet to be fought. It concerned the desire of the Jewish DPs to be recognised formally by the authorities as Jews.

As has been established in previous chapters, the majority of the British people, whether at home or serving abroad with the forces, did not fully realise the particular nature of the Nazi policy towards the Jews, nor its consequences. The Jews had received sympathy but only so far as they were survivors of the terrible concentration camps given prominence in the newsreels; not in recognition of their suffering as Jews. The army authorities and the press did not highlight the unique character of the Jewish persecutions or the 'Final Solution'. Similarly, as DPs the Jewish survivors were destined to disappear into national statistics. Both the British and American authorities refused to recognise religious divisions when dealing with the DPs and so Jews were classified by their country of origin and grouped thus in the assembly centres before repatriation. Polish Jews, then, were placed with Poles, German Jews with other Germans, and so on. In effect the policy sanctioned further Jewish suffering. Very often German Jews and other pre-war nationals from Axis countries, although many were camp survivors, were, nevertheless, classified as enemy nationals and thus denied privileged rations. It was expected that ex-internee German Jews would return home to be cared for by German civilian authorities, with little thought given to the implication of that policy. Furthermore, those who remained in the camps sometimes found themselves among former guards or tormentors, anti-semites and collaborators.[36] The Jewish Committee in Belsen from the beginning set out to oppose the policy which left the Jews suffering from 'the curse of national anonymity'.[37]

Israeli and American historians writing on the Jewish DPs in Europe and the period before the establishment of the Israeli state, have tended to concentrate on the American zone of Germany and the reactions and responses to the DPs from all levels of American authority. This concentration on the American zone is understandable given that, as from 1946, the greatest number of Jews in Germany resided in this area. The result, however, has been the neglect of the significant Jewish community in Belsen and others in the British zone.[38] The role of the British in the lives of the Jewish DPs tends to be considered only at the governmental level by these historians. The British attitude to the Jews in Europe is seldom reviewed and then only in respect of the British policy on Palestine. Often the British authorities are portrayed as ogres and it is infrequently that an attempt is made to explain the rationale behind their actions. British postwar attitudes are often presented very simplistically: the British government held the Palestine Mandate; it did not want to see an Israeli state; all action concerning Jewish DPs in Europe reflected this attitude. One would not attempt to suggest that the issue of Palestine did not become important in the expression of British attitudes towards the Jewish DPs, only that this is much too simplistic a view. Initially, the British regarded the two questions –

the situation of the Jewish Displaced Persons and the matter of Palestine – as quite separate issues. The refusal to link the two problems became unworkable and absurd as the months went by, and events unfolded in Europe and in Palestine. Nevertheless, this refusal was a fact and must be understood when examining the treatment of the Jewish DPs in the British zone. Further, such generalisations do not allow for the consideration of everyday relations with the lower levels of British authority or for the existence of human sympathy in dealing with the Jewish DPs.

It is not necessary to repeat at length the history of the British Mandate in Palestine here. Briefly, the British were constantly torn between the commitment of the Balfour Declaration in 1917 to establish a Jewish National Home in Palestine and the protection of British interests in the Middle East. It was the latter consideration, the appeasement of Arab opinion, which precipitated the 1939 White Paper restricting Jewish immigration to Palestine and which led the government to reject plans for the establishment of a Jewish fighting force in 1940 and throughout the war. Jewish public opinion in the Middle East was greatly angered at these moves, yet differences had to be set aside during the war. The soldiers of Jewish Palestine joined the British and American armies and fought for an Allied victory; the implicit understanding was that further consideration would be given to the Palestine question when victory was secured.[39] As the war came to an end, the Jewish Agency had every reason to believe that a Jewish state would soon be reality. In 1944 Churchill announced the formation of a Jewish brigade and talks were resumed between the Prime Minister and Weizmann. Following the Labour Party's victory in the general election immediately after the war Jewish hopes for a settlement of the Palestine question were raised further. The Labour Party had opposed the White Paper and at the party conference in 1945 had reaffirmed its commitment to rescinding it. Once it was in government, however, the decisions no longer seemed quite so simple and the protection of British interests took precedence once again.[40]

Outside of party politics in Britain and outside discussions with respect to Palestine, regarding the Jewish DPs in Europe, the policy agreed between the British and Americans before the end of the war was simple enough. It was thought undesirable (or illiberal) to echo the Nazi theory that the Jews were a separate race. They were a religious group and in common with other such groups they should be classed according to their nationality. Any form of racial or religious segregation would only confer credence on Nazi ideology and give rise to anti-Jewish feeling amongst the DPs in general.[41]

This viewpoint can be better understood if one returns to the argument of the previous chapter, where it was demonstrated that in general Britain had little understanding of the level and nature of the Nazi persecution of the Jews. It was acknowledged that the Jews had suffered in the concentration camps but then so had other groups. The idea of special treatment was a notion unacceptable to British liberal monoculturism. What is more, segregating the Jews would seem in accordance with the theories propounded by the Nazis and sit uncomfortably with the policy of denazification. And finally, such a policy was thought to be detrimental to the interests and security of the Jews themselves – it was felt that any policy which appeared to favour the Jews over other DPs would lead only to disruption and racial persecution in the camps. In any case, Military Government did not make provision for special cases. Jewish DPs were DPs none the less, and the army, as a huge bureaucratic organisation, was concerned simply with getting the assembly centres to run as smoothly as possible. It did not see any need to complicate matters further in what was already an administrative and logistical nightmare. Unfortunately, the British could not see the irony of their policy. So, as long as the Jews were forced to live in camps with their fellow nationals they would be exposed to anti-semitic feeling. As long as the non-fraternisation order applied to all Germans then Jewish German nationals were to suffer unfairly.

The British view of the Jewish people is a further consideration in reviewing the British policy towards the survivors. The only Jewish community, if any, British personnel would have been familiar with was the Anglo-Jewish community, which was largely assimilated. The main distinction between Jews and non-Jews in Britain tended to be viewed as a religious one, and it was presumed that the same would be the case with the Polish Jews in Belsen. Yet the Polish Jewish community had largely not been assimilated, and had lived in close communities, often in towns where 90 per cent of the population were Jewish. During the war, these communities had been destroyed, and many Polish Gentiles were alleged to have supported Nazi policy. These factors combined to ensure that the Polish Jews had no desire to return to Poland nor even to live in the same DP camp as their fellow nationals.

Typical of the British viewpoint on the Jewish DP question is a letter written by a senior member of Montgomery's office at the Control Council. The Jewish Committee in Belsen had made contact with various prominent members of American Jewry and Anglo-Jewry in an attempt to bring publicity to their situation. As a result, during the next few months there was a flurry of correspondence between prominent members of the Anglo-Jewish community and those responsible for the policy concerning the Jews in Germany. On 13 July, the Marquess of Reading wrote an anxious letter to General Weeks, Deputy High Commissioner in Germany, regarding the poor treatment received by the Jews and requiring a reply to the demand that all Jewish DPs should receive preferential treatment and be segregated irrespective of their nationality. The informal reply, to be regarded as an 'unofficial communication', was sympathetic but implacable. 'Your comments have had very careful consideration at this headquarters and all of us are only too anxious to relieve the suffering which has been caused in Germany, whether to Jew or non-Jew.' Nevertheless, 'segregation would result in a large body of Jews of many nationalities who would probably refuse repatriation and constitute a continuous embarrassment'. Furthermore, preferential treatment for the Jews would be unfair to the many non-Jews who had suffered at the hands of the Nazis and 'it would also cause irritation and anti-Jewish feeling on the part of non-Jewish displaced persons which might well have far reaching results and give rise to persecution at a later date'. Weeks continued, 'I am the first to admit the cruelties and hardship to which the Jews in Germany have been subjected but equally it is true that there have been many other sufferers.' This then was the position of the British authorities. On humanitarian grounds they shared sympathy for the Jews but against the background of the 'gigantic' DP problem in Europe they could not see the justification for according the Jews special consideration. The view had little connection with the Palestine question at this stage.[42] Adding further comment to Lord Reading's letter, the Chief of the Political Division of the Control Council concluded in a communication of 24 July, 'In short we cannot accept the theory that the Jews are a separate race – and as it was one of the principal tenets of the Nazi creed it is rather odd that they should now be trying to put it across.'[43] It is clear that the claim of the Jewish DPs for a distinctive handling of their situation in Germany was not based on a claim that they were a separate race, but on the fact that as a group they had suffered particular persecution. The latter was a fundamental reality in the lives of the Jewish DPs. For the majority, there could be no returning to pre-war norms. And no amount of British liberal conviction would change the situation.

Against the Occupation authorities, the Belsen Jewish Committee, and the rabbis in the camp with whom its members forged close links, continued in their attempts to alert the Jewish press to the plight of the DPs. In particular, they were distressed at the way the British policy discriminated against Jews of German nationality; if they had been liberated, and continued to live, outside a camp then often they were treated as enemy nationals and denied privileged rations.[44] On 4 May 1945 Rabbi Levy addressed a letter to the *Jewish Chronicle* in which he outlined the conditions in which the Jewish survivors lived. In the same issue a letter from Leslie Hardman explained why the Polish Jews refused to return to Poland.[45] Two weeks later Levy wrote to Mr T. Scott, attached to the DP Section of UNRRA in London, bringing to his attention the problems affecting the Jews of Belsen. He explained that the openly anti-semitic views held by the Hungarians and Poles in the camp added to the suffering of the Jewish internees. Levy had already asked the military authorities that special consideration be given to the Jewish victims of the Nazi regime and he reiterated the plea here. That a solely Jewish transit centre be opened up, he wrote, 'seems so obviously the only solution'.[46] As we have seen, his plans for the Lingen camp did not come to fruition, but Reverend Richards's account of the affair, published in the *Jewish Chronicle* under the headline, 'Belsen Sufferers Still Suffer', gave further publicity to the Jewish plight. In June the revisionist *Jewish Standard* criticised a situation in which liberated Jews suffered from a lack of food and from continued anti-semitism, and were allowed no communication with the outside world. The *Jewish Chronicle* in July published a report from the Jewish Telegraphic Agency (JTA) detailing the 'cruel and callous treatment' received by the Jewish survivors in Europe from their liberators.[47]

The pressure for action was continued in July when the World Jewish Congress (WJC) alerted the public to the plight of the Jews with an appeal sent direct to the Potsdam Conference. The WJC asked that immediate steps be taken in order that the situation of the Jews be improved, as they were presently being treated with a 'callous and shameful neglect and indifference'. It was inadmissible that over three months after liberation, Jewish people were still virtual prisoners in conditions of 'abject misery', unable to receive food parcels and without liaison officers to represent their views.[48]

The Americans, too, were being alerted to conditions in Germany. Protestations about the fate of their co-religionists were made by Jewish politicians and community leaders to various government departments. As a result President Truman appointed Earl G. Harrison, the American representative to the Intergovernmental Committee on Refugees, to visit the camps and the assembly centres and to report back on the conditions in which the DPs, particularly the Jews, were living.[49]

The Harrison Report was damning and sent shock waves around Washington. Harrison and his entourage visited around thirty camps, including Belsen, and found the majority to be less than satisfactory. According to the report, liberation for many survivors equated to living in Nazi-built camps behind barbed wire fences, wearing concentration camp clothing and suffering malnutrition whilst, at the same time, being unable to make contact with the outside world or any relatives who might have survived. 'As matters now stand', Harrison concluded disturbingly, 'we appear to be treating the Jews as the Nazis treated them except that we do not exterminate them.' The report insisted that the Jewish DPs should be given recognition as Jews:

> When they are now considered only as members of nationality groups, the result is that special attention cannot be given to their admittedly greater needs because, it is contended, doing so would constitute preferential treatment and lead to trouble with the non-Jewish portion of the particular nationality group.
>
> Thus there is a distinctly unrealistic approach to the problem. Refusal to recognise the Jews as such has the effect, in this situation, of closing one's eyes to their former and more barbaric persecution, which has already made them a separate group with greater needs.

Further, Harrison highlighted the wish of the Jews to leave Germany and Austria with haste, the majority to Palestine. 'They want to be evacuated to Palestine now, just as other national groups are being repatriated to their homes.' His main recommendation amounted to a fundamental change in policy: that the United States government should press for the issue of a significant number of immigration certificates. Meanwhile, pending evacuation, he recommended that separate camps be set up for Jews under the auspices of UNRRA; that a programme of activities be organised to aid in the rehabilitation of the DPs; and also that facilities be made available to enable DPs to trace surviving relatives.[50]

The Harrison Report could not have expressed the political views of the Jewish leaders in Belsen more persuasively. Reactions to the report, however, were to lead to the first divergence in Anglo-American zonal policy with regard to the Jewish DPs. Ahead of the full version of the report, which did not reach President Truman until 24 August 1945, Harrison sent his preliminary thoughts to the Secretary of State on 28 July. Washington was shocked at the condemnatory nature of this first telegram (so much so that orders were imme-diately issued through the Secretary of War's Office that those of Harrison's recommendations which could be implemented immediately should be realised in the American zone). With direction from General Eisenhower, Jewish DPs were segregated, their rations were increased to twice those of the German civilians and attention was given to the improvement of facilities for recreation and rehabilitation. Further, Eisenhower overturned a previous decision in agree-ing to the appointment of a Jewish liaison officer who would serve to advise the army on problems specifically relating to the Jewish DPs. The general, however, articulating the resentment of his officers, was loath to accept all of Harrison's criticisms without comment. He defended the military and their achievements since the liberation, noting that the Jewish DPs were only a small minority of the total and that the first priority of the army had been to repatriate the majority.[51]

There is no doubt that the Harrison Report was in part exaggerated and unfair to the military; to compare the Allied armies with the SS was unjustified. Never-theless, for the first time a figure with political standing (the importance of the fact that he was a non-Jew should not be underestimated) had spoken to the Jews. With such a singular agenda, Harrison, perhaps, could not have failed to be touched by the pathetic situation of the Jewish DPs. This, however, was the first recognition from a *military* authority that, in view of their specific and terrible persecution by the Nazis, the Jews deserved a great deal more sym-pathy and special consideration than had hitherto been afforded them. The acknowledgement was a crucial turning-point, but it was not one that the British felt able to make.

The contents of the 28 July telegram from Harrison were cabled to the War Office in London on 3 August 1945.[52] The telegram was less damning than the final report but, nevertheless, the major recommendation was that separate camps for Jews should be established. On this point the War Office sought the advice of Montgomery's office but no change in policy followed.[53] The reply to the War Office, dated 6 September, reiterating existing British policy, stated that the DPs were to be treated on the basis of nationality. On the other points raised by Harrison's telegram, the letter assured the War Office that the DPs were, in fact, given priority over Germans as regards food and accommo-dation; that a winter accommodation scheme for the DPs was in hand; that a Tracing Bureau for missing persons had been set up; and that every encourage-ment was being given to the speedy hand-over of responsibility for the DPs to UNRRA. The letter concluded, 'It will therefore be seen that Mr Harrison's report . . . is not in accordance with the facts, at any rate as far as the British zone is concerned.'[54]

Yet the British were not immune to the mounting criticism of their policy towards the Jews. A report in the *News Chronicle*, alleging inhuman treatment of the DPs in Germany, along with various protestations by Eleanor Rathbone, MP, prompted the Foreign Office to contact the Chief of Staff once more, anxious that as little ground as possible be given to the complaints.[55] The reply gave the assurance that the newspaper article was 'mischievous in the extreme and grossly exaggerated'. General Britten, writing for Montgomery, was particularly keen to refute the claim that it had been a deliberate policy to make the conditions so uncomfortable that the individuals concerned would go anywhere rather than remain in the camps.[56]

There is little doubt that many of the reports that reached Britain, as with the Harrison Report, were exaggerated and overly critical of the military authorities. The claim, this time by Lady Reading in a letter to the Chief of Staff, that in the autumn the Jews were forced to live in tented accommodation was untrue. Neither was it entirely correct to claim that the Jews in Belsen were living in an ex-concentration camp. The concentration camp proper had been burned to the ground and the internees moved to the improved, if still grossly overcrowded, Panzer Training School barracks. On the other hand, many criticisms were valid. In particular, the existence of barbed wire around the camps was an unnecessary security measure. Designed to keep the local German population out rather than the DP population in, it nevertheless added to the feeling of the DPs that they were liberated but not free.[57] Shortages in everything from clothing – forcing internees to remain in the striped concentration camp pyjamas – and shoes to books and pencils caused understandable resentment. Further, there was some truth in the charge aimed at the military authorities that they were often reluctant to inconvenience the German population for the benefit of the DPs. By the winter of 1945 Allied policy had softened towards the Germans. The policy decision in the Western zones to facilitate the regeneration of the German economy meant that the authorities were loath to increase the disruption to German life for the sake of people whom they expected to repatriate within months. Only rarely was German civilian accommodation requisitioned for the use of DPs in the British zone.

Yet the situation of the DPs had to be viewed against the background of the general situation in Germany. The lack of food and variety in the diet was an issue of major contention among the DPs, who received only 2,000 calories a day.[58] As has been noted, statistics concerning the German economy illustrate that the German population suffered heavy shortages after the war. They too were on strict ration scales. In Celle, near Belsen, the civilian ration scale was cut to only 1,300 calories.[59] Only perhaps in the countryside, where the war had made a lesser impact and farmers were able to grow some food, was the population better off. These well-fed and well-clothed people understandably caused resentment to the DPs living close by and the contrast must have been striking to visitors to the camps.

The formal reply to Washington from the Foreign Office concerning the Harrison Report came on 5 October 1945, by which time Truman had ordered that the recommendations be implemented in the American zone. The Foreign Office requested that the decision to segregate Jews in the American zone be reversed to avoid the embarrassment a divergence in policy would bring. It is worth quoting the telegram at length. To accept the policy advocated by Harrison, the Foreign Office stressed,

> is to imply in effect that there is no future in Europe for persons of Jewish race. This is surely a counsel of despair which it would be quite wrong to admit at a time when conditions throughout Europe are still chaotic and when effect of antisemitic policy sedulously fostered by Nazis has not yet been undone: indeed it would go far by implication to admit that Nazis were right in holding that there was no place for Jews in Europe.
>
> Above policy would also mean that we were ready to reverse decision reached with so much difficulty at recent UNRRA Council that displaced persons must be given time in which to decide freely and after full information as to conditions which were likely to await them whether to return home or not. It means accepting and indeed requiring them to make irrevocable decision now on this point at a time when conditions in which a balanced judgement can be taken are completely non-existent.
>
> We should thus be faced with a vast increase in the number of those displaced persons who will ultimately have to be resettled at a time when there is a crying need for all possible displaced persons, Jews no less than Gentiles, to return home (unless the objection in any given case is overriding) to build up their native lands where they all have their own part to play. Our task surely is to create conditions in which they will themselves feel it natural and right to go home rather than to admit at this stage that such conditions are impossible to create. Nor must it be forgotten that the Jews are not the only persecuted group and that groups of German Christians have suffered almost as badly.[60]

Once again, the arguments used by the Foreign Office were based on Military Government working policy – not on British government policy regarding Palestine. Clearly, one might argue that it was not in the interests of the British government at this stage to agree to the segregation of the Jews as that was only a small step away from recognising them as a national group. But the telegram of 5 October shows that there was more to this policy. There was a genuine feeling that to admit that the Jews were a separate race and to advocate their leaving Europe was to concede victory to the Nazis. Throughout the war, the interests of the Continental Jews had been placed second behind the primary aim of winning the war. The plight of the Jews was not highlighted by the British government. Yet, when the war was over and the concentration camps were liberated, the horror then revealed suddenly became the reason why the war had been fought, both in government propaganda and in the public mind. In government circles there was a genuine sympathy for what the victims of the Nazi regime had endured. Those kinds of conditions would not have existed in a democracy and the thinking was that if the DPs gave the Allies time, democracy would be restored in Europe and life for the victims would return to normal. British liberal principles were such that officials simply could not accept that

Jews or any other religious grouping could not lead an ordinary life free from persecution in Europe. The British could not ally themselves with a concept they believed to be Nazi in origin. We must recognise this if we are to understand fully British reactions. It is far too simplistic to look at British policies towards Jewish DPs (in the early months after the war at least) *only* against the background of Palestine. The genuine fears of the British have parallels in more recent history. With the fall of the Iron Curtain and the opening of USSR borders, there has been a great exodus of Russian and East European Jews to Israel. Often the émigrés have not had a true idea of what conditions in Israel are like or what life holds in store for them. Meanwhile, back in Europe sadness is expressed that these people, whose roots in these countries go back generations, should feel that they must leave. There is a fear that soon there will be no living communities left in these countries and certainly no one to remember or preserve the rich heritage of the Jewish people which is so much a part of the history of, for example, Poland or the Baltic states.[61] Attempts in the past and the present to maintain the Jewish link with the continent of Europe often stem from the best, if sometimes the most naive, of motives.

## III

What was missing from the British analysis of the situation in Germany was an understanding of the deep feeling of the Jewish DPs concerning their own future. In Belsen, where many of the surviving Jews were Polish, the majority view was that a return to Poland was out of the question. As early as 26 May 1945 a Military Government weekly summary stated, 'There are . . . many Jews of all nationalities, including Germans and Hungarians, who wish to go to Palestine.'[62]

Over the summer months the Jewish Committee had been increasingly active. Jewish relief organisations arrived in the camp in June and played an effective role in setting up and equipping nurseries, schools and welfare centres. Links were established with other Jewish communities in Germany and on 8 July 1945 a conference was held at Belsen at which representatives of the known fifty-four camps in the British and American zones were present. Having received reports on the situation in various camps, those present decided that, as Jewish DPs, they needed to present a united front to the outside world. Unanimously, the meeting agreed to elect a Central Jewish Representative Council which would be representative of all of the Jews in western Germany in dealings with the Military Government, the Allied governments and UNRRA. In addition three resolutions were confirmed. First, that due to continued anti-Jewish discrimination, economic rehabilitation difficulties and 'the complete extermination of their families', Jewish DPs should be afforded every facility in order that they might emigrate to Palestine or a country of their choice. Second, that until such time as the first resolution could be implemented, immediate steps should be taken in order to normalise their existence. Thus, there was a call for the establishment of centres where vocational training and religious and cultural activities could be encouraged. The third resolution was a statement of unity. It requested that the Military authorities acknowledge the constitution of the Central Jewish Representative Council as the only authorised voice of the Jewish DPs and understand that the council was working closely with British and American Jewry to the same end.[63] In fact, no Jewish Committee which claimed to represent *all* the Jews in the British zone, German and non-German, was ever acknowledged by the British zonal authorities in the whole of the postwar period.

A second conference was held on 16 July. In the intervening week several delegates had made visits to various camps and reported back on the conditions they found there. Some camps were found badly wanting in adequate facilities. At this second meeting, the first tentative plans for a congress were discussed and a number of delegates were elected to organise it.[64] The congress was to be a high-profile event designed to focus world attention on the claims of the Jewish DPs. Jewish leaders and representatives of all the major Jewish organisations were to be invited, together with the press. Held in late September and lasting two and a half days the congress was a great success and received a good deal of publicity. It was officially opened by Rosensaft on 25 September after a ceremony on the site of Camp I at Belsen to consecrate the newly-erected Jewish monument to the dead. The main theme of the congress was the revival of the Jewish faith and national spirit, and a reiteration was made, though in more forceful terms, of the resolutions passed in July. Complaints were voiced about the conditions in camps all over Germany. The lack of bread and green vegetables in the diet; overcrowding; the staffing of the hospital with German medical staff; and a general feeling of being regarded as second-rate human beings: these were just some of the complaints specific to the Belsen DP Centre. The delegates demanded the removal of guards and barbed wire from the camp; the right to exercise freedom of speech; and the right to publish a Jewish newspaper. A great deal of resentment was voiced against the fact that five months after the liberation they were still unable to correspond freely with relatives and friends abroad.[65]

In the week following the congress in Belsen, the Board of Deputies of British Jews and the World Jewish Congress continued to exert pressure on the British authorities in London. Alexander Easterman, for the WJC, put forward his arguments in a letter, and Brodetsky, president of the Board, met with Lt-Gen. Robertson of the Control Commission, on a visit to London from Germany.[66] Once again Robertson presented the chief argument of the Control Commission that segregation of the Jews in Germany would revive and perpetuate anti-semitism. According to his report on the meeting to the War Office, however, this reasoning carried 'no conviction' with Brodetsky. Convinced that the British would be forced to accept segregation sooner or later, Robertson agreed to stand down and recommend such a policy on administrative grounds only – so long as the War Office raised no objections on political grounds.

If the War Office accepted the compromise, the Foreign Office most certainly did not. In fact, the whole Jewish DP question generated a long but reasonable letter from the latter on 24 October. The FO agreed that administratively there was good reason to arrange for Jewish DPs to worship, eat and live 'in self-contained groups within the quarters which are allotted to them in common with their fellow displaced persons possessing the same nationality' and hoped that this would be done. It was argued, however, that this was quite different from the idea of segregating Jews on racial grounds and to this the FO continued to object strongly. In his defence, Robertson admitted that he had no idea that the Foreign Office had such strong views on the matter, an indication, perhaps, that the officials in Germany thought of the Jewish DP question as an internal matter. He apologised for encouraging Brodetsky to believe that segregation was a possibility.[67] The FO, however, did welcome the decision of Robertson to have a Jewish Advisor on his staff. Colonel Solomon was subsequently appointed to the post in London.[68] This was a major concession but, in fact, Solomon was never able to play the same proactive role as his American counterpart. As it was, British and American policies towards the Jews remained largely disparate. By this time, however, events had taken off at a higher level. After receiving the Harrison Report in August, President Truman repeated in writing to Attlee the request that he had made at Potsdam in July: that restrictions on Jewish entry to Palestine be lifted. The letter of 31 August suggested that 100,000 certificates be issued to the refugees in Europe. The Americans saw clearly the link between the Palestine question and the Jewish DP problem in Europe. One offered the solution to the other (with the added gain that the US Senate would not have to warrant an increase in immigration quotas). The British continued to prefer to consider them as separate issues.[69]

The Zionists, both in Palestine and America, had come to expect positive action from a Labour government over the Palestine issue since the party had publicly pledged support for the Jewish National Home at several party conferences.[70] At the World Zionist conference in early August, Weizmann was still optimistic that the pledge would be met. Yet even the pro-Zionists within the new Labour Cabinet found that political responsibility for the increasingly difficult problems Palestine presented forced a change in attitude. On 6 September, despite Truman's intervention, the Cabinet's Palestine Committee decided that it was impossible, at least in the short term, to advocate mass Jewish immigration to Palestine, or to rescind the 1939 White Paper. On advice from the Foreign Office, the committee decided that to antagonise the Arabs would be to risk almost inevitable civil war. The Cabinet agreed: the best policy lay in deferring a long-term decision, in the hope that pressure for Jewish immigration would lessen.[71]

In the short term, however, the Zionist lobby in the USA was exerting great pressure on the American government. As a consequence, on 29 September the American press were informed of Truman's request that 100,000 people be admitted to Palestine. This occurred despite Attlee's call for caution in publicising details of the talks without due consideration of the consequences in the Middle East. The press release added that Truman had yet to receive a response from Attlee. The ball was now firmly in the British court.[72]

Ernest Bevin, Foreign Minister, disappointed at the negative nature of Truman's intervention, was increasingly keen that Britain should not shoulder the burden of Palestine alone. It was on his suggestion that the Cabinet agreed to invite the USA to join Britain in setting up an Anglo-American Commission of Inquiry to examine the position of the Jewish DPs in Europe and how the situation could be relieved. On 13 November, Bevin announced the terms of reference of the commission in the House of Commons.[73] The enquiry would be concerned with the Palestine question and the position of the Jews in Europe, the recommendations to be presented within four months. The British reluctance to link the two issues completely was still apparent. In his statement, Bevin made it clear that he was not prepared to accept that opening the gates of Palestine was the only solution to the predicament faced by the Jews in Germany. He felt sure that once the American contingent of the commission was made to understand the complexity of the question, it would no longer be prepared to welcome uncritically the naive solution presented by the Zionists.[74]

The Palestine statement was well received in Britain but the Zionist reaction in America, where Bevin had already been cast as a staunch anti-semite, was bitter. Worse, in a press conference later that day, he unthinkingly labelled the Jews as queue-jumpers, only strengthening Zionist opinion against him. In fact, Bevin was reiterating the Foreign Office line that if the Jewish DPs were seen to be treated differently, an anti-semitic reaction would follow. Regardless, to the American Zionists the enquiry in itself was a ruse in which they held no faith; Bevin was simply stalling for time, intent on discrediting and disregarding Zionist demands.[75]

In Belsen too, the Palestine statement was received with bitter disappointment. On 15 November the Belsen Committee informed the local Military Government authorities that a strike had been called for the following day in protest at Bevin's announcement. Other protests were to take place in Hanover, Hamburg and Celle at the instigation of the Central Jewish Committee. The demonstration in Belsen was permitted but the camp leaders were warned that if the Jewish employees did not work they would receive no rations for the day. Elevated to a hunger strike, the protest, nevertheless, passed off peacefully; 1,500 people, led by members of the Jewish Committee, marched from the camp to the office of the Military Government Detachment and a deputation then presented a resolution to the officer in charge.[76]

In Hanover on the same day, Majer Lipka, president of the local Jewish Committee, attempted to lead a similar protest and he requested that the Jews working at the offices of the former Concentration Camp Prisoners Association be allowed to attend. The situation became heated when the German administrator of the association, Herr Grande, refused and called in the British Military Police. One hundred Jews had gathered to protest. When the German arrived with two British policemen intent on arresting Lipka the crowd became violent and the British used truncheons to protect Grande, the focus of the attacks. Lipka and others were taken into custody. In a further incident, when military police entered the Jewish Committee offices to confiscate documents concerning the protest, they arrested six other Jewish DPs for hindering the investigation.[77]

The episode was an unfortunate one and must have soured relations between the Jewish community and the local British detachment. There is little doubt that the incident could have been handled better and that both sides shared the blame. The Jews, on their side, failed to get a permit from the British to enable them to hold a public protest and then allowed their anger and frustration to escalate into violence. The British, on the other side, displayed a definite lack of tact and restraint in the handling of the situation.[78]

News of the Hanover episode reached the United States. On 7 December a full-page advertisement appeared in the New York *Post* strongly condemning the British authorities in Germany. A scathing attack, it went so far as to accuse the British of attempting to finish the job begun by Hitler and so solve the Palestine problem for ever. The advertisement, however, mistakenly (though perhaps deliberately) reported the incident as taking place in the Belsen camp:

> There are no Arabs in Bergen Belsen [*sic*]. One incident in Bergen Belsen and the whole British policy towards the Hebrew peoples stand revealed [*sic*]. The date is November 16 1945. . . . The place is that very camp where thousands of Hebrews died and where today the survivors are still compelled to live. The incident occurred not under the swastika but under the liberating Union Jack. . . . On that day the representatives of the Hebrews of Bergen Belsen voted to submit a protest against the statement of Foreign Secretary Bevin. . . . However, the German administrator of the camp, one G. Grande, learning of the plan, appeared with British military police who arrested Lipka the President of the Hebrew committee. . . . The military police then let loose with their rubber truncheons striking indiscriminately at men, women and children who had managed to survive that sort of treatment over a period of many years and who thought that at last, half a year after VE Day, they had finally been liberated.[79]

The report was exaggerated and economical with the truth.[80] It was effective, however, and further blackened the British name. The British were always aware of the influence that the powerful American Jewish lobby might be able to exercise. Such a fear had been expressed by one official in somewhat sinister terms on 15 October:

> it is worth bearing in mind that the Jews have considerable influence over the press both in Britain and the USA, so that if a case can be made against our treatment of the Jews at Belsen we shall come in for very sharp criticism. We should therefore be well advised to make sure that we are doing all we reasonably can for these unfortunate people.[81]

The name 'Bergen-Belsen' was a useful publicity tool in itself, a detail which did not escape the Central Committee. In June 1945 the British authorities, having burned down the main Belsen camp, decided to call the new Displaced Persons' centre Höhne Camp. The name Belsen was associated with misery and suffering and it was deemed better to sever all connections with it. The Jewish leadership resented the change and continued to refer to the 'Belsen camp' for the whole of its existence. The camp representatives on the Central Committee called themselves the Belsen Committee and had their stationery printed with a Belsen address.[82] They did not want to sever connections with the name. Like an advertising logo, the name Belsen encapsulated the horror of the Nazi regime and the sympathy felt for the survivors in countries all over the world. Höhne meant nothing to anybody. If they were not to be forgotten, the Jewish Committee knew they had to keep the name of Belsen alive. Certainly, this 'device' was used to good effect abroad. As in the New York *Post* example above, it was not always made clear in the press that in fact the scene of the worst Nazi atrocities in Belsen was not the same site as that occupied by the DPs after the war. On 20 November the *New York Times* carried a report on the Jewish Displaced Persons in the British zone. Quoting Rosensaft, the paper reported that unlike American camps run by UNRRA, the British camps were still under the control of the army. Conditions were said to be very poor with a shortage of clothing (many DPs did not have shoes, socks, or overcoats) and no provision was made for heating the cold barracks. Finally, it was alleged that Zionist activities were discouraged and that the British authorities censored the news-sheets of the DPs. For the officials at the British CCG this report was the last straw. A memo concluded:

> We, therefore, think that we should adopt a policy of removing all Jews from Belsen camp to other camps in the British zone . . . the Jews seem to be using Belsen as a focal point for world agitation to emigrate to Palestine. If we move Jews from Belsen they will not be able to use the magic word Belsen in connection with this propaganda.[83]

The Central Committee members were not the only offenders in continuing to use the Belsen name. The Foreign Office was sharply reprimanded in a communication from the CCG at Lübbecke: 'Belsen is a misnomer and Belsen camp no longer exists. DP camp is at Höhne ten miles from Belsen.'[84] Ironically, the authorities in Lübbecke did not seem better informed. The DP camp was actually only a mile and a half from the original Belsen camp and, in fact, not in the village from which it took its name.

Meanwhile, the British attempted to correct the poor impression of the British camps presented in the foreign press. On 20 December in the House of Commons, the Chancellor of the Duchy of Lancaster made a lengthy statement concerning the treatment of displaced persons, carefully answering the criticisms directed at the British policy. Although he admitted that deficiencies still existed in some supplies, everything possible was being done – including levying the German people – in order that the shortfalls be made good. Hynd made clear that there was no censorship of newspapers, no restriction on political activity and complete freedom of movement in and out of the camps.[85]

In the British press, compared with the US, very little attention was given to the camps in Germany. Even in the Jewish press, only the *Jewish Standard* consistently raised the issue.[86] The lack of interest in the controversy was illustrated when the Foreign Office attempted to secure a reporter from the British press to visit Belsen and send home an impartial story to correspond with Hynd's statement. Despite strong persuasion, not a single British foreign correspondent accepted the invitation.

The consensus was that the story would be stale and have little news value. One reporter, however, a journalist representing Amalgamated Press, did agree to visit Germany and arrived in Belsen on 18 December. The report, sent confidentially to Hynd, was objective and the general impression presented was that everything possible was being done for the DPs, particularly since the arrival, in November, of a new Military Government commander, Major Murphy. The reporter, Sam Goldsmith, interviewed the leaders of both the Jewish and Polish communities. He found that although the *New York Times* report had been exaggerated, the main complaints of the internees – concerning the lack of variety in the rations and the shortage of clothing, footwear and fuel for the winter – were legitimate. The clothing situation was improving with the help of the relief organisations, but Murphy confirmed that some children were still required to go barefoot. In the middle of December this was obviously unacceptable and the camp leaders were rightly indignant. As to the allegations made by Jewish sources in America that the British authorities were attempting to dissuade the Jews from wishing to emigrate to Palestine, Goldsmith reported that they were not corroborated by the Jewish Committee.[87]

Nevertheless, relations between the Central Jewish Committee and the British authorities were often pressured, particularly in the first two years after the liberation. With its members' commitment to settlement in Palestine and their close links with Zionist organisations, it is little surprise that Rosensaft's committee did not endear itself to the authorities. The British zonal authorities did not formally recognise the Central Jewish Committee as representative of the Jewish DPs in the British zone as a whole, nor, initially, the separate camp subcommittees as representative of the individual Jewish communities. The Belsen Committee was no exception and for almost two years worked without formal recognition from the authorities.[88] In the controversy over the Lingen camp, Rosensaft had proved to be a provocateur. Throughout 1945, as the campaign to highlight the situation of the Jewish DPs and the publicity surrounding the Palestine issue were stepped up, the British authorities in Germany became increasingly aware of Rosensaft's powerful influence in the Jewish community. In the period following Bevin's statement, relations became particularly strained.

In December Rosensaft requested permission from 30 Corps District to travel to the United States in his capacity as the president of the Central Jewish Committee, having already secured the necessary permits from the American and French authorities. He was informed by the local authorities that he was free to leave the British zone in accordance with normal regulations, but having done so would then be regarded as having elected resettlement in the United States. In effect, therefore, he would cease to be a DP, cease to be president of the Jewish Committee and would certainly not be encouraged to return to

Germany. Not surprisingly Rosensaft found these conditions unacceptable and, in spite of the British authorities, he proceeded to America without permission, returning to Belsen some time later.[89] Outraged, officials in Germany were quick to inform the Foreign Office when Rosensaft disappeared from Belsen. In turn the Foreign Office cabled the British Embassy in Washington:

> please report anything you may hear regarding his political activities. He is an extreme Zionist inimical to (? Social Democratic) Jewry and has done his best to blacken British treatment of the Jewish displaced persons in Germany doubtless with a view to influencing the Anglo-American Commission of Enquiry.[90] [The brackets are original; the Foreign Office evidently struggled to describe non- or anti-Zionists.]

As Zionism became more of a perceived threat to the status quo in the British zone, so the British policy became more cautious. Careful distinctions were made between Jewish organisations on a political basis. Thus, representations from non-Zionist groups tended to be more welcome, and greeted less suspiciously, than those from overtly Zionist bodies. In September 1945, the World Union for Progressive Judaism addressed a letter to Bevin requesting that a rabbi, a German refugee living in Palestine, be permitted to return to Frankfurt so that he might aid the revival of religious life in Germany. In the chaos of postwar Europe, the standard reply to such an application was that no facilities for private travel to Germany were available. In this case, however, it was felt that an exception should be made:

> The WU is a sensible and moderate body, whose objectives do not conflict with the policy of His Majesty's Government. . . . For this reason we should like to give the Union any facilities that we reasonably can, more particularly as we wish to discourage the view that Jews would be unable to establish themselves in Europe after the present period of emergency. There is reason to believe that the Zionists in Palestine are exerting pressure on this ground to prevent Jews from applying for permission to return to Europe.[91]

In October 1945 the War Office was wary of allowing a visit to the British zone by Ben-Gurion, then chair of the Jewish Agency for Palestine.[92] Further, in February 1946, following a decision to invite a community leader from England to live and work among the survivors of the Jewish community in Berlin, it was stated by an official that no objection would be raised as long as the candidate was carefully vetted: 'we do not want any Jews who are likely to conduct Zionist propaganda.'[93]

The names of those chosen to serve on the Commission of Enquiry were announced on 10 December. Although all male and so not truly representative, the twelve individuals held a wide range of opinions on the Palestine question. Generally speaking and rather predictably, the American delegation tended towards a pro-Zionist stance and the British were pro-Arab. Beginning in Washington in January and travelling to London, Europe and the Middle East, the commissioners heard representations from all interested parties. In

Europe, visiting Belsen and other camps, they gained a clear understanding of the need and determination of the majority of Jewish DPs to emigrate to Palestine. When the time came, in April 1946, for the final report to be written, great differences of opinion still existed between the delegations. Nevertheless, the commission was determined that only unanimous recommendations should be presented. Eventually, the British yielded to American persuasion and a report emerged which endorsed Truman's original entreaty that 100,000 Jews be admitted into Palestine.[94]

For the DPs, the recommendations of the Commission of Enquiry brought new hope after their first winter of liberation in the camps. Needless to say, the British government was disappointed at the result. It continued to believe that to accept the recommendation and allow wide-scale immigration to Palestine would be to invite an Arab revolt and it pointed to the technical difficulties in rapidly moving 100,000 people. Terrorist attacks in Palestine during the summer, most notably the bombing of the King David Hotel in Jerusalem by the Irgun, only strengthened British feeling further. The publication of the committee's report heralded only more high-level talks.

## IV

A full twelve months after the liberation of the concentration camps, the future of the Jews in Europe was as uncertain as ever. Had the British government made the connection between the DPs and the Palestine question and issued 100,000 certificates in 1945, then the Jewish DPs would no longer have constituted a problem. By 1946 the initiative had been lost; the number of Jewish people in the Western zones was increasing, both as a proportion of the DPs as other groups were repatriated, and in absolute terms, due to a new influx of 'infiltrees' from Eastern Europe.

A great many of the 83,000 Jews remaining in Poland after the war resolved that they wanted to leave that country. Large numbers did in fact flee and, by their actions, justified the decision of those Polish Jews who, liberated in German camps, had refused to be repatriated.[95] The decimation of the pre-war Jewish communities and the presence of a hostile anti-semitic population, combined with a bleak political and economic outlook, compelled the Jewish population to leave. By December 1945, the number of Jews arriving in Berlin was thought to be in the region of 250 a day. During that month the Directorate of the Allied Control Authority concerned with DPs met to discuss the situation. In a meeting on 11 December, the Soviet and British representatives were quite clear that the refugees should be returned to Poland. The Americans, however, were reluctant to return people to 'possible death' and persuaded their colleagues that temporary refuge should be afforded to the Poles, at least as a short-term measure.[96]

Initially, the spontaneous flight of people from Poland and the USSR was hurried and *ad hoc*, becoming more organised only in 1946.[97] Certainly, agents of the B'richa, the name given to the illegal Jewish rescue organisation under the direction of Haganah, were active in Kovno and Vilna from as early as 1944 but their activities were on a small scale. Nevertheless, during 1945 escape routes were established through Romania, Hungary and Yugoslavia into the DP camps in Germany and Italy from where agents organised sea passages to Palestine.[98]

By mid-August it was estimated that over 750,000 people had passed through Berlin. This was despite concerted efforts to keep them out of the city, due to overcrowding. The refugees, mostly German nationals expelled from Poland, were in a terrible physical and mental state, and many died on the journey. Correspondents described the scenes at the Berlin railway station as 'being like Belsen all over again' with carts on the platform having to be loaded with the dead.[99] The Polish Jews among these refugees all gave persecution as the reason for their fleeing Poland. British officials, however, were becoming sceptical and in December 1945 they contacted the embassy in Warsaw requesting evidence of this alleged persecution. They suspected the movement was more likely the result of Zionist organisations trying to influence the Anglo-American Enquiry; by encouraging Jews to cross into Germany the 'pressure of would-be immigrants may appear to be increased'.[100]

In January 1946 a report reached Berlin which confirmed growing British suspicions that the illegal movement was not spontaneous.[101] On 4 January, forty-five Jews, mostly young Poles, were arrested in the British zone attempting to cross a deserted spot on the German-Dutch border. From an examination of their documents and following subsequent interrogations, it became obvious that they were following an organised underground escape route. Soldiers of the Jewish Brigade formation based in the Netherlands were also implicated. Four soldiers were detained when they were found to have driven two lorries to the German frontier 'for no very convincing reason . . . and in direct line of the arrested party's advance'. Jewish Brigade soldiers were indeed involved in the illegal operation, and to an even greater extent when stationed in Italy in 1945. They often provided food and accommodation for the refugees and, more crucially, transport, of which there was a great shortage. When the brigade was formally disbanded in 1946, many of the soldiers stayed on in the DP camps and, together with individuals working with the voluntary relief organisations, continued to help the infiltrees.[102]

The proof the British had sought of Polish anti-semitism came most forcibly in July 1946 with the shocking reports of the Kielce pogrom.[103] A senseless and unreconstructed ritual murder accusation, reminiscent of the medieval period, sparked the pogrom in which forty-one people were murdered. The involvement of local Polish officials in the violence and the lack of condemnation from the Church gave further evidence of the deep-rooted and murderous nature of Polish anti-semitism. The direct result of the pogrom was a marked increase in the numbers of Jews crossing the Polish border into Germany. By September 1946 almost 65,000 people had left Poland, many with the aid of B'richa.[104]

Even before the Kielce incident in July, the level of illegal immigration into the British zone had greatly increased and boat loads of people were reaching Palestine.[105] British policy in dealing with the new influx into Germany was repressive. Refugees were refused entry to the zone and those who got through were denied DP facilities and the means to continue their journey. Many did get through. Reliable reports were reaching the British that a great many of the infiltrees were finding refuge in the Höhne camp. Jewish refugees arrived in the camp with forged papers and were cared for illegally under the auspices of the Jewish Committee. A stratagem practised by the committee, whereby the rations of genuine DPs continued to be drawn long after their departure from the camp (usually on illegal journeys to Palestine), helped feed the infiltrees.[106]

In June, the British announced there would be no further registration of new DPs after 1 July 1946 in the British zone.[107] In addition, orders were issued that food and transport should be supplied only to the authorised DP population and that steps should be taken to confiscate all illegally procured stocks of food.[108] Yet the Polish Jews continued to pour into the zone, and into the Belsen camp, confident that they would be provided for. In August, 1,064 people were thought to have arrived in Belsen in just one week. They had travelled on forged papers as part of 'Operation Swallow', an official Allied programme which transported German expellees from Poland. British suspicions that the new arrivals had been briefed on what to say if questioned were confirmed after interviews with refugees. Many infiltrees gave the same story; that they were born and had lived in Germany until 1938, when they were placed into concentration camps, before being moved during the war to Poland. It should be added that these histories might have been credible had the infiltrees been able to speak German.[109]

The British orders were ignored by the Jewish Committee at Belsen and it continued to draw rations for the infiltrees illegally. In August, a further instruction from the headquarters of the Prisoners of War and Displaced Persons (PW and DP) Division of the Control Commission ordered that from then on the ration strengths of all DP camps would remain at 2 July levels. At the same time it was explained to the inmates of Höhne that ordinary German ration cards would be available to all those living in the camp who were not registered DPs (provided that they complied with the regulation for the issue of ration cards; that is, lived with the civilian German population outside of the camps). The British received no positive response from the camp. From this time onward, as far as the authorities were concerned, the Jewish Committee was solely responsible for the presence in Höhne of the 2,000 illegals. If they were starving to death, as alleged by a Swedish Zionist organisation in the press in December, then it was not the result of any Military Government policy but because of the choice of the Belsen Committee to disobey orders.[110]

In August 1946 the illegal traffic formed the subject of correspondence between the Control Office in London and the British authorities in Berlin. London requested reports on the illegal migration and recommendations as to how it might be stopped, going so far as to hint that force might be the solution. Dealing specifically with the Belsen camp, a telegram from London recommended that the Polish Jews who had entered the Höhne camp illegally should be 'dispersed' and others 'prevented' from entering. In this telegram there was certainly an intimation that the use of physical coercion might be coun-tenanced by London, but the authorisation was not implicit enough. Force had not been a sanctioned British policy hitherto and in view of the inevitably serious consequences in taking such a step, Berlin felt it needed further confirmation:

> To change our present policy for one of forcible ejection is a step which we do not feel justified in taking unless we are clear that it is your wish. The alter-native is to continue the discouragement policy as rigorously as possible which would include as close a control over neighbouring frontiers and zonal boundaries as is practicable in present conditions.[111]

In fact, a change in tactics was not authorised. Indeed, it is difficult to see what could have been gained at all by following a policy of forcible ejection and repatriation. More than the fact that it would have been difficult to implement for relatively little reward, the negative publicity generated by such a policy would have caused terrific embarrassment. Any attempt to expel the 2,000 infil-trees in Belsen would have met with opposition in the camp and outrage in the American press. In the words of one official: 'fun and games at Höhne camp in casting out unauthorised inhabitants, will achieve nothing except political diffi-culties and should not be attempted.'[112]

If the infiltrees were a direct threat to British authority then so too was the Jewish Committee who gave them sanctuary. A report based on an interview with Captain McAllen, acting Military Government commanding officer at Höhne camp, portrayed 'a horrifying state of affairs' as far as the bureaucrats in Lübbecke were concerned.[113] McAllen admitted that Military Government no longer had any control over the camp. The British officials in the area were convinced that Höhne was used as a major transit centre for the movement of illegal immigrants. More disturbing was the evidence that food and transport facilities for the illegals were provided by the American Joint Distribution Com-mittee (AJDC), Jewish Relief Units (JRU) and UNRRA.[114] British suspicions about the camp as a collection point for those people making the illegal journey to Palestine were correct.[115] McAllen's opinions of Josef Rosensaft, however, were less objective and seem to have been based on a fear of the power Rosensaft was perceived to have in the British zone. Thus Rosensaft, on his emergence as 'the leader of the European Jews', was in this report transformed from a Polish Zionist, and chair of the Poale Zion party in Belsen, into a much more menacing threat: a Russian communist! The damning 'proof' of the accusation was that it was thought Rosensaft was fluent in Russian – and he had once been sighted as taking 'the communist salute of the clenched fist at a demonstration'. The British administration in Germany was evidently not free of the anti-semitic, anti-Bolshevik propaganda which had been so much a part of Nazi dogma. That the actions of the Jews in Germany should be viewed in terms of a Jewish communist plot reflects the early fears of the Anglo-Americans of the perceived Russian menace. Infiltrees into the Western zones in particular were viewed with sus-picion; Anglo-Americans were fearful that communist penetration would not only be extended in eastern Europe but also begin to threaten the security of the West.[116] To cite one example in the American zone, intelligence officers noted that a jeweller had been given an order to make 1,650 copies of a pin for a nearby DP camp. The pins were to display a hammer and sickle, a torch and the name of Borochov, the Labour Zionist. The Americans, however, instantly assumed Borochov was a communist and took no little persuading otherwise.[117]

The PW and DP Division in the Control Commission was sharply criticised when this latest report reached the Political Division. It had allowed its authority to be undermined to such an extent that it no longer had any control over the Jews in the British zone. The Political Division proposed that on the strength of this new evidence a serious effort should be made to get rid of Rosensaft who was 'clearly the chief nigger in the woodpile'.[118] In November, when Rosensaft and Norbert Wollheim were invited to visit London by the World Jewish Congress, the chiefs in the Political Division in Germany raised serious objections to the visit. They were convinced that as a 'dangerous trouble-maker' he would be bound to use the visit to embarrass the government 'by spreading malicious untruths about the British administration'.[119] A senior official wrote concerning Rosensaft to the Foreign Office in September: 'The difficulties our authorities have had in dealing with Jewish DPs in the British zone are in large measure directly attributable to him'. Unlike the officials in London, increasingly influenced by Colonel Robert Solomon, the Jewish Advisor and former Chair of the Jewish National Fund, and by correspondence and deputations from representatives of the Anglo-Jewish community in favour of the Jewish DPs, the officials in Germany did not see Rosensaft as an asset in dealing with the Jews at Höhne. Instead, they were hoping for an instruction 'to remove him' from his position.[120] In the event, the Foreign Office, to the consternation of the British administration, allowed the visit.

Against all the odds, and despite British efforts to the contrary, the Jewish Committee actually held a strong position in the British zone. Nowhere was this better illustrated than in an incident earlier in 1946. In April, to mark the first anniversary of the liberation of Bergen-Belsen, a ceremony was held to unveil a memorial on the site of Camp I. Seven thousand Jews from the Höhne camp, various relief workers and army officials attended to hear addresses by members of the Central Committee. All went smoothly until Norbert Wollheim, vice-chair of the Central Committee, rose to give a speech, in English, guaranteed to offend the British members of the audience. Wollheim, pre-empting the recent historical debate concerning the role of the Allies in the Holocaust, alleged that as the British had done nothing to prevent Hitler's extermination of 6 million Jews, they shared some guilt in the crime. The speech, indeed, caused a great deal of distress to the British spectators. When questioned later, Wollheim claimed that in the excitement of the moment he had omitted to include that page in his speech, which praised the British for all they had done since the liberation. Such blatant criticism of the British was a new extreme for the Central Committee. Wollheim's excuse was not accepted and the local Military Government officials called for harsh reprisals. They recognised that the Jewish Committee was a powerful organisation and that, unless something was done to control its activities, it could be a cause of considerable trouble in the British zone. Nevertheless, 'the political implications' of the Jewish situation in the zone were also 'fully realised'.[121] In this, the Central Committee had the British over a barrel. Any action taken against them would have certain serious political repercussions at home and abroad. Ultimately, there was only one solution to strive for. 'Höhne is a festering ulcer,' professed one British official, 'the sooner it is closed and its contents dispersed the better.'[122]

British policy in dealing with the Polish infiltrees was not terribly effective, not only because of the defiance of the DPs and the Jewish organisations, but also because the policy was followed in isolation. By far the greatest number of Jews fleeing from Eastern Europe headed for the American zone. The Americans recognised the plight of these people and, unlike the British, offered them rations and accommodation.[123] UNRRA policy, too, was to provide the new influx of people with full DP status and privileges.[124] Any firm British action against the infiltrees only served to direct more refugees into the American zone.

Moreover, the Americans were not the only ones to hinder the British policy of 'maximum discouragement' to the illegal immigrants. Intelligence Division reported in August that French officials, 'swayed by somewhat misguided humanitarian considerations', had been allowing illegal Jewish DPs to cross the Belgian border.[125] On another occasion, 440 Jews bound ostensibly for Costa Rica (but quite obviously headed for Palestine) were stopped.[126] When it transpired that the exit visa for the group was granted by the head of the Soviet Administrative Section of the Allied Control Council, the British strongly protested at 'Soviet collusion' with an 'enemy country in illegal measures directed against her ally Great Britain'. It was later verified that a collective visa alleged to have been issued by a Costa Rican representative in Bucharest was in fact a forgery.[127]

Meanwhile, all through the summer of 1946, high-level negotiations continued in London between newly appointed British and American delegations over the recommendations of the Anglo-American Commission of Enquiry. Only now did the British begin to admit the link between the question of Palestine and the question of the DPs was inevitable. On 1 August the Control Office informed Berlin that the government had authorised, as part of a wider plan for the solution of the Palestine problem, the issue of 100,000 immigration certificates.[128] In the summer of 1945 the movement of 100,000 Jews to Palestine would certainly have emptied the DP camps in Germany and Austria. A year later, however, emigration from the East had increased the numbers of Displaced Jews to around 250,000. Hundreds of people had already attempted to reach Palestine illegally. As a reaction to the British refusal to implement the recommendations of the enquiry, militants in Palestine had begun a bombing campaign culminating in the serious explosion at the King David Hotel in Jerusalem, the British military headquarters.[129] The British response was unrestrained. Mass arrests were made and curfews enforced. On 13 August, the government announced that refugees would no longer be allowed into Palestine. Any illegal immigrants henceforth arriving in Palestine would be taken to Cyprus and housed in detention camps there.[130] In the same week the Control Office sent a letter to Berlin asking for information on B'richa and on the involvement of the American Joint Distribution Committee in its activities.[131]

In Germany, in the meantime, the Central Committee continued its fight for official acknowledgement by the British. A full twelve months after the formation of the committee, it had still received no recognition from the British authorities. In May 1946, however, the chief of the Division responsible for Displaced Persons decided that the time had come when it had either to recognise the Central Committee or suppress it altogether. 'All other nationalities in the British Zone are represented by Liaison Officers or their respective Government representatives,' he wrote to the Deputy Chief of Staff, 'it seems the time has arrived to recognise one Jewish authority.'[132] To the people working on the ground it seemed the obvious policy. Following a survey of the British zone conducted in March, UNRRA had made such a recommendation.[133] It was strongly supported in London by Colonel Solomon, the Jewish Advisor to the Control Office, who was considered to be an even-handed man. To those in the Political Division, however, the policy was as preposterous now as it had been a year previously. To treat Jews as a separate race by recognising a committee which represented German Jews and non-German Jews alike, was contrary to the policy of His Majesty's Government (HMG). Moreover, the Political Division was at pains to point out to its colleagues in Germany and to the Foreign Office the folly of giving official recognition to a committee led by such an unsuitable character and 'ardent Zionist' as Rosensaft.[134]

If the authorities were looking for an ally in their attempt to dispose of Rosensaft and the Central Jewish Committee then they did not find it in Colonel Solomon, the Jewish Advisor. He immediately alienated himself from officials in the Political Division of the CCG with his early suggestion that German and non-German Jews were in the same boat as members of a persecuted minority for whom a refuge must be found in Palestine or elsewhere.[135] In his official recommendations on the Jewish question, based on his visits to the British zone in 1946 and interviews with all the parties concerned, he made the differentiation between the two groups of DPs. Thus, his first two points, that early arrangements should be made to resettle the Jewish DPs in Palestine and elsewhere so that the Jewish centres, especially Belsen, could be closed, and that encouragement should be given to the German Jews to resettle once more in the German community by providing restitution and returning community buildings, were long-term goals and met little opposition. The third proposal, that the British administration in Germany should employ four liaison officers, one concerned with orthodoxy, one with welfare, the third with German Jews and the fourth with Jews of other nationalities, was less well received.[136] Requests for liaison officers had been rejected in 1945 by the Military Government. Yet on this occasion, it was less the suggestion itself than the names put forward for consideration, among them Rosensaft and Wollheim, that caused distress to the officials in Germany. 'All four names have been unmitigated nuisances to Military Government for a long time', wrote an official from the Political Division to the Control Office. He also doubted Solomon's reliability and impartiality and in the same letter continued:

> It is probably a pity a Jew was ever appointed 'Jewish Adviser'. Almost any honest Jew will admit that no Jew can be really objective about Jewish affairs; and anyone who is not objective cannot be expected to advise H.M.G. reliably. . . . I am not suggesting we should necessarily try to get Solomon replaced at present, though if he commits any serious gaff we may have to do so. But I thought you ought to know that these difficulties do exist, and that we are apt to be faced with somewhat naive instructions from the Control Office, based on an implicit acceptance of Solomon's advice.[137]

It was precisely this kind of attitude which led to Solomon's resignation as Jewish Advisor in August 1947. Having spent twelve months in the job, Solomon felt complete frustration at the lack of progress on his recommendations for Germany. None the less, one very important proposal *had* been put into effect; the authority of Josef Rosensaft was finally officially recognised by the British. Certainly, this recognition went some way to improving relations between the Jews in Germany and the British authorities in 1947.

## V

In the international arena there had been marked developments since 1945 in reaching a permanent solution to the Palestine question. The British on their part had showed a willingness to deviate from the 1939 White Paper policy – by extending Jewish immigration (set at a quota of 1,500 per month) beyond the original five-year period without the consent of the Arabs – even if they did not go nearly as far as required. The Zionists were also willing to compromise on their 1942 decision at the Baltimore Conference to accept nothing short of a Jewish state encompassing the whole of Palestine, and to negotiate for an acceptable partition solution. Yet the two sides could not agree. In July 1946 the British Cabinet endorsed a compromise proposal drafted by Morrison which was categorically rejected by both Jews and Arabs. Finally, in February 1947 the British government returned the Mandate over Palestine to the United Nations. That year, 1947, undoubtedly marked the lowest point in postwar Jewish–British relations. In particular, Jewish terrorism in Palestine, instrumental in the extremist Irgun and the Stern group and directed towards British military and civilian authorities, caused an immense amount of ill feeling.[138] These groups were a minority of the Yishuv in Palestine. The majority, who followed the more moderate line advocated by the Jewish Agency Executive, wished to keep the door of political negotiation open. The main effort of the Hagana, the military wing of the Jewish Agency, in the second half of 1946 and in 1947 was focused on the organisation of illegal immigration of Jews from Europe and the destruction of such targets as radar installations which enabled the British to track illegal ships and intercept them. Some boats did get through the British nets but others were prevented from reaching Palestine and instead the DPs were transported to internment camps in Cyprus.[139] The famous exception was the *Exodus 1947* which became the focus of the world's press in the summer, when the British decided to make an example of the prospective illegal immigrants on board and sent them back to Germany. This long-drawn-out incident, which will be discussed shortly, in fact had the effect of regaining for the Jews' cause much of the sympathy that had been depleted by the widespread publicity given to the atrocities against British targets in Palestine.

The Jews in Belsen were directly affected by the negotiations and conflict in the international arena and in general did not have any sympathy for the British policy. At the same time, however, as far as local politics was concerned, some improvements in relations did occur during 1947. In January 1947, Rosensaft had written a worried letter to Solomon concerning the infiltrees in the camp who were still not receiving official rations. Shortages in the camp were becoming more acute. As camp leader, Rosensaft was in a difficult position. He had already been forced to turn away new arrivals to Belsen but he could not ask those who were already settled to move on – most were old or sick and many were Orthodox Jews who refused to leave. As a 'final plea' Rosensaft asked that Solomon put before the authorities the proposition that the remaining 1,868 infiltrees be allowed to stay as refugees and receive German rations distributed to the camp. In return Rosensaft would do his utmost to prevent any further influx into the camp and to reduce the numbers of internees already present.[140] Solomon was sympathetic. So too were officials at the Control Office for whom 'common humanity' demanded that the hardship of the DPs should not be 'needlessly increased any more'. In fact, Hynd, as Chancellor of the Duchy of Lancaster, and the Control Office were under quite some pressure from the Anglo-Jewish community over the question of the infiltrees and therefore welcomed the opportunity provided by Rosensaft's proposal to solve the problem.[141] If Rosensaft failed to make good his undertakings, then the authorities in Germany could 'discard him finally'.[142]

Characteristic of the bureaucracy of the British administration was the ensuing delay; it was May 1947 before a conference between Rosensaft and the PW and DP Division was arranged. The meeting, though not entirely built on trust, did establish an important dialogue and the two parties reached agreement on several issues. Rosensaft assented to produce, with the assistance of the local Military Government Detachment, accurate figures of the camp population and in return the CCG agreed to the provision of German rations for the camp refugees. Both would work together to ensure the population did not increase any further. In addition, the British confirmed that official recognition had now been given by HMG to the elected Jewish Committee at the Höhne DP Assembly Centre, as representing the DPs of that centre. Members of the Jewish Committee were given direct access to British officers on all matters affecting Höhne. The British were steadfast, however, in their refusal to recognise the Central Jewish Committee as the one authority representing German and non-

German Jewish opinion throughout the zone. Nevertheless, the committees in other DP centres would also be recognised as the authorities in their own communities and the chairs of the various committees would be received together in matters affecting the whole zone.[143] There was a marked change in the level of co-operation between the two sides. In December 1947 Rosensaft even received a letter of thanks from Major-General Franshaw of the International Refugee Organisation (IRO – which had taken over the role of UNRRA) for his personal assistance in helping staff to document people in Höhne.[144]

An air of good feeling was further promoted in 1947 with the beginning of 'Operation Grand National', the code name given to the legal emigration of Jews to Palestine. The choice of name reflected the number of hurdles that had been met on the way. The first group of 395 people, all from Belsen, left Borcholt transit camp *en route* to Palestine on 1 April. An order of priority was established – for example, those persons who had been receiving DP care since before October 1945 were the first to go – and the transports were chosen by a selection board comprising representatives from the PW and DP Division, the Jewish Agency, the JRU and UNRRA, together with the camp president.[145] Only 300 certificates per month were issued by the Colonial Office but they were all restricted to the Jews in the British zone. The British were keen to clear their zone of occupation as quickly as possible and to close down the Jewish DP camps, particularly Belsen, altogether. This was also a response to the decision of the Americans to reserve for their own zone the entire quota of emigration certificates for the USA. As far as the British were concerned the Americans had deliberately encouraged the flow of illegal immigration into their zone and they only had themselves to blame for the enormous DP problems there.[146] In addition to 'Grand National', the 'Westward Ho!' scheme also operated from the British zone. It also gave encouragement to the DPs that their expectations of a new life would shortly be realised. In terms of the wider DP problem in Europe the number of certificates was not sufficient but in the relatively small community of Belsen, the impact of witnessing fellow DPs leave the camp legally for a new life was tremendous and improved the morale of those who remained.

Yet although 1947 saw some improvement in the relationship between the Jews in Belsen and the British Control Commission a number of events and incidents ensured and illustrated that the thaw was not complete. In spite of the emigration and resettlement schemes in operation for DPs, there still remained in Germany a great number of Jewish DPs who were prepared to risk reaching Palestine illegally rather than wait indefinitely for a legal passage. The majority of illegal immigrants to Palestine left from the southern European ports. The British zone, however, also offered opportunities for clandestine Jewish emigration. In 1947 the provision of a maritime training school on the coast at Neustadt caused a political row in the British zone and in London. In the House of Commons, Sydney Silverman, MP, had raised with Hynd the question of the lack of fishing opportunities for the DPs in Germany since the closure of a Jewish fishery school in Hamburg in November 1946.[147] A proposal to open the school at Neustadt, however, met with strong opposition from the Control

Commission in Germany. The Political Division, backed by the Naval Division, believed it 'highly undesirable that there should be an organisation in Germany which by training potential blockade runners, will further complicate the task of the Royal Navy in the Mediterranean'.[148] In July the maritime training school was opened despite further very strong objections raised by the Deputy Military Governor to the British zone, Lt-Gen. Bishop.[149] Bishop presented his opposition to the proposal in a meeting with a high-ranking Foreign Office official in London. It was impossible to dissociate this new school from its Hamburg predecessor which had been closed on orders from the Commander-in-Chief. On investigation, it had been found that the first school, sponsored by the AJDC, had been opened without authority and was home to DPs from the Russian zone who had not been screened and held no papers. They were fed by AJDC workers, who had been drawing rations illegally. In a report of 1 November 1946, the Regional Commissioner claimed that the occupants appeared to be a disciplined, militant organisation, acting under orders received from the Central Committee in Belsen. Telephone intercepts had proved that they were engaged in procuring and falsifying identity documents, while the police, on visiting the house, found excessive stocks of food and money. The report had recommended that the fishing school be closed. This was done after some initial opposition from the occupants who had been given instructions by Rosensaft, Bishop was told, not to vacate the premises.

Despite the political implications, however, the Chancellor of the Duchy of Lancaster was determined that plans for the school should go ahead. Under considerable pressure from the Jewish community in Britain, Hynd did not want to invite further criticism of British policy and the charge that he had deprived the Jewish DPs of the chance of earning their living in a useful and honourable way. The authorities, however, watched the DPs very carefully. The Commander-in-Chief closed down the school's deep-sea activities when it was suspected that Neustadt was being used as a transit centre for illegal emigration between the Höhne camp and Sweden and Denmark.[150] Nevertheless, it was quite a hopeless task to prevent any great number of DPs from leaving the British zone illegally. 'In our view', wrote one senior official, 'the only restrictive measures which would be truly effective in overcoming the determined spontaneous movement of Jewish emigration would be such as can only be undertaken by regimes approximating to that of the Nazi government.'[151]

The deteriorating political situation in Palestine in 1947, when, as already noted, the level of violence escalated to new heights, did not help foster goodwill between the British and the Jewish DPs on the Continent. For the first time, the repercussions of the violent aspect of the fight for the Jewish state were felt directly in Europe. In June 1947 small explosive packages, posted from Rome, were sent to prominent persons in London.[152] In July rumours circulated in camps in the American zone that a Jewish group intended to blow up the British consulate in Frankfurt.[153] The murder of two British sergeants on active duty in Palestine caused a great deal of upset and unrest in Britain. In the summer of 1947 riots occurred against the Jewish communities in several British cities[154] and on 4 August, the British consulate in Frankfurt received an anonymous warning letter: 'You are being warned, that if your Government does not do anything about the riots now happening in the UK life will not be easy for any Britisher over in Germany. Also threats being made by our organisation to kill one Britisher for one Jewish Patriot will be strictly carried out.' It was signed 'A Jew'.[155] Josef Rosensaft, in the spirit of goodwill, sent telegrams to the Regional Commissioner, Land Niedersachsen, and to London expressing the horror of his committee at the murder of the two British sergeants in Palestine and their opposition to terrorism in general. Read aloud in Parliament by Michael Foot, MP, the telegram was reported to have made a great impression.[156]

In Belsen itself, more mundane matters caused friction between the Central Committee and the Control Commission. In July 1947 the committee planned to hold its annual congress and in the spirit of the new relationship with the British, it invited the Commander-in-Chief and other prominent officials in the British zone. In addition, Rosensaft asked the local military commander for the facilities needed to hold the congress, four days' rations for 300 people, 500 gallons of petrol and a Military Police presence. All facilities were refused, however, and CCG representation withheld on the grounds that the British did not recognise the authority of the Central Committee. Once again Silverman used his influence to intervene on behalf of the DPs, complaining to Hynd of the general obstructiveness of the CCG.[157]

One subject on the agenda at the congress – which went ahead regardless – was the noticeable emergence of anti-semitism in the British zone. The major theme of a campaign launched by certain sections of the German press presented Belsen as the centre of operations of a black market smuggling ring. In February 1948 the Belsen camp did come under suspicion when British Intelligence intercepted a lorry carrying a large quantity of contraband cigarettes destined for Höhne. When interrogated the German driver stated that he had delivered three previous truckloads, totalling 13 million cigarettes in all. As a consequence, the British authorities raided the camp. The search by British soldiers went smoothly (although Rosensaft complained in the strongest terms at use of German police to surround the camp) and the Belsen committee was thanked for its co-operation. In fact, little evidence of black market activity was uncovered and there were no arrests made. Among the few items confiscated was a cow for which no one claimed ownership. Off the record, Rosensaft later quipped that anyway the cow had no right to be in the camp since it had no DP card.[158]

Despite the lack of firm evidence linking the Jewish population in Belsen with smuggling activities, the Jews were branded as black marketeers.[159] In London, *The Star* claimed that the Belsen camp was a centre of large-scale racketeering in Germany and a junction in the underground trading route to Palestine. 'Each twenty cigarettes and 1 lb of coffee', warned the paper, 'might have meant another gun in the hands of a "Fighter for Israel".'[160] Reports circulated that the goods had been found in the vicinity of the camp when in fact the lorry was stopped on an autobahn near Hanover, 68 km from Belsen. The official account of the incident, however, stressed that the lorry was the fifth in a series, at least two of which were witnessed by a customs official unloading at the camp. Nevertheless, as Colonel Solomon pointed out in defence of the Jewish population, the report was silent on where the lorries unloaded, the Jewish portion of Belsen constituting only a fraction of the camp. He argued with the authorities that as the raid had brought nothing to light, Belsen was entitled to be cleared publicly of all suspicion. Solomon was reminded of a previous incident when, after a series of robberies at local farms, suspicion fell on the Belsen community. In fact, the culprits turned out to be British personnel. Both Rosensaft and Solomon strongly suspected that propagandists were at work to denigrate the name of the Jewish DPs and at the same time divert attention away from the true centres of black market activity.[161]

Anti-semitic activity manifested itself in a multitude of other forms. In July, Rosensaft wrote to the Chief of the PW and DP Division asking that concrete steps be taken to alter this worrying trend.[162] Rosensaft pointed, as evidence, to the desecration of Jewish cemeteries, a whispering campaign regarding the new currency reform (in which it was alleged that Jewish people received 'Mark for Mark' redemption of new currency for old) and the press campaign over the smuggling allegation. On 9 July, the *Nordsee Zeitung* had reported that 1.5 million cigarettes had been stolen from Hamburg port and claimed that 'all clues lead to the DP camp at Belsen where criminals are being protected by special treatment enjoyed from the Military Authorities'.[163] Yet, Rosensaft's memo impressed the British officer as 'propaganda not truth' and in his reply he concerned himself with the illegal status of the Central Committee under whose banner Rosensaft had written. Rosensaft failed to see the connection. 'Non recognition of the Central Committee', he wrote in a second letter, 'should not release the authorities from the responsibility of stamping out Nazi tendencies.' He then listed thirty-eight Jewish cemeteries desecrated in the British zone in recent months. The currency lie, he continued, had reached such proportions that crowds had collected outside Celle banks in protest, and the headline in the Hamburg *Allgemein Zeitung* of 2 February had read, 'Bergen-Belsen, Centre of Black Market'.[164] It was in the summer of 1947 that Oswald Mosley, the British fascist, was able to smuggle 10,000 copies of a news-sheet into the Western zones of Germany, although it is unclear if there was any connection between the events.[165]

Certain members of the Jewish population in Belsen certainly were involved in black market activities. As long as shortages existed in Germany and there was a demand for commodities such as food and cigarettes the existence of a black market was inevitable. Certainly goods such as cigarettes were in greater supply in the DP camps than elsewhere in Germany because they were allowed to be included in relief parcels. Yet the anti-DP, and especially anti-Jewish, propaganda affecting the camps was unjustified. Allied personnel were often guilty of dealing on the black market and of course the civilian population who bought the goods, often travelling long distances on illegal journeys, were equally incriminated but rarely prosecuted. A local officer, while not refuting the level of Jewish involvement, regretted very much that the official report on the Belsen incident had 'conveyed the impression that full responsibility for black market activities in Höhne must be placed on the shoulder of the Jews for indulging and on the British for allowing them to indulge when the Germans get away with a pat on the back for integrity and good behaviour'.[166] Local British officials were well aware of anti-semitism amongst the German population but even they were surprised when the Minister of the Interior at Niedersachsen asked that restrictions be placed on the import of coffee, claiming that 200 tons was sent every month to Jewish DPs in gift parcels and ended up on the black market. The figure of 200 tons was a gross exaggeration. Nevertheless, the PW and DP Branch replied that it was strongly opposed to any legislation where discrimination against DPs, whether Jewish or otherwise, could be practised, noting as an aside that the minister made no mention of restricting the number of gift parcels to the German population.[167]

Of all the incidents that soured relations between the DPs and the British in this period, perhaps the most well publicised was the *Exodus* affair. By mid-1947, the detention camps in Cyprus were filling up with illegal immigrants who had been intercepted in the Mediterranean by the Royal Navy. In May 1947 the Foreign Office took the step of writing to thirty-eight British embassies in Europe and around the world in order that they give full publicity to the ongoing illegal traffic. The object of the publicity was to illustrate that the infiltrees were jeopardising the possibility of finding any solution to the problem. The American Zionists who organised the movement, it was claimed, enticed the refugees with tales of Palestine as 'the land of milk and honey' when in fact all they faced were dangerous journeys on unseaworthy ships and an uncertain future.[168] Indeed, the expectations of the DPs, whilst living in and on departure from Germany, is an interesting subject area requiring further research. No number of lectures on life in Palestine could have prepared the average East European for the realities of the drastic changes in environment and culture. The assumption that the émigrés reached Palestine without qualms about their future in that country is surely a false one. Certainly, one reason given for the decision of Josef Rosensaft not to settle in Israel, is his disappointment at seeing the conditions there under which the survivors were forced to live.[169]

The *Exodus*, owned by Mossad, the Jewish intelligence service, arrived in Palestine in July 1947 carrying over 2,000 illegal passengers from Europe. They were forcibly disembarked by the British at Haifa on 18 July. Instead of being taken to Cyprus, however, they were returned in three cargo ships with a naval escort to Port-le-Bouc, the French port near Marseilles from where they had begun their sea journey.[170] Bevin had taken the decision to make an example of them in order to discourage further attempts at illegal immigration.[171] The plan backfired, however, and the British found themselves dealing not only with an international incident but with one that played right into the hands of the Zionists.

When the ships arrived at Marseilles the majority of the DPs, under the persuasion of the Jewish leadership on board, refused to disembark in protest at their treatment. Not only had they been repatriated, the conditions on the boats were truly appalling. In order that people might be allowed to lie down in the caged holds on the *Runnymede Park*, 150 women and children and those suffering from heat and exhaustion were moved to sleep on the upper deck. Sanitary facilities were grossly inadequate and some of the food supplies were out of date, containing weevils and maggots.[172] The ships remained anchored for three weeks and the DPs, including small children and pregnant women, continued to live in overcrowded conditions while negotiations took place between the British and French governments as to their future. Meanwhile, the Jews were frequently fired up with heroic speeches from the leaders on board so that their resolve to stand their ground would not be broken.

Nevertheless, it was a serious blow to morale when in August the British Cabinet made the decision to order the DPs back to Germany. American protests, unaccompanied by an offer to take the refugees, were ignored by Bevin and on 7 September the three boats finally reached Hamburg.[173] This time most of the DPs disembarked peacefully although some had to be forced off the ships by British Military Police. From Hamburg they were taken to Am Stau and Poppendorf camps where their ordeal continued, with conditions initially cramped and unhygienic. The reaction in Germany, from the Jewish relief organisations and the DPs, was one of disgust at the treatment the émigrés had received. Jews throughout the British zone held a one-day general strike combined with a fast in protest.[174] The international press, which followed the story closely, was overwhelmingly critical of British government actions and particularly of Bevin. In short, the affair drew an immense amount of sympathetic attention to the Jewish refugee problem in Europe at a crucial point in negotiations over the future of Palestine.[175] Moreover, it did not deter further DPs from making the journey to Palestine.[176]

Initially, the Jewish relief agencies working in the British zone decided collectively that they would refuse to co-operate in caring for the *Exodus* victims as a protest against British actions. In late August, however, the British gave Sam Dallob, director of the AJDC in the British zone, an ultimatum: either to promise to help the *Exodus* immigrants, or to face the cessation of all AJDC activities in the British zone. Personnel were also demanded from the JRU and it was agreed as a compromise that both organisations would provide medical staff but only to those immigrants who requested such help.[177] On 7 September the Belsen Committee organised a demonstration where several speakers protested against the return of the Jewish people to Germany but there was little in the way of incidents. Conditions in the *Exodus* camps were improved following the widespread condemnation of British policy and as the winter approached, the DPs were moved to better accommodation at Sengwarden and Emden.[178] For most, the stay in these camps was not a long one; they received priority in further legal and illegal transports from the British zone.[179]

Meanwhile, legal emigration programmes were in progress. 'Grand National' continued and in 1948 'Grand National Junior' was put into operation finally taking the orphan children from the camps to Palestine.[180] In January 1949, however, there were still 7,000 Jews awaiting evacuation from the British zone.[181] For a short period in the winter of 1948–9, during the conflict following the declaration of the Israeli state, male DPs who were of military age (18–45), were not issued with exit permits from the British zone.[182] Illegal transport routes continued to be utilised, however, to ensure that DPs who wished to fight in the 1948 war reached Palestine. A number of former Belsen residents lost their lives in the fight for Israeli independence. In February 1949, the ban was lifted and all Jews were permitted to leave Germany without restriction.

In fact, the Jewish camp at Belsen did not finally close until 1950, just weeks short of the fifth anniversary of the liberation of the camp. Rosensaft and Bimko, two of very few DPs still in Belsen who had been inmates of the Bergen-Belsen concentration camp, remained until the end. In March, the remaining occupants, many of whom were TB patients, were transferred to the Jever transit camp where some continued to live until December 1951.[183] On 12 December 1951 the British Section of the World Jewish Congress addressed a letter to Rosensaft to mark the closing of the Jever camp and the 'final liberation of nearly 40,000 Jewish survivors of the Nazi anti-Jewish terror'. The letter sought to pay tribute

> to the courageous and devotedly selfless service which, for the past six years, the small group of men and women of the Central Committee of Jewish Displaced Persons in the British Zone gave to their fellow Jews who endured with them the trials and afflictions of the Nazi horror camps of Auschwitz and Belsen.[184]

## VI

During the final two years in the life of the Belsen DP camp relations between the British authorities and the Central Jewish Committee had improved a great deal, indeed, enough for Rosensaft to comment later that the British had shown them 'much goodwill'. In the years immediately after the war, tensions were far more apparent. Despite the attempts by a powerful Zionist lobby to link the Palestine question with the issues of the Jewish DP question British policy was often short-sighted and insensitive and, in their attempt to be non-discriminatory and follow pre-determined policy guidelines, the British authorities refused to see the specific Jewish tragedy.

This chapter cannot be concluded without first recording a prime example of how the recognition of the Jewish tragedy became embroiled with the political realities of the postwar situation. During the three years after the war, the CCG published a monthly Intelligence Review to be circulated among CCG officials for information. The issues of November and December 1946 carried a two-part article on Auschwitz, the first part prefaced thus:

> *Following is the first instalment of a report by an SS eye-witness who was employed at Auschwitz camp. This gruesome record is as originally written and is published here for the benefit of those in this Zone who are being daily mis-*

*lead into a kindness for and misplaced leniency towards one of the most barbaric races of the world.* [original italics]

The fact that the editor found it acceptable to print a Nazi account of the camp rather than one by a survivor, is typical of the era. Moreover, the article makes absolutely no mention of the gas chambers and the word Jew is mentioned only once. For these reasons it is an interesting piece. Of equal note, however, is the disclaimer which appeared in the February 1947 issue of the review. On the front cover, placed in a box and marked 'IMPORTANT', it read:

> The preface to the first instalment of the article on Auschwitz, published in the November issue of the Review, will be struck out of all copies. Its wording does not correspond with the views of His Majesty's Government, nor of the Control Commission for Germany.[185]

Thus the Jewish question was merged with the general DP problem and had it not been for the protests of the survivors, it would have been lost from sight. The DPs themselves were drawn into the arena of international politics. Their desire for better conditions, as well as their hope for emigration, placed them further at odds with the zonal authorities. What is more, their presence kept the pressure on American opinion and ultimately helped swing the UN behind the partition of Palestine.

The British government showed it was capable of some compromise on both the treatment of the DPs and the handling of the Palestine question. However, it refused to capitulate totally to Zionist pressure and emerged with some of its more important liberal principles intact. Even after the establishment of the Israeli state (and the British refused to recognise it initially) officials continued to insist that Jews in Germany – German Jews and Jewish DPs – could not be lumped together as a single entity.

The tenacity of the Jewish DP leadership was quite remarkable. They worked extremely hard for their own community and fought the local British authorities for the rights they felt they deserved. As far as the future was concerned, high political negotiations were largely out of their hands. Nevertheless, they exerted considerable pressure on the Jewish representatives in Britain, America and Palestine to protest on their behalf. To continue the theme of examining British responses to liberation of Belsen, the next chapter will examine the various ways in which the Anglo-Jewish community met the challenge posed by the existence of the Belsen DPs and the general threat posed to Jewish–British relations, by which they had a lot to lose.

# 4 Anglo-Jewish responses

It is not the purpose of this chapter to give a general history of the Anglo-Jewish community before 1945, which can be found elsewhere.[1] Instead, it will concern itself with the period immediately following the war and propose that this was arguably one of the most testing times in the history of modern Anglo-Jewry. The chapter deals with British Jews and their response to Belsen but will do so within the wider context of Jewish political debates in Britain. The postwar years were a time when changes in the community, which had been taking place since the late nineteenth century, such as the shift in communal power and the geographical relocation of the Jewish population, might have, on their own, caused considerable internal debate. The community, however, having been paralysed during the *Shoah* (the Holocaust), was in the postwar period expected to come into its own on an international level. In six years the Anglo-Jewish community, from its position as one of the smallest and least prominent Jewish communities in Europe, rose to find itself after the war one of the biggest; in fact, behind the USA and the USSR, the third largest in the world. It was a difficult era, a time when co-operation was needed and sought over the rescue and relief issue, but when the political considerations and differences concerning the creation of the Jewish state rendered co-operation out of the question. In fact, it was a period of tremendous conflict for British Jewry, a time when 'the fundamental question as to how a British Jew was to judge his Government's Palestine policy objectively led to constant upheaval in the community'.[2]

## I

The wartime outlook of Anglo-Jewry was expressed by Chief Rabbi Hertz, himself a Zionist, in a letter addressed to the whole community in July 1943: 'Though we can do little to render immediate help to our brethren suffering in Nazi hands, we should be preparing for the day of liberation.' Leonard Stein when presenting the Annual Report of the Anglo-Jewish Association (AJA) (the body representing non-Zionist opinion in the mainstream of Jewish politics), had taken the same line a year earlier.[3] In short, British Jews saw themselves as powerless in the face of the Nazi control of Europe but accepted that they must be prepared for the time when the Nazis were defeated.

In 1942 it was not too soon for the community to be thinking ahead, about the question of immediate relief but also, fundamentally, about 'the still more formidable problem of the place to be occupied by the Jews in the permanent structure of the postwar world'.[4] Seven years later, in September 1949, a meeting of the Council of Christians and Jews was called upon to discuss a crucial issue of some consequence for the postwar world, the matter of restitution legislation. Disappointed at the limited nature of the law passed by the British zone authorities compared with that of the American zone, the council resolved to write to the Foreign Office. This is not remarkable. What is noteworthy in the context of this chapter is the minuted comment in September 1949, which lamented that this was the first time in Anglo-Jewish history when there seemed to be a conflict between the British and Jewish points of view.[5] Bearing in mind the period of almost five years that had preceded this comment, it is quite remarkable. This chapter will contend that the postwar period, perhaps more than any other, highlighted gaps that existed in the so-called symbiotic relationship between the British Jews and the host community.

Against the general background of helplessness during the war, there were some members of the community who were involved in rescue work: people such as Alex Easterman working for the European Section of the World Jewish Congress (WJC) and Rabbi Dr Solomon Schonfeld, executive director of the Chief Rabbi's Religious Emergency Council (CRREC), set up by his father-in-law. Yet they were exceptions, holding politically or religiously radical views. They were individuals who tended to work outside the realm of mainstream Anglo-Jewish politics. The WJC, formed in 1936 as a sister organisation to the World Zionist Organisation, claimed to be an international, independent, all-party organisation which sought to 'foster the unity of the Jewish people' throughout the Diaspora. The organisation had its roots in the Paris Peace Conference in 1919 when the Committee of Jewish Delegations to the Peace Conference was formed; at that time only two Jewish delegations separated themselves from the others: the Alliance Israélite and the body representing British Jewry, the Joint Foreign Committee of the Board of Deputies (BOD) and the Anglo-Jewish Association. Both wished to dissociate themselves from the claim for Jewish national rights. The Anglo-Jewish elite in particular loathed the ascension of political Zionist ideas in Europe and, indeed, in Britain as advocated by many in the new immigrant population who had fled from Russia: 'Jewish nationality in a political sense seemed inconsistent with premises and promises on which emancipation had been sought' and thus threatened and compromised the position of the Anglicised ruling elite.[6] The political outlook of Easterman and that of Schonfeld could hardly have been more opposed. Schonfeld, a rabbi of the Union of Orthodox Hebrew Congregations and the ultra-orthodox Adath Yisrael Synagogue in North London, was an uncompromising man and rigorously defended and promoted his orthodox, anti-Zionist world-view. Both Easterman and Schonfeld, however, particularly in the face of the emergency which faced European Jewry during (and after) the war, were prepared to reject established communal procedures and instead, using their own political connections, to approach the government directly and independently of the BOD. As we have noted, their actions proved to be anomalous.[7] For the most part those who followed the fortunes of the European Jewish community in Britain felt that they could do nothing except prepare for the end of hostilities.[8]

To this end, community leaders continually reminded the Jewish community of its obligations to the Jews in Europe and began a programme to train relief workers. A booklet produced during the war by the Jewish Committee for Relief Abroad (JCRA), entitled 'Aspects of Jewish Relief', detailed information on the extermination policy of the German state. Under the section 'Our obligations', the booklet then outlined the responsibilities of Anglo-Jews:

> Why do we give this account, why do we . . . recall the memory which already belongs to the past, knowing the anguish they bring to those who are safe in Allied lands . . . it has to be said again and again, because we Jews in Great Britain, the last large Jewish community in Europe, must realise and remember how fortunate we are to be on the other side of the Channel. But that is not enough; we are burdened with great duties and heavy responsibilities; with the duty of doing everything in our power to contribute to a victorious end to the war. . . . We who are privileged by fate . . . are under an obligation to consider and plan how help can be brought at the earliest possible moment. Help, not as charity given to the poor, but as relief given by brothers, members of the same family.[9]

In September 1943, the Chief Rabbi made his first call for volunteers and the JCRA elected a Volunteer Committee appointed to the task of selecting and training those who came forward and of organising training weekends, discussion groups and lectures.[10] The booklet asked for volunteers to join the JCRA training courses in order that teams could be sent to Europe as soon as they were needed. In January 1944 Hertz specifically appealed to members of the clergy who might be able to go to Europe after the war.[11] The CRREC began a food collection in 1944 and British Jews were asked to put aside one tin of kosher food per week. In a letter to the *Jewish Chronicle* Schonfeld tried to alert the public to the fact that even a small sacrifice could save lives. If every second person in the Anglo-Jewish community gave up only one item per month, it was insisted, then a million packets would be available within six months. A leaflet campaign carried the same message under the slogan 'A little less for you means A LOT MORE FOR THEM'.[12]

Despite all of these appeals and more, the response of the Anglo-Jewish community at the individual level was limited. The account presented by Norman Bentwich in which the revelations of Belsen and Dachau 'stirred . . . a wave of compassion and a yearning to give direct personal help to the survivors' must be challenged.[13] Volunteers did not come forward in droves from the Anglo-Jewish community. Bentwich himself admits that of the 400 people who responded to the JCRA call for volunteers in 1943, only half were British.[14] Refugees who had emigrated to Britain in the 1930s obviously still had very strong language and cultural links with the Continent and would consider it natural to return. More crucially, most had left family members behind. This translated into two more 'push' factors: they did not generally have close family ties in Britain preventing them from travelling, and also they were keen to take up the opportunity to trace the fate of their relatives on the spot and help the survivors generally.

In June 1945, four volunteer rabbis, funded by the CRREC, were sent to the camps but all were European refugees who had sought asylum in Britain before the war. Rabbi Baumgarten, for example, who worked in Belsen after the war, was an Austrian refugee to Britain in 1938 and fortunately had been excluded from general internment at the request of the Chief Rabbi.[15] Very few Anglo-Jewish rabbis answered Hertz's call. The *Jewish Monthly* in a review of 1946/7 complained, 'Not withstanding the needs of the DP camps in Europe no Rabbi has been prepared or his congregation ready, to spare him to serve in this sphere.'[16] In May 1945 a candid appeal was made to the minister of Amersham and District Synagogue to volunteer for a two-month attachment to the Belsen camp. Less than three weeks after the terrible pictures of Belsen were published in the British newspapers, the executive officers wrote to the United Synagogue:

> While we realise to the full the importance of Welfare and Rehabilitation work amongst the survivors of our Continental brethren, the members of our committee whom we have consulted on this matter unanimously agree with us that the position of this Community renders the service to it of the Rev. J. Indech of greater importance.[17]

There were those who did answer the appeal, such as the Rev. Carlebach from the Golders Green congregation, but they were the exception and tended to stay only for a short time rather than the period of years arguably necessary in order to aid the re-establishment of a religious community. Significantly, like Baumgarten, Carlebach was also a refugee.[18]

The most spontaneous fund-raising events seemed to be also generated by the refugee community. In July 1945 a concert in aid of the victims of the German concentration camps was organised by the Free German Youth in Great Britain and the Anti-Nazi Refugee Youth Organisation. Initiated, composed and executed by Jewish refugees, the concert was to express the abhorrence they felt at hatred and suffering perpetrated by the Nazi state.[19]

It is all too easy to criticise a group of individuals or its separate members for what is perceived as an inadequate response to an intensely difficult situation. One must be careful to consider the real difficulties involved. The sacrifice one made to become a volunteer – for example, with the JCRA – was none too small. To enter the selection and training procedure necessitated giving up weekends and often taking additional days off work; that is not to mention the months one was committed to spend in the field working in potentially appalling conditions. Edith Greenberg, who worked voluntarily for the Manchester Co-ordinating Committee of the JCRA, had expressed a willingness to go to Europe; her reservations, however, were also very real: 'I'd just love to go, as you can imagine and see some continuation of our work, but I could not see the horrors we have been reading of in the Press.'[20] Indeed, it was a grave and difficult decision to give up a relatively comfortable life and overcome personal commitments in order to help others on the Continent. Nevertheless, it is difficult to reconcile oneself to the attitude of the officers of the United Synagogue in the face of the unique calamity presented by the Jewish situation in Europe.

The relief work, if it was to be effective, was in need of proactive individuals, but there were also numerous roles in which many other Anglo-Jews (and indeed non-Jews) could offer support and material assistance. After all, as Charles Zarbac of the JCRA remarked, 'without a steady flow of substantial help from Jewry in this country all the willing hands in the world . . . cannot achieve the gigantic task that faces us'.[21] There were people who gave up large amounts of their time to raising money for the Central British Fund (CBF), to the collection of food and clothing and to maintaining public awareness of the voracious need. Nevertheless, they were, once again, relatively a select few. The same nucleus of people campaigned tirelessly to keep the issue of European Jewry alive amongst the Anglo-Jewish community.

The workload in the London offices of the relief organisations was phenomenal. The CRREC in particular was a very small operation and its running depended on just a few dedicated workers.[22] Many of the organisations offered an unofficial free postal service. Correspondence was received from around the world in many different languages asking that letters be passed to family and friends on the Continent or that family members be traced.[23] In the same way the internees communicated with their contacts abroad. The UNRRA Central Tracing Bureau and the UK Search Bureau for Germany and Austria, situated in Bloomsbury House, were inundated with requests, while the Jewish press ran missing persons columns. When a family was reunited, if not in person then at least by letter, the hard work was proved to be worthwhile. Sadie Gold from New York was overjoyed to hear that her nephew was alive and in contact with the CRREC:

> there are times when words are futile and wholly inadequate and I find that this is one of those times. To express thanks to you would not nearly convey our heartfelt gratitude for this incredible achievement of locating my nephew from whom I haven't heard for more than five years.[24]

Parcels in great numbers were dispatched from the London offices to all over Europe destined for persons inside and outside of camps. Those people living in Britain with relatives abroad were able to purchase and have sent on their behalf parcels of food or clothing. For example, a food parcel containing 10 pounds (4.5 kilos) of tinned food, including cocoa, milk, fish and jam, would cost the sender £27 including postage. The scheme was calculated on a basis which enabled the CRREC to send free of charge a quarter of the parcels available to individuals in Germany and Austria who had no relations abroad. Difficulties were caused by the fact that there was no official postal service to the concentration camps until several years after the liberation. Thus parcels

were sent through official channels, to UNRRA personnel, Jewish Brigade officers or relief workers, and then distributed to the addressees. With rationing still
in force, the food situation in Britain dictated what items could be sent abroad;
very often it was impossible to obtain export licences for rationed goods such as
fats and cocoa.[25] The British government also refused permission to send kosher
meat out of the country, the only way to do so was through the channels of the
'Save Europe Now' campaign. Parcels could be sent to any address in Germany,
although such meat could be given only by people who were sacrificing their
own meat rations, in order to help friends or relatives.[26] In February 1946 the
relief organisations were prevented by the British and American authorities on
the Continent from forwarding private parcels at all due to the congestion in
the postal service. Thereafter, only bulk consignments could be sent.[27]

The Chief Rabbi and the community as a whole were particularly concerned
about the fate of the surviving children in Europe. A Commission on the
Status of Jewish War Orphans in Europe was set up with Chief Rabbi Hertz
in the chair. Most of the relief organisations were represented and they met at
regular intervals to discuss the relief work as it applied to children.[28] In particular
the estimated 10,000 children thought to be in non-Jewish homes and religious
establishments, were cause for concern; the feeling was very much present that
they 'can either be saved for Judaism or lost for ever'.[29] It was felt that an important role the Anglo-Jewish community could fulfil was to bring a number of children to Britain in order that they could be nursed back to bodily and mental
health. In the summer of 1945 the Home Office agreed that up to 1,000 children could be brought to Britain. The CBF was responsible for their maintenance and care. In fact it soon became apparent that 1,000 suitable children
under 14 could not be found.[30] In the event 300 children were flown from
Theresienstadt and taken to Windermere to be cared for. In December 1945
the first batch of children left for England from Belsen and later other groups
from Germany followed. In total the number transported reached over 700.
A working Committee for the Care of the Children from the camps was set
up by the CBF and they were able to acquire houses around the country in
which the children were cared for. Regular visits were made to the houses and
such arrangements as were necessary, such as with the local education authority,
were made.[31]

The community also played host to those people who were allowed into the
country by the Home Secretary under the tightly controlled Distressed Persons
scheme.[32] This allowed those people on the Continent who had close relatives in
Britain willing to guarantee their upkeep, the opportunity to travel to Britain for
a period of recuperation. The success of these initiatives was dependent on the
goodwill and tireless energy of a small number of people from the Anglo-
Jewish community.

Anglo-Jewry in many ways reacted to a unique and critical situation in a traditional and philanthropic manner. The community made the predictable decision
to take on all liability for the Jewish relief, in keeping with the established
premise of the emancipation contract that Jewish obligations would never fall

on the host community. Hence, the CBF did not advertise in the non-Jewish national newspapers – this was thought to be 'ill-advised' – and as a result the majority of the British population did not hear of the major fund in the country for the relief of European Jewry.[33] In general, Anglo-Jewry viewed the relief of their co-religionists in Europe as an issue to be kept within the community, the 'burden' (as it was actually labelled) was one for them only. Thus, a member of the JCRA was able to write with all sincerity,

> It is perhaps not outside one's understanding of human nature to forgive the British public, deeply moved as they were on reading the first eye-witness reports of the German concentration camps, for turning their attention to more domestic matters. . . . But for Anglo-Jewry this cannot be so. . . . The newspapers are telling us that thousands are expected to die this winter.[34]

Society as a whole was indeed concerned with domestic matters in the postwar years. Nevertheless, there are no reasons to believe that an appeal on behalf of the Jewish DPs in Europe would have triggered a wholly negative response. As early as March 1945, a well-informed non-Jewish student, on hearing about the appeal for food for European Jewry, single-handedly collected sixty-three tins of food in Nelson in Lancashire.[35] Perhaps we can use as a comparison the 'Save Europe Now' campaign, endorsed among others by Victor Gollancz, which sought to raise funds and collect food donations on behalf of the starving millions in Europe and particularly the German population. A wide section of the population responded generously.[36] If an appeal on behalf of the German people could gain a positive response, how much more popular could have been an appeal on behalf of the concentration camp victims? The decision not to appeal to the general public was rooted deep in the collective consciousness, in the general perception and interpretation of the liberal contract between the Jews and the 'host' community. Forever playing the defensive role, the dominant attitude of the Jewish community leaders was that to seek financial support as well as sympathy from the British people as a whole, would have an detrimental effect on Jewish/non-Jewish relations. Such an attitude, it might be said, was understandable in the terrible shadow of the *Shoah*. Against the backcloth of the way in which British society was embraced by the Jewish community as the most liberal and civilised of nations, however, it is also quite ironic. Indeed, it is possible that had the Jewish community approached British society as a whole over the question of relief, this might have facilitated greater debate and understanding about the Holocaust in Britain.

It is difficult to imagine what an adequate response to the catastrophe that had befallen European Jewry could have been. Here we are concerned with practical responses. On one level, the degree of success in meeting the needs of the survivors would undoubtedly depend on how far the British Jewish communal leaders and organisations, in light of the unique situation, could overcome past differences and rivalries and find some common ground. This question will be further discussed below. On a second level, funds would be crucial in the European relief effort. In this respect targets (presumably thought to be realistic) were set by contemporary Jewish leaders. On every count the community failed to meet its own expectations. The response was never overwhelming even immediately after the liberation of Europe. By January 1945 the CRREC had collected only 50,000 packets of food and it was necessary for Schonfeld to write to the editor of the *Jewish Chronicle* on more than one occasion to call for donations.[37] In the newspapers there appeared regular reports on the conditions in the camps from journalists, relief workers and rabbis. In the Agudist paper *The Jewish Weekly* Baumgarten's letters from Belsen were published in an attempt to procure a response: 'In the face of these horrors we should be ashamed of our petty troubles', he wrote.[38] The major relief appeal, that by the Central British Fund, was launched in March 1945 with the aim of raising £1 million. Large advertisements in the Jewish press informed the public that although the council had practically no funds, the patrons were confident that British Jewry, 'which has been spared a like fate', would respond generously: 'The need is immense: the duty of each and every one of us is plain: the moment is now.'[39] Nevertheless, despite the urgency of the call and the fact that this was the first collection on behalf of European Jewry for over five years, by the end of 1945 the appeal had produced the sum of £700,000. In the words of the 1945 CBF Annual Report, this was 'an inadequate response to the gravity of the cause'; if the Anglo-Jewish community were 'to continue to take a worthy share of the work of rehabilitation' then it was felt a further effort would have to be made.[40] The CBF Women's Campaign was no more successful in reaching its target of £100,000 and in fact in the first year, 1946–7, managed only a disappointing £12,000. In 1948, it fell £20,000 short of the target.[41] Whilst general advertisements for donations were placed in the Jewish press and elicited some response, the majority of the money was contributed by the traditional givers, the families of the 'Cousinhood' and wealthy business people in the community.

If the task of fund-raising was difficult in 1945 it only became harder as the years went on.[42] The needs of the Jewish DPs did not decrease – in fact, with the arrival of thousands of infiltrees in 1946 and the natural increase in population, they multiplied – but, to compound the matter, they lost their 'newsworthiness'. Many of the new camp inhabitants were Orthodox Jews and thus not only was there more pressure on kosher food supplies but also on such items as religious requisites.[43] In addition the CBF was in direct competition with various Palestine appeals which gained more prominence after 1945.[44] The outcome of a conference of the North London synagogues, called in order to appeal once again to the Jewish community to donate money to the CBF, was an indication of the struggle. For the event, held in October 1947, 250 invitations had been issued. Only fifty people replied and fewer attended. The speaker, the Rev. Elton, who had worked with the Jewish Relief Units (JRU) in Europe, told of the frustration of the relief team at not being able to do all the work necessary due to a lack of funds and support from the Anglo-Jewish community. Elton told the meeting that he felt sure the attendance that evening did not represent North London's response to European Jewry, but what other conclusion could be drawn?[45] Sir Henry d'Avigdor Goldsmidt was correct when he commented at the North London Conference that the contributions of the very wealthy members of society no longer sufficed. Nevertheless, in stressing the necessity for every member of the Jewish community to realise his or her responsibility to the Jews of Europe, he could not have been optimistic about the response. The wealthy families had shouldered the relief effort alone for too long, it was very late in the day to be appealing to the wider community. A few months earlier, in April 1947, only three people had responded and made a donation following a direct mailing by the CBF to some of the wealthier members of the community.[46] By 1950 it was very difficult for the relief organisations to find new funding for ongoing projects and it was almost impossible to get straightforward donations – 'now-a-days they want much more than a receipt for their money', commented one frustrated fundraiser.[47]

The scale of the relief work which could be undertaken by the British Jewish organisations was restricted by a shortage of funds. The CBF required £5,000 per week simply to maintain the children under its care in Britain and to fund the activities of the JCRA in the field. The work of the CRREC was also regularly frustrated. It received limited funding from the United Jewish Relief Appeal but this allocation was small compared with the level of the committee's commitments.[48] In addition to its pre-war activities, the CRREC had taken on the responsibility of partly funding the religious community (*Kehilla*) in Belsen but by 1947 Schonfeld was finding this increasingly difficult.[49] In 1945 Schonfeld made plans to travel to the USA in order to raise £50,000 independently: 'All our widespread promising activities threaten collapse' he cabled his brother in America.[50] In particular, Schonfeld was concerned that his activities in rescuing children from Poland should not suffer. He visited Poland several times between 1945 and 1947 and brought more than 500 children into Britain and Ireland, once again seeking independent funds for their maintenance at home and abroad. In 1948 the CRREC was £9,000 short of the £17,500 needed to support the children.[51] Financial backing in America was increasingly difficult to attract; in view of the political situation, the Jewish population there had 'taken a very belligerent attitude to anything connected with Britain'.[52]

Why the response was so poor in Britain is a complex question. Some members of the community undoubtedly took the view that the government should not be relieved of its duty to the Jewish populations in the liberated countries by means of Jewish charity at home. In Chapter 3 it was shown that Britain was unwilling to recognise the Jews as anything other than a religious grouping. The likelihood of the British government's affording the Jewish DPs the kind of welfare that the Jewish relief organisations sought to provide, therefore, was remote to say the least. The government was of course piling money into the British zone of Germany as a whole and also into UNRRA funds. Another opinion in Anglo-Jewry believed that the much larger American Jewish community should be the ones to bear the cost.[53] Far more worrying, however, and far more difficult to combat was the fact that many people within the Anglo-Jewish community – at whom the major fund-raising drives were directed – did not understand the true nature of the conditions on the Continent and were not prepared to confront them. For those people who were closely involved in relief work the attitude of impassivity was terribly disheartening. A relief worker related her experience when she and a colleague had been asked to speak on behalf of the CBF at a Ladies Guild meeting:

> I think we both felt a visible sigh of relief when we had finished harrowing them and they could get on with their beastly tea . . . the big amounts [of money] we should get are difficult, because, quite candidly, people don't know and don't want to know. Consequently they won't let you talk to them, nor will they come to meetings and life becomes very depressing.[54]

In Ireland the situation seemed little better. Olga Eppel, the organising secretary of Clonyn Castle, a home for Polish orphans of the *Shoah*, wrote to Schonfeld in despair:

> I work tooth and nail to get money from the community here, and it is not easy . . . the collection from the community this month slackened on account of Xmas. That may seem strange to you but . . . the pleasure bound Jewry of Dublin are very unorthodox, and I am afraid Xmas comes before charity.[55]

Fund-raising was difficult no matter what the time of year, particularly when the public were not fully acquainted with the cause. On this point, Alex Easterman maintained there were even those Anglo-Jews who professed to know little about what had happened in Europe during the war.[56] This group must have been limited in numbers (although it may be pertinent to recall the Chief Rabbi's remark in 1944, with respect to the 'Final Solution', that 'Anglo-Jewry does not know what is going on; and the few who do, do not seem to care much').[57] Certainly, the evidence suggests that the view encountered by the woman addressing the CBF meeting was commonplace after the war. Mayer Stephany, secretary of the CBF, wrote bitterly in 1947:

> No Jew in this country is entirely unaware of the plight of his co-religionists on the Continent, but there are, unfortunately, many who are not well informed enough and who – we must face it – do not wish to be well informed. It might disturb their comfort, to which they feel entitled after six years of total war.[58]

If the burden was to fall on the Jewish community in the time-honoured way, then, also in keeping with tradition, it was to fall on the very wealthy families first. The Anglo-Jewish establishment approached the CBF appeal as they had any other: there was no sense of spontaneity in the giving to match the profound or unique nature of the tragedy. As had always been the way, the patriarchs of the leading families waited to be approached and then made 'a few enquiries' as to what their friends were doing 'on this occasion'. Leonard Montefiore, treasurer of the CBF, had the unenviable task of writing personal letters on behalf of the appeal; he was forced to be polite and accommodating in his official communications no matter how tiresome he found the persons concerned. His scribbled private notes on certain individuals, however, are illuminating. The majority of the wealthy families agreed to take out generous covenants but others did not always set a good example. In the old days, according to Montefiore, one group of gentlemen could never agree on what to give and usually agreed it would be better to give nothing. He feared the same attitude in this case. One of the men approached was certain to 'give as little as possible'. On another member of the elite who was less than generous he remarked, 'Tiresome old woman. However I wrote back . . . and resisted the temptation to enquire about her new mink coat.'[59] The complacency and indifference of such people arose from the divide they perceived between themselves and the Jewish DPs, not only in social status but also in terms of birthplace and culture. The perception was misplaced and elitist; in the words of Richard Bolchover, 'The philanthropic ethos and strategy developed by the Anglo-Jewish community . . . had engendered an attitude of benevolent superiority toward the Jews of Eastern Europe'.[60] This conviction is evidenced in the fact that as late as 1947, the CRREC was still passing on to stateless women in Germany notice of vacancies for domestic employment offered by Anglo-Jewish families. Such a response had been common during the refugee crisis in the 1930s and the government continued to encourage it in the postwar period.[61]

Many people in the community believed that the multiplicity of appeals launched by different sections of Anglo-Jewry did much harm, both in terms of the image presented to the public and thus in the success of the appeals. Particular disaffection was felt with the fact that the Chief Rabbi had given his signature to two appeals: the CBF campaign and another by the United Jewish Relief Appeal. In addition, of course, the Chief Rabbi was fully behind his own Religious Emergency Council, which although partly funded by the CBF, did also raise some funds independently. In July 1945 a Conference of the Provincial Representative Councils of the Jewish community was 'unanimously and strongly' of the opinion that the CBF should be recognised as the whole instrument for European relief.[62] Similar criticism came from elsewhere but Hertz refused to be persuaded that one large central effort would necessarily yield the best results. The United Jewish Relief Appeal, he maintained, appealed to different groups, and particularly the overseas communities, who might not respond to a comparatively new body such as the CBF.[63]

A plethora of Jewish bodies and organisations worked within the broad umbrella of European relief and rehabilitation. Leonard Cohen of the JCRA attempted to cut through the confusion and reassure the public that although there was a multiplicity of organisations, there was still a great deal of co-operation between the relief workers: 'One of the happier features of Jewish communal life is that cooperation for the common purpose of the relief of our brethren is increasing.'[64] Some of the bodies, most notably the Board of Deputies and the World Jewish Congress, had a political role; some, such as the CBF, were purely concerned with relief work; and many had a dual interest. Some groups were small with a very specialised role, such as the CRREC, which concerned itself largely with religious relief. Many of the bodies were interconnected in some way either through funding, alliances or the prominent personalities who gave support to more than one organisation. The extent to which there was true co-operation between the relief organisations and the communal bodies, at home and in the field, is the subject of the rest of this chapter. First, however, it is necessary to address the validity of criticisms that have been made of the delays in the initial relief effort after the liberation of the camps.

## II

The speed, or rather slowness, of the response of the Jewish communities in the 'free world' to the urgent situation in Europe after the war has been the subject of some comment.[65] The liberated Jews themselves protested at the lack of Jewish representation among the relief workers between April and June 1945. As we shall see, there is foundation in this criticism, although with some qualification. Particularly while the war was still on and even when it was over, the voluntary relief organisations, including the Jewish, were at the whim of the government and military authorities. As we have already seen, the main organ of relief, the United Nations Relief and Rehabilitation Association (UNRRA), had not been fully prepared for the scale of the DP problem in Europe and the same was true of British Jewry. The military authorities were not keen to have groups of civilians under their feet and the relief organisations were dependent on their goodwill. There were mitigating circumstances to explain the seemingly slow response. In January 1945 the Executive Committee of the JCRA had intended to form a mobile hospital team. It was, however, unable to proceed with the idea because of the impossibility of getting the necessary releases for doctors and nurses from the Ministry of Health and the Ministry of Labour.[66] The JCRA, in conjunction with the CRREC, bought and fitted out several synagogue ambulances. One was meant for Belsen and was handed to the War Office on 30 April 1945 in order to be transported to the Continent. By July the vehicle had still failed to arrive and there was little the JCRA could do except write to the War Office pressing the urgency of the matter.[67] Indeed, the four rabbis flown to Germany had relied entirely on the goodwill and hospitality of Whitehall. The Ministry of Food similarly imposed strict restrictions on food supplies sent out of the country. Nevertheless, taking into consideration these limits on action and the dependence on bureaucracy, the fact remains that the community was singularly unprepared for the magnitude of the task at hand. The truth of the matter was that those who had followed events during the war simply did not expect to find very many Jews alive in Germany. The information received by many who were planning the relief effort was that the surviving population in Germany was very small.[68] Neither did the community expect the delays in repatriation, and the compulsory and prolonged stay in Germany faced by many of the Eastern Europeans, which required more than the immediate emergency relief or rehabilitation. When the reports on the Western camps came out, however, it was clear that more than simply relief in the form of food consignments was going to be necessary; the survivors would need all manner of other supplies and psychological support. During May the personalities connected with the JCRA were forced to make approaches to the British Red Cross about giving assistance in the camps through its organisational structure.[69]

Perhaps uncertainty over the conditions in Europe goes some way to explaining why, only in May 1945, did the Board of Deputies approach government officials with a view to setting up a Jewish section within the Civil Branch of the Administration in Germany. In considering this request came the realisation that a centralised approach by the Jewish bodies would be more profitable and desirable. Thus, Brodetsky, on behalf of the BOD, sought the co-operation of the Jewish Agency, the CBF, AJA, WJC, Agudah Israel and the Federation of the Polish Jewish Relief Organisation and arranged a meeting to take place on 23 May.[70] Brodetsky reported at the meeting that the response of the Foreign Office had seemed favourable towards their desire for a Jewish section but that the matter would have to go to the Cabinet. It was agreed that Brodetsky and Lord Reading should draft a formal set of proposals to Whitehall. The organisations at the meeting also established themselves as a consultative committee to which any future Jewish section could apply for advice and assistance. These proposals were very ambitious, particularly when one considers that at this point of time, there were no Jewish relief workers in Germany working under the auspices of Anglo-Jewry. Certainly, representatives of the British section of the WJC believed that initially the committee should concern itself with more practical matters. Having received a copy of the draft memorandum proposed by Brodetsky and Lord Reading, Ben Rubenstein, treasurer of the British section, wrote on 29 May to the Board that, as a great deal of valuable time had already been lost as far as bringing relief to the Jews in the camps was concerned, the committee should be more pragmatic in its outlook. The letter received no reply and he followed it with three others stressing the urgency of the situation in Europe. The most pressing task, Rubenstein stressed, was to get relief teams to Germany immediately; he urged that the committee be reconvened at once with the agenda limited to this one question. The suggestion was ignored and Rubenstein's letters, on behalf of the WJC, became more angry and frustrated with the conventional and bureaucratic manner in which the Board chose to approach the matter: 'May we point out we consider the delay absolutely unjustifiable and harmful to the interests of the liberated Jews whom we want to serve.'[71] The dissatisfaction expressed by Rubenstein was independently echoed, with even greater feeling for having witnessed the conditions in Belsen, by Rabbi Isaac Levy. Addressing a rally of the Zionist Youth Council, while on leave from Germany, he told that he had visited the representatives of the Jewish organisations but had been appalled at 'the inertia and complete lack of vital interest' which had been shown.[72] In fact the committee did not convene for a second time until 13 June, a full three weeks after the first meeting.[73] An approach to UNRRA, to increase the number of Jewish relief workers in Germany (there were then twenty), was not made until the end of the month.[74]

The Committee for Jews in Germany (CJG) was formally established at this meeting on 13 June and the memorandum to the Foreign Office, when it finally reached its destination, informed the government that the committee was at its disposal for the purpose of consultation. The main proposal of the memo, as discussed in the previous chapter, was that Jewish officers be attached to a division of Military Government with the specific duty of collecting information concerning Jewish problems and offering advice. Further, they requested that consideration be given to the desirability of appointing a liaison officer in various camps to maintain close contact with the Jews in the area.[75]

In July 1945 Brodetsky and A.G. Brotman, the secretary of the Board of Deputies, were called to the Foreign Office for informal talks with the Under Secretary of State Lord Dunglass, Paul Mason of the Foreign Office and General Anderson from British Army Headquarters in Germany.[76] The Jewish community was thanked for giving the authorities the chance to deal with the unified opinion of Anglo-Jewry and in a positive move Anderson agreed to appoint Jewish officers, responsible to Military Government, to deal with Jewish affairs in Germany. Concerning the question of liaison officers between Military Government and Anglo-Jewry, the response was less positive. Military Government could not possibly agree to the appointment of persons not entirely responsible to the military authorities on the spot. Moreover, on consideration of the complaint that the German Jews were treated as German citizens, the officials, while accepting it would cause a certain amount of hardship, could not consider changing the policy. In his report of the meeting to the Committee for Jews in Germany, Brodetsky explained that he thought it better not to press the matter and thus endanger losing the valuable concession of the appointment of officers of Jewish affairs. In fact, the concession was never granted. During the summer of 1945 the British authorities in the Control Commission for Germany were closely consulted on the proposals and were generally antagonistic.[77]

The formal reply to the Brodetsky–Brotman memorandum did not come from Paul Mason until the latter half of September and contained the news that the British authorities could no longer advocate the appointment of Jewish officers, as we have seen in Chapter 3.[78] Brodetsky registered his disappointment about the change of heart in a letter of reply shortly after returning from Germany.[79] He had attended the congress organised by the Central Jewish Committee. Whilst in Belsen he met with and was impressed by the Jewish camp leaders, but he also spoke with Military Government personnel, notably General Robertson and General Templar. On the questions of the appointment of a Jewish Advisor, separate camps for Jews and the acceptance of camp leaders to act as liaison officers, he gained the impression that the two men were inclined to accept these measures. He indicated this impression to both the Foreign Office and the War Office in further correspondence. By November, the decisions concerning separate camps and the Jewish Advisor had been passed to Hynd, the Chancellor of the Duchy of Lancaster. More weeks passed and in January a deeply disappointed and no doubt frustrated Brodetsky contacted Hynd directly, asking for an early appointment to discuss matters. In the American zone at this time the recently appointed Jewish Advisor was working efficiently. In Belsen, meanwhile, the grave concerns voiced over the proximity of the Polish and Jewish communities seemed to be vindicated when a local synagogue was desecrated.[80]

The back-pedalling of the British authorities was a blow to the Jewish community leaders. Nevertheless, they continued to work for the benefit of the Jewish DPs under the auspices of the Committee for Jews in Germany. On most issues concerning the DPs the committee was able to work harmoniously. Throughout 1945 and 1946 it met regularly, usually holding speaker meetings and, despite differing outlooks on some issues, the organisations involved were usually able to put joint and unified resolutions to government offices. When members of the community visited Germany they were encouraged to report back to the committee on their findings.[81] More importantly, the committee gave a forum for representatives of the Jews in Germany to address the Anglo-Jewish community as a whole. Thus, all the organisations interested in the relief and rehabilitation of the Jews on the Continent were kept abreast of the conditions in Belsen and the other smaller communities in the British zone. In a meeting in February 1946, the committee prepared for a meeting with Sir Arthur Street at Hynd's office. In the light of the Harrison Report (discussed in Chapter 3) they were able to agree that they should press the government for improved food, housing and clothing arrangements for the Jewish DPs in addition to an increase in the facilities for movement throughout Germany, recreation, education and vocational training.[82] Similarly, when the committee came together in November 1946, it was to hear statements by Colonel Robert Solomon, the recently appointed Jewish Advisor, together with Josef Rosensaft and Norbert Wollheim, for the Central Jewish Committee, on the problems of the 3,000 infiltrees in Belsen whom the British authorities would not assist unless they were dispersed from the camp. The committee agreed to address a resolution to the Control Office seeking modification of the ruling on humanitarian grounds.[83] The fact that problems arising from the relief programme were raised openly to the whole group provided an added incentive to any organisation that ran into difficulties to sort them out quickly. Thus, for instance, at a meeting in June 1947, Rosensaft complained that the distribution of food in Belsen by representatives of the CRREC was unfairly weighted in favour of certain religious groups. The committee ensured that a meeting between Rosensaft and Solomon Schonfeld was arranged in order that the situation be rectified.[84] Given the nature of the Anglo-Jewish community and the discord within it after the war, however, it was inevitable that there should be dissension in the committee.

The Committee for Jews in Germany had, sown within it, the destructive seeds acting against its unity. The various representatives of the Anglo-Jewish community were generally able to overcome the religious, political and social differences which usually segregated them, in order to arrive at a consensus on humanitarian issues concerning the DPs; however, as soon as the delegates were faced with more controversial matters – in particular, with the demand from the DPs for a Jewish state in Palestine and the British government's response – all consensus was lost. Norman Bentwich, in his early history of the

Anglo-Jewish relief effort of the 1930s and 1940s, noted that in reaction to the Nazi anti-semitism of the pre-war period, 'the whole community united; there was not Zionist or anti-Zionist, Orthodox or Reform or Liberal. The common responsibility to help in rescue was accepted.'[85] In subsequent studies of the period this rather too rosy picture of communal politics in the pre-war period has been shown to be inaccurate.[86] In the 1930s real differences and divisions existed in the community and they were exposed by such complex issues as the boycott of German goods, the establishment of the WJC, the refugee crisis and the Zionist takeover of the Board in 1939. Splits, although by no means always clear-cut, existed between Zionists and non-Zionists, between rich and poor, between British and foreign-born Jews, and between religious and secular groups. Intercommunal relationships could be complex. While it was often the case that the most ardent political Zionists were non-orthodox, middle-class and first- or second-generation East European immigrants, and that many of the wealthy members of Anglo-Jewry, the British-born members of the elite or 'Cousinhood', preferred to take an anti- or non-Zionist position, such categorisation is problematic. The complex nature of Anglo-Jewry was epitomised in the lives of some of the most prominent individuals within the community: Dr Joseph Hertz had to reconcile his belief in political Zionism with his position as the Chief Rabbi of the United Hebrew Congregations of the British Empire; Leonard Stein, a self-confessed Zionist, found himself leading the non-Zionist Anglo-Jewish Association, in direct competition with the Zionist-dominated Board of Deputies; the Marchioness of Reading, though born into the Anglo-Jewish elite, controversially became the president of the British Section of the World Jewish Congress. By the end of the Second World War the ideological and political divides within the community were as wide as ever; the Palestine issue and British government policies served only to highlight the divisions further and placed Anglo-Jewish communal leaders under great strain.

Such divisions manifested themselves in the founding of the Committee for Jews in Germany. At the first meeting of the committee on 13 June the delegates had agreed that all separate approaches to government officials would then cease. At a second meeting on 18 June the final draft of the memorandum for the Foreign Office was ratified. Altercations over who should be signatories to the letter, however, delayed its dispatch. Dr Zelmanovitz, representative of the British section of the WJC, refused to add the name of his organisation when the Zionist Federation, Poale Zion (the Jewish Socialist Labour Party, Zionist in outlook) and the Mizrachi Federation (a Zionist organisation based on traditional Judaism) were not invited to the meeting and were left off the approach to the Foreign Office because the AJA, Agudas Israel and the CBF objected. Zelmanovitz wrote to Brotman at the Board asking him not to send the letter immediately:

> I understand that the participation of the British Section of the Jewish Agency for Palestine is still not yet definitely secured . . . the representative of the BCF

[*sic*: the CBF] stated at the last meeting that his organisation would have to reconsider its relationship to the committee if the three Zionist organisations were admitted. The representative of the Agudah declared after the meeting that in the event of the three Zionist organisations being admitted he would suggest that a number of Agudah organisations be included in the committee as well. It is felt therefore that to submit a letter to the Foreign Office at this stage of the confusion within the community would be very inadvisable.[87]

The memorandum was not sent immediately. When it was mailed, the list of signatories included the WJC and the British section of the Jewish Agency. Yet the time taken to reach a consensus – well over a month – and the internal disputes it caused were indicative of the difficulties to come.

By 1947, a most difficult year for Anglo-Jewry when terrorist violence against the British authorities in Palestine increased and the issue of dual loyalties was inflamed, the Committee for Jews in Germany was floundering. In 1947 no meetings were held between June and October. Its inaction was raised at the General Purpose and Foreign Committee of the AJA and resentment was voiced that since the last meeting the WJC and the BOD had been discussing matters regarding the Jews in Germany with British ministers, without first consulting the committee. If the committee was not to function effectively, it was argued in the AJA, then it should be disbanded altogether.[88] This split between the AJA on one side and the WJC and BOD on the other, was to form a major feature of postwar Anglo-Jewish political life.[89] Nevertheless, the committee continued to function intermittently. There was an impetus to come together in 1949 over the issue of restitution and a certain amount of unity was restored. In November 1949, Jewish organisations in Britain, together with representatives from the American Joint Distribution Committee (AJDC) and the Jewish Agency, agreed on a set of proposals for the establishment of a Jewish Trust Corporation for the British zone of Germany to which the government was agreed in principle. There was general agreement that the American model, whereby all property was placed in the hands of a Jewish successor organisation to provide surviving European communities with their basic needs, was a good one. By 1949, however, the majority of representatives felt that the CJG had ceased to fulfil a useful role, particularly as the relief work in Germany was almost at an end, and the committee was officially disbanded. It was remarkable, given that the relief effort became so embroiled with politics, that the committee had survived so long.

## III

If ideological differences severely hampered the ability of the major representative Jewish organisations in Britain to work together, the same can be said of their representatives in Germany. The following section examines the relationships between the agencies directly involved in relief work on the ground and what influence the same political, social and religious conflicts had on the work of these groups. Arguably, disunity in the field could have a more serious and direct effect on the Jewish DPs.

Not surprisingly relations between relief bodies in the field were not always smooth. Indeed, observations were made that the chaos caused by the various organisations working apart was to the detriment of the actual relief work.[90] In particular, there existed antagonism between the British and American relief bodies. In the final analysis this came down to money. At a meeting of the CBF in October 1945 some concern was expressed about relations between the Jewish Committee for Relief Abroad (JCRA) and the American Joint Distribution Committee (AJDC). Leonard Cohen was keen to co-operate with the American body but he did not find this goodwill replicated. The Joint, who considered themselves professionals, regarded Cohen's much smaller voluntary organisation as rather insignificant in the overall scheme of relief.[91] The attitude was rather unjust. In the areas in which they were concentrated, the JCRA staff carried out important work and in fact the majority were salaried (although generally were paid less than AJDC workers). The Joint tended to measure quality of work according to the amount of money an agency spent each year and in this respect the JCRA did not impress. As Cohen remarked, the JCRA might have been more welcome to its American colleagues had it had £3 million to spend rather than the hope of £1 million.[92] In 1945 the AJDC spent $45 million on Jewish relief work and over $50 million in 1946. The increase in the contribution of American Jewry was an acknowledgement of the ever-growing need for Jewish help in restoring the struggling Jewish communities on the Continent. It has been noted that this benevolence did not seem to have been shared by the Anglo-Jewish community. The position of the JCRA also suffered at the expense of the immense amount of publicity received by the Joint. The American body knew itself to be the most prestigious. In consequence, it did not see the sense in an independent body such as the JCRA existing and sought to amalgamate its workers; indeed a considerable number of the JCRA volunteers left to take up positions as highly paid salaried officials with the Joint.[93] The JCRA, meanwhile, was determined to cling tenaciously to its independence as the representative of Anglo-Jewry in Europe.[94]

The bodies with representation on the Committee for Jews in Germany often worked independently according to their own agendas and information was often not disseminated among the organisations. The CRREC, influenced by the Chief Rabbi while he was alive but always dominated by its director, the committed and zealous Rabbi Schonfeld, in particular worked very independently and on several occasions came into conflict with other bodies. During the war the CRREC had maintained spiritual leaders from Germany and Austria and many of the children brought to Britain after the *Kristallnacht* pogrom in 1938. In addition the council provided a kosher parcel service to Jewish troops and needy clergy and war victims.[95] After the war the CRREC was concerned that, among the survivors on the Continent, the Orthodox Jewish life might be allowed to diminish through a lack of facilities. It worked tirelessly and single-mindedly in Belsen and elsewhere to see that this should not be so.

In Belsen, after the liberation, there was a great split between the Central Jewish Committee, more secular and political in its outlook, and the religious orthodox community.[96] This will be discussed at greater length in the next chapter but it is of relevance here due to the involvement and conflict with Cohen of the JCRA.

The CRREC sent rabbis, rather than trained relief workers, to the British zone. The Chief Rabbi believed it was important to give the religious Jews in the camp support and counsel at the earliest opportunity. The wisdom, however, of not co-ordinating British relief efforts, whether general welfare or religious, must be questioned in the light of the confusion that it caused. The Belsen camp leaders, for example, in the first summer after liberation when there were so few relief workers in Belsen, had pressing priorities to feed and clothe people. They did not recognise distinctions between the different relief organisations in Britain and could not understand why the CRREC was not sending urgently needed food supplies in the place of religious requisites. The Central Committee inundated London with requests for more help. When in August 1945 Schonfeld addressed a frustrated letter to the Jewish community in Belsen, that they must 'understand once and for all', that his council was 'strictly a religious body', his feelings of frustration were no doubt echoed amongst those in Germany.[97]

Schonfeld did not find many allies in Britain for his cause. He was a vocal critic of the CBF, 'a self-appointing ad hoc' body which he felt handled the urgent situation in Europe in 'a lethargic and petty manner'.[98] The two bodies ran into opposition in the summer of 1945 when the CBF wrote to the CRREC that it wished to see the purchase of food supplies in Britain for the Continent centralised within the JCRA. The CRREC, who had already begun to send consignments of food to Europe before the end of the war, resented this suggestion and felt it to be an attack on orthodoxy: 'Had this been any other body the CBF would have trusted the consignments. Instead you wish to hand them over to an organisation already over worked.' Schonfeld added, with a caustic aside, 'The JCRA agreed from the outset that relief food supplies (in Jewish circles we call them Kosher Food Supplies) were our concern.'[99] The result was that the two bodies bought and dispatched food consignments separately. In October 1945 Brodetsky felt compelled to intervene in a matter concerning the work of the CRREC. He wrote to Chief Rabbi Hertz on the matter of orthodoxy in Belsen. In particular, he highlighted his concern that as the Jews in the camps were from many different sections of the community, Jewish observances should not be of the extreme type. It was necessary, he argued, to attract people to faith, not push them out with extremism. Whilst in Belsen, Brodetsky had heard numerous complaints that the rabbis working under the CRREC had adopted the policy of giving kosher food, cigarettes and comforts only to those claiming orthodoxy; such actions were patently unfair and unprofessional. Brodetsky asked Hertz that he lend his support to the principle that distribution of supplies from Jewish sources to Jews should be centralised and carried out with no discrimination.[100]

Here was a major point of contention which was closely linked with the rift between the Central Jewish Committee and the orthodox community in Belsen. The two bodies, the former a political group and supported by the Board of Deputies and the other a strict religious community backed by the ultra-orthodox Schonfeld, were poles apart in the ways in which they viewed the situation faced by the DPs. The Chief Rabbi, in his reply to Brodetsky, repeated the complaints he had heard from his rabbis. The CJC, it was claimed, practised the very reverse of the policy the rabbis were accused of; supplies sent by REC were confiscated and religious Jews were refused *Tefillen* and other important requisites – instead they were given away for barter purposes to irreligious Jews. Naturally Hertz denied all allegations of inducement and was not keen to co-operate in centralising supplies in Belsen:

> Our purpose is not to differentiate or to bribe Jews into becoming Orthodox, but to lend some standing and authority to the Jewish religious community. We differ as to which channels are best to carry out this centralization and fair play.

Hertz's added remark did little to promote a positive atmosphere of co-operation within the relief organisations:

> I draw your attention to the conclusion I must draw from this complaint, namely that supplies sent by my REC and by the Associated Orthodox bodies form a large proportion of those reaching Belsen. This is indeed a sorry comment on the efficiency and activity of the larger bodies whose duty it is to look after the welfare of the needy persons.[101]

In November 1946 a report by the JCRA complained that food supplies sent from the CRREC and the other orthodox bodies such as Agudas Israel and Vaad Hazalah were still put at the sole disposition of the individuals or groups in Belsen who were connected with these organisations. The report urged upon the organisations involved the necessity of avoiding even the appearance of favouritism. The amount in each assignment and its destination should be declared to the Central Jewish Committee, now officially recognised by the military authorities, so that they could alter the allocation of supplies accordingly.[102] Schonfeld, however, could not be persuaded that all supplies that left the CRREC should reach anyone but those intended by their benefactors: the rabbis and other orthodox groups. The relief workers on the ground generally favoured pooling all resources entering the British zone meant for the Jewish population. Particularly in 1946, when the population was increasing and food was in short supply, this policy made sense. The distinction between religious and non-religious Jews made by orthodox groups in Britain and America concerned that the new *Kehillas* should receive the maximum support, seemed overstated when the want in Germany was so universal. To distribute parcels sent by the CRREC and Agudas Israel exclusively to the religious population, when they formed only a small part of the whole and there were others in greater need, seemed unjustifiable. The ridiculous nature of the situation was best illustrated in Celle where the population of only 400 Jews received 500 large parcels for their sole use.[103]

At a meeting in London to discuss the matter, Schonfeld went so far as to accuse Henry Lunzer, the director of the JRU in Germany who advocated and encouraged the pooling of resources, of embezzlement. In a subsequent letter to Lunzer, Schonfeld put forward his case more rationally:

> the main points remain that the CRC entrusted to you certain stocks of food with specific instructions to hand them over to certain organisations and individuals. Instead of doing this you dealt with the supplies in accordance with your own good judgement. No argument can justify this.

The situation was a difficult one. Schonfeld's argument that the CRREC received monies on the understanding that they would be used for a specific purpose, in this case for the use of Belsen *Kehilla*, was sound.[104] Schonfeld's own fundamental commitment to Orthodox Jewish life absolutely precluded him from campaigning under a universal banner, for religious and non-religious Jews. He fought doggedly on the issue. In January 1947, another letter was penned to the JCRA that kosher supplies, this time sent to southern Europe, had been handed to the AJDC for distribution. The reply when it came back was firm:

> However great the volume of your supply programme may have been to help and encourage religious organisations and communities . . . it seems to me that the condition to which I have drawn attention is fundamentally different. The conditions in the camps, as you are well aware, present special problems and I cannot see any justification for favouring any particular group, especially in the case of food.[105]

In reality, disregarding principles, it was the group who first gained possession of the supplies who decided the manner in which they should be distributed. Nevertheless, the clash of beliefs caused a great deal of bad feeling amongst the leaders of the relief effort in Britain.

The relief agencies clashed over another issue which was far more political in its nature. Rabbi Vilenski, a European refugee who had resided in Manchester during the war, caused a great deal of turmoil – and correspondence – between those involved in the relief effort, when he publicly aligned himself with Rosensaft's Central Committee. Some level of co-operation had been established between the CRREC and the JCRA. It was agreed that the rabbis sent to the Continent should go out as from the Department of Religious Reconstruction of the JCRA, and be nominated by the CRREC. In practice, however, difficulties arose with the question of whose authority the rabbis were under when in Germany. Leonard Cohen, as director of the Jewish relief work in the British zone, thought that it should be himself. Cohen believed he had cause to complain when Rabbi Vilenski refused to recognise his authority and avoided Cohen when he visited the camp. Vilenski did not co-operate with his colleagues, showed a lack of consideration and confused the military authorities by visiting German towns without first consulting with the JCRA. In July, Cohen asked the

Chief Rabbi that Vilenski be replaced.[106] Schonfeld received a report from Cohen in the field, detailing the progress and work of the ministers. With regard to Vilenski, he was unable to document his achievements, but commented nevertheless:

> his activities in Belsen seem to have been limited to certain synagogue services and to conferences with the Central Jewish Committee. . . . Rabbi Vilenski seems to be under the impression he enjoys the confidence of the Military Government in Belsen. In fact just the contrary is the case. He has acted most unwisely in connecting himself so closely with the Central Jewish Committee which has not yet been approved by the authorities. I am afraid that his indiscretions have done much to destroy the esteem which the Jewish chaplains and Jewish relief workers had won.[107]

Salaman reiterated this view to the Chief Rabbi. The JCRA had grave misgivings about the appointment of Vilenski before he started and events in the field, claimed Salaman, had proved them right: 'He is a danger to the good name of the work for Anglo-Jewry and we want him removed.'[108] Schonfeld, needless to say, was not impressed with Cohen's letter and claimed dogmatically that nobody should be giving orders to the rabbis least of all Cohen.[109] Rabbi Vilenski, according to Schonfeld, was simply being victimised for his loyalty to Zionism: 'Yet our so-called Zionists in this country seem to think that it is their duty to join his opponents.'[110]

There was some truth in Schonfeld's claim. The leaders of the JCRA did face a difficult problem in dealing with an overtly Zionist relief worker. The personal politics of the committee's Executive – most notably Cohen himself who was a committed non-Zionist – undoubtedly influenced the way in which they viewed the situation. Yet there was a far more complex dimension. The JCRA obviously worked closely with the Jewish DPs and thus gained an acute awareness of the urgency of their political demands that the gates of Palestine be opened. The JCRA also faced the disappointment of the DPs when the British policy on the issue became clear. Naturally, every relief worker would have his or her own view on the Jewish problem; many it seems were sympathetic to the objectives of the Central Jewish Committee. At an organisational level, however, the JCRA was mandated to be apolitical and to work strictly as a relief body. This was a line Cohen felt had to be promoted at all costs; after all the JCRA was a British body and worked in the British zone only due to the goodwill of the British government.

The clash of loyalties experienced by the political representatives of the Anglo-Jews in London was no less felt by those involved in relief. In fact, their position was possibly more acute; not only were they in daily contact with the victims of the British policy but they were under the watchful eye of the British authorities who suspected every Jewish relief worker as a Zionist conspirator. In theory, the neutral position of the JCRA Executive on the political issue was necessary. In practice, it was completely unworkable. British relief workers inevitably did choose to get involved not only in Zionist politics but also in aiding the illegal immigration programmes sponsored by the Central Jewish Committee in Belsen. The grave mistake of the JCRA Executive was in not coming to terms with the situation in Germany as it was rather than how the JCRA would have liked it to be. They were not prepared to discuss political issues at the highest level, instead leaving the problems to the JRU to resolve. Such a policy directly led them to dismiss their field director in Germany, Henry Lunzer, in the winter of 1946. Lunzer, on termination of his appointment, addressed a lengthy letter to the CBF Executive in an 'attempt to save a potentially great and important work from disintegration or even collapse'. Lunzer highlighted a major problem in the organisation of the JRU:

> There was [on the part of the Executive Committee] an ever present fear of becoming involved in a political situation and there was never any real attempt at coordination of work or policy with that of the AJDC or the Jewish Agency, although I repeatedly pointed out that any such attempts at coordination in the field were greatly hampered by the lack of such negotiation at the head.

Lunzer's task of directing his JRU in policy and administration was in addition to that of dealing with the difficult problem arising out of the lack of emigration from Germany and increased immigration of refugees from Poland. Despite repeated requests for policy guidance through the German Department of the JCRA, he received no instructions. Moreover, 'there seemed to be some suspicion about the JRU activities in Germany, which though never voiced made for an uneasy atmosphere'. Lunzer had been criticised by Rose Henriques, a non-zionist leading a JRU in Celle, when the names of certain JRU workers had appeared on an official black list of persons suspected of disobeying British Control Commission orders, making negotiations with the British authorities very difficult. Lunzer continued in his letter:

> It is unavoidable that certain suspicions should arise in the very difficult atmosphere of Germany. One or two instances were brought to my notice and satisfactorily allayed. If other suspicions have arisen and were not referred to Germany for investigation it is, perhaps, just because it was feared that those suspicions were justified. It must be categorically stated that everything possible was done at all times to ensure that members of the JRU abided by rules and regulations as laid down by the authorities. This was not made easier by failure on the part of the JCRA even to reply to certain suggestions put forward by me as a result of restrictions imposed in Germany.[111]

The understandable reluctance of the JCRA to become involved in the politics of the DP situation was nevertheless fainthearted and rather naive. The JCRA refusal to support the Central Jewish Committee before it had been acknowledged by the British authorities, immediately influenced the DP leaders against it and allied the DPs even more strongly with organisations such as the Jewish Agency and the WJC. The WJC for its part had no time for the JCRA. In a 'strictly confidential' letter to Easterman, Noah Barou complained of the situation in Germany:

The JRU instead of helping the Central [Jewish] Committee really is showing a very 'objective' and luke-warm attitude; it does not stand up to the authorities and in my opinion does a lot of political harm. . . . I have explained to [Norbert] Wollheim he should explain clearly to our friends in America that if they would have to rely on the help of so-called British Jews their position would probably be ten times worse than it is now.

I cannot be too happy with the progress we are making, but still if things are moving they are moving chiefly by our efforts and the rest are much more a ballast than a help.[112]

The representatives of the WJC, the Jewish Agency and the AJDC, by their actions, all unofficially and clandestinely supported the illegal immigration of Jews to Palestine as a means of placing political pressure on the British government. The fact was generally well known, not least by British Intelligence. The conflict in political interest was probably a more significant factor, other than the financial one already noted, in the poor relations between the JCRA and the AJDC. Ironically, Lunzer maintained that it was because of the non-cooperation policy of the JRCA 'even though it was the second largest Jewish body in Germany at the time' that the British organisation 'was not invited to the discussions on the allocation of $22,000,000 accruing from confiscated German funds in neutral countries and allocated to the work of Jewish rehabilitation'.[113]

Many of the AJDC workers were well known to be sympathetic to the illegal measures pursued by the Jewish DPs. In judging the attitude of the JCRA by comparison, we must be careful not to underestimate the unofficial support or backup that the American relief workers inferred from the official policy of their own authorities. The Americans allowed unrestricted access for East European Jews into the American zone and thus the actions of the AJDC relief workers did not fundamentally bring them into conflict with their government. The same could not be said of the JCRA; its predicament was far more complex and its position, arguably, less secure. A final example will illustrate the viewpoint of the JCRA Executive in matters concerning the relief work in Germany, in addition to explaining how the relationship between the JCRA and the CRREC finally became untenable.

We return to the problem of Rabbi Vilenski, the CRREC representative in Belsen introduced earlier. Cohen and Salaman, the latter also an honorary officer of the JCRA, initially requested a meeting with Schonfeld to complain of the conduct of Rabbi Vilenski, who had associated himself with the Zionist CJC and, it was claimed, brought the British relief effort into disrepute. In addition to his Zionist activities, at this meeting they also incidentally questioned the legitimacy of Vilenski's carrying a gold cigarette case. Their complaints reached a new pinnacle when it emerged that, indeed, Schonfeld had advised the rabbis travelling to Germany to take with them certain articles which might be sold on the black market – as a reserve for any emergency which might arise in a country where currency was practically non-existent.[114] Schonfeld agreed to take back his advice to the rabbis but the matter did not end there, in large part due to the personal animosity between Salaman and Schonfeld. Having contacted the rabbis concerned, Schonfeld penned a letter to Salaman:

> You still seem unable to observe decent manners where I am concerned. I repeatedly told you that I was quite prepared to tell the Rabbis not to make use of the suggestion I originally made to them. . . . Instead of writing a cooperative letter you proceed in a pompous manner to 'countermand my instructions'.[115]

The incident escalated further when Salaman contended in a meeting with the Chief Rabbi that the director of the CRREC had advised the rabbis to use the articles to 'bribe officials', and in retaliation Schonfeld instructed his solicitor to send a letter to Salaman warning him of slander.[116]

The moral rights and wrongs of the episode are perhaps incidental. Neither man emerged unblemished. Salaman was probably correct to view as very serious the fact that a religious leader encouraged four of his colleagues to break the law and to devote £400 of public funds to the same end. More than anything he was keen to dissociate the JCRA from any scandal and misdoing in the eyes of the British authorities. Yet, in the context of the situation in Germany, the episode was very small fry, and in fact the rabbis had expressed little interest in using the articles in any illegal way. The outcome of the incident certainly served no party, not least the Jews in Belsen. During September the executives of the JCRA and the CRREC jockeyed with one another as to who would sever relations first. When the JCRA threatened to make public the facts, the Chief Rabbi withdrew a letter informing it of the CRREC's decision to dissolve their partnership.[117] However, after consultation with others who had attended the initial meeting at which Schonfeld and Salaman were present, and having spoken to people who disagreed with Salaman's version of events, Hertz decided that his letter should stand. He wrote once more, 'I trust you share my desire to see the "separation" carried out with the least possible publicity and unpleasantness.'[118] Two months later, Schonfeld penned a confidential letter to Handler of Bachad asking if he knew of any relief workers who would like to be incorporated into CRREC teams. He planned to make his own arrangements with UNRRA and have the rabbis working independently of the JCRA.[119]

The humanitarian drive and strict orthodoxy of Schonfeld combined led him to care warmly for the fate of his co-religionists but tended to set him apart from other sections of the Anglo-Jewish community. There was another proposal, given much consideration, on which Schonfeld did not seek the support of the other organisations. He and prominent members of the Agudah believed that an ideal solution to the problem of the DP camps in Germany would be to buy a piece of territory outside Europe. The survivors could be taken there and cared for until which time they were able to emigrate permanently. In February 1946, he put forward a proposal for a Jewish reserve on an island in the Azores. He was confident that he would be able to provide the funds to build the colony and arrange for migration facilities.[120] In March 1947 the scheme was overtaken by another, this time for an island in the Bahamas. Together with a friend, Schonfeld 'acquired' an island named Stranger Cay and wrote to the Colonial Office to lay out the main points of the plan.[121] The intention was to develop a transit and rehabilitation centre for Jewish refugees from Europe, who were destined for America. A comfortable transit home, it was argued, would greatly improve the chances of the survivors' spiritual and physical rehabilitation. The society would be a self-contained unit. Schonfeld was prepared to purchase a ship and all food supplies and materials, even the prefabricated houses, would be supplied from outside the West Indies. The entire responsibility for covering the costs would fall to the CRREC. Schonfeld asked for the approval of both governments.[122] The scheme did not come off, not least because, although some of his colleagues thought it a good idea, they were afraid to back it for fear of the Zionist reaction.[123]

## IV

The postwar years proved to be a tumultuous period in the history of Anglo-Jewry, a time when long-held allegiances were called into question and perspectives had to be changed. British Jews had their opportunity, having felt so powerless during the war, to come to the aid of their surviving European brethren. Their response in the early months after liberation was not faultless. There seemed a reluctance on the part of Anglo-Jewry, traditionally a relatively small community, to appreciate that it was now the largest in Europe and was expected to undertake a large part of the responsibility for the rehabilitation of the Jewish DPs. The money necessary for such a programme simply was not forthcoming. The connection of the DP question with demands for a Jewish state was inevitable but it placed further strain on all British Jews, and not only the arch-assimilationists, forcing them to reassess their own position both as British citizens and as Jews.

There remained in Germany Jewish DPs after the establishment of Israel as we have seen. As an epilogue to this chapter it is worth examining briefly the approaches adopted by the various Jewish organisations in Britain to the question of Jewish settlement in Germany. The non-Zionist AJA unsurprisingly attached a great deal of importance to the existence of this community. In a report on 'The Future of German Jews', written in the summer of 1945 and submitted to the European Committee of the AJA, Rose Henriques had posited, with reference to pre-war German and Austrian nationals, that their 'present disinclination to return might not prove to be as permanent as some Jewish circles seem at present to suppose' and, further, that it 'might be wise to envisage some attempt being made to offer inducements to them to return'.[124] This alternative to the hard-line Zionist view that Europe could no longer accommodate a Jewish community was important and one which was rightly made. Not every Jewish DP on the Continent wanted to go to a Jewish state, nor for that matter to Britain or America. The appeal of Anglo-America for DPs tended to be the presence of surviving relatives; and for wartime refugees, that they had laid down permanent roots. The old and the sick DPs were undoubtedly forced to stay in Europe but many others made a positive choice to remain. There is even evidence that a number of Jews who left for Palestine after the war returned again to Europe.[125] Thus, post-1948, the AJA continued to be concerned with domestic issues in Germany and particularly followed trends in anti-semitic behaviour. In a characteristically paternalistic manner the AJA commissioned reports on anti-semitism and discussed the matter endlessly with the aim of promoting the re-establishment of the tolerance necessary in Germany if a Jewish community was able to thrive. Other organisations, who saw no future for Jews in Germany, invested little time in the affairs of the community there at all. The Zionists chose to believe that those who remained did so only because they were old or infirm. At a council meeting in April 1950, the AJA noted with concern that a number of former Nazis had been appointed to the new government of Land Schleswig-Holstein. They discussed ways of securing closer contact with the Jewish communities in the British zone. One suggestion was to send qualified speakers to improve morale and show that the Jews of Britain maintained their interest in them.[126] The Board also took up the issue, sending a letter to Defence Committees around the country asking them to publicise the conditions in Germany.[127] The Anglo-Jewish Association continued to protect its true loyalties. When the *Daily Express* carried a story on the production of a new film in America which was to portray Israeli antagonism towards Britain, the AJA was keen that measures were taken to see that the film was prevented from being shown. As it happened, *Sword in the Desert* was not so anti-British as had been believed, although it did sympathise with terrorism. Nevertheless, the AJA would regret the film's being shown as it would 'remind the public of terrorism in Palestine' and thus presumably resurrect anti-semitic feelings in Britain.[128]

Rose Henriques, showing a continuity between ideology and practice, took particular interest in the small community left in Germany five years after liberation. She liaised between the CBF and the leaders of the community in an attempt to provide them with a rabbi and a team of religious leaders and officials.[129]

The JCRA had expected the work in Europe to be completed and its organisation disbanded by the middle of 1947. In fact, the office did not close down until 1952 and there were relief workers in the field in Germany, including Belsen, as late as 1950 when the last of the Jewish DPs were preparing to leave. Those five years since the end of the war had proved to be most troublesome for the Jews of Britain. In the addressing of the needs of the survivors and the issues raised by the Palestine question, internal political and ideological divisions had been exposed and were intensified by personality clashes and rivalries.

This chapter, concentrating on the Anglo-Jewish community, has made little reference to the survivors themselves. In the next and final chapter we return to them, reviewing the liberation and rehabilitation process from the perspective of the survivors and also examining briefly the way in which the refugees who came to Britain were received by the Anglo-Jewish community.

# 5 The survivors

The theme of this book has been liberation, as staged at Bergen-Belsen camp. This term has been used frequently, so far without question. Yet what do we mean by liberation in the context of the Holocaust? If we attempt to interpret the word literally then we might arrive at a definition such as 'freedom from captivity or slavery'. This would be perfectly apt. Whether liberated by British tanks in a concentration camp or by a Russian regiment in an extermination camp, whether on an abandoned train or from a farmhouse cellar, once the territory was taken by the Allied forces then all surviving victims of the Holocaust were literally set free from the physical enslavement of the Nazi regime. The time of 'liberation' in any war is traditionally perceived as a time of great joy, of happiness and jubilation. Indeed, this was the experience of many victims of the Second World War. For those Holocaust survivors who were physically well enough to understand the event, then liberation meant a great deal too; it was what many had been living for, clinging on to, the belief in imminent liberation kept them alive. For many, however, liberation marked the beginning of a great deal more suffering and pain, of soul-searching and rebuilding and adjusting to many changes. This chapter will challenge the view presented so often in popular perceptions and representations of the Holocaust, including Holocaust testimony, texts and interviews, that when studying the *Shoah* we can simply conclude our survey in May 1945, when the last camp was liberated, and assume that life resumed 'normal' status in Europe. Millions of the victims of war lost members of their family, yet rarely did an individual have to face up to the loss of the whole of their immediate family, a whole community and a whole way of life. For the majority of the survivors of the Holocaust this is the reality that faced them after their liberation. This final chapter, thus, will be concerned with the experience of the survivors at liberation and after. It will look at the period of immediate liberation and rehabilitation in Belsen. It will explore the flourishing life which grew in the Displaced Persons' (DP) camp as the former inmates found strength and independence and will examine those people who found their way to Britain and the reception they received there. In no way does this chapter seek to deny the joy and freedom which liberation did indeed bring to many, but rather than concentrating on that it looks in more depth, again through the prism of one camp, at what is a very complex issue – one which raised a whole range of conflicting emotions in different individuals and which deserves a more thorough treatment than has thus far been afforded it in the existing literature.

The concern here is with Belsen survivors within an historical rather than a psychological framework. The stress is not on an examination of any notions of 'survival' – that is, on possible explanations of why some lived when millions more perished, a question that has so intrigued some scholars – but on an investigation of the challenges, attitudes and decisions which faced the remnant of Continental Jewry in the postwar years. To date we can identify two historical models or standard representations of these people in the historiography. The first is in the earliest descriptions of the liberated camps by the Allied troops and other observers. We have encountered this already in Chapter 1. The distressed soldiers, faced with 'animal-like' behaviour, felt sure that these deranged people would never again return to be useful members of society. This view was shared by many in the contemporary media and also by the Jewish communities in the 'free world', particularly in Palestine. The second model is that generated more recently by some Zionist historians. It is one which seeks to counteract the image of despair with an ultimately more positive one. In studying the era of the Jewish Displaced Persons' centres, these historians have recognised the speed with which these communities reformed themselves and regained a passion for life. Indeed the Israeli historian Ze'ev Mankowitz has pointed to the 'affirmation of life' in the DP camps in order to add further weight to the school of thought which seeks to recognise and venerate the contribution of the 'Saved Remnant' to the establishment and development of the Israeli state. Moreover, the dynamism of the Surviving Remnant is presented as a further means of counterbalancing the 'negative' (in terms of Zionist historiography) characterisation of Jewish behaviour – that of passivity – during the Holocaust.[1]

One need not contest the opinion of Mankowitz that the 'tenacious negative stereotype of the "survivor"' needs to be readdressed, nor can one reasonably deny that the leaders of the *She'erith Hapleita* did indeed emerge from the Holocaust with (among other characteristics) 'a special blend of strength, determination and daring'; their achievements in pursuit of their primary goal, the establishment of a Jewish state in Palestine, were truly remarkable. Yet, it is suggested here, we should also be disturbed by some of the implications of Mankowitz's argument, and the Zionist perspective he presents should not go unchallenged. The Zionist 'fighting model', restated in his article, is a political response. It teaches us very little about the Holocaust and offers only a partial history of the DP camps in Germany. The Holocaust was fundamentally a human experience. Those Jews who entered the death camps entered a world beyond imagination. Those who entered the gas chambers were not weak and not necessarily passive; neither were they necessarily noble. They were simply human – and no more or less so than the resistance fighter. An accurate narrative of the role of the resistance fighter is essential to the history of the Holocaust but it cannot be the sole focus of our attention; we cannot neglect those who were liberated in the camps and who survived without taking up arms and, of course, we cannot ignore the dead. Similarly, the experience of the Zionist leaders, who established themselves in the DP camps and strove for Jewish sovereignty, will constitute a crucial chapter in the history of the postwar period. So, too, should the experience of the thousands of others, the majority in the DP camps. One doubts that the Zionist model is capable of encompassing their experience to a convincing political end. Mankowitz rightly states that 'the inner history of *She'erith Hapleita* has been sadly neglected' and yet, in his article, he expresses 'the collective identity of the 300,000 survivors' under consideration only in terms of '[t]he leaders of *She'erith Hapleita*'. Finally, Mankowitz pre-empts such criticism as has been expressed here by reconsidering whether his emphasis on the 'constructive and defiant' side of *She'erith Hapleita* is a 'distortion of the past'. He thinks not:

> the truth about the survivors emerges when the history of the *She'erith Hapleita* is seen as a continuous struggle between opposing forces, a struggle wherein, for the most part, the affirmation of life came out on top. . . . They had every cause to surrender themselves to blind anger and cynical destructiveness. But this, by and large, was not the case: while the suffering and losses they sustained were their point of departure their best energies were given over to grappling with the fundamental causes of Jewish catastrophe.[2]

There is much truth in these words. The survivors of the Holocaust have proved that the human being is capable of withstanding a great deal of trauma (although no one came out unharmed) and, indeed, this is a theme which extends through the following pages. Nevertheless, there are qualifying clauses in both of the quoted sentences, perhaps suggesting that Mankowitz recognises that there is (at least) a group who do not fit the mould created by Zionist historiography. One is forced to speculate, for example, whether those individuals, who after the war saw no alternative in their desperate situation other than to take their own lives, will be excluded from the Zionist narrative altogether. Is the work of Primo Levi, perhaps one of the most important and gifted writers on the Holocaust period, destined to be shunned by Zionist scholars because his life did not fit with a rigid, politically constructed model? (Or will his name be rescued? He was after all a partisan in Italy before being transported to Auschwitz.)[3] We will return to an examination of this Zionist model as it affects the history of the Belsen DP camp later in this chapter.

Before we move on to examine the reactions of the survivors to the liberation of Belsen, we ought to consider briefly the problematic question of survivor testimony, on which this chapter is largely based. Despite the fact that numerically the liberated far outnumbered the liberators, when examining the liberation period in Bergen-Belsen we have at our disposal much more primary source material – in all forms – from the military side. This should not come as a surprise. For the majority of the Allied soldiers the entry into Belsen was the most moving and memorable experience of the war, if not of their lives as a whole. It was a catastrophic shock; the sights and smells defied imagination. The liberators were compelled to write. Whether as part of their duty as army personnel, or simply as a coping mechanism, whether in order to refute disbelievers at home, or simply for posterity, the liberators recorded the events which took place on 15 April and in the weeks that followed. Conversely, our source material from the survivor side tends not to dwell on the liberation period. The accounts that do exist often end their story on the day of liberation or shortly after and we do not have the same range of responses as from the liberators. Moreover, there follows a second obvious point. Unlike the majority of liberator accounts which were written on the spot and thus record immediate feelings and responses, the survivor accounts are generally written from memory months or usually years later. As historians we must always be aware of the characteristic shortfalls and merits of various types of source material. In this case the problems inherent in accounts written after the war need to be borne in mind. In the survivor accounts what we read is the memory of the events. Often details are missing or events are chronologically distorted. More crucially, the writer, as her or his own censor and writing for a perceived audience, will undoubtedly give a modified, even stylised account. Primo Levi was both a witness to the events of the *Shoah* and a story-teller but he was very aware of the pitfalls of his craft. '[A] memory evoked too often', he wrote in his powerful and authoritative work, *The Drowned and the Saved*, 'and expressed in the form of a story, tends to become fixed in a stereotype, in a form tested by experience, crystallised, perfected, adorned, which installs itself in the place of the raw memory and grows at its expense.'[4] Hence, with regard to the liberation period, although the survivor might assert that the day of liberation was unforgettable, any description which follows must be the product of memory, unconsciously embellished or altered over the years. Indeed, the very structure of the story form can dictate a formula for Holocaust testimony – every story is in need of a beginning, a middle and an end and what more convenient 'end' than liberation? The accounts that adopt this formula only reinforce expectations and false impressions that the liberation of the Holocaust survivors can be satisfactorily equated with the arrival of the Allies. Needless to say, by drawing attention to these considerations we in no way detract from the memoirs' value as historical sources. The point is simply that we cannot on the whole expect to compare the liberator and liberated accounts of the same event as like with like. Some of the clandestine diaries kept by Belsen internees in the camp, enabling them to record spontaneous sentiments, have been published in their original form, while others appear as the basis of or as a prelude to memoirs written after the war.[5] It would not be surprising to discover that even these excerpts had been altered in some way. The memoir writer would not have been the first and will not be the last to make 'cosmetic' alterations to diary material originally not intended for public consumption.

I

The conditions in the Belsen camp on 15 April have already been described and we need not recount them again here. The situation, in terms of food supplies, sanitary facilities and overcrowding, had progressively worsened over a number of months. The health of those people who had been in the camp for three months or more had deteriorated badly and many of those who had arrived with health problems were already dead. In many cases, those early arrivals who had held on to life did not recognise their liberation on 15 April; for them it simply did not register. Those who were delirious with typhus or unconscious because of their starved state did not realise the situation until days or weeks after the liberation. Generally, the more recent arrivals, albeit very weak and infirm, were in better shape and had not yet succumbed to the deadly typhus. They were far more aware of events and were able to register changes in the camp during the final days of German control.

Most prisoners in Belsen knew in the first months of 1945 that the front was very close. For weeks before the liberation, prisoners were able to hear the 'sweet music' of bomb attacks and gunfire in the distance and guessed that it was Hanover or Hamburg under attack. 'Formations of Allied bombers soared over the camp, unchallenged in broad daylight', remembers one prisoner.[6] Some internees, such as the transport of women transferred in March from an armaments factory in Hamburg, had experienced air raids first hand and were aware that the Allies were closing in.[7] Many prisoners had been transported from other camps by goods trains which had been mistaken for supply trains and had often been the target of Allied bombing raids. Bergen-Belsen camp itself was subject to several red alerts.[8] The transports of men who arrived at Belsen in April and were accommodated in the *Wehrmacht* barracks (named Camp II by the British) had strong reason to believe the war was nearing its end on seeing the German Army leave the barracks *en masse*.[9] Thus, latent hope of impending liberation was fostered for weeks.

The camp abounded with rumour. For all those who dreamed of liberation and believed reports that the Allies were very close, there were others, interminably pessimistic, who were convinced that the SS would rather blow up the camp with the internees in it than surrender to the Allies such indelible evidence of atrocity.[10] 'Rumours began to travel from mouth to mouth, wonderful, encouraging rumours', wrote Gisela Perl, alluding to the resuscitating breath of new life felt by many prisoners: 'Those who had the strength to get up came out of the barracks and went from group to group to listen to the news. "We are going to be free! We are going home! . . . We can eat-drink-eat-drink . . . ".' Only the 'incorrigible pessimists', according to Perl, 'did not believe in life' and talked of bombing and bloodshed.[11] According to Werner Weinberg, 'the prisoners agonised about the way the camp would fall into the hands of the Allies'. One rumour had it that the SS would lay down their arms and hand over the camp peacefully. 'The other version said that the SS would put up a last stand at the perimeters of the camp while we would be locked up in our barracks and burned together with them.'[12] In the second week of April there was some excitement as prisoners began to notice a real change of atmosphere in the camp. The SS guards became less in evidence, some disappeared altogether. One day those that remained, mostly the Hungarian guards, appeared in white armbands while white flags were hoisted and flown from the watch towers. At night the sky glowed red and there was much talk 'of the end' amongst the prisoners in the huts.[13] Even then, in unawareness of the truce negotiations taking place between the *Wehrmacht* and the British, there were a great many mixed emotions: 'The camp was seething with joy, fear, uncertainty, hope [and] expectancy.'[14] Thoughts now more than ever were on survival. In the last few days, people took to staying inside the huts during the daytime, not only because of failing health, but because it was deemed safer. Many decided that they did not want to jeopardise their life during the final hours and they avoided the camp guards at all costs.[15]

The experience of liberation differed greatly from one individual to another, even within a single camp such as Bergen-Belsen. As we know, several Allied vehicles entered the camp before the official liberating unit. Each was met by a crowd of excited and jubilant onlookers, those who were in the vicinity of the camp gates and roads and had the physical strength to run or walk.[16] The joy at recognising a British uniform for the first time was tremendous.[17] The internees cheered and applauded the horrified soldiers, cried and embraced each other in the knowledge that, if nothing else, they had made it to the end of their own personal war. A Czech woman described the chaos in her hut in Camp I after the first British motorbikes had been spotted. Tanks rolled down the camp street causing the whole hut to shake and women poured out to meet them, some falling unconscious in the excitement. Jostled out of the hut with the others she urged her heart to hold out, the joy was so hard to bear.[18] The moment of which these women had dreamed, and had talked endlessly, was here. Those able to do so were determined to welcome their liberators personally. Samy Feder, a Belsen survivor and later a member of the Central Jewish Committee, recalled:

> We could not speak. Tears choked us. There we were, completely stunned with the news of freedom. Those of us who could stand on their feet walked to the jeep of Lt. Sington and saw another British soldier on it. He spoke in Yiddish: 'Jews? Are you Jews? Who of you is Jewish?' . . .
> Most of us were dangerously ill, and the rest were emaciated. . . . We had no strength to express our joy.[19]

It was probably in Camp II, where the internees were all recent arrivals and relatively fit, that the British received the most animated reception. Paul Trepman, a Polish Jew incarcerated in Camp II, managed to keep a diary and recorded the 'joyous shock of deliverance' in his entry for 15 April. From his bunk he heard wild shouts as people 'crazy with joy' met the first tanks and army vehicles crying, laughing, hugging, kissing and rolling on the ground.[20]

Although Bloeme Evers-Emden was liberated in a factory in Upper Silesia (and not in Belsen), the recollection of her release is nevertheless worthy of quotation for its passion and embodiment of the sentiment which touched some of the survivors, despite the ugly and filthy surroundings:

I have always considered that to be the most beautiful day of my life: To stretch and feel your body and, with your face turned to the sun, to have it penetrate that it was all over, that you had made it. All of this was simply impossible to comprehend, that intense feeling of happiness sweeping over you because you had survived. . . . You couldn't think of anything beyond that.[21]

The Belsen inmates who were able to celebrate, however, also noted the reaction of their liberators to their appearance. 'The British soldiers stared at us in repulsion and pity, as though unable to believe their eyes.' 'They were horrified. The young soldiers, they couldn't believe their eyes', echoes another testimony.[22]

News of the liberation spread quickly throughout the camp. Many had heard the commotion outside from their huts but did not have the strength to greet the soldiers. Hedi Fried only managed to totter to the window of her hut having heard with disbelief the hysterical cry of 'British tanks!' from a fellow internee. 'At that moment I felt only an indescribable weariness. I walked back to the bed and wanted only to sleep.'[23] Mala Tribich, still a child when liberated, remembers lying in her bunk near a window in the children's block and seeing people running. Ill and weak, her only thought was of incredulity that there were people with the strength to run.[24] Mr Dessau, a Pole, was one of hundreds of those emaciated shapes which lay almost motionless along the roadside of Camp I and which added to the shocking scene which met the British on 15 April. He remembers seeing soldiers coming towards him and he heard the cheering, but the 18-year-old was simply too weak to move or show any emotion at what unfolded around him. 'In Belsen', recalls Dessau, 'I lost faith altogether, I didn't care what happened to me.'[25] Indeed, for the majority of people in Camp I there was no celebration on the arrival of the British. Agnes Sassoon, a Hungarian who had been enslaved late in the war in November 1944, nevertheless five months later was completely crushed having endured hard labour in Dachau and a series of forced marches before reaching Belsen. In April, just conscious but unable to move, she was counted for dead and thrown on top of a pile of corpses. Unaware of the liberation, she awoke delirious and hysterical in the camp hospital.[26] Others shared her experience, falling ill prior to the surrender of the camp and regaining consciousness to find themselves liberated.[27] It could prove to be quite terrifying; patients awoke disorientated in hospital surroundings and often immediately panicked in the fear they were to be used in some ghastly experiment.[28]

Traditionally, the account of the liberation experience by historians, if handled at all, has ended there. The Holocaust is wrapped up neatly with the almost clichéd image of the tank rolling in. Primo Levi was conscious of this 'stereotyped picture, proposed innumerable times, consecrated by literature and poetry and picked up by the cinema' whereby 'to deliver us from imprisonment "our boys" arrive just in time, the liberators, with waving flags'.[29] Yet, the stereotypical views of the liberated, the bizarre concentration camp victim greeting his or her Allied saviours with crazy ecstasy or, alternatively, with indifference, lying oblivious on the grass verge, both skeletal but both, if able to recover their health, looking forward to a fresh future and a new life, are far too simplistic and need to be readdressed. The liberation experience, it will be argued here, was far more eclectic. The immediate reaction of the survivor to liberation was often one of rejoicing that he or she had endured the war and was able to experience freedom from the National Socialist regime. Yet, this was quite often only an initial, short-lived reaction, only one aspect of a multi-faceted, long-term response which we must be prepared to examine. For many victims of the Holocaust liberation did indeed mark the end of a punishing and hateful ordeal, yet for many it was also the inauguration of a further period of anguish, which some claim was *even more damaging* than what had gone before.[30]

## II

As has already been described in Chapter 1, relief did not reach the victims of Belsen immediately. As we have seen, for those who could not leave their bunks, daily life was little changed under the British. Those who were relatively fit continued, in the traditional *Lager* manner, to 'organise' their own food. In the first few weeks, before the British began to enforce the ban on leaving the camp, the prisoners made expeditions into the surrounding area. The act of simply walking out of the camp, into the woods, free of guards, induced a tremendous sensation.[31] Prisoners, usually in small groups, approached local farm-houses and demanded food and clothing. Some DPs gained a reputation for dispensing harsh treatment to the local German population and there are reports that German farm workers were killed in reprisal. An ex-Belsen internee admits being involved in a shooting incident; a German farmer who had protested he was an anti-Nazi was shot with his own gun when it was found in a barnyard with a picture of Hitler. Clearly struggling with the guilt of this action many years later, Mr K. attempts to describe his feelings at the time: 'I know it was something quite inhuman . . . we wanted to fight the Germans . . . we somehow did what the next best thing was.'[32] In fact, the primary targets of internee rancour were fellow ex-prisoners – the Kapos who worked for the SS from inside the huts and barracks delivering punishments and thus keeping the camp running smoothly. Initially, until the camp administration had been properly established, these acts of reprisal went unpunished by the military authorities and often it fell to the chaplains and rabbis to try to calm the liberated internees down and to impress on them that they were re-entering the free world where law and order should prevail.[33]

Liberation from the National Socialist regime was important but the major reality in Bergen-Belsen was hunger. During their incarceration, the internees had dreamed of freedom in terms of the lavish meals they would savour.[34] Often, in this respect liberation was disappointing. For many, gorging on too-rich foods was fatal while for others it was a setback in their physical recovery. When one woman awoke from a coma to find she was liberated, her unbelieving eyes saw three pieces of bread and a tin of Nestlé condensed milk before her. She had been hungry for six years, she had dreamed about eating constantly and yet, when the food was before her, she could not take a single bite.[35] Those who did feel capable of eating were still feeling hunger pains a week after the liberation and expressed discontentment at the seeming unwillingness of the British to feed them.[36] As was the case before the liberation the camp economy was based on exchange and bartering, although now the currency was of a higher quality. Those who raided German farms stole the livestock and slaughtered them. The meat was then sold within the camp for cigarettes or other goods which had been distributed by the soldiers.[37]

Disappointment concerning food was not the only cause of despondency in the camp after its liberation. Fela Bernstein, a young woman in relatively good health, had been amongst the elated women to welcome the first of the Allied soldiers into Camp I; years later she described that day as one she would never forget. Nevertheless, once the excitement had died down, Bernstein found herself dejected and lonely. Before 15 April she had somehow lost contact with her sister with whom she had shared every experience during the war. She found some comfort in the companionship of two older girls who were liberated in the same hut and with whom she was eventually moved to Camp II. Older than Bernstein, they took advantage of her vulnerability and used her as a 'runner'. She spent her days finding food and cooking on an open fire for the others while they smoked cigarettes at leisure. Bernstein was fortunate. Weeks after liberation she was quite by accident reunited with her sister, who, very weak with typhoid, had only recently been released from hospital.[38] The experience of other survivors was not so positive. In her memoir, Bertha Ferderber-Salz, a survivor of Camp I, is bitter and there are few joyous sentiments to be found in the account with regard to her liberation. In fact, she is very critical of the British relief effort: 'they did not even do the little they could have done. . . . There were no doctors, paramedical aid was not provided, and very little food was supplied.' The liberation for Ferderber-Salz was coloured by one overarching milestone, the death of her sister-in-law in Belsen after the liberation. The tragedy of this event and the obvious anguish that it caused her influence her whole memory of the liberation period. The death, just one of thousands the British were to deal with, was almost too much for this individual to bear. The struggle, at the time and subsequently years on, to come to terms with the sheer cruelty of the death of one so close, *after freedom had been attained*, is evident throughout the text of the memoir. The fact that when she approached a member of the liberation force for medicine for her ill sister-in-law she was turned away empty-handed, gave Ferderber-Salz some outlet for her grief and enabled her to direct her anger and resentment toward the British. 'Our liberators', she noted, 'excelled at one thing, collecting the dead . . . they were ready to take me to their rubbish heap, too, and an English soldier dragged at my leg, calling to his companion to come and help him.'[39]

Any joy felt by Ferderber-Salz on liberation day was not recalled. She had been liberated but, 'What did this mean?'[40] Her narrative, written in 1980, is launched with an introductory chapter taken from a journal written in Bergen-Belsen in May 1945. The words do not disguise her anguish:

> In every limb of my pain racked body I feel that freedom is not possible for me. . . . It has been two weeks since we were liberated . . . and even more wagonloads of corpses are being wheeled from the camp than before. There they lie on the wagons, the liberated people, their shaven heads lolling, shaking slowly with the steps of the person pushing them.
>
> The spectacle gives me no rest. . . . I see neither the rays of the spring sun nor the green of the trees. . . .
>
> It is true that there is a difference between the funerals of today and those of yesterday. Now it is Germans who are pushing the wagonloads of corpses. Formerly we did that. But how great is the difference, the dead are laid in mass graves whether they died as prisoners or as free men.

Thus, although her physical strength and that of her companions began to return, still, 'We could not understand what had happened to us; there was only pain in our hearts and minds.'[41] These feelings of loneliness and isolation were a common part of the liberation experience and not only for those who lost close ones so cruelly in the final days.

A great number of people had arrived in Belsen without any family members or close friends to help them through. Many survivors had seen all of their close relatives go to their deaths in other camps or perhaps had heard from other prisoners that this had been their fate. For these people too, liberation was a time of mourning. Able at last to feel they could let go of that single preoccupation which concerned them prior to the liberation, staying alive, their thoughts were now filled with the future. As Sarah Bick-Berkowitz recalls, it was an unforgettable day but one cast with sadness: 'I was happy to be alive. But what about my parents, my brother, my sister who had met with such disgraceful deaths?'[42]

Even the immediate feelings of elation at liberation were accompanied by an undercurrent of fear, and often this turned to a swell as the DPs further recovered their health and faced the future. The survivors had fought hard for freedom but when it came they were afraid of it. Paul Trepman, writing in his diary, fretfully considered his future and echoed the thoughts of hundreds of others as the relief operation got under way:

> Where is my home? To whom shall I go? How shall I start life again without the people and the things I've lost? Sure, I'm alive, I've survived the war – but was it worth it? What kind of life will I have with my heart bleeding and my spirit broken? Now that I am free all I feel is a terrible ache of loneliness.[43]

Norbert Wollheim wrote in the same vain:

> how could we jubilate knowing that we were not able to share this day, for which we had been yearning so desperately all these long and bitter years with those who had been closest to us, our parents, our children, our brothers and sisters. We were free from the whip and the pistols and machine guns of

the SS criminals – and yet the invaluable gift of the new freedom could not entirely make up for the sense of frightening personal isolation, the certainty of the infinite loneliness within ourselves.[44]

Those who survived alongside close relatives or friends in Belsen clung on to them and found the strength in them to go on. Two women, a mother and daughter, lived to see the liberation together and were placed in adjacent beds to recover. Though the elder woman was delirious with typhus, whenever she spoke, of the past or of the future, it was always in connection with her daughter. Her whole future was invested in her offspring. Together they had survived Auschwitz, a labour camp in Hamburg and now Belsen. For two years the mother had protected her child, had given up her bread, her soup and her energy so that her daughter might stay alive. In liberated Belsen the 16-year-old was taken away from her by death. Liberation brought this woman only the freedom to mourn for herself and her tragic loss.[45]

For the people who did not know for sure the fate of their relatives, there was still hope. Sometimes it was the case that unbeknown to one another members of the same family were imprisoned in Belsen. After the liberation when the internees were able to wander around the camp at will, they would find one another. In a bid to find surviving family members other DPs were forced to leave Belsen, either as part of an official repatriation transport or as individuals by their own means. Amidst the chaos that was Europe after the cessation of hostilities they made the long journey back to their home towns. Often such a quest would be in vain. On returning to their former homes, DPs would sometimes find them occupied by other tenants with no trace of their family to be found. This was a particularly common outcome for those who returned to Poland. With prospects of finding their loved ones dwindling, the DP would dejectedly make his or her way back to the camp, to the security of other people in similar circumstance, or fall back on the Red Cross or another voluntary agency. For a significant few the long journeys were not in vain and happily resulted in the reuniting of families.[46] Rehabilitation then seemed a less daunting prospect. Eventually, each camp and DP centre compiled and circulated lists of the names of people living there. As people began to leave Belsen, they were replaced by new arrivals from other camps and communities across Germany who were in search of loved ones they had heard were safe in Belsen. 'The first intimation I had of their coming', recalls Hardman, 'was on the day I found a woman lying on the ground in a state of complete collapse. A youth was bent over her, patting her white hair, and murmuring over and over again, "Mama, Mama." He had come to Belsen in search of his mother, but at the sight of him she had fallen prostrate.'[47]

Slightly more certain of discovering surviving relatives were those people who had family connections abroad, outside of the Continent, perhaps in America or Palestine or Britain. The difficulties in contacting these people were immense, however, due to the general breakdown in communications across Europe.

The frustration at their inability to send freely letters abroad was just one complaint among many of the DPs living in Belsen and other such camps.

During the period following the liberation, after the initial celebrations had died down, rumours and anxieties did not completely disappear. Despite the presence of Allied troops, the fear of the Nazis remained. When the over-eating of the first few days caused some people to suffer terrible diarrhoea, the rumour spread that the Germans had poisoned or added powdered glass to the last bread ration.[48] In Camp II the rumour was rife, and became further embellished, that a group of German soldiers or SS men had broken through the forests around the camp and were attempting to kill the camp inmates before they had the opportunity to tell of the atrocities they had witnessed. The rumour came to nothing but nevertheless it did add to the anxiety of some of the internees. Indeed, the rumour affected one man in a very unique way. Paul Trepman's liberation had a double edge. Although a Polish Jew, Trepman had managed to survive the war by successfully concealing his Jewish identity. Through Auschwitz and then Belsen he had lived among Poles and kept his true identity a closely guarded secret. A whole week after the liberation in Belsen he still lived among the Poles. By that time the British had begun to group the internees in Camp II into nationality groups and the ex-inmates with nationality in common had themselves tended to cluster together. Within just a few days of liberation there were internee committees working on behalf of the Poles or the Jews with the British authorities. Trepman was keen to approach the committee of Jewish ex-inmates and unburden his secret but his fear of the Germans nearby prevented him from doing so; he did not want to be recaptured as a Jew at this stage in the war. In fact it was two full weeks after the liberation before Trepman approached the 'Jewish' barrack and asked to speak to the Czech block leader, Kurt Fuchs, in private. In a shaking and impassioned voice he confided the story of the last four years of his feigned life. Perhaps this was as much liberation for Trepman as the sight of his first British soldier. He visited that barrack every day before leaving on a transport to Celle and noted in his diary: 'How good it is to be with Jewish people again!'[49]

Weeks soon passed into months for the former concentration camp internees who were unable to be repatriated. Very quickly they began to question just how much freedom their liberation had gained them. Although renamed assembly centres, the camps which housed these DP communities continued to be contained by fences and gates, and in some cases even by barbed wire. Restrictions were placed on people leaving the camps and then the gates were closed and passes required in order to leave. For the mobile and healthy and particularly for the young DPs this was too much to bear. In Belsen a heated demonstration was staged at the main gate by a group of young people who felt strongly about the harshness of the ruling.[50] The DPs increasingly felt cut off from the outside world. They strongly resented the fact that no postal service was made available to them so that they were prevented from making much-needed contact with relatives abroad. They also felt indignation at what they perceived as the unhelpful attitude of the authorities. For months, the only way internees were able to get mail abroad was through army chaplains, soldiers and co-operative relief workers. When the pressure on these unofficial postal services became too great, the authorities began to clamp down on this route too.[51]

There were strict rules in Belsen Displaced Persons' Camp, administered as it was initially by British Military Government. Although generally these regulations caused resentment among the camp inhabitants, and as we shall see led to charges of inhumanity, the rules did in the early days provide some stability and security for the DPs. Early repatriates from Belsen appreciated the freedom that other camps afforded. In Celle, for example, where temporary nationality repatriation centres were established, the Czech and some Polish DPs from Belsen were able to come and go around the small town as they pleased. Some DPs were placed in quite comfortable quarters once occupied by German soldiers but life was still fairly basic. Nevertheless, the simple sensation of walking free through the middle of a German town was indulgence enough. It was often the case that DPs would form groups with those people from the same home town and thus find strength and protection in numbers.[52] They walked into shops and demanded food without queuing or paying the unresisting Germans, enjoying this mild form of revenge. Garrisoned soldiers, British, French and Canadian, handed out their cigarette allowances which in turn the DPs traded for food. The DPs continued to 'organise' as vigorously as they had in the camps.

From the earliest stage of rehabilitation the goal of many survivors was to be as independent as possible. Following years of captivity they wanted to use their freedom to the full and to live in their own way. This theme of independence is one we will return to again, both in the context of life in the Jewish Displaced Persons' Centre and when examining those who settled in Britain. Some survivors, however, sought to express their liberty by offering their assistance during the initial relief effort.

From the very early days after liberation, some of the more healthy ex-prisoners had taken on roles in aiding the British to establish a working administration. Doctors and nurses, some formally qualified and others not, who had tried to run hospital blocks under the SS regime, continued to work in the new hospitals after the liberation. Bilinguists acted as interpreters for the army and helped in the taking of statements and in issuing orders. This was a way of improving one's English and was a help to those who eventually settled in Britain or America. Other workers acted as cooks and cleaners and took on other similar tasks.[53] Often the work, although unsalaried, would pay well in tips in the guise of extra food and additional clothing. Sometimes the work acted as a displacement activity; by keeping occupied the individual had less time to dwell on the uncertainty brought by liberation.

Dr Gisela Perl took on a crucial role in post-liberation Belsen and was kept very busy. She had worked in a hospital block in the Auschwitz complex, before being evacuated to a women's labour camp in Hamburg. From there, in 1945 she was transported to Belsen and amongst the filth and misery tried to administer the most basic form of health care. Perhaps of all the prisoners liberated in Belsen on 15 April Perl and her patient are truly unique. Against the background of intermittent cheers from outside and surrounded by squalor, Perl assisted a young woman to give birth and then struggled successfully to save her life.[54] This event alone is quite remarkable. It is given an added poignancy when one knows the background of Perl; her memoir is perhaps the most onerous that one will ever read. In Auschwitz she was responsible for saving the lives of many women but at a horrendous cost not only to life but to her own mental well-being. Amidst the filth of the barracks and with no medical instruments she secretly terminated pregnancies and induced early birth in order that the babies would not survive and by their existence imperil their mothers. Later in her camp life she was forced to deliver babies and give them up to be used in perverted experiments. 'No one', wrote Perl in 1946, 'will know what it meant to me to destroy these babies.' Yet by her words she implores that the reader attempt understanding:

> After years and years of medical practice, childbirth was still to me the most beautiful, the greatest miracle of nature. I loved those newborn babies not as a doctor but as a mother and it was again and again my own child whom I killed to save the life of a woman. Every time when kneeling down in the mud, dirt and human excrement . . . to perform a delivery . . . without the most elementary requirements of hygiene, I prayed to God to help me save the mother or I would never touch a pregnant woman again. And if I had not done it, both mother and child would have been cruelly murdered.[55]

Perl would obviously carry with her the horror of that experience for the rest of her life. What had sustained her in Auschwitz, and later in Belsen, was the thought that she had to survive until the day she could be reunited with her husband and her own son.[56]

In Belsen, Perl continued to place her own emotions and anxiety about the fate of her family aside as the relief operation got under way. She began work in the newly established gynaecological clinic. Only in the autumn of 1945 did the doctor leave Belsen to seek out her husband and son, after being informed that she had qualified for a priority certificate to Palestine. For the first time since her liberation Perl was faced with the realities of her own life as opposed to those of others. Having travelled from camp to camp for almost three weeks she came across news of her family. Devastatingly, neither had survived the war. 'When I returned to Belsen Bergen [*sic*] I did not want to live', admits Perl in her memoir. 'There was enough poison at the hospital, poison which in small quantities served as a medicine. I took some of it.' The suicide attempt failed when she was discovered by a young priest who worked in Belsen with the Vatican Mission. He attempted to instil new hope into this woman who had done the same for so many others in her position. She returned to her work in the hospital although 'half insane with pain and sorrow'. Not until she was able to leave the camp for Paris and subsequently the United States did she begin 'to feel human again'.[57]

It would be wrong to imply that in the weeks after the liberation there was no room for happiness in the lives of the Belsen DPs. The experience of Fela Bernstein was quite different from that of Gisela Perl; she has a very positive memory of the summer of 1945. She and her newly reunited sister were part of the Lingen transport which left Belsen in July. Although facilities were poor there the weather was warm and they made the best of the situation. The locals had fled the nearby village and the Lingen DPs helped themselves to luxuries from the houses (the Bernstein sisters even carried a bed back to the camp) and crops from the fields. Later they were moved to Diepholtz where their recuperation continued. Bernstein was 18 and free for the first time in her adult life. In Diepholtz the women were visited by English soldiers stationed nearby and they revelled in the attention that was given to them.

The liberating soldiers played an important part in the recovery of the internees, particularly, it could be argued, in the case of the women. The latter used their natural advantage over the male DPs in order to procure delicacies of food and cigarettes from the soldiers. Flattery and presents made recovery and recuperation easier for some women and for many life at this time was exciting and enjoyable. Attempting to communicate in sign language was a constant source of amusement.[58] When Hedi Fried's younger sister decided it was time she contributed to the 'family income' she placed herself in front of a mirror, 'rouged her cheeks, applied lipstick, brushed her again-luxuriant hair and practised ogling looks'. Fried records her memory of the ensuing conversation:

'What are you doing?' I asked. . . .

'You know it's easier to get a Tommy interested if you look pretty. Otherwise they won't notice me. How else can I get cigarettes?'

I did not think she understood the implications, and tried to explain, but she would not listen.

'What does it matter if they kiss me?'[59]

Fela Bernstein describes life in Belsen in the summer of 1945 as quite carefree: 'the times of crying was [*sic*] past. Now was the time for the good life. . . . I was young, I had no worries. I didn't think a great deal of anything.'[60] Hedi Fried, having taken the lead from her younger sister, echoed this feeling, 'I was a young girl again. One interest eclipsed all others: boys.' She too found herself trying to attract the British soldiers and 'life flowed easily' over the summer:

On the surface it seemed almost normal, a woman's world of gossip and intrigue, centred on food and men. We thought neither of the past nor of the future. Only today mattered: filling our bellies, and a little romance.[61]

In Hanover, one group of ex-internees, who had been taken to a hospital there, were assigned officers to entertain them and to help them readjust. Thus they were taken swimming and to dances or the theatre. The soldiers tried to will the women back to health. Usually these relationships were innocent and close friendships resulted from the time spent together, some becoming like brother and sister.[62] Not all relationships were platonic of course. Affairs did begin and on more than one occasion the relationships between liberator and liberated ended in marriage.[63]

That there was a darker side to these encounters was inevitable. On occasion the soldiers were unacceptably 'fresh'.[64] Promiscuity was not absent from post-war Belsen and all residents, survivors and servicemen alike, were implicated. In the words of one survivor, '"Love" was cheap' in the Belsen camp. Women, many of whom had not ovulated for some years, began to have periods again as they put on weight. Sexual relations undoubtedly played a role in rehabilitation but as contraceptives were not widely available then the result for some was unwanted pregnancy. Venereal disease was an additional peril. Gisela Perl observed the behaviour of the camp residents in the months after the war:

> Some sought love because it made them feel like human beings again; others because they wanted to prove to themselves that they were still men and women; others again because they wanted to enjoy their newly won freedom to the fullest. Then there were those who sold their bodies for cigarettes, chocolate and other small comforts.[65]

The birth in Belsen on the day of liberation was not an isolated case and other babies were born in the months following. Members of the clergy who spent time in the camp felt it their moral duty to attempt to persuade couples to think about the future before beginning sexual relationships and about the hardship they would have to face even without the added complication of a pregnancy. 'Why don't you try to start this new life, free and unencumbered?' pleaded a young Catholic priest who worked in the camp. Usually the response was laughter and mockery from people who did not want to hear his moralising.[66] Women did become pregnant in Belsen and for some, perhaps paradoxically, this was a form of liberation. The gynaecological hospital was the place 'where sick mothers, suffering from typhus, starvation, exhaustion, revived at the sight of their newborn babies and gained new strength from the knowledge that their children needed them'.[67]

Relationships, although obviously playing an important role, often induced more problems than they solved. The survivors held their Holocaust experience in common but all were affected in unique ways. Fela Bernstein became involved with a Polish boy of 22 on her return to Belsen from Diepholtz. The psychological scars left by his incarceration in Auschwitz were too much for her to cope with. In Belsen he had become a heavy drinker. He proposed marriage but feeling herself to be too young (and no doubt unwilling to become the wife of an alcoholic) she looked for ways of ending the relationship. Rather drastically, when an opportunity came up in October 1945 to join a six-month transport to England, she jumped at the chance to be able to escape the man's unwanted advances, pretending to be under 16. Her departure was traumatic, he had cried so much when she told him of her decision that she was forced to say her goodbyes in secret, hiding in case he tried to prevent her from leaving, even nervous when she got as far as Celle. On one level this incident illustrates the sheer unpredictability of life in the camp and the way in which decisions were made. It is simply not the case that every survivor had a clear notion of what he or she would do with their freedom. In numerous cases one capricious decision changed completely the direction of a person's life. Perhaps, the episode also represents some of the difficulties in forming relationships whilst at the same time carrying the psychological burden of such suffering, a burden not removed by the physical liberation from the regime that had imposed it. One can only guess at the motivations of these two young people. He felt he was expected to take responsibility for his life as a man of 22 but in reality sought security in alcohol and an unsuitable marriage. She, on the surface, though four years his junior, seems the stronger of the two, determined to protect her independence and refusing to be tied into a marriage she did not want. But her motivations for running away may have been more akin to his feelings than at first appears. Bernstein, also deeply scarred by her experience, coped with her insecurity not by opening up but conversely by fiercely protecting her emotions: she built a wall around herself and allowed no one in lest she got hurt again.[68]

In post-liberation Belsen ordinary situations were made extraordinary by the very nature of the survivor's experience. The usual ups and downs involved in forming and breaking close ties were there for couples in Belsen, but they were often further exaggerated and the emotional turmoil was even greater. Before the war, the young Pole described above as in love with Bernstein, might have been upset and disappointed at such a rejection but it is unlikely that it would have caused any form of psychological ruin. Yet, as Leslie Hardman, the army chaplain, discovered, even 'the strongest . . . could collapse under a psychological straw'. One man who throughout his incarceration had determined to survive and remain strong for the day he would be reunited with his wife, became 'a weak and defenceless creature' after discovering her in another part of the camp, as Hardman describes in his book, *The Survivors*:

> After months of stifled longing and apprehension the imagined meeting had become reality. Here before him was his wife, prematurely old, almost unrecognisable. . . . She put out a trembling hand to him; and as her thin, wasted fingers touched him, he almost sank to the ground. He gasped out something, he could not remember what, then dragged himself to his hut and collapsed on to his bunk.

The shock at seeing his wife so ill and apathetic, the realisation that she had been so close for so long and his own sense of failure by running away from her, left the man feeling depressed, and he became as listless as his wife. It was some days before either was fit enough to appreciate their fortune.[69] Picking up the threads of past relationships could be more upsetting than forming new ones. One young woman, who was reunited with her fiancé when he came to look for her in Belsen, was distraught to discover that she could no longer love this weak and skeletal figure who bore no resemblance to the man she had agreed to marry. The man eventually regained his health but he was prepared for further difficulties. 'I know things can never be as they were', he confided in Hardman. 'I love her still, but desperately, not joyfully as I used to. She must have changed; I don't expect her to be the same, but together we could take up living again'.[70]

Many people sought 'new bonds' in order to replace lost families or lovers. Like the young Pole that Bernstein encountered, men and women wanted intimacy so much that they often imagined that their affections were reciprocated. This Hardman observed as 'love garnished with illusion'.[71] The related desires to escape from loneliness, to replace lost loved ones and at the same time to return to 'normalcy' resulted in a great many marriages in the camps. Hedi Fried, soon after liberation, met a widowed British sergeant, who, lonely himself and touched by her story, asked her to marry him. They had known each other a very short time, yet

> I almost said yes on the spot, without reflecting that I did not know him, that he was much older than I, that I knew nothing about his background. My hunger for a family, to feel that I belonged, to share my life, was such that I would have done anything to still it.[72]

She turned him down. For other survivors, the need for regeneration was so strong that it pushed them into impetuous and unsuitable marriages which sometimes they lived to regret.[73]

## III

We shall return at the end of this chapter to life as it was in the DP camp for the Jews who remained there, but the majority of people liberated in Belsen left in the first six months after liberation. They did so by a variety of means and in many different directions. All shared an uncertainty about their future. Quite a number of patients ill with TB were taken to make a full recovery in sanatoriums in Sweden. One Pole who was taken to Celle could not bear to wait around there while the fate of his family was unknown to him. He set out on the long journey walking and hitching lifts. He found no one in Poland and instead of welcome in his home town he encountered only intolerance. Hundreds like him shared the same experience and thus rejected and dejected had seriously to rethink plans and make life-changing decisions alone. Most sought the advice of the local Jewish authorities who remained and the *Brichah* organisation (formed in 1944 in Lublin by Jewish resistance fighters) who guided Jews across Europe to Italy, Austria and Germany. Mr Dessau was advised to leave Poland and travel on to Prague where there were agents arranging transport to Palestine. In August 1945 he found himself in Theresienstadt where he had learned there were people who held permits for Palestine. In fact his future was to be very different. He arrived in the camp just before a transport of children left for England and managed to get himself included on it.[74] Mr Abisch, on the other hand, remained in Celle until the end of June 1945 and was then taken on a Canadian transport through Germany and on to Prague.[75] From there he travelled to Budapest where he signed up with the American Joint Distribution Committee (AJDC) and was happily reunited with his sister. Together they travelled on to their home town in Czechoslovakia but found no trace of other family members. Instead they perceived a great deal of anti-semitic feeling and no longer felt comfortable there. In addition, it was rumoured that people were being forcibly repatriated to Russia and thus frightened Abisch and his sister returned to Budapest and the relative security of the AJDC. It was there that they were made aware of an opportunity to go to England and they grasped it.[76]

People planned as much as they could but often in the tumult of postwar Europe their goals were easily deflected. People simply sought a future for themselves and they were willing to take anything that was offered to them. Zionist historiography stresses the fact that the majority strove for Palestine. Indeed, contemporary reports leave the reader in little doubt that this was the case.[77] Whether the motivations behind the choice were so clear-cut, however, is more difficult to establish. Many people were political and ideological in their outlook and actively chose to try for entry to Palestine for those reasons. It is also true that many more strove for the same end – simply because Palestine offered them a new start and seemed to be the place which offered the highest chance of receiving a visa. Fela Bernstein relates the experience of her sister; she emigrated to Israel 'not because she was a Zionist but because she had married a Russian Jew in the DP camp at Belsen and started a family there. There was nowhere else for them to go.'[78] If whilst a DP was waiting for a visa or for an illegal passage, however, an offer of settlement to another country came along, more often than not he or she would take it. These people sought independence and security rather than the uncertainty of a prolonged wait in Europe and the possibility of settlement in Palestine.[79]

Those who left the security of the DP camp to begin a new life abroad did not usually find this to be an easy adjustment. Resettlement in another country was tremendously difficult and took a great deal of orientation. The young in particular found it very onerous. On the one hand, they were perhaps more resilient than the older refugees and more open to change, but on the other, they were extremely vulnerable and deeply scarred by their experiences.

A small number of people came from the camps to Britain in order to live with relatives who agreed to act as sponsors. Others, mostly young people under the age of 18 (some were older but lied about their age), arrived under the auspices of Jewish voluntary agencies, usually the Central British Fund.[80] The scheme was originally devised in order that the children might recuperate away from the camps but many of them ended up staying indefinitely. The Refugee Children's Movement, based in Bloomsbury House in London, as well as caring for the prewar refugees, after the war had to find homes for hundreds more children who had survived the camps. The committee, which functioned officially until 1948, represented children of all religions although the majority under its care were Jewish. Although the headquarters of the organisation was in London, several sub-committees were located around the country and these regional offices were responsible for the children living in their vicinity. In the event of a query or problem arising with a particular child then the regional workers were compelled to consult the relevant religious committee – whether the child be Catholic, Church of England or Jewish – before taking further action. A great deal of work was accomplished by a few dedicated workers, many of whom continued to run the local offices long after the central London headquarters was closed.[81]

The experience of these refugees and immigrants, not only those who settled in Britain but in other countries too, was one of being encouraged to 'forget' their past.[82] Only rarely did relatives and acquaintances in the host countries attempt to understand the trauma which survivors of the Holocaust had endured. This silence lasted until perhaps the late 1970s, when there was a burgeoning of interest in the lives of survivors; since then a succession of accounts have been published around the world in many different languages. Although mostly concerned with life during the war years some of the authors do discuss briefly their lives after the war, but this is more unusual. Only recently have historians begun to show an interest in the postwar experience. Oral history projects set up in recent years now use extended interview schedules to include experiences encountered after the war in the country of domicile. Interest has also been generated with respect to the second generation of Holocaust survivors and scholars are investigating the way in which their lives have been affected by the experience of their parents.[83] This renewed interest in the survivors has in a way proved to be a 'liberation': survivors after many years of burying their past altogether or confining talk of their experience to just a small circle of close family and friends, appreciated the opportunity to discuss or write down their stories. Others had written down their memoriess very soon after the liberation. From the 1950s onwards those people who settled in Israel were encouraged to record their experiences by Yad Vashem (although at this stage Israeli society as a whole was still hostile to the survivors – with the important exception of the ghetto fighters – as not conforming with the image of strong nation-builders).[84] Writing could be a cleansing experience. Those in Britain and America were rarely given the opportunity to speak and on the contrary were encouraged to forget their past altogether. While today some still prefer to remain silent, finding it too painful to remember, others find a release in the new interest generated by Holocaust studies.

Not until many years after the war was Kitty Hart encouraged to talk about her wartime ordeal; in 1985 she published the second of two memoirs.[85] In this book, *Return to Auschwitz*, realising it must seem 'grotesque' in view of her extermination camp experience, Hart, none the less, gives a quite damning and heartbreaking observation on her reception in Britain: 'this was one of the unhappiest times of my life. . . . This was the nearest I ever came to total despair.'[86]

A survivor of Auschwitz and Belsen and bereft of almost all ties with her past except her mother, Hart arrived in Dover in 1946, aged 19, and was met by her uncle with whom they were to stay. She was doubtless simultaneously nervous and excited at the prospect of her new life in Britain. Perhaps to a certain extent she wanted to leave the past behind her and look ahead. She was not, however, prepared for the words of her uncle before they left Dover for Birmingham: 'there's one thing I must make quite clear. On no account are you to talk about any of the things that have happened to you. Not in my house. I don't want my girls upset. And *I* don't want to know.' It seemed no one wanted to know. Hart remembers this period of her life with bitterness:

> I was soon to discover that everyone in England would be talking about personal war experiences for months, even years, after hostilities had ceased. But we who had been pursued over Europe by the mutual enemy and came closer to extermination at the hands of that enemy, were not supposed to embarrass people by saying a word.[87]

Fela Bernstein also found that she did not speak of her past in any detail, even to her husband and children, until she was approached by a journalist and historian and encouraged to remember.[88] Until then she had effectively tried to bury her past.[89] Bernstein travelled to Britain in October 1945 as part of a children's transport and once she had found employment, stayed on. She lodged in London with a Russian Jewish household in Hampstead but despite mixing with a large group of interesting people she was never asked about her ghetto or camp life. Thus, she 'remained frozen' and placed a protective barrier around herself, defending herself from distress.[90]

Some survivors who continue to live in Britain, are still bitter about their reception, particularly by the Anglo-Jewish community. The most common complaint is made at the lack of understanding that people afforded them, despite knowing their background; 'they didn't make allowances for anything'.[91] The refugees were different, culturally and in the languages they spoke, but they had also been profoundly affected by their camp ordeal. Edith Birkin, born in Prague and a survivor of Auschwitz and Belsen, arrived in Northern Ireland in 1946 and then moved to London eighteen months later. Like other survivors she felt a tremendous sense of isolation:

> I had acquired a completely new set of values from the camps: there was no one who understood those values, and I felt desolately lonely. . . .
>
> I had all those experiences inside me, and I needed to get them out of my system – just by sharing them – and no one let me do it. . . . Then you felt that you were supposed to close the door on the past and be normal, and it made you sick.[92]

Kitty Hart has her own theory on why the Anglo-Jewish community appeared to ignore the recent past of the survivors: 'Maybe they were a little afraid for themselves; being Jews maybe they thought they'd have to be more English than the English.'[93]

The predilection on the part of people not to listen was a phenomenon by no means restricted to British society. Initially in Israeli society, the camps were a taboo subject and the emphasis was on talking of the future rather than the past. 'That I'd been in the Warsaw ghetto was a kind of scandal', remembers

Aviva Unger who arrived in Israel in 1948. The people 'neither understood us nor forgave us. For what we had been through.'[94] Similarly, Rachel van Amerongen-Frankfoorder discovered on her return to the Netherlands – 'we were a miserable lot of women' – that 'no one was very interested in what we had gone through'. She felt 'written off' and decided at an early stage not to talk about her past, not even to her children. She was eventually to talk many years later and that decision 'proved to be a catharsis, a totally unexpected liberation'. In fact, she admitted, 'It was much more difficult to remain silent'. For years she had lived with her memories alone and no matter how she tried to bury them, they were always there.[95] In her book, *New Lives*, Dorothy Rabinowitz examines the lives of survivors of the Holocaust in the USA. She too found evidence of friends and relatives who were 'intent on hearing nothing' and concedes that this may have been perceived by these individuals as a generous act on their part. This attitude, however, only 'served to isolate those survivors who could not successfully pretend that they had been nowhere'.[96] In the words of a survivor, 'It hurt more to have our experience seemingly ignored.'[97]

Yet even when survivors were questioned about the war it seemed just more proof that their experiences were utterly incomprehensible to those who had been far removed from them. As Rabinowitz found, echoing Hart's feeling:

> They soon learned that they might be asked, by friends and relatives, what it was like to starve, and after being told that starvation was very bad, the friends and relatives might respond that yes, they knew, because there had also been shortages of many things in America during the war, such as sugar.[98]

Curiosity was often bred of ignorance. The most difficult response to deal with, however, was the query, 'But why did they send you to a concentration camp? You must have done something wrong?'[99]

Esther Brunstein, an Auschwitz and Belsen survivor, arrived in England in 1947, aged 18, after spending two years recuperating in Sweden. She found the adjustment difficult. In particular it was hard to make contact with Anglo-Jews, again because of the kinds of questions she was asked and the reactions she received. She maintains that it could not have been out of ignorance. The family who were sponsoring her stay in England would ask, 'Did the Germans, did they interfere with you?' Brunstein, only a young girl at the time, found this a very morbid curiosity: 'What they meant was, were you experimented on in Auschwitz? Were you raped by some Germans? . . . these were the questions they were really asking.'[100]

Nevertheless, despite these negative encounters, perhaps some of the most fortunate survivors of the Belsen camp (in terms of their immediate postwar lives) were those children who were taken to Britain in order to recuperate. In the initial scheme fifteen girls and thirty-five boys left Belsen at the end of October and flew to Southampton where they were met by representatives from the Jewish Refugee Committee (JRC). To the tired and dishevelled youngsters these wealthy, beautiful women dressed in fur coats were a remarkable sight.

It seemed the privation of the previous years was finally over. Each member of the party was given a fresh orange and a hot meal before being taken by coach to a large house near Durley in Hampshire. Already there were 150 boys from other camps in Germany. The house begged no comparison with the DP camps the children had left behind. It had tennis courts and stables and a large common room full of toys and games. Food, always kosher, was in abundance: in fact the children were fed five times a day. The Jewish Refugee Committee rented property around the country, housing refugee children brought to Britain both before and after the war. The Belsen children were moved from Hampshire to Great Chesterford near Cambridge where they mixed with pre-war refugees and in the summer of 1946 they moved again to a hostel situated in a mansion house in Kings Langley, Hemel Hempstead. Some of the older ones were able to spend some time in London, staying for a time in an East End Shelter.[101]

Fela Bernstein remembers this period as pleasant and happy. She had originally thought the trip to England would last only six months but was pleased to be able to stay on when she was told she would be able to stay indefinitely. Although these months were happy, it was a time when she had to begin to face up to her life. The youngsters swapped stories of the camps and to a certain extent gave each other the support they needed. During this time Bernstein began to open up and felt the need to be independent and ready to make her own decisions. She decided to go into nursing and a Miss Pearlman from the JRC managed to get her an appointment at the London Jewish Hospital. Her first experience of working life, however, was lonely and miserable. Her romantic ideal of a job where she would be able to help and care for others, perhaps as a means of assuaging the treatment she herself had endured, proved to be illusive. A combination of an anti-semitic matron who made her 'life hell', and the actual realities of the job, handling deceased and dying people and cleaning dirty beds, proved too much for Bernstein and she was forced to resign after a little over six months.[102]

Bernstein was not the only refugee from the concentration camps to experience anti-semitism in Britain. Mr Abisch arrived in England in June 1946 also under the Jewish Refugee Committee, based in Bloomsbury House. For the first few months he stayed at an East End Jewish Shelter and after tuition in English he attended college to study engineering and found work helping a car mechanic. Almost two years after his liberation Abisch felt confident enough to live independently and moved to lodgings in Stamford Hill whilst securing a job as a typewriter mechanic. Initially his relationship with his boss was very good and as a favourite he was allowed to sit at the front of the workshop with the foreman. The situation changed drastically when the young mechanic asked for two days' holiday in order to celebrate the Jewish New Year. The holiday was granted but this was the first the foreman had learned of his Jewishness. On his return to work Abisch found himself relegated to 'sitting at the back with the Africans'.[103]

Making a living was very difficult for the refugees. Often those youngsters who had their education interrupted by the war were not able to return to it until years later, if at all. Some of the refugees were allowed to enter the country only because the Jewish agencies had managed to procure permits to enable them to do domestic work. They were grateful for this opportunity to leave Europe at the time, but after a number of months of what many felt to be degrading work, they became resentful that they were not allowed to pursue a more rewarding career.[104] Labelled 'refugees' although their experience was far removed from those who had fled from Germany before the war, the DPs had to deal with the same problems and prejudices as the earlier arrivals. The shocking story of the wife of a Cambridge don who, when outdoors with the refugee in her employ, made the woman walk three paces behind, was atypical but nevertheless, many refugees and later survivors were overworked and treated as inferior beings. Ironically, although victims of the 'Final Solution', the DPs (like the refugees before them) were discouraged from speaking German in the street.[105] The bigotry faced by the DPs from the non-Jewish community was one thing but more hurtful was the intolerant attitude adopted by sections of the Anglo-Jewish community. Some DPs sought to deny their origins in order to avoid prejudice. In the 'matchmaking' section of a British Yiddish newspaper advertisements could be found from young men who sought partners, specifying that refugees need not apply. This sort of attitude, coming as it did from fellow Jews, needless to say caused a great deal of pain to the survivors.[106]

Life was not easy for the DPs but they did have the benefit of a strong support network in each other. Several transports of young people arrived at various times throughout 1945 and 1946 and were accommodated at various places around the country including Windermere in the Lake District and Alton in Hampshire.[107] The country was divided into districts and both paid and volunteer workers were employed to look after the interests of the children in their district, whether they were in a hostel or living with a family in a private home. The young people under the auspices of the Cambridge Refugee Committee were able to make use of a large house which had been donated to the committee by Jesus College. The facilities included a canteen, reading rooms and enough space in which to hold dances. The committee offices were upstairs in the same building. Here the local youngsters, often students from the university, would meet the DPs to socialise. A similar facility for those living in London, set up by the survivors themselves, was the Primrose Club in Belsize Park where again young people were provided with cheap food, lessons and sporting facilities as well as the all-important social contact.[108] Ben Helfgott, now chair of the Yad Vashem Committee in Britain, was a regular at the Primrose Club, and regarded the warmth and support he received from his fellow survivors as vital to his rehabilitation: 'We had . . . an understanding of the past which no one else, however sympathetic, could possibly share.'[109]

For many of the children, particularly those who were placed in private homes, there was often no psychological help, professional or otherwise, in enabling the survivors to come to terms with their trauma and their new life. Although talking of her two years in Sweden, before arriving in England in 1947, Esther Brunstein nevertheless describes the attitude encountered by many in Britain: 'They didn't understand. There was no such thing as therapy and trying to help you emotionally but they were interested in your physical well being and with the rest you had to cope.'[110] The relief agencies working in Europe did often question the survivors in order to produce recommendations in their reports. Charity Blackstock was working in a Paris home for ex-camp children when it was visited by women from the AJDC collecting material for a survey. They were cold and clinical in their approach, and the questions they asked were 'monstrous':

> I do not know how they compelled their lipsticked mouths to frame them. Have you lost both your parents? How did they die? . . . What camp were you in? Were you afraid of being gassed?

The finished reports Blackstock maintained were unhelpful. 'They dealt with the past and offered no solution for the future.'[111] As the type of questioning and comments from relatives have illustrated, the extreme polarity in wartime experience acted as a barrier between survivors and others.

The Refugee Committee workers and those who worked in residential homes, usually inadequately qualified, had to work closely with the camp survivors and deal with complex situations as they arose. Margareta Burkill identified two types of child from the camps. There were those who 'didn't want to know anything more about it', who seemed to want to forget and start a new life, and a second group 'who wanted to live it and who didn't want to get away'. These people 'became intensely orthodox, intensely involved with Israel'.[112] In reality the spectrum of emotional responses was much wider. The way in which individuals coped obviously depended on a range of considerations. Ester Brunstein arrived in England to be reunited with her brother. Able to give each other mutual support, they decided that they 'were going to live and try to make the best of it. This is what our parents would have wanted.'[113] Other children, whether 'fantastically lonely little girls' or 'embittered young adolescents', found it more difficult to adjust.[114] Often as important to rehabilitation as the state of mind of the child, was the home in which they were placed. Charity Blackstock in her role as secretary of the Jewish Children's Scheme had the task in 1947 of finding homes for 150 ex-camp children. They were from children's homes in France and the plan was that they stay with English Jewish households for a couple of months in order to help them convalesce. Blackstock's task was not simple and the placing of 'neurotic [and] disillusioned . . . adolescents on to kindly middle class bosoms was sometimes disastrous'.[115] The sponsoring families were usually not prepared for the difficulties involved in caring for the children. Many seemed much older than their young age and they were often rebellious, few having any respect for authority. Even those who on the surface seemed to be well adjusted concealed a deep-rooted unhappiness. Blackstock doubted whether in fact the scheme benefited either side at all and wondered whether it was not simply a charitable 'attempt at self justification'.[116] With hindsight she wrote:

How in the name of sanity could a kindly, well-intentioned woman who had lived in the suburbs begin to understand the state of mind of a boy who had, six years back, been dragged out of a gas chamber by his hair, and flung into a mountain of corpses where he lay for a day and a half until it was safe for him to crawl away? She could be pitiful, desperate to help, but neither she nor anyone else could in the brief time of the holiday really reach out a hand to someone whose mind and heart and spirit had been corrupted by so stinking and evil an experience.[117]

Those people who did decide at an early stage to try to liberate themselves by attempting to forget the past were sometimes prevented from doing so by subsequent circumstances. For a number of people illnesses related to the camp experience were diagnosed years after the liberation. Often it was TB, which can lie dormant in the body without any obvious symptoms. When it does appear, however, the disease can be extremely disabilitating and often calls for months of complete rest. The effect of the illness on those survivors who had attempted to rebuild for themselves a normal life was frequently devastating. Not only was the TB a reminder of the camps but it could also destroy the newly won independence of the victim.[118] Survivors who felt at the time they were in full control of their future after the liberation, nevertheless lived to regret the decisions made in that period for the rest of their lives. So traumatised by the death of his wife and children was one survivor, that he could not face having reminders of his past in his life. He decided after emigrating to America that he could not marry a fellow survivor and that he could not bear to have more children lest he could not love them. He did indeed marry an older woman who could not have children. He lived to regret this as one of the biggest mistakes of his life.[119]

Unlike many of those who reached Britain, for the vast majority of survivors who left Belsen their first destination after departure from the camp was not their final one. A great many were repatriated to their country of origin (although figures are impossible to estimate – for so many this journey proved to be only the first leg of a long migration). As we have already noted, many repatriates eventually returned to the camps in Germany designated as Stateless persons. After the war there were very few governments around the world who came forward to offer citizenship to the Displaced Persons. Those people with sole surviving relatives in a foreign country usually obtained visas enabling them to settle there. Like Britain, although on a much greater scale, Sweden offered short-term hospitality to Belsen survivors so that they might recuperate away from the camp.[120] After a number of years many of these people then moved on to join relatives in America or Palestine/Israel, but some were allowed to stay on and made their lives there.[121] A significant minority felt no inclination to leave the DP centres. They might travel between them looking for relatives but they had no other option than to wait for an exit visa to become available, although certain individuals devoted their time and energy to facilitating the illegal movement of DPs towards Palestine.[122] Indeed, thousands of people from the British zone and elsewhere moved to the American zone where the chances of obtaining an illegal passage to Palestine or a visa for America were judged to be greater. Nevertheless, a large number of people, a small nucleus of the original concentration camp prisoners and a majority of postwar arrivals, did make a temporary home in the Belsen, or more strictly Höhne, Displaced Persons' Centre. They numbered perhaps more than 10,000 people and that is the community, the largest Jewish community in the British zone, to which we now turn.[123]

## IV

When Bertha Ferderber-Salz returned to Belsen in March 1946 after an absence of six months in Poland, she found that the camp 'had become a miniature Jewish kingdom – a vital Jewish community had been established'.[124] During that first autumn and winter in the DP camp, the Jewish DPs began to take control of their own community and set up the institutions which enabled daily life to run smoothly. In Chapter 3, the establishment of the Central Jewish Committee (led by Josef Rosensaft) was discussed, particularly in reference to its political role in highlighting the plight of the Jewish DPs in Belsen and the British zone of occupation. In this section, the focus will be on the domestic workings of the camp and the ways in which individuals coped with life as Displaced Persons in Belsen.

In examining the history of the DP camp in Belsen we are faced with the same difficulties as with studying most periods. The few accounts of postwar Belsen that we have are those written by the camp leaders – those closely involved in the political struggle of the Central Jewish Committee. Indeed, material from the thousands of ordinary members of the Belsen DP community is almost non-existent (to the knowledge of the writer; unfortunately, such an avenue of enquiry was outside the scope of my research). Yet, in this case there is a more complex explanation for the imbalance in the historiography than simply the usual workings of the historical process. It is linked with the peculiarity of the position of the Jewish DP community in postwar politics, and also with the prominence that the DPs' struggle for political representation in 1945–8 has gained in Zionist historiography. The Central Committee of Liberated Jews in the British zone was a unique experiment in Jewish politics. From the very beginning, the men and women – of many nationalities and differing political opinion – who met together to form the first Jewish DP committee decided that their only course was to present a united front to the British authorities and indeed to the world. The common goal was, of course, to have the gates of Palestine opened for Jewish settlement and, at the same time, to demonstrate the logic of the Zionist argument. As events unfolded, it became clear that the original decision of the committee had been a right one. It became even more crucial to the political struggle that the Central Committee was recognised as the sole combined voice of the Jews living in the British zone. Moreover, Josef Rosensaft was the chair of the committee, his voice was heard as speaking for every Jewish voice in Belsen and beyond. Thus, the maximum pressure was exerted on the British government, and any attempt to divide the Jews was heavily resisted. This is the version of events we have from the core Central Committee members. It is a very convenient account. It is also one which fits very easily into the Zionist model of the creation of the Israeli state: the 'Saved Remnant', risen from the embers of the concentration camps and with the same fighting spirit that has come to represent the model of the Jew since the founding of the Israeli state, who fought for their freedom with unerring courage and determination. Thus, postwar Belsen has a very special place in Zionist history, a symbol of rebirth and heroic struggle. 'In many ways Belsen was a kind of miniature Jewish state', wrote an emissary of the Jewish Brigade. He continued (almost as though the *shtetls* of Eastern Europe had never existed):

> It preceded the state of Israel by some years and it was, in a weird way, a kind of pattern for a community ruled exclusively by Jews. There was in Belsen a kind of Jewish Government, with its head and its members responsible for various departments, and its diplomats responsible for foreign contacts, and its apparatus for State.[125]

Almost all of the survivor accounts we have of the DP camp, then, are told by one of the camp leaders. For these people the 'cornerstone for a new beginning of Jewish work' was the 'explicit desire to pave the way for liberated Jews into ultimate freedom outside of Germany'.[126] In fact, their aspirations were far more specific; they fought for the 'realisation of the ultimate goal . . . which the *Sheerit Hapleita* had set for itself: the final liberation'.[127] Needless to say, this goal was the founding of the Israeli state.

The attitude of the Central Jewish Committee, then, was that all religious, cultural and political differences which usually made for divisions in a Jewish community should be placed aside for the good of the united Zionist cause. The achievement was a remarkable one. To unite under one umbrella simply the various *political* factions represented in the British zone was no mean feat, and one of which the Belsen camp leaders was immensely proud. 'The distinctive mark of its [the Central Committee's] activity', wrote Rosensaft, 'was its general above-party nature; all the multi-colored threads of Jewish endeavor wound towards it. The committee represented *all* the community and not any one part.'[128] This way of organising, however, did not always meet with understanding from the leaders of the individual political parties based outside Europe. In particular, returning again to Rosensaft, 'our friends from Eretz Israel' – where party politics was very much the norm – 'did not agree with us on this point. . . . With the best will in the world they could not grasp the simple truth that party politics did not make sense in Belsen.'[129] In actual fact political unity in Belsen lasted only until the official call for camp elections came in 1946 (although they did not take place until spring 1947). Until March 1947 the affairs of the Belsen camp were run by the same Central Committee which had been nominated to administer Jewish activities in the British zone as a whole in September 1945. There were repeated demands that a local election should take place and indeed, elections were proclaimed and postponed several times during the course of 1946.[130] When it finally did take place, the election was fought on a party political basis and each elected committee member represented his or her party rather than the community in which he or she lived.[131] Nevertheless, this new Belsen Committee did not, as was feared, undermine the united front presented by the Central Committee to any great extent. Indeed, the election of Josef Rosensaft as the chair of the Belsen Committee, too, ensured a certain amount of continuity and endorsed his qualities as a leader. There did, however, exist another more significant threat to the status quo: the rift which existed in Belsen between the Central Committee and the orthodox religious community. Moreover, it is precisely because the details of this rift do not concur with Rosensaft's assertion that 'The [Central] committee represented *all* the community' that no mention is given to it in the most detailed book so far published on Jewish life in the Belsen DP Camp.[132]

The split between the Belsen religious community and Rosensaft's committee became apparent as early as September 1945, when the first Central Committee of Liberated Jews in the British Zone was nominated at the Belsen congress of survivors. From the beginning the committee was overtly political. Thus, although the religious Jews attended the early sessions of the congress, the majority soon boycotted the event, protesting at the 'illegality and intolerance' of the proceedings.[133] In the first two months after liberation, just as there had been established a temporary political committee to make representations on behalf of the Jews to the authorities, so too had the Orthodox Jews among the survivors established a religious community along the lines of a *Kehillah*.[134] At the congress, however, the representatives of the congregation, known as *Adath Sheerith Yisrael* (ASY), felt that their views and concerns were marginalised. Henceforth, the orthodox religious groups such as the Agudah and the Mizrachi refuted the claims of Rosensaft and his supporters that the Central Committee represented the entirety of the Jews in the British zone, and they campaigned tirelessly for a formal election of a Belsen Committee to be held, in the hope that they would attain greater control in camp affairs.[135]

The friction created between these two blocs was a continual backdrop to life in the DP camp. Each side found allies in sympathetic organisations abroad. The influence of the organisations which gave backing to the Central Committee, most notably the World Jewish Congress and the Jewish Agency, was formidable. The religious congregation were strongly supported in Britain by Rabbi Schonfeld and the Chief Rabbi's Religious Emergency Council (CRREC) as well as by individual orthodox groups, especially in Britain and America. From the very beginning of the life of the *Kehillah*, Rabbi Meisels, a founding member, was given recognition by the office of the CRREC as the elected ecclesiastical head of the Jewish communities in and around Belsen in north-west Germany.[136]

By November 1945 the Central Committee and the *Kehillah* had become two completely distinct groups. Each body had its own post office, search bureau and stores of food, clothing and other commodities. The *Kehillah* was in dispute with the committee in almost all religious matters pertaining to the camp: for example, the religious education of the children and the observance of *Kash-ruth*.[137] Both sections of the community recognised different men as the author-ity on religious matters.[138] Rabbi Meisels, a vocal opponent of Rosensaft's tactics, was given acceptance by the ASY but was, unsurprisingly, rejected by the Central Committee. Needless to say, the latter was met with indignation; as the committee was not a religious body it should have no standing in such matters. Any hope of reconciliation seemed futile when, in the words of one observer,

> The distinction between the so called orthodox and unorthodox has reached a stage that the Kehilla considers it wrong, in fact almost a crime, for any of their members to visit the Beth Chalutz or the Children's Home or to be friendly even personally with any who work in the Central Jewish Committee. This attitude is producing a sharp reaction in the so called 'other' camp.[139]

As the divide deepened, each side criticised the actions of the other. The issue of the separate stores became a particular bone of contention. As another eye-witness noted, the *Kehillah* was 'far from collaborating with the Central Committee on such "religious" matters as cocoa and clothes'.[140] The Central Committee maintained that while the food and other supplies under its control were distributed to every single member of the Belsen community, those people who applied to the *Kehillah* for supplies were asked first if they were *Shomrei Hadath* (strictly orthodox). Thus the ASY were accused of bribery in order to win DPs into the community. Moreover, it was claimed, the minority of ortho-dox DPs in the camp, were receiving a disproportionately large share of the total supplies which were sent to the Belsen camp. These accusations were put in writ-ing to Chief Rabbi Hertz in London, under whose jurisdiction the rabbis in Belsen acted. He repeated the assurances, given by these rabbis, that they made a special point of dispensing equal facilities to the whole community. Furthermore, he echoed the counter-claim of the rabbis that the Central Com-mittee appropriated supplies sent directly to the *Kehillah* by the CRREC. It was the policy of the CRREC to deliver supplies to religious communities rather than to general bodies but the intention of this, Hertz was keen to emphasise, was 'not to differentiate or to bribe Jews into becoming orthodox, but to lend at least some standing and authority to the Jewish religious community'.[141] The disagreement continued for the next two years and eventually all the agencies and bodies working in the British zone became involved in a protracted debate over the question of whether or not supplies to the camp should be pooled in a central store to be distributed by a single body to all DPs. Rosensaft repeatedly appealed to the CRREC to help put a stop to the practice of distribut-ing supplies preferentially to minority groups. If such practices were not ended, he threatened, the Central Committee would be compelled to retaliate by deny-ing the supplies the committee had from other sources to the groups favoured by the CRREC. The Central Committee, Rosensaft maintained, was party to mem-bers of Mizrachi and Agudas Israel and was not prejudicial in regard to the strictly orthodox members of the Belsen population; in fact the committee did all it could to facilitate the observance of their religious requirements. Dr Schonfeld's response was as usual uncompromising: the CRREC could not, as a matter of principle, allow the religious orthodox section of the Belsen community to be dependent on the goodwill of a body which in his view was anti-religious. The sole interest of the CRREC in this regard was the fostering of religious life and organisation.[142]

The debate over the distribution of resources was obviously crucial, and indeed is one which deserves a more detailed analysis than has been possible here. Nevertheless, for the purposes of this study, it is important to realise that the major criticism of the ASY by the Central Jewish Committee, the true agenda behind the dispute did not fundamentally concern distribution networks. Rosensaft's major complaint was that the establishment of a separate orthodox community undermined the unity of the Belsen population.[143] In a meeting in London in 1947 with the committee for Jews in Germany, the chair of the Central Committee stated that the activities of the CRREC representatives in the British zone had in certain respects compromised the Jewish name, made the work of the committee very difficult and also created a good deal of conflict amongst the DPs. Moreover, because the rabbis of the *Kehillah* worked in isolation and without any consultation with the Central Committee, they upset the regular working of the organisation in the camp and, by their actions, harmed the cause of the Jewish DPs *vis-à-vis* the military and UN authorities. The claims of the Central Committee against the ASY were not without some truth. Yet, the rights and wrongs of the actions of the religious leaders is not the issue under consideration here. The question must be addressed, however, as to what extent the fears of the Central Committee, as regards the threat posed by the *Kehillah*, were justified.

Certainly, the opposition of the religious community to the Central Committee did focus a great deal of attention on the internal workings of the camp. Particularly in 1946, when illegal activity surrounding the work of the Jewish Defence Force, *Haganah*, reached its peak, such scrutiny was unwelcome and unsettling. During the same period, as was illustrated in Chapter 4, the complaints from a dissenting group of DPs who rejected the authority of Rosensaft, gave valuable ammunition to the British officials in the Control Commission at a time when they were seeking reasons not to give formal recognition to a manifestly political Jewish body. Once the British government acknowledged the Central Committee, however, the claim of Rosensaft to speak for all Jews was finally given official sanction. Thus, when the ASY appealed for British intervention on *its* behalf (and to authorise recognition of its community as a separate body), the Military Government refused to become involved in what it considered a religious problem. 'The question of a free and democratic election of a separate central committee within the camp to handle the affairs of the Jewish religious congregation (ASY)', wrote a British officer in reply to an appeal for support, 'must be the sole concern of either UNRRA on the spot or the Jewish people as a whole who are living in the camp.'[144] The religious community did not receive any special privileges and, unlike the Central Committee, were even forbidden to use the Military Government Detachment address on their letter-headings.[145]

The position of the Central Committee as the majority representative voice in the British zone of occupation was not and could not today be questioned. Yet, as we have seen, it was not the only voice. Furthermore, it is clear that any valid historical examination of the Belsen DP camp must be prepared to challenge, no matter how appealing, the narrow Zionist perspective of a completely harmonious DP administration. It has also to be suggested that there is still a great deal of research work to be conducted in this area, particularly in respect of the grass-roots level of the community.

Yet, there was more to the Belsen DP camp than these struggles over political power. It had indeed grown into a small town under the auspices of the international relief organisations and the British authorities. The following pages attempt to give a brief profile of the Jewish experience of the DP camp and to sketch the achievements – administrative, educational and cultural – of which the population were so proud and which were a vital part of the liberation experience. The Jewish community in Belsen became a stable, if only temporary, community. Some of the camp facilities, such as hospitals and clinics, grew naturally from the relief effort. As relief turned into rehabilitation and the acknowledgement came that the wait for visas to leave Germany could be a long one, other facilities were established. Community centres, schools, libraries, a theatre, sporting facilities and associations, a printing press and a Jewish police force eventually thrived.[146] Although initially the majority of services were set up and staffed by relief and welfare workers from abroad, very quickly the DPs began to utilise their own talents in administering the new Jewish community and worked in close co-operation with the relief agencies.[147]

The general level of supplies and basic necessities in Belsen improved greatly over the course of 1945. Yet, conditions in the Displaced Persons centre were generally substandard throughout most of the five years of its existence. The DPs resigned themselves to making a temporary home in Belsen in the hope that what they perceived to be their liberation – a visa out of Germany – would come quickly. Meanwhile, they faced several difficult months or years in the camp as Stateless DPs; physically, there were shortages of most things whilst, in addition, their future remained uncertain, dependent on the political machinations of foreign governments. The DPs lived on an emotional roller-coaster with times of high optimism, such as when the first children's transport left Belsen for Palestine in April 1946, followed by events which caused much anguish and despair, most notably the *Exodus* affair in the summer of 1947.

The shortages which still prevailed generally in postwar Germany and the inability of the Jewish relief agencies to fully meet the needs of the camp meant that the winter of 1945–6 was a difficult one for the DPs. Selig Brodetsky, president of the Board of Deputies, reported on the conditions in Belsen following his attendance at the first Jewish Congress in the autumn of 1945. The clothing, he related to the committee for Jews in Germany, was bad and insufficient. The food, although not totally unsatisfactory, was dull and meagre; some people had spoken to him of their continuing hunger.[148] Similar observations concerning the basic shortage of food, clothing and accommodation were often made, not least by Josef Rosensaft and fellow members of the Central Jewish Committee. In March 1946 Rosensaft addressed a meeting in London of the committee for Jews in Germany. He highlighted the lack of freedom afforded to the Jews in Belsen and the conditions which were 'incompatible with human dignity'. In the camp, four people were forced to share a small room; eight could be found in one of a larger size. Moreover, the housing situation was made worse by the infiltrees, approaching 15,000 in the British zone, who had travelled from Eastern Europe. The DPs also had cause to resent the restrictions on their personal liberty. The fact that the Belsen camp was patrolled by Polish guards, said Rosensaft, was an affront to the DPs. The Jews in the camp had no confidence in them as they were known to abuse their power, discriminating between Jews and non-Jews. Moreover, although the DPs were able to travel freely within the British zone, their movements were greatly restricted by the necessity of special passes – very difficult to obtain – in order to travel further afield.[149] That Rosensaft should have highlighted the shortages in Belsen is hardly surprising given his agenda of gaining the best possible facilities for the people in the camp. Yet other eyewitness reports and accounts confirm that Rosensaft had little need to exaggerate in order to prick the conscience of Jewish officials abroad.

At the request of UNRRA, the AJDC undertook a survey of the Jews in the British zone in the early months of 1946. In all, 14,000 Jewish people resided in the zone, of whom 4,000 were German. There were found to be 6,000 living in Belsen.[150] The survey noted that the food situation was poor, with a particular lack of fat and sugar in the diet, and that as the majority of the DPs lived in barracks, they were afforded little or no privacy. Furthermore, psychologically the DPs were found to be in a poor state of morale. In addition to supplementary food, the most urgent needs recommended by the AJDC were homes for the aged, TB sanatoria, Jewish farm-training centres, and educational facilities and supplies such as textbooks.[151] The latter two in particular were important in the rehabilitation of the DPs who, as the months in Germany rolled on, became increasingly frustrated at the lack of facilities for recreation or useful employment. This was to become a serious problem which needed to be addressed by the relief agencies.

A Jewish Relief Unit volunteers' newsletter regretted that in April 1946 conditions with regard to food, accommodation and clothing in Belsen were worse not better. The DPs had endured the winter without sufficient pairs of shoes and there had been no allocations of fuel to individuals: only recently had they been permitted to go into the surrounding forests to cut their own wood. Subsequent volunteer newsletters all told the same story: 'medical treatment is urgently required', 'the food situation is poor [and] the small amount of clothing we have been able to give people is hardly worth mentioning', the 'shortage of furniture . . . and household equipment such as mattresses, blankets and utensils is horrifying'.[152] In April 1947 there were 615 children under the age of 6 in Belsen and a further 210 pregnant women. The shortages in milk, fresh fruit and vegetables, soap and baby and maternity clothes, however, remained acute.[153] One welfare worker wrote in November 1946, over eighteen months after the liberation,

> I am at the end of my wits . . . health visiting, teaching, supervision of can-teens and sewing classes, all these items which are so important have to suffer or be left undone because I have to beg for some old dirty blankets to put the new born babies in.
>
> I may sound bitter, but if you work with young children you have to bear in mind that they are not machines which one can take out of operation on account of lack of fuel, the babies will be born whether we are prepared or not.
>
> The diet for young babies is atrocious . . . you will understand that $\frac{1}{2}$ lb milk and porridge is not an adequate diet.[154]

The medical facilities that existed in Belsen were relatively good. By 1946, alongside the well-equipped Glyn Hughes Hospital, there was established a dental surgery, medical stores and a dispensary, two consulting rooms, and a bandaging and treatment room. There did remain a problem with the Glyn Hughes Hospital, however. Although it was run by UNRRA officials it was actu-ally staffed by German doctors and nurses. Many of the internees were nervous of these Germans, and consequently many ill Jews were reported as preferring to stay in their rooms rather than be admitted.[155]

Beyond essentials such as food and medical care, the way in which the majority of Belsen residents became involved in communal activity was through educa-tional, cultural or sporting pursuits. The level of achievement impressed all who visited the camp. One American observer noted that 'everywhere, the emphasis was on creating an atmosphere of living, living for the future and not in the past'.[156] Education in Belsen was felt to be of crucial importance and a great deal of attention was given to it. The first school, in fact, was estab-lished just six weeks after the liberation of the camp. The children were classed not according to age or ability but according to their first language.[157] At this early stage the teaching aids were almost non-existent but volunteer teachers drawn from the camp survivors did all in their power to bring normalcy into the lives of the children. The school system had matured a great deal by July 1946 when Professor Weingreen, from Trinity College, Dublin, who as a relief worker had been in Belsen for two months in 1945, returned and took up the newly created post of Director of Education. His education office set out to co-ordinate, improve and expand the school facilities which had already been established. The primary and secondary schools were already running well and the facilities there were relatively good. A gift of twenty Meccano sets had been gratefully received from the youth of Dublin and a twice-weekly club was held where the children could use it under guidance. In addition to the primary and secondary schools there were also two Beth Jacob schools, a Talmud Torah and a thriving Yeshiva.[158] In the evenings the students could meet in the recrea-tional rooms or attend one of the various youth groups which existed. The small number of orphaned children who had survived the war and were still living in Belsen in 1946, were sent to a newly established children's home at Blackenese near Hamburg, accompanied by teachers and guardians. The house, owned by the Warburg family, was set in a large estate and offered the children a perfect opportunity to recuperate and learn in a Jewish atmosphere.[159]

Whilst an education was thus provided for the younger children, the needs of those young people between 17 and 25 could not be forgotten. Many had been denied six years or more of their formative education by incarceration in the ghettos and camps, whilst others had been dragged out of university or vocational training. The world, however, would not wait for them and as young people with the need to earn an income, they sought to learn new skills in Belsen which would enable them to begin a career immediately on leaving. This is where the technical school came to the fore, teaching basic crafts such as carpentry, tool-making, locksmith work, motor mechanics, tailoring, cobbling, building and cookery. The school was strongly backed by the Central Jewish Committee and by UNRRA as both bodies recognised not simply an educational opportunity but also a 'potent instrument for real rehabilitation'.[160] The technical school gave practical importance to the priority of giving young people the skills necessary to build their lives outside the camps, particularly in Palestine. At the same time, the school dealt with the immediate problem of the boredom and restlessness in the camps. Understandably the DPs refused to work for the German economy but, although many were anxious to work in the camps, the lack of material resources available enforced unemployment for most of them.[161] This was one of the major complaints of the Central Jewish Committee to the relief agencies.[162] There were in February an estimated 6,000 able-bodied workers in the British zone but the majority were kept idle. Thus the technical school became a central institution in the camp and indeed throughout the British zone as a whole when eventually a residential block was established so that those people living outside Belsen could benefit from its services. The students followed quite rigorous courses and after completion received an ORT certificate, a formally recognised qualification.[163] Usually the instructors would find useful work to do in maintaining the camp and surroundings. The building of a wall around the cemetery of mass graves where Camp I had stood was one such project.[164]

Adult education was also given prominence in the programme of Weingreen and his colleagues. It was decided that the guiding principle of the new committee established to co-ordinate adult education should be 'As people cannot take their place in normal society we must bring it to them'. As part of the programme language classes were held in Hebrew and English, and there were others in crafts and public speaking. Popular lectures on subjects such as contemporary Palestine, general discussion groups and musical evenings, attracted a great many interested students. Additional courses in religious and cultural education were directed by Reverend Greenbaum and special classes were provided for hospital patients.[165]

Cultural life in Belsen was surprisingly rich and varied given the shortage of resources which inevitably existed. Books sent by the relief agencies and collected from the nearby towns helped to establish an extensive library in the camp. Sporting equipment was also eventually procured and various clubs – boxing, football and volleyball amongst others – were established. At an early stage the British military had been instrumental in encouraging entertainment in the camp as a means of rebuilding confidence and expediting psychological restoration. As early as May 1945, the first International Cabaret, with the full participation of the camp internees, took place in a canteen in Camp III. The performers – actors, singers, musicians and dancers – were drawn from all nationalities in the camp and Jewish and non-Jewish entertainers shared the same stage. The second production, a much larger affair held on 4 June in the tented theatre of the Panzer Training School, was tremendously popular and all 800 seats were filled. The events were greatly appreciated, restoring as they did a degree of 'normalcy' to life in Belsen and imbuing the performers with a tremendous sense of accomplishment.[166] Arguably, however, it was another production, not given until September 1945, which caused many in the Jewish community the most satisfaction. This was the first Yiddish theatre, organised and produced by Samy Feder.[167] Feder had a great deal of experience, and not only from before the war. Even in the concentration camps he and his colleagues had been able to fashion dramatic performances in the barracks. The 'Kazet'-Theatre, as it was called, was a tremendous success and came to symbolise the rejuvenation aspect of the liberation experience. Feder experienced among his troupe a real 'need to play'; and on that first night, the audience were the most grateful crowd he had ever played to. 'They clapped and laughed and cried. When we gave, as our last item, the famous song "Think not you travel to despair again", the thousand people in the hall rose to their feet and sang with us.'[168]

Initially, the motivation behind the company was to dramatise the camp experience. Eventually, however, they began to produce classics of the Yiddish theatre – and not only in Belsen; tours took the company to other parts of Germany and also to France and Belgium where they were very well received.[169]

Religion, of course, was an important aspect of liberation for some people. Many DPs were non-religious and others had lost their faith as a result of their time in the camps. Yet others held on to their faith. They were often the same people who had attempted throughout their imprisonment to mark in some way the religious holidays, either in small groups or alone. After the liberation some of the most memorable dates were those which marked the first Jewish holidays celebrated in freedom. Even those people who were not particularly religious took part in these festivities, important as they were in allowing people to publicly celebrate their Judaism. The first *Rosh Hashana* celebrated in the hospital or the first *Chanukah* party held in the children's block were events of great psychological importance. This was no less true of the last such celebration than of the first. The first day of *Chanukah* in 1949 coincided with Boxing Day and several functions were held in joint celebration. A giant Menorah was erected 20 feet (6 m) high in Freedom Square and a large party given for the children in the camp.[170] Yet who would have believed four years earlier that there would still be a Jewish community in Belsen?

Although the community had drastically dwindled in numbers by 1949 and, thus, there was less demand on resources, at the same time food parcels from the AJDC had ceased to be provided. A JRU welfare worker reported in January 1949 that there was still a distressing amount of poverty in the camp. The psychological strain on all of the so-called 'hard-core' DPs who had not yet procured a visa must have been tremendous. Undoubtedly, the most desperate were the bedridden patients with TB; even Israeli immigration officials had strict rules concerning the emigration of Jewish TB cases. For these people liberation from their wartime ordeal had not come in 1945. Five or six years later they still awaited their liberation, this time without any of the joy and with even greater trepidation than in the spring of 1945. As a welfare report noted, 'the atmosphere amongst the patients, especially the chronic cases, is one of despair, everyone wants to know what will happen to him or her and so far there is no answer'.[171]

The conditions endured by the survivors in the DP centres surely could never have formed a part of the wartime hopes of liberation. Indeed, as Norbert Wollheim wrote later, '[t]he enforced stay in mass billets, under camp-type conditions, could not mean the kind of freedom which we had yearned and longed for.'[172] Nevertheless, despite the difficulties the DPs faced in Belsen they showed a great deal of self-reliance. After their liberation they began what Rosensaft called 'the tortuous climb back to normalcy' and began to organise their own lives.[173] An important turning-point was the Belsen Jewish Congress in September 1945. This event marked the changeover from the relief of the Belsen victims to rehabilitation proper. Certainly, one of the first tasks of the newly nominated Central Jewish Committee was to attempt to change the attitude of the aid organisations. The majority of the Belsen internees no longer required aid on a philanthropic basis but sought instead the means with which once again to develop their own skills and talents in order that they might contribute to the Jewish community.

The camp leaders, like Rosensaft and Norbert Wollheim who, after the liberation, quickly found strength in the political struggle for a Jewish homeland, strongly resented the free Jews who came into the camp and looked upon them only as objects of pity and in terms of their imagined psychiatric problems.[174] When the secretary and the vice-chair of the Central Jewish Committee, Berl Laufer and Wollheim, visited Anglo-Jewish leaders in March 1946, they made a point of expressing this resentment. '[T]he welfare workers from England . . . looked upon them as though they were just miserable, broken victims of the concentration camps', note the minutes of the meeting. 'They, however, were not broken in spirit, they were independent men [*sic*], knowing their own minds, wishing to conduct their own political affairs.'[175] This was certainly true of those who were politically active in the camp. At the September Congress, Selig Brodetsky, in rather exulting tones which fitted the occasion, told the delegates:

I had feared your grief and your tears, but your tears are cradled in the smile of the eternal Jew. I had feared your despondency and helplessness, but instead you have displayed a resoluteness that should be emulated by Jews throughout the world.[176]

When Norman Bentwich returned to England from a lecture tour of Germany he too reported his strong impression of the 'driving energy and determination of the leaders of our Jewish survivors to help themselves'. 'Those who have survived the agonies of the concentration camps', Bentwich wrote, 'have a sense that they have lived for a purpose . . . they possess, as it were, a human atomic energy.'[177] There is absolutely no denying that the Jewish leaders who emerged from the camps were extraordinary men and women. Certainly, as ever, there were thousands of individuals who passed through Belsen who were not leaders. They may well have shared similar aspirations but, so far, that variety of experience is missing from the story.[178]

All Jews who found themselves in the British zone after the war had at least one reason to be grateful to the dedication and hard work of the Central Jewish Committee. One of the earliest accomplishments of the temporary Jewish committee, who established their first headquarters in a small room in Camp IV of the former Panzer Training School, was the founding of an information centre for all those people seeking lost relatives. The committee produced a card index of all the Jewish people who survived in Belsen and they also kept similar lists brought by representatives from other camps and communities in Germany.[179] Once the Central Committee was fully functioning it was strongly felt by the members that they needed a voice. Another early achievement, therefore, was the successful publication of a regular newspaper, despite the fact the committee had no legal allocation of paper and no typewriters until they managed to procure their own. Paul Trepman became the editor of *Unzer Sztyme* (Our Voice) a Yiddish newsletter and the first Jewish journal to be published in the British zone of Germany after the war. The first issues were written by hand and reproduced for distribution in the British zone and eventually outside Germany as well. Later Trepman also edited the successor to the first journal, *Vochenblatt*, a six-page weekly which began production in December 1947. Both were organs of the Central Committee of Liberated Jews in Bergen-Belsen and thus were generally used for transmitting propaganda and raising morale among the widespread Jewish communities in the British zone.[180] The Central Committee also produced numerous books and leaflets on the Holocaust and life in Belsen DP Camp.[181]

## V

The Zionist history of the Belsen camp thus far written, of the Jews rising heroically, almost mythically, from and in spite of the desolation and destruction of the concentration camp is an impressive one. As we have seen, it corresponds well with the Zionist hegemony model of events leading to the 'restoration of Jewish national sovereignty'.[182] This rendering of the history of the DP camp has been born of an eagerness to counter popular perceptions, superficially reinforced by the 'Final Solution', of the Jew as victim. Also there is a necessity to see something wholly strong and positive emerge from the destruction. Moreover, those few who survived the camps and, firm in their Zionist beliefs, succeeded in rebuilding temporary Jewish communities in Germany, have been equally eager to have the world recognise the role that they played in the creation of Israel. Yet, as we have seen, it is questionable how far the 'fighting model' holds in Belsen. That the camp leaders and indeed all of the DPs displayed an immense strength and tenacity after the liberation cannot be repudiated. Neither can we deny the courage of the Central Jewish Committee who were prepared to confront the British occupation authorities and, indeed, the British government, in order to attain improvements in the situation of the Jewish DPs, nor that of those people who left the Belsen DP Camp for a new life in Palestine only to lose their lives in the War of Independence.[183] In the history of the Belsen DP Camp, however, there are many other shades of experience which, although they may not fit easily into the leadership model of a strong and united community, nevertheless cannot be ignored. The history of events constructed by the camp leadership clearly excludes the experience of the strictly orthodox in the camp. In the same way, it can be argued that the account also excludes those people who were not leaders and do not fit the restricted and even shallow image of the zealous and spirited, fighting Jew. Does the Zionist model not exclude the *Exodus* passengers who on their miserable return to Germany, were admitted into the Glyn Hughes Hospital in high numbers; these people, who left Germany so optimistically, but returned suffering from psychologically related illnesses and directing all their aggression, in understandable sheer frustration and disappointment, against their own members and leaders?[184] Does the model allow for the existence of the Polish Jew, and others like him, who almost five years after being liberated in Belsen, was transferred to Switzerland with little hope of recovering from his condition (due to the camp experience) of complicated TB together with serious heart, liver and kidney diseases?[185]

The Belsen DP Camp in its short history was an exceptional place. The uncertainty under which people lived, the injustice they felt at their treatment by the British authorities, and clouds of personal tragedy could make Belsen a bleak camp. Yet, at the same time, it was also a lively and often even an exciting community which drew strength from its internal organisations and Jewish way of life. In the final analysis, however, perhaps the only single factor which linked every member of the community, was the hope, surely dwindling for some, that their stay in the Belsen DP Camp truly would be temporary.

When the British troops entered Belsen they wondered at the apathetic reception provided by the prisoners compared with the tumultuous welcome received elsewhere. This chapter has examined the phenomenon of liberation from the viewpoint of the survivor; what is most apparent is that the freedom delivered by the Allies was for the survivors only one aspect of the liberation. The reality of liberation for the Belsen victims was often difficult and complex. A myriad of feelings and experiences were associated with it, and almost always they involved sorrow, loneliness and anxiety. Furthermore, the notion of liberation as providing 'a neat ending' to the Jewish suffering of the wartime years is simplistic and misleading; the very length of the Belsen DP camp's existence is evidence enough of that.

# Conclusion

## I

Yehuda Bauer, in his own work on the last months of the war, has stressed the need for further research in this area.[1] Historians of National Socialist Germany and the Holocaust have tended largely to ignore the final stages of the war, including the death marches, or briefly pass over the events of the period in order to 'tie up' a wider account.[2] This book has attempted, through the example of Bergen-Belsen, to advance research on the liberation period and the years following the end of the war.

The book's overriding theme is clearly the fact that the liberation of Bergen-Belsen or any of the western concentration camps did not mark the 'end' for any of the parties involved. The fighting units in the British Army who first entered the Belsen camp had to move on from the camp and rejoin the fighting at the front. The war continued for almost a month after the liberation. Having taken some time out in the satisfying, if desperately difficult, task of trying to save lives rather than destroy them, a number of soldiers, nevertheless, had to return to battle after Belsen. Far more crucially, on a personal level, the liberating act was not an end in itself for the soldiers, war correspondents and medical staff. The experience had a tremendous impact on a great many individuals and the memory of those days spent in Belsen has stayed with them throughout their lives. Some, like Mervyn Peake who was haunted by the guilt he felt, or the Mass Observation diarist who became an atheist after hearing of Belsen, were led to reconsider the way they lived their own lives. The experience of witnessing the horror of Belsen did not have a uniform impact. As we have seen in Chapter 1, whilst the majority of liberators in the main 'horror' camp at Belsen struggled to relate to the victims on a human level, a small minority, most notably Rabbi Leslie Hardman, were able to overcome their feelings of horror and shock and view the survivors as individual beings. Similarly, we can differentiate between the experience of men and women in Belsen, and indeed, Chapter 1 has examined the gender aspects of the liberation of the camp. Male and female liberators played very important roles in the camp and yet the female experience, until now, has largely been unexplored in the historiography.

A common reaction on the part of the liberators was to document what they had witnessed, either in writing or on film, in order to convince the home front that the appalling conditions in the camps were authentic. The communication of the news of the liberation was the subject of Chapter 2. The army and the news media together set out to prove beyond doubt to the British public that the reports of German atrocity were not propaganda stories. They largely succeeded. Indeed, the photographs and films shot in Belsen and the other liberated camps have gained a prominent place in Holocaust documentation as rare examples of pictorial evidence of the interior of the Nazi camps. The footage of the liberation has survived the event and is used again and again, though often misplaced, in the telling and retelling of Holocaust history. As with the initial liberators, the journalists covering the liberation story, though more adept in the art of descriptive narrative, were still to discover the failure of language in dealing with the scenes in the camps. The newspaper reports represented a serious attempt to inform the reader but at the same time there was also a tendency to exploit and sensationalise the material. This tension is present throughout many of the immediate postwar accounts of the Holocaust; in the 1950s the sensationalism gained an upper hand with the publication of some Holocaust narratives in paperback form together with lurid covers and titillating sub-titles.[3] A further important aspect of the reporting on Belsen was the downplaying of the Jewish aspect of the camp. In the initial reports there was rarely an attempt to link Belsen, and its high percentage of Jewish internees, with the Nazi design to exterminate all of Europe's Jews. Instead, the message of Belsen was universalised and used as a weapon: by the right as a means to establish the war guilt of the barbarous German nation and by the left to discredit those who had supported the appeasement stand of the pre-war Conservative government.

An unwillingness to relate to the particularity of Jewish suffering can be further observed in the postwar policy of the British authorities towards the Jewish DPs under their jurisdiction. In much the same way as the wartime plight of the Jews and the calls for specific rescue operations were subjugated to the more universal goal of winning the war, Chapter 3 has demonstrated the way in which the British attempted to bury the specific claims of the Jewish DPs within the general DP issue. Thus, for example, by refusing to acknowledge that the Jewish DPs were deserving of special privileges through virtue of what they had endured, or by removing the 'Belsen' title from the camp which housed the largest single Jewish community in the British zone, the British government helped to delay further the perception of Belsen's (and British) links with the Holocaust.

Chapter 3 also explores a sub-theme, which is further developed in the final chapter, that we must be aware of the limitations of a crude Zionist interpretation of the Belsen DP Camp. Such a representation fails to do justice not only to the complexity of the survivor's aspirations and activities in the post-liberation period but also to the complexity of British government responses to the postwar situation. The link between the DP camp and the Palestine issue was not straightforward by any means.

The history of the Belsen camp is an important part of British history but within that broad umbrella, also a significant episode in Anglo-Jewish history. The postwar era was a troubled time for the Jewish community in Britain, a time when not only had it to come to terms with the enormous European loss and assess what the future for Diaspora Jewry would be, but also the Palestine issue brought anti-Jewish violence to the streets of Britain together with accusations of dual loyalties. Chapter 4 has offered a critical account of the contribution of the Anglo-Jewish community to the relief and rehabilitation of the DPs. The community in its response to the emergency failed to present a united front on many issues, yet it would be too simplistic to provide undifferentiated criticism. Thus the chapter has attempted to place the response of the community in the context of the complex political, social and economic divisions which prevented the community from co-operating in a cohesive manner. The response in terms of volunteer personnel and monetary donations, on the whole, was not commensurate with the great need; as we have seen, those who actually worked with the Jews in Germany were a relatively small nucleus of people. Nevertheless, it is clear that the experience of working closely with the DPs in Belsen made a deep and lasting impression on many of their lives.

On an even more fundamental level, liberation certainly did not mark the end for the survivors of Belsen. Tragically it was the end for those thousands of people who lived to see 15 April 1945 but died in the weeks that followed as a result of their previous torment. For those who did live, as with the liberators, there was no immediate return to normalcy. The vast majority could not return to their former homes and all faced a future of uncertainty. A large number were forced to remain in camps under the care of UNRRA and the British authorities, as far as they knew, indefinitely. The liberators were unable to wave a magic wand so far as the survivors were concerned and their suffering went on. At the individual level, the liberation brought time to reflect on the immense tragedy which had befallen them, their families and their culture. The liberation period was a time of mourning. For most, looking forward was difficult and did not inspire feelings of joy but of fear and loneliness. Similarly, survivors continued to meet indifference or a lack of understanding from those around them. As discussed in Chapter 1, the liberators had difficulty relating to the survivors and many believed that the emaciated figures would never return to normalcy. This view was proved to be prematurely pessimistic by the subsequent actions and achievements of the Belsen Jewish community and the life the survivors made for themselves. Those who emigrated to Britain, America or Palestine/Israel met with a different but equally disheartening response to their situation. Generally, the societies did not want to know about the wartime experience of the survivors and they were left to get on with their lives with little or no support network outside their fellow survivors.

The second major theme of this book is that Belsen, and the Holocaust in general, is very much a part of British history. In terms of the British historical narrative, the liberation of Belsen equally did not bring an end to the ambivalence with which British society greeted the realities of the 'Final Solution'.

On the contrary, 1945 marked a determining point in – or perhaps even the beginning of – the long, ongoing development in British understanding of the Holocaust. It has been established that the publicity surrounding the liberation of Belsen and of the other camps convinced the British public that the Nazi state had been capable of an appalling level of atrocity: 'its name resonated as the exemplar of Nazi evil'.[4] Further, Belsen helped prepare the British mind to be able to accept the truth of the 'Final Solution' and the 6 million dead when such terms became more widespread than was the case at the end of the war. Jon Bridgman asserts that 'The photographs of the [Belsen] camp littered with 13,000 bodies, the hollow-eyed, emaciated prisoners, the sleek and brutal-looking guards fixed indelibly on the Western consciousness the grim reality of the Final Solution'.[5] This statement is clearly untrue. The photographs fixed indelibly the grim reality of Belsen camp as it was in April 1945. It is only with the passing of time, allowing for the formulation of a Belsen myth in British society, that the camp has become directly and inaccurately associated with gas chambers and the murder of millions.

## II

Vast strides have been made in the western world during the 1980s and 1990s in attempting to come to terms with, and formulating ways of properly remembering, the Holocaust, a process speeded with the commemorations surrounding the fiftieth anniversary of the end of the war. In 1981 a conference was held in Washington, USA which brought together liberators and survivors from several different countries in order to bear witness to the horror they had experienced and confronted.[6] Thirty-five years on, in marked contrast to the camps, the survivors and liberators were able to talk on an equal level and, to an extent, communicate their respective ordeals. The conference lasted two days and needless to say it proved a deeply emotional event. The liberators – soldiers, medical personnel, journalists, chaplains – formed a significant number of the witnesses. When one examines their testimony one is struck by the similarities between them. Few of the delegates felt able to describe what they saw or their feelings at the time in any detail. Instead most talked of how they had come to be in the camps, their total unpreparedness for what they encountered and the importance of keeping the facts of the Holocaust alive. An overriding theme of the conference, a point that many of the delegates stressed again and again, was the responsibility held by the eye-witnesses to make their voices heard; not only to counter the charges of Holocaust denial, which, it emerged, was a subject of major concern to the delegates, but also to raise a united voice against such genocide occurring again.

These were genuinely held and noble sentiments and are shared by veteran liberators of Belsen in Britain.[7] The question, however, of how far the liberators' testimony and, more crucially, their interpretation of material can stand alone is one that should be addressed. In 1945 the liberators struggled to find an adequate language for what they witnessed. The words of Marvin Kalb, American journalist, on the *Shoah* can be quoted to remind us of the great difficulties faced by contemporaries in coming to terms with the atrocities: 'It pushes the writer's ability, the speaker's eloquence, the witness's testimony, the listener's credulity, beyond what is natural, beyond the outermost limits of tolerance to absorb the enormity of the crime.'[8]

The liberators found difficulty in vocalising their feelings. But what they felt they could do was document the scene with photographs and film and (inadequate) written and oral testimony. Indeed, the major concern of the British and American witnesses was to corroborate as much as possible what they saw in the camps so that no one in the future could deny that it had happened.

For these actions the historian will be eternally grateful. The evidence was also crucial, as we have seen, in convincing the public in 1945 that the Nazi atrocities had occurred. Fifty years on it should not be used in the same role. Indeed, to do so might be dangerous; much of the contemporary evidence, the way in which material was interpreted and presented by the liberators at the time, has helped to promulgate the Belsen myth in British society. For example, the common view that there were gas chambers in Belsen probably originated amongst the liberators or early visitors to the camp who misinterpreted the stories the survivors told of gassings in camps they had been prisoners in previously, or subsequently imposed a gas chamber on their memory of the crematorium chimney. Another erroneous view held by liberators at the time, one which has appeared in published form since the war and does not aid in the establishment of an historical narrative of Belsen, is that the conditions in the camp were in no way attributable to the German authorities. According to one extreme account, written by one of the medical students who worked in the camp in May 1945, there had never been a deliberate policy of starvation in Belsen. The reasons for the breakdown of the camp as presented by Dr Russell Barton (the article was written in 1968), illustrate a marked unfamiliarity with the facts of the Holocaust and a lack of imagination concerning the capabilities of the Nazi regime:

> The irresponsibility of overcrowding living conditions by central authority, *the failure of warders or nurses to maintain a framework of law and order in which justice could be exercised*, and the powerful instruments of defence which institutions develop for their protection and perpetration – these were factors which resulted in *cruelties and sometimes atrocities*. [My italics][9]

Barton's view was similarly expressed by George Bernard Shaw. In September 1945 he wrote:

> Belsen was obviously produced by the incompetence and breakdown of the military command. The concentration camps are always left to the refuse of officers' messes, for whom the job of feeding and sanitating the deluge of prisoners is too much. The result is always the same more or less.[10]

The collapse of Germany in the final stages of the war certainly did contribute to the conditions found in Belsen in 1945 but it does not explain the underlying reasons for the generally appalling nature of the camp. This can be explained only by the Nazis' determination to humiliate and wipe out European Jewry. The factors outlined by Barton and Shaw did not contribute to the conditions found in the Warsaw ghetto three years earlier when hundreds of Jews died of cold and starvation on the streets nor did they contribute to the decision to march thousands of prisoners aimlessly around central Germany without food or water with a view to seeing them die. Lastly in this respect, we should remember that in the officers' mess at Belsen in the last four months of the war was an ex-commandant from Auschwitz-Birkenau extermination centre.

It is clear that all liberation testimony needs to be integrated into a wider context if it is to be applicable to the modern day. Such testimony is important for what it can tell us about British responses to the Holocaust. As John Ezard reminded us in the *Guardian* newspaper in April 1995, in his introduction to the moving contemporary testimony of a Belsen liberator printed therein: 'Most of us have grown up in a moral world haunted by the extremes of Belsen. . . . We forget what it must have felt like if you had never thought humans capable of such deeds; if the term "concentration camp" was so new to you that you spelt it with initial capitals.' Yet clearly, when we use the testimony we must be aware of its ability to distort the facts and be prepared to examine it free from the myths created about Belsen at the time of the liberation and subsequently.

This book has attempted to bridge the divide which has existed between British history and Holocaust studies with the hope that the two will eventually be integrated. The move towards a wider understanding of the Holocaust, and the lessons that can be learned from it, has been made in Britain over the decade of the mid-1980s to the mid-1990s. A great step forward has been the introduction of the subject into the National Curriculum at school level and on to higher education courses. The first version of this book was written as we were approaching the fiftieth anniversary of the liberation of Bergen-Belsen. One hoped that the debate, both academic and popular, that was inevitably to accompany the anniversary would be constructive and progressive, forging a wider understanding of the central place of Belsen in modern British history, and not simply restating old myths without interpretation.

Indeed, the press reporting of the liberation commemorations in 1995 demonstrated a willingness, on the whole, to make some moves to explain the complex history of the Holocaust and the starkly different roles imposed on distinct categories of camps within the Nazi system. As one might expect, the major coverage of the Holocaust commemorations appeared in January 1995, focusing on the Auschwitz-Birkenau complex and the unequalled level of Jewish loss during the Nazi period. Nevertheless, the anniversary of the liberation of Belsen did receive independent coverage in British press reporting in April 1995, and on two levels: that the Belsen camp was among the first camps to be liberated by the Allies and the first to be unforgettably described and filmed for the home front, and that it was the site chosen for the official German commemoration of the Holocaust on 27 April 1995, attended by Chancellor Helmut Kohl and President Herzog. Although the similarities in the reporting of the official ceremony between the British newspapers suggested that the correspondents were simply repeating facts of Belsen's history issued by the Belsen Memorial Centre, nevertheless they served to inform the public of Belsen's place in the Holocaust narrative, distinct from the extermination camps in the Eastern territories (or the sites where the *Einsaztgruppen* murdered one million Jewish men, women and children).[11]

In 1945 myths about Belsen sprang from the genuine shock experienced by soldiers who stumbled across the camp without warning and the perceived need to universalise the message of Allied good overcoming Nazi evil. Reporting of the liberation often served to highlight the testimony of the few British prisoners in Belsen and hence to disguise the role of the camp in the 'Final Solution'. The reporting fifty years on, in contrast, attempted to reflect the subtleties of the camp's history and, crucially, showed a sensitivity towards recording Jewish testimony. Many of the reports were careful to document the words of Jewish survivors respectfully and specifically, carrying brief biographies, memories and reactions and reflecting the development in awareness about the Holocaust and how it should be remembered.

The press in 1995 only hinted at complex histories and memories but largely avoided distorting them. However, it will fall to historians rather than journalists to preserve the truth about the relationship between Britain and Belsen. We can afford to be proud of and thankful to the British men and women who risked their lives to enter Belsen, who testified to what they saw and were destined to be haunted by their memories for many years. At the same time we must hold in our minds the words of Belsen survivor Ester Brunstein, 'I can't bear it when people tell me I must have been brave. I wasn't brave. I was lucky. If the British had come a week later, I would have been dead.'[12]

Britain did not have as its war objectives the saving of European Jewry. The British liberation of Belsen indicates the role of accident in history. This book has highlighted how the liberation of Belsen, rather than forcing a British recognition of the horrors of the *Shoah*, served only to reinforce the self-satisfaction of the British with their war effort and its moral justification. Such an interpretation is no longer acceptable. Belsen in the future must be seen as part of British history and of Jewish history, and of the two in combination. Ultimately, however, and in contrast to perceptions in 1945, it must be analysed properly as an important and complex part of what we now call the Holocaust.

# Notes

## ABBREVIATIONS

CMAC   Contemporary Medical Archives Centre, Wellcome Institute, London
HU     Hebrew University, Jerusalem
ICH    Institute of Contemporary History, Jerusalem
IWM    Imperial War Museum, London
MJM    Manchester Jewish Museum, Manchester
MO     Mass-Observation Archive, University of Sussex, Falmer, Sussex
SU     Southampton University Archive, Southampton, Hampshire
YV     Yad Vashem Archive, Jerusalem

## INTRODUCTION

1 M. Bunting, 'How Memories of Old Wars Distort our Moral Certainties', the *Guardian*, 16 July 1994; comments on bombing by Bob Nelsen (a member of Bomber Command during the Second World War) in the *Guardian*, 18 May 1992.
2 See the work of T. Kushner, *The Persistence of Prejudice: Anti-semitism in British Society during the Second World War*, Manchester, 1989.
3 J. Keegan (ed.), *Encyclopedia of World War II*, London, 1990, p. 120. In a similar publication, [no author] *The War Years, 1939–1945: Eyewitness Accounts*, London, 1994, it is stated that over one million people died in Belsen. The actual figure is thought to be nearer 70,000 (including 18,000 Russian prisoners of war who died on the Belsen site 1941–42): M. Godecke *et al.*, *Bergen-Belsen. Explanatory Notes on the Exhibition*, Hanover, 1991.
4 See the brief discussion in S.D. Ezrahi, *By Words Alone: The Holocaust in Literature*, Chicago, 1980, pp. 4–7.
5 A.J. Nicholls, 'Lessons to be Learned from Nazi Germany', *The Times Higher Education Supplement*, 27 March 1992; the *Observer*, 20 March 1994.
6 See W. Laqueur, *The Terrible Secret*, London, 1980; T. Kushner, 'The Impact of the Holocaust on British Society and Culture', *Contemporary Record*, 1991, no. 5, pp. 349–75.
7 G. Steiner, 'Book-keeping of Torture', *Sunday Times*, 10 April 1988.
8 A. Sharf, *The British Press and the Jews under Nazi Rule*, London, 1964; A.J. Sherman, *Island Refuge: British Refugees from the Third Reich, 1933–1939*, 2nd edn, Ilford, Essex, 1994; B. Wasserstein, *Britain and the Jews of Europe 1939–1945*, Oxford, 1979; M. Gilbert, *Auschwitz and the Allies*, London, 1981; L. London, 'British Immigration Control Procedures and Jewish Refugees,

1933–1942', unpublished PhD thesis, University of London, 1992; T. Kushner, *The Holocaust and the Liberal Imagination*, Oxford, 1994.

9 R. Bolchover, *British Jewry and the Holocaust*, Cambridge, 1993; G. Alderman, *Modern British Jewry*, Oxford, 1992; M. Berghahn, *Continental Britons: German-Jewish Refugees from Nazi Germany*, Oxford, 1988, a reprint of *German-Jewish Refugees in England: The Ambiguities of Assimilation*, Basingstoke, 1984; A. Gill, *The Journey back from Hell: Conversations with Concentration Camp Survivors*, London, 1988.

10 Y. Bauer, 'The Death Marches, January–May 1945', *Modern Judaism*, Feb. 1983, vol. 3, pt 1, pp. 1–21.

11 R. Abzug, *Inside the Vicious Heart: Americans and the Liberation of Nazi Concentration Camps*, Oxford, 1985; B. Chamberlain and M. Feldman, *The Liberation of the Nazi Concentration Camps 1945: Eyewitness Accounts of the Liberators*, Washington, DC, 1987.

12 J. Bridgman, *The End of the Holocaust: The Liberation of the Camps*, London, 1990; P. Kemp (ed.), *The Relief of Belsen, April 1945: Eyewitness Accounts*, London, 1991.

13 See the British press; Y. Kleiman and N. Springer-Aharoni (eds), *The Anguish of Liberation: Testimonies from 1945*, Jerusalem, 1995 brings together a number of short testimonies from individuals liberated in many different circumstances together with photographs and an intelligent introduction by Yaacov Lozowick.

14 For work predominantly on the American zone see: Y. Bauer, *Out of the Ashes. The Impact of the American Jews on Post-Holocaust European Jewry*, Oxford, 1989; L. Dinnerstein, *America and the Survivors of the Holocaust*, New York, 1982; A.L. Sacher, *The Redemption of the Unwanted: From the Liberation of the Nazi Death Camps to the Founding of Israel*, New York, 1983; L. Schwartz, *The Redeemers*, New York, 1953. Hagit Lavsky (Hebrew University, Jerusalem) is currently working on a research project examining the British zone. She has published 'The Day After: Bergen-Belsen from Concentration Camp to the Centre of the Jewish Survivors in Germany', *German History*, 1993, vol. 11, no. 1, pp. 36–59.

15 Despite its age, H. Krausnick *et al.*, *Anatomy of the SS State*, London, 1968 is perhaps still the best introductory text to the creation and evolution of the concentration camp system. See also Y. Gutman (ed.), *The Nazi Concentration Camps: Proceedings of the Fourth Yad Vashem International Historical Conference in Jerusalem, January 1984*, Jerusalem, 1984; M. Broszat, *The Hitler State*, London, 1981; I. Kershaw, *The Nazi Dictatorship*, London, 1989.

16 For a far greater depth of analysis than is possible here, the reader is directed through the end notes to the relevant texts on individual aspects of the discussion. For general introductory texts on the Holocaust see: M. Marrus, *The Holocaust in History*, London, 1988 and also his (ed.), *The Nazi Holocaust*, vols 1–9, Westport, CT, 1989, a collection of previously published articles by numerous well-known scholars; M. Gilbert, *The Holocaust: The Jewish Tragedy*, London, 1986 and *Atlas of the Holocaust*, London, 1982; C. Supple, *From Prejudice to Genocide: Learning about the Holocaust*, Stoke-on-Trent, Trentham Books, 1993.

17 Numerous texts cover issues of racial theory and anti-semitism. For example: G. Mosse, *Toward the Final Solution: A History of European Racism*, Madison, WI, 1985; L. Poliakov, *The Aryan Myth: A History of Racist and Nationalist Ideas in Europe*, New York, 1974 and *idem.*, *The History of Anti-Semitism*, Oxford, 1985, especially vol. 4, *Suicidal Europe, 1870–1933*; H. Graml, *Anti-semitism in the Third Reich*, Oxford, 1992; J. Noakes, 'Social Outcasts in Nazi Germany', *History Today*, Dec. 1985, pp. 15–19 offers a simple introduction to the subject.

18 Krausnick, *Anatomy*, pp. 134, 408–10; A. Weiss, 'Categories of Camps – Their Character and Role in the Execution of the "Final Solution of the Jewish Question"', in Gutman, *Nazi Concentration Camps*, pp. 117–18.

19 R. Hilberg, *The Destruction of the European Jews*, rev. edn, New York, 1985, p. 864; Krausnick, *Anatomy*, pp. 421–8; Weiss, 'Categories of Camps', p. 118; For conditions in Dachau see the unpublished memoir of A. Laurence ('Dachau Overcome', Parkes Library, Southampton University Archive [hereafter SUA]), who experienced the camp as a prisoner in the 1930s and also as a liberator with the American forces in 1945. On life in pre-war Buchenwald see the unpublished, untitled and undated memoir in the Lindsay Papers: L153, University of Keele Archive.

20 Weiss, 'Categories of Camps', p. 119.

21 Supple, *Prejudice to Genocide*, p. 80. See K.P. Schleunes, *The Twisted Road to Auschwitz*, Urbana, IL, 1970 for 1930s anti-Jewish legislation; also M. Burleigh and W. Wipperman, *The Racial State: Germany 1933–45*, Cambridge, 1991 and L. Davidowicz, *The War Against the Jews, 1933–1945*, London, 1975 on this period and the Holocaust in general.

22 See Graml, *Antisemitism*, pt one. Also: W.H. Pehle (ed.), *November 1938 Pogrom: From 'Reichskristallnacht' to Genocide*, Oxford, 1991; A. Read and D. Fisher, *Kristallnacht: Unleashing the Holocaust*, London, 1989.

23 There are numerous secondary sources covering the 'Final Solution', some of which have already been referenced (see the works by Hilberg and Davidowicz, in particular). See also: D. Cesarani (ed.), *The Final Solution: Origins and Implementation*, London, 1994; N. Levin, *The Holocaust: The Destruction of European Jewry, 1939–1945*, New York, 1973; L. Yahil, *The Holocaust: The Fate of European Jewry, 1932–1945*, New York, 1990; G. Hirschfeld (ed.), *The Policies of Genocide: Jews and Soviet Prisoners of War in Nazi Germany*, London, 1986; C.R. Browning, *Fateful Months: Essays on the Emergence of the Final Solution*, rev, edn, New York, 1991; C.R. Browning, *The Path to Genocide: Essays on Launching the Final Solution*, Cambridge, 1992.

24 See R.C. Lukas, *The Forgotten Holocaust: The Poles under German Occupation 1939–1944*, Lexington, KN, 1986. Specifically on the ghettos see, for example: Y. Gutman, *The Jews of Warsaw, 1939–43: Ghetto, Underground, Revolt*, Bloomington, IN, 1992; R. Hilberg *et al.*, *The Warsaw Diary of Adam Czerniakow: Prelude to Doom*, New York, 1979; J. Sloan (ed.), *Notes from the Warsaw Ghetto: The Journal of Emmanuel Ringelblum*, New York, 1974; L. Dobroszycki (ed.), *The Chronicle of the Lodz Ghetto 1941–1944*, New Haven, CT, 1984; Y. Arad, *Ghetto in Flames: The Struggle and Destruction of the Jews in Vilna in the Holocaust*, New York, 1981; M. Gilbert (ed.), *Surviving the Holocaust: The Kovno Ghetto Diary*, Cambridge, 1990.

25 See Y. Arad et al. (eds), *The Einsatzgruppen Reports: Selections from the Dispatches of the Nazi Death Squads' Campaign against the Jews, July 1941–January 1943*, New York, 1989.

26 Specifically on these camps see, for example: Y. Arad, *Belzec, Sobibor, Treblinka: The Operation Reinhard Death Camps*, Bloomington, IN, 1987; A. Donat (ed.), *The Death Camp Treblinka*, New York, 1979; P. Levi, *Survival in Auschwitz*, New York, 1960.

27 Hilberg, *Destruction*, pp. 865–70; For one of the few studies of women in the Holocaust see R. Schwertfeger, *Women of Theresienstadt: Voices from a Concentration Camp*, Oxford, 1989.

28 WVHA D-IV to WVHA-B, 15 Aug. 1944, Nuremberg Documents, NO-399 (organisation of Nazi Party and SS) cited in Hilberg, *Destruction*, p. 871.

29 D. Czech, *The Auschwitz Chronicle 1939–1945*, London, 1990, pp. 753–805; Bridgman, *End of the Holocaust*, p. 26; E. Kolb, *Bergen-Belsen: From 'Detention Camp' to Concentration Camp, 1943–1945*, 2nd rev. edn, Göttingen, 1986, pp. 40–1 (hereafter *Bergen-Belsen*).

30 Bauer, 'Death Marches', pp. 1–21; S. Krakowski, 'The Death Marches in the Period of the Evacuation of the Camps' in Gutman, *Nazi Concentration Camps*, pp. 475–89; L. Rothkirchen, 'The "Final Solution" in its Last Stages', *Yad Vashem Studies*, 1970, vol. 8, pp. 7–28; Krausnick, *Anatomy*, p. 504; D.J. Goldhagen, *Hitler's Willing Executioners: Ordinary Germans and the Holocaust*, New York, 1996.

31 For example, G. Reitlinger, *Final Solution*, 2nd rev. edn, London, 1961, p. 365. Kolb, *Bergen-Belsen*, p. 11 (this is an abridged, more accessible version of Kolb's research, based on an original monograph now out of print: *Bergen-Belsen. Geschichte des 'Aufenthaltslagers' 1943–1945*, Hanover, 1962). Also, Kolb, 'Bergen-Belsen, 1943–1945' in Gutman, *Nazi Concentration Camps*, pp. 331–42.

32 Kolb, *Bergen-Belsen*, pp. 20–1; see B. Oppenheim, 'The Chosen People: the Story of the 222 Transport', unpublished account, Wiener Library, pp. 78–81, 90–8; Wasserstein, *Britain*, pp. 223–8; Reitlinger, *Final Solution*, p. 363.

33 See comments by Abel J. Herzberg in Kolb, *Bergen-Belsen*, pp. 72–3.

34 Kolb, *Bergen-Belsen*, p. 24; circular decree WVHA-DI, 29 June 1943, Nuremberg Documents, NO-1291 cited ibid., p. 22; Hilberg, *Destruction*, p. 985.

35 On first exchange Jews see Yad Vashem Archive [hereafter YV] 033/1566: Korngold, survivor testimony (Yiddish): South American documents were for sale on the Aryan side after the Warsaw Ghetto uprising; subsequently 2,800 Jews who held South American documents were persuaded by the Germans to emerge from hiding on the pretext that they would be exempt from deportation. See also Reitlinger, *Final Solution*, p. 276n and Gilbert, *The Holocaust*, p. 620 for brief mention of this incident. The majority of these Jews arrived in Belsen but a smaller number were sent to the French transit camp at Vittel. Korngold states that 1,800 were deported to Auschwitz from Belsen, Gilbert notes 1,750. The majority of the Vittel Jews were also deported to Auschwitz but some were included in an exchange scheme and reached Palestine. On forged documents see Reitlinger, *Final Solution*, p. 364; Wasserstein, *Britain*, pp. 229–33; D.S. Wyman, *The Abandonment of the Jews: America and the Holocaust, 1941–1945*, New York, 1984, pp. 276–80. See the testimony of B. Spanjaard, '*Don't Fence Me In!*', Los Angeles, CA, 1985, p. 36 and H. Kruskal, 'Two Years behind Barbed Wire. Factual Report of a Dutchman Describing his Experience under the German Oppression', unpublished memoir, Wiener Library, Palestine, 1945, p. 6 for evidence of these practices in the Netherlands. Also, N. Eck, 'The Rescue of Jews with the Aid of Passports and Citizenship Papers of Latin American States', *Yad Vashem Studies*, 1957, vol. 1, pp. 136–41.

36 Kolb, *Bergen-Belsen*, pp. 25–6.

37 Reitlinger, *Final Solution*, p. 362; Kruskal, 'Two Years', pp. 5–9; Wasserstein, *Britain*, pp. 228–9.

38 Oppenheim, 'Chosen People', pp. 82–7; Y. Bauer, *American Jewry and the Holocaust: The American Jewish Joint Distribution Committee, 1939–1945*, Detroit, 1981, p. 276. The role of the Jewish Councils (*Judenräte*) in the deportations has become the centre of a controversial historical debate. See Y. Gutman and C.J. Haft (eds), *Patterns of Jewish Leadership in Nazi Europe, 1933–1945: Proceedings of the Third Yad Vashem International Historical Conference*, Jerusalem, 1979 and, specifically, in ibid., J. Michman, 'The Controversy Surrounding the Jewish Council of Amsterdam', pp. 235–57; see also Kruskal, 'Two Years',

p. 14 for criticism of the council leaders. On submissions to the Swiss Legation see I. Taubes, 'The Persecution of the Jews in Holland 1940–1944', London, Jewish Central Information Office, 1945, pp. 17–18; Kruskal, 'Two Years', p. 13.

39  For Pick-Goslar see W. Lindwer, *The Last Seven Months of Anne Frank*, New York, 1991, p. 21; see also the example of Paul Oppenheimer in Z. Josephs, *Survivors: Jewish Refugees in Birmingham 1933–1945*, Oldbury, 1988, p. 181: his family were given privileged status because his sister had been born in London; it seems that in Westerbork, prisoners knew that Belsen was within the Reich and not in Poland. It was also rumoured that there were no gas chambers and that the camp was under the control of the Red Cross: see L. Brilleman, 'This Is the Story of my Life and that of Others', unpublished memoir, Wiener Library, p. 42 and Kruskal, 'Two Years', pp. 18–19, 21; on numbers see Netherlands State Institute for War Documentation: details of first five transports from Westerbork to Belsen in 1944: 11/1/44 – 1037; 1/2/44 – 908; 15/2/44 – 773; 15/3/44 – 210; 5/4/44 – 101, cited in Spanjaard, *'Don't Fence Me In!'*.

40  Life in the Star Camp has been well documented by a number of survivors who were able to keep diaries in the camp or who documented their experience immediately after the war. Some have been published; for example: S.H. Herrmann, *Austauschlager Bergen-Belsen. Geschichte eines Austauschtransportes*, Tel Aviv, 1944; A.J. Herzberg, *Amor Fati. Zeven opstellen over Bergen-Belsen*, Amsterdam, 1947 and *Tweestromenland*, Amsterdam, 1950 (an English translation of *Amor Fati* by J. Santcross is available; *Between Two Streams*, London, IB Tauris in assoc. with the European Jewish Publication Society 1997; Renata Laqueur, *Dagboek uit Bergen-Belsen maart 1944–april 1945*, Amsterdam, 1965 (or *Bergen-Belsen-Tagebuch 1944/1945*, Hanover, 1983); Hanna Levy-Hass, *Vielleicht was des alles erst der Anfang. Tagebuch aus dem KZ Bergen-Belsen 1944–1945*, ed. E. Geisel, Berlin, 1979 (or *Inside Belsen*, trans. R.L. Taylor, Brighton, Sx, 1962). English excerpts from these diaries and reports are published in Kolb, *Bergen-Belsen*, pp. 59–91.

41  For punishments see Taubes, 'Jews in Holland', p. 32 and Kruskal, 'Two Years', p. 23; on kitchen workers see B. Ferderber-Salz, *And the Sun Kept Shining . . .*, New York, 1980, pp. 146–7, Brilleman, 'This Is the Story', pp. 50–2 and Laqueur's account (22 July 1944) in Kolb, *Bergen-Belsen*, p. 69; on the crematorium workers see YV 033/7 (German): because the young men were so isolated they were able to keep a diary (dated 8/3/44–16/4/44) as a record of their experience; Taubes, 'Jews in Holland', p. 33 reports that they were 'kept busy every day'; Spanjaard, *'Don't Fence Me In!'*, p. 132 refers to the workers as Frans and Pieter and notes that although they were well fed he would not have wanted to swap places with them.

42  Brilleman, 'This Is the Story', p. 32; Kruskal, 'Two Years', p. 23; Spanjaard, *'Don't Fence Me In!'*, p. 153.

43  Taubes, 'Jews in Holland', pp. 32–3; D. Dwork, *Children with a Star*, New Haven, CT/London, 1991, pp. 123, 131; Levy-Hass, *Inside Belsen*, pp. 36–8 (23 Oct. 1944); on faith in the exchange plan see Brilleman, 'This Is the Story', p. 4, although some did become very depressed – see Taubes, 'Jews in Holland', p. 33.

44  Kolb, *Bergen-Belsen*, p. 30; Bauer, *American Jewry*, pp. 398–9, 414–18, 427; Dwork, *Children*, p. 131: Gabor Czitrom was on this transport.

45  See Kruskal, 'Two Years', pp. 25–8 for details of the departure from Belsen and the journey to Palestine via Istanbul; S. H. Herrmann gives a powerful account of the anticipation and disappointment felt by the internees waiting for news of the exchange: see Kolb, *Bergen-Belsen*, pp. 59–65. See also YV 033/928: Mainz (German); YV 033/750: Jania (Hebrew). See the *Jewish Telegraphic Agency*

*(JTA) Daily News Bulletin*, 13 July 1944, pp. 1–2 for the arrival of the group in Palestine and their descriptions of the 'Bergenbelzen' camp. Barry Spanjaard was on the transport that reached Switzerland: *'Don't Fence Me In!'*, pp. 159–62. In the last months of the war negotiations to free Jews in the western concentration camps took place between Nazi officials on one side and the Red Cross and Jewish organisations on the other. Bauer, *American Jewry*, provides a good overview and is particularly concerned with the role of the AJDC in these final attempts to save lives. Wasserstein, *Britain*, pp. 341–2 deals briefly with the subject. See R. Hewins, *Count Folke Bernadotte: His Life and Work*, London, 1949 for an early account of negotiations which took place between Bernadotte, representing the Swedish Red Cross, and Himmler. Following the release of 1,210 Jews from Theresienstadt to Switzerland on 7 Feb. 1945, the World Jewish Congress representatives in Stockholm heard rumours that 3,000 Jews were about to be released to the Swedish authorities from Belsen. These people in fact did not reach Sweden: see WJC (Br Sect) C2/308: confidential report, Rubenstein and Zelmanovits, Relief and Rescue Dept, WJC, 3 April 1945.

46 Ferderber-Salz spent nine days in an overcrowded and stinking train from Auschwitz: *And the Sun*, p. 140; See also S. Bick-Berkowitz, *Where Are My Brothers?*, New York, 1965, pp. 76–84; Brilleman, 'This Is the Story', p. 59: See A. Lasker-Wallfisch, *Inherit the Truth*; Ferderber-Salz, *And the Sun*, p. 142; Lindwer, *Last Seven Months*, pp. 26, 102; Hanna Levy-Hass managed to talk to the Auschwitz women through the fence and learned about the liquidations there: *Inside Belsen*, pp. 51–2.

47 Dwork, *Children*, p. 147; Levy-Hass, *Inside Belsen*, pp. 48–50. SUA, Schonfeld 192: 'The Concentration Camp for Sick People at Bergen-Belsen', undated, a report compiled by the internee doctors at the camp; for secret cell see Lindwer, *Last Seven Months*, p. 75.

48 Imperial War Museum [hereafter IWM] (Sound Dept [hereafter S]) 9181/11: Abisch, reel [hereafter r.] 8; see also IWM (S) 10732/4: Lauth, r. 3–4; IWM (S) 9236/4: Dessau, r. 3; YV 033/135: Lichenstein (German), and the testimony of Fred Baron and Felicia Weingarten in R.G. Lewin, *Witnesses to the Holocaust: An Oral History*, Boston, MA, 1990, pp. 8, 79; P. Trepman, *Among Men and Beasts*, New York, 1978, p. 177; G. Perl, *I Was a Doctor in Auschwitz*, Salem, NH, reprint edn, 1992, pp. 163–4; IWM (S) 9122/5: Brunstein, r. 5; YV 033/6 (German); YV 033/449 (German). See also the account of Rudolf Küstermeier, who arrived in Belsen from Sachenhausen in Feb. 1945, in D. Sington, *Belsen Uncovered*, London, 1946, pp. 99–144.

49 YV 033/29, Gutman (German); *Bergen-Belsen, Explanatory Notes*, p. 9; Lindwer, *Last Seven Months*, p. 74.

50 See K. Hart, *Return to Auschwitz*, New York, 1985, pp. 144–5 on turning away; YV 033/1057, Rosensaft Papers: she was one of 500 Jewish women in Belsen chosen for transfer to an aeroplane factory in March; see also Brilleman, 'This Is the Story', pp. 74–6, who left Belsen with a transport of Hungarians on 7 April. After five days the train was stopped by heavy fighting and the prisoners were liberated when they walked to the nearest town, Wolmirstadt. See Kolb, *Bergen-Belsen*, p. 40 and W. Weinberg, *Self Portrait of a Holocaust Survivor*, Jefferson, NC, 1985, pp. 85–115 for the fate of the people on the April transports; on arrivals from Dora see IWM (Sound) 9181/11, r. 8 and Trepman, *Men and Beasts*, p. 220.

51 On the Gypsy population in Belsen see W. Günther, *'Ach Schwester, ich kann nicht mehr tanzen . . .' Sinti und Roma im KZ Bergen-Belsen*, Hanover, 1990. He is critical of Eberhard Kolb who gives no mention to the Gypsy prisoners in Belsen in the abridged standard version of his work. Quote is from Lindwer, *Last Seven Months*, pp. 105–6.

## 1 THE MILITARY AND MEDICAL LIBERATION

1 Poem by J.W. Trindles in V. Selwyn (ed.), *More Poems of the Second World War*, London, 1989. Trindles wrote the poem in 1945 having spent nine weeks in Belsen as a nursing sister with 29th British General Hospital.

2 J. Harris, 'An Elegy for Myself: British Poetry and the Holocaust', *English*, Autumn 1992, vol. 41, no. 171, pp. 213–33.

3 L. Langer, *Versions of Survival: The Holocaust and the Human Spirit*, Albany, NY, 1982, p. 11.

4 See the discussion in Ezrahi, *By Words Alone*, pp. 4–7.

5 ibid., p. 181.

6 J.E. Young, *Writing and Rewriting the Holocaust: Narrative and the Consequences of Interpretation*, Bloomington, IN, 1988, p. 3.

7 F. Kersten, *The Kersten Memoirs 1940–45*, London, 1956, p. 276.

8 See H. Trevor-Roper, *The Last Days of Hitler*, London, 1947.

9 R. Breitman, 'Himmler and Belsen', paper delivered at the Wiener/Parkes 50th anniversary Liberation of Belsen conference, April 1995, pub. in J. Reilly *et al.*, *Belsen in History and Memory*, London, 1997.

10 Bridgman, *End of the Holocaust*, p. 47. Himmler appointed SS *Standartenführer* Kurt Becher as *Reichssonderkommissar* for all concentration camps on 4 April 1945. See Kersten, *Memoirs* for details of the negotiations. He claims to have been influential in persuading Himmler of the importance of producing evidence of humanitarianism in the Reich; see also P. Padfield, *Himmler*, London, 1990, p. 582: Ernst Kaltenbrunner, chief of the RSHA, personally informed the commandants of the western camps that it was the Führer's order that no prisoner should fall into enemy hands alive. He told Kramer in Belsen on 7 April. Kersten claims that after lengthy negotiations he was able to persuade Himmler to reverse the order.

11 Public Record Office [hereafter PRO] WO 171/4773: Lt-Col. Taylor, DSO, MC, Report, April 1945.

12 PRO WO 171/4773: ibid., App. C.

13 J. Lucas, *Last Days of the Reich*, London, 1986, pp. 183–4.

14 PRO WO 171/4773: Taylor's report.

15 PRO WO 171/4957: War Diary, 113th Light Anti-Aircraft Regiment, April 1945.

16 D. Sington, *Belsen Uncovered*, London, 1946.

17 See P. Fussell, *Wartime: Understanding and Behavior in the Second World War*, New York, 1989, pp. 155–9 on the importance of taking credit for wartime actions; *The RAMC Journal*, February 1984, claimed that Glyn Hughes was the first to reach the camp but this was disputed by a Lt-Col. Spencer who maintained that, in fact, he was the first Allied soldier to enter Belsen: see Contemporary Medical Archives Centre [hereafter CMAC] Royal Army Medical Corps [hereafter RAMC] 1801 1/6, file 2: letter from Spencer to editor, 28 May 1984.

18 P. Kemp, 'The Liberation of Bergen-Belsen Concentration Camp in April 1945: the Testimony of those Involved', *Imperial War Museum Review*, no. 5, 1990; IWM (Docs) 85/9/1: Brig.-Gen. R.B.T. Danielle.

19 PRO WO 171/4773: Taylor in his report mentions that there were both SAS and Phantom officers in the camp on 15 April. An SAS officer reported that he had found a man from his unit in Camp I. The man, named Jenkinson, was removed immediately. See also PRO WO 177/322: Brig. Glyn Hughes who arrived in Belsen in the late afternoon of 15 April had received prior intelligence reports giving him some idea of what to expect in the camp.

20 PRO WO 171/4773: Taylor's report; Sington, *Belsen Uncovered*, p. 12.

21 Sington, *Belsen Uncovered*, p. 16.
22 Perl, *Doctor in Auschwitz*, p. 168; See also the testimony of Clara Greenbaum, cited in Bridgman, *End of the Holocaust*, p. 129.
23 By 16 April, Taylor had decided that the SS made no material difference to the administration of the camp. On the following day they were arrested and subsequently formed into burial parties. Kramer was removed from the camp altogether. In a war crimes trial at Luneburg six months later, eleven members of the SS, including Kramer, were sentenced to death by hanging for their actions at Belsen and Auschwitz. See R. Phillips, *The Trial of Joseph Kramer and Forty-four Others*, London, 1949.
24 'Belsen', no author, in a supplement to *British Zone Review*, 13 Oct. 1945.
25 PRO WO 171/4773: Taylor's report.
26 The figure of 40,000 is generally accepted. K. Feig, *Hitler's Death Camps: The Sanity of Madness*, New York, 1979 talks of 40,000 while Bridgman, *End of the Holocaust* cites 39,500. M. Gilbert, *The Second World War*, London, 1989 claims that the whole of the Belsen complex, Camps I and II, contained only 30,000 people at the time of liberation, a figure which by all contemporary accounts seems far too low. Nevertheless, as Glyn Hughes remarked: 'Estimates are pure guess work; the true figures will never be known': PRO WO 177/322: Medical Diaries, DDMS 2nd Army, 30 May 1945, App. A.
27 Kolb, *Bergen-Belsen*, p. 46.
28 ibid., pp. 46–7; Sington, *Belsen Uncovered*, pp. 48–9.
29 Phillips, *Trial*, p. 60; Rudolph Küstermeier in Sington, *Belsen Uncovered*, p. 112. See L. Cotterall, 'The Man From Belsen' in L. Gilliam, *BBC Features*, London, 1950: the Channel Islands capitulated to Germany in 1940. In June 1944 de Druillenec was found guilty of listening to enemy news and subsequently imprisoned in Neuengamme, Wilhelmshaven and Belsen concentration camps.
30 PRO WO 177/322: Medical Diaries, 30 May 1945, App. A; Manchester Jewish Museum [hereafter MJM] Sound Archive C410/005/06: Bernstein, r. 7A, trans. p. 67.
31 Phillips, *Trial*, p. 32.
32 PRO WO 177/322: Medical Diaries and also report by Major Waldron, 1 May 1945.
33 Phillips, *Trial*, pp. 31–2.
34 PRO WO 177/322: Medical Diaries.
35 11th Light Field Ambulance, led by Lt-Col. Gonin took responsibility for medical measures in Camp I, aided by 567 Coy American Field Service Unit, 32 Casualty Clearing Station, No. 30 Field Hygiene Section and No. 7 Mobile Bacteriological Laboratory. Lt-Col. Johnston became Senior Medical Officer at Belsen responsible for the supervision of all medical arrangements throughout the camps: CMAC RAMC 1218/2/15: 'Early Measures at Belsen: Observations' by Glyn Hughes at the Inter-Allied conference, 4 June 1945.
36 'Belsen', *British Zone Review*.
37 IWM (Docs) 84/59/1: Sgt W.J. Barclay, Personal Report on Belsen April 1945.
38 'Belsen', *British Zone Review*.
39 Phillips, *Trial*, pp. 53–4. At his trial Kramer claimed that he had taken every course of action open to him in order to try to deal with the situation in Belsen in the spring of 1945. He insisted that the stores in the *Wehrmacht* barracks were for the use of the *Wehrmacht* only and that his supply system depended upon a civilian base. He blamed the cold weather and air raids for the lack of food and general conditions in the camp. In fact, as Kolb insists,

'It was grave acts of neglect and a cynical contempt for human suffering by innumerable SS members which led to the catastrophe', *Bergen-Belsen*, p. 50.

40 IWM (Docs) 75/55/1: Major-General W.F.J. Eassie, 'The Administration of Second Army in the NW Europe Campaign, App. B – 'Belsen Concentration Camp'.

41 'Belsen', *British Zone Review*.

42 Phillips, *Trial*, p. 21; 'Belsen', *British Zone Review*; IWM (PB) K85/3364: Captain Pares, 'The Story of Belsen', 113th Light Anti-Aircraft Regiment, RA, 1945. The Royal Electricians and Mechanical Engineers repaired the electricity supply and restored the original water supply.

43 IWM (Docs) 84/50/1: Sgt Midgley, letter written in Belsen, 18 April 1945.

44 IWM (Docs) 85/38/1: Lt-Col. Gonin, 'The RAMC at Belsen Concentration Camp'.

45 Sington, *Belsen Uncovered*, pp. 52–3. The term *Muselmann* was part of the concentration camp language. Primo Levi in *If This Is A Man*, London, 1987 noted: 'The word "Muselmann", I do not know why, was used by the old ones of the camp [Auschwitz] to describe the weak, the inept, those doomed to selection' (p. 94). They formed the backbone of the camp: 'an anonymous mass, continually renewed and always identical . . . if I could enclose all the evil of our time in one image, I would choose this image . . . an emaciated man, with head dropped and shoulders curved, on whose face and in whose eyes not a trace of a thought is to be seen' (p. 96).

46 Ezrahi, *Words Alone*, p. 184.

47 'Belsen', *British Zone Review*. F.A. Riches, a driver with 11th Light Field Ambulance, was a witness to the burials and claims that the bulldozer was used on more than two occasions, IWM(S) 9937/03.

48 Phillips, *Trial*, p. 65.

49 See Lucas, *Last Days*, pp. 183–4; Also L. Miall (ed.), *Richard Dimbleby, Broadcaster*, London, 1966, p. 42: Wynford Vaughan-Thomas, a fellow BBC war correspondent, decided against going into Belsen with Dimbleby thinking that it was going to be a 'normal prisoner-of-war camp'.

50 Levi, *Survival in Auschwitz*, pp. 106–7.

51 IWM (Docs) 84/50/1: Midgley.

52 Sington, *Belsen Uncovered*, p. 37.

53 Phillips, *Trial*, p. 35.

54 G. Turgel, *I Light a Candle*, London, 1987, p. 106.

55 IWM(S) 7481/3: Lawrie.

56 See Abzug, *Inside the Vicious Heart*, p. 138; for the similar feelings of a photographer in Buchenwald see M. Bourke-White, *Deutschland, April 1945*, Munich, 1979, p. 90.

57 Review of his work, Radio 4, *Kaleidoscope*, 29 Sept. 1994; See the interview with him in the British Library National Life Story Collection.

58 Comments in J. Watney, *Mervyn Peake*, London, 1976, p. 127. Peake enrolled as a war artist in the army in July 1940 but had a nervous breakdown and was discharged in April 1943. When the war was over he was commissioned by Charles Fenby, editor of *Leader* magazine, to tour western Europe in the immediate aftermath of war and record his impressions. See Peake's drawings in *Leader*, 30 June, 14 July and 4 Aug. 1945.

59 From M. Peake, *The Glassblowers*, London, 1950 cited in Watney, *Mervyn Peake*. The girl is also thought to be the inspiration for Black Rose, a character in the third book of Peake's Gormenghast trilogy, *Titus Alone*, Harmondsworth, Mx, rev. edn, 1970. See also M. Peake, *Writings and Drawings*, London, 1974 and also comments by Harris, 'Elegy', pp. 227–8.

60 See J. Dimbleby, *Richard Dimbleby, A Biography*, London, 1975 and Miall, *Broadcaster*, London, 1966.

61 Phillips, *Trial*, p. 31; IWM (Docs) 84/50/1: Midgley.

62 Perl, *Doctor in Auschwitz*, pp. 166, 170.

63 For example, Sington, *Belsen Uncovered*, p. 46: 'The scene in some of the over-crowded blocks during the days following our arrival resembled Dante's Inferno' and Phillips, *Trial*, p. 58: 'A night in those huts was something maybe a man like Dante might describe, but I simply cannot put [it] into words.' See also IWM (Docs) 84/59/1: Barclay's report; once 'decent people', the prisoners now seemed to Barclay 'little more than animals'.

64 See Langer, *Versions of Survival*, pp. 9–11. Langer is concerned with the study of language and offers interesting and critical perspectives on writings by or about survivors of the Holocaust. His work might also be applied to liberator accounts. See also Ezrahi, *Words Alone*, p. 218.

65 IWM (Docs) 82/24/1: Col. F.M.V. Treagear, Draft Report on Belsen Camp, April 1945.

66 IWM (S) 9093/5, r. 4–5.

67 Abzug, *Inside the Vicious Heart*, p. 40.

68 A.H. Rosenfeld and I. Greenburg (eds), *Confronting the Holocaust: The Impact of Elie Wiesel*, Bloomington, IN and London, 1978, p. 19.

69 Langer, *Versions of Survival*, p. 8.

70 See P. Wyand, *Useless If Delayed*, London, 1959, p. 161.

71 IWM (Docs) 85/9/1: Danielle.

72 IWM (Docs) Misc. 105, Item 1657: Lt-Col. Gonin, Special Order of the Day, 1945.

73 IWM (Docs) p. 435: Sqd. Ldr F.J. Lyons, letter, 18 April 1945.

74 IWM (Docs) {Con Shelf}: Gen. Sir M. Gow; IWM (Docs) 91/1/1: Flying Officer F.T. Tatlow. See also 'The Belsen Story', the official illustrated publication produced by the American Field Service Unit: it is claimed that 7 million people died in Belsen between 1933 and 1945, picture 22N, p. 2.

75 See Introduction, pp. 2–5.

76 IWM (PB) K85/3364: Pares.

77 On 25 April seven Irish army nurses arrived, as well as six British Red Cross teams, each with one doctor, one nurse and five nursing aides; plus a small transport team of British Quakers. Following an SOS from the British Red Cross a medical mission of the International Red Cross – six Swiss doctors and twelve nurses – left Brussels for Belsen on 2 May: CMAC RAMC 1218/2/18: Annig Pfirter, 'Memories of a Red Cross Mission'.

78 PRO WO 177/849: War Diary, 11th Light Field Ambulance.

79 IWM (Docs) 75/55/1: Eassie; Lt-Col. F.M. Lipscombe in E.E. Vella, 'Belsen: Medical Aspects of a World War II Concentration Camp', *Journal of the Royal Army Medical Corps*, 1984, no. 130, pp. 38–40.

80 Early in May, 102 Control Section assumed control of Belsen from Headquarters 10 Garrison, while Inland Depot took over responsibility for all supplies for the camp from 155 Detail Issue Depot. Advance parties of 9 British General Hospital arrived on 28 April and 163 Field Ambulance on 8 May. By 16 May advance parties of 35 Casualty Clearing Station and 29 British General Hospital had arrived. The 113th Light Anti-Aircraft Regiment was relieved by another anti-aircraft regiment of the 103rd Anti-Aircraft Brigade and on 29 May 35 Pioneer Group relieved 102 Control Section. Finally, on 8 June Belsen Camp passed to the command of 30 Corps District as an area in the British zone of occupation in Germany: IWM (Docs) 75/55/1: Eassie; IWM (PB) K85/3364: Pares; 'Belsen', *British Zone Review*.

81 Leslie Hardman, interview with author.
82 PRO WO 171/4604: War Diary, 10 Garrison HQ, Report on Belsen, 18–30 April.
83 PRO WO 171/4031: War Diary, 8 Corps.
84 PRO WO 171/7950: War Diary, 224 Military Government Detachment, Ann. 1, Report on Belsen Camp. The delay came in clearing the barrack area in Camp II: 'owing to a lack of appreciation of Military Government methods by the Military Commander'. The task of clearing, cleaning and re-equipping the *Wehrmacht* buildings to make them resemble a hospital area was not an easy one and realistically delays were to be expected. However: 'At this stage it was the morale that was keeping people alive and nothing else, if they saw that we did not keep our word they just lost again the will to live': IWM 85/38/1: Gonin, 'The RAMC at Belsen Concentration Camp', pp. 7–8.
85 R. Pearce (ed.), *Patrick Gordon Walker: Political Diaries 1932–1971*, London, 1991, pp. 152–3. An interesting point is that when Gordon Walker himself published his diaries in 1945, he felt it appropriate to omit these criticisms of the British Army: see *The Lid Lifts*, London, 1945.
86 PRO WO 171/4604: Notes on Taking over a Concentration Camp.
87 ibid.
88 On 29 April, 10 Garrison handed the running of Belsen over to No. 2 Control Section and on 30 April moved to Luneburg with the intention of taking over another concentration camp at Neuengamme as soon as that camp was liberated. On 3 May, however, the information was received that Neuengamme camp had been found empty: PRO WO 171/4605: War Diary, S & T Branch, 10 Garrison. Many of the inmates of Neuengamme had in fact been marched to Belsen in the weeks before the liberation.
89 PRO WO 171/7950: Miles's report.
90 The usual ambulances used to carry the internees from Camp I to Camp II could hold two stretchers, and the bigger ones four, but if blankets were placed on the floor then the capacity could be increased to three and six. In an effort to speed up the evacuation, the orderlies began to optimise the number of patients they could carry only to be reprimanded for disturbing the routine when they arrived at the hospital: IWM (S) 9937/3/2: Riches. In the same way, Hardman was reproached by an officer when he stopped an ambulance and had a man he found wandering in the camp placed inside: interview with author.
91 IWM (S) 9937/3: Riches. For their tireless work, seventeen ambulance personnel were mentioned in dispatches: PRO WO 177/849: War Diary, 11th Light Field Ambulance.
92 CMAC RAMC 1790: Prescott, article on the clearing of Belsen; a BBC 'Open Space' programme in May 1985 documented the experience of the Belsen medical students.
93 See IWM (S) 8935/2: Horsey, r. 1 and 8924/1: Trimmer.
94 IWM (S) 8909/3: Dossetor, r. 2, and 8930/2: Garstin, r. 1.
95 IWM (S) 8924/1: Trimmer.
96 PRO WO 171/4604: Notes on Taking Over a Concentration Camp.
97 IWM (S) 9309/2: Proctor, r. 2.
98 Dr A.P. Meiklejohn in Vella, 'Medical Aspects'.
99 See PRO WO 171/7950: War Diary, 224 MGD. The death rate in Camp I fell steadily:

28 April – 304     9 May – 118
29 April – 259     10 May – 118
30 April – 260     11 May – 61

100 IWM (Docs) 76/74/1: Hargrave, diary, 3 May 1945.
101 IWM (S) 8996/02/01: Dixey, trans. p. 6.
102 IWM (S) 8925/2: Raymond, r. 2.
103 IWM (Docs) 76/74/1: Hargrave, 5 May 1945.
104 IWM (S) 9232/2/1: Bradford, trans. p. 8.
105 IWM (S) 8996/02/01: Dixey, trans. p. 4.
106 IWM (Docs) 86/7/1: Bradford, diary, 9 May 1945.
107 IWM (S) 8924/1: Trimmer.
108 CMAC RAMC 1790: Prescott.
109 IWM (S) 8924/1: Trimmer; IWM (Docs) 86/7/1: Bradford, 23 May 1945.
110 J. Hankinson, 'Belsen', *St Mary's Hospital Gazette* 1945, no. 51, p. 76. Captain Winterbothom's main achievement was in equipping the first 7,000-bedded hospital area in Camp II by combing the district around Belsen and requisitioning materials.
111 IWM (S) 8932/1: MacAuslan.
112 IWM (S) 8930/2: Garstin, r. 2.
113 See R. Collis and H. Hogerzeil, *Straight On (Journey to Belsen and the Road Home)*, London, 1947 and also Collis, *To Be a Pilgrim*, London, 1975.
114 IWM (Docs) 86/7/1: Bradford, 15 May 1945.
115 See diary entry for 19 May 1945 in A. Paton, *British Medical Journal*, December 1981, vol. 283, pp. 1656–9.
116 See, for example, IWM (S) 8909/3: Dosseter, r. 1: 'the language barrier was almost complete'; IWM (S) 9309/2: Wand, r. 4: he remembered that the internees talked about Auschwitz but in his interview he describes the camp only in terms of the cold weather and the poor rations. It is probable that the internees told him more than that about the camp; whether Wand understood more at the time but failed to assimilate the information, or whether the only words he could understand concerned the weather and the food, we cannot ascertain; IWM (Docs) 91/6/1: Coigley: he became familiar with the name of Auschwitz when he began to compile short records on each internee. A typical card would read: 'Rosalina Levi, Hungarian, 34 yrs, 5 months in Birkenau on bad food. Worked hard. Walked 20km day. 4 mth in Belsen, no illness 'til three weeks ago.'
117 Ezrahi, *Words Alone*, p. 184.
118 IWM (Docs) 76/74/1: Hargrave, 23 May 1945.
119 CMAC RAMC 1218/2/14: letter, Major R.J. Phillips to Glyn Hughes, 31 May 1945.
120 IWM (Docs) {Con Shelf}: Horsey, diary, 10 May 1945; See also IWM (Docs) 91/21/1(R): Horwell, letter, 4 May 1945 and the comments by Collis in the *British Medical Journal*, 9 June 1945, p. 815.
121 L. Hardman, *The Survivors: The Story of the Belsen Remnant*, written by C. Goodman, London, 1958.
122 Lipscombe in Vella, 'Medical Aspects'.
123 IWM (Docs) 86/7/1: Bradford, 12 May 1945.
124 IWM (Docs) 76/74/1: Hargrave, 21 May 1945.
125 E. Taylor, *Women Who Went To War*, London, 1988, p. 15.
126 J. Smyth, *The Will to Live: The Story of Dame Margot Turner*, London, 1970, p. xxi.
127 G. Brayburn, *Women Workers In The First World War: The British Experience*, London, 1981.
128 ibid., pp. 31, 232.
129 P. Summerfield, *Women Workers in the Second World War*, London, 1984, p. 1; A. Marwick, *Britain in the Century of Total War*, London, 1968.

130 K. Millett, *Sexual Politics*, London, reprint 1989, p. 26 and discussion which follows.

131 R. Wilson, *Quaker Relief: An Account of the Relief Work of the Society of Friends 1940–8*, London, 1952, p. 222; J. Greenwood, *Quaker Encounters*, York, vol. 1, 1975, p. 319; *The Times*, 16 May 1945; see IWM 11540/2: Hughes, r. 1: by the time he had arrived in May 1945 'things were more civilised and we were able to have British nurses'.

132 See the comments by Maureen Gara on her part in the Normandy Landings – 'it was dust, dirt, blood and mud' – in 'Angels of D-Day', *Outlook*, April/May 1994, p. 25 [published by South West Trains]; Taylor, *Women Who Went to War*, *passim*.

133 PRO WO 171/4604: 10 Garrison Report, 18–30 April, App. E; Hankinson, 'Belsen'.

134 Hardman, *Survivors*, pp. 35–6 and interview with author.

135 T. Moi, 'Feminist Literary Criticism' in A. Jefferson and D. Robey, *Modern Literary Theory*, London, 2nd rev. edn, 1988, p. 213; See S. de Beauvoir, 'Dreams, Fears, Idols' in *The Second Sex*, London, 1988, pp. 171–229.

136 The British press were fascinated by the female SS guards and particularly Grese. See, for examples of the reporting on the women: *News Chronicle*, 19 April 1945; *Daily Herald*, 19 and 27 Sept. 1945.

137 IWM (Docs) 880: Cayley, letter, 5 May 1945.

138 See, for example, Pearce, *Patrick Gordon Walker*, p. 152 referring to Hardman's anguished feelings.

139 IWM (Docs) 91/13/1: Forrest, 'An Experience of Belsen'.

140 See Ch. 5 on the relationships formed between the female internees and the soldiers.

141 Wilson, *Quaker Relief*, p. 227; B. McBryde, *Quiet Heroines: Nurses of the Second World War*, London, 1985, p. 182.

142 W.R.J. Collis, 'Belsen Camp: A Preliminary Report', *British Medical Journal*, 9 June 1945, p. 814.

143 IWM (Docs) 76/74/1: Hargrave, 26 May 1945.

144 McBryde, *Quiet Heroines*, p. 184.

145 ibid.

146 CMAC RAMC 1218/2/18: Pfirter; see the comments by a Belsen nurse in *The Times*, 16 May 1945.

147 ibid., Pfirter.

148 E. Kahn-Minden, *The Road Back: Quare Mead*, New York, 1991, p. 11.

149 McBryde, *Quiet Heroines*, p. 184; CMAC RAMC 1218/2/18: Pfirter.

150 McBryde, *Quiet Heroines*, p. 184; Kahn-Minden, *Road Back*, p. 8.

151 Collis, *Pilgrim, passim*; Kahn-Minden, *Road Back*, p. 11.

152 CMAC RAMC 1184/3: Report on Sandbostel Political Prisoner Camp.

153 M. Korzak, 'Women at War – a Celebration', *History Workshop*, Autumn 1977, no. 4, pp. 239–40.

154 Vella, 'Medical Aspects'.

## 2 BRITISH POPULAR RESPONSES

1 Kushner, *Liberal Imagination, passim*.

2 Kushner, 'Different Worlds: British Perceptions of the Final Solution During the Second World War' in Cesarani, *The Final Solution*, p. 253.

3 Kushner, 'Impact of the Holocaust', pp. 350–1.

4 Kushner, 'Different Worlds', p. 251.

5 Sharf, *The British Press, passim*.

6 ibid., p. 77.
7 ibid., p. 58; for an example see *Picture Post*, 26 Nov. 1938.
8 R. Griffiths, *Fellow Travellers of the Right*, Oxford, 1983, p. 339.
9 Commission of Enquiry of the Labour and Socialist International: Communications on the Conditions of Political Prisoners, issued 22 Dec. 1938, cited in Sharf, *The British Press*, p. 84.
10 White Paper, *Concerning the Treatment of German Nationals in Germany 1938–1939*, Cmd. 6120, London, 1939 cited in Wasserstein, *Britain*, p. 163. See *Daily Express*, 31 Oct. 1939 for an example of press reaction to the White Paper.
11 See Wasserstein, *Britain*, p. 163; T. Kushner, *The Persistence of Prejudice: Antisemitism in British Society during the Second World War*, Manchester, 1989, p. 157.
12 See, for example, *The Times*, 31 Oct. 1939: editorial.
13 Wasserstein, Britain, p. 164.
14 Sharf, *The British Press*, pp. 88–9.
15 *Daily Herald*, 15 Jan. 1942.
16 *The Times*, 11 June 1941; *Sunday Times*, 8 June 1941.
17 *Daily Telegraph*, 25 June and 30 June 1942.
18 See Y. Bauer, 'When Did They Know?' Midstream, April 1968, no. 14, pp. 51–8; Sharf, *The British Press*, pp. 92–3; Kushner, *Liberal Imagination*, p. 168.
19 Laqueur, *Terrible Secret*, pp. 77–9. Mention of the Riegner telegram is to be found in most standard works on the Holocaust; for example, see Hilberg, *Destruction*, vol. III, pp. 1116–17.
20 See Wasserstein, *Britain*, pp. 166–82 for the events leading to the declaration by the Allies and the response to it. Also R. Breitman, 'The Allied War Effort and the Jews' in *Journal of Contemporary History*, 1985, vol. 20, pp. 135–56.
21 SUA Parkes Papers 15/057, file 2: Harold Nicolson, 24 Nov. 1943, cited in Kushner, 'Different Worlds', p. 258.
22 *Sunday Times*, 3 Nov. 1943.
23 On Oswiecim see *Daily Telegraph*, 20 June 1944 (although the piece is only 1 cm in length); *Manchester Guardian*, 27 June. For 'notorious' see *Sunday Dispatch*, 25 June 1944; the article reported that hundreds of thousands of Jews had perished at Oswiecim. On Majdanek see *The Times*, 8 July 1944; *News Chronicle*, 30 Aug.; *Manchester Guardian*, 12 Aug.; *Sunday Express*, 13 Aug.
24 Laqueur, *Terrible Secret*; Gilbert, *Auschwitz and the Allies.*
25 Laqueur, *Terrible Secret*, p. 203.
26 Kushner, *Liberal Imagination.*
27 Kushner, 'Different Worlds', p. 261.
28 Laqueur, *Terrible Secret*, p. 99.
29 Mass-Observation Archive [hereafter MO]: D 5443, 15 April 1945; see Chamberlain and Feldman, *The Liberation*, pp. 42–5 for the transcript of Murrow's account.
30 *Evening Standard*, 16 April 1945; also *Manchester Guardian*, 16 April 1945.
31 For Belsen reports see, for example: *News Chronicle*, 18, 19 April 1945; *Daily Herald*, *Daily Worker*, *Glasgow Herald*, *Manchester Guardian*, *The Times*, *The Scotsman*, *Yorkshire Post*, all 19 April 1945.
32 *The Times*, 19 April 1945; see also, for example, the *Daily Herald* for the same day.
33 *Daily Mail*, 19 April 1945; *Evening Standard*, 16, 18 April; *Daily Sketch*, 18 April; *Sunday Times*, 22 April.
34 Miall, *Richard Dimbleby*, p. 193.
35 *The Times*, 19 April 1945; *Daily Mail*, 19 April 1945.

36  *Evening Standard*, 20 April 1945.
37  *News Chronicle*, 18, 19 April 1945; Wills's account was also used by some of the provincial papers; see, for example, *Western Mail*, 18 April 1945.
38  *Daily Worker*, 19 April 1945.
39  *Evening Standard*, 16 April 1945; for the Reuter comment see the *News of the World*, 22 April and the *Yorkshire Post*, 21 April; for Monson see the *Evening Standard*, 20 April 1945; *Observer*, 22 April 1945.
40  *Daily Sketch*, 18 April 1945.
41  See Fussell, *Wartime*, pp. 269–70.
42  *The Times*, 19 April 1945; see also the issue of 24 April: R. Donnington, letter to the editor: 'We owe you a debt for printing those terrible photos which bring home the full meaning of the Nazi concentration camps as none of the verbal descriptions of the past ten years and more could do.'
43  *Daily Mail*, 19 April 1945; *Daily Herald*, 20, 21 April 1945.
44  *Picture Post*, 5 May 1945. The *Post* did publish artists' impressions of the Belsen camp at the time of the Nuremberg War Crimes Tribunal, see the issue of 22 Sept. 1945, pp. 13–17; *Illustrated London News*, 28 April 1945: 'These revelations of coldly-calculated massacre and torture are . . . intended for our adult readers only.'
45  See Bolchover, *British Jewry*, introduction. For an example see *Jewish Chronicle*, 19 Jan. 1945.
46  *Jewish Chronicle*, 9 Feb., 13 April 1945.
47  ibid., 27 April 1945.
48  MO: D 5270, 21 April, 5 May 1945; D 5205, 20 April 1945; D 5239, 21 April 1945; D 5110 and D 5378, 23 April 1945, all verify that the 'atrocities' were widely discussed.
49  MO: D 5344, 21 April 1945.
50  MO: D 5261, 21 April 1945; see D. Hawkins (ed.), *War Report: A Record of Dispatches Broadcast by the BBC War Correspondents with the Allied Expeditionary Force, 6 June 1944–5 May 1945*, London, 1946, pp. 401–2 for Dimbleby's report.
51  *Daily Express*, 29 April 1945.
52  *The Times*, 28 April 1945.
53  See *The Times*, 19 May 1945: C.G. Bernstein, letter to the editor.
54  C. Seymour-Ure, *The British Press and Broadcasting Since 1945*, Oxford, 1991, p. 2.
55  *Daily Telegraph*, 1 May 1945.
56  For example, see MO: D 5443, 29 April or D 5270, 5 May 1945; also IWM (S) 9937/3: Riches; and M. Caiger-Smith, *The Face of the Enemy: British Photographers in Germany 1944–52*, Berlin, Nishen, no date, p. 15.
57  *Manchester Guardian*, 23 May 1945: J.B. Dunn, letter to the editor.
58  MO: FR 2248, 'German Atrocities', 5 May 1945.
59  M. Gilbert, *Road to Victory*, London, 1988, p. 1304.
60  *Hansard*, 410 HC DEB 5s, cols. 390–1, 19 April 1945.
61  Gilbert, *Road to Victory*, p. 846. It was Eden who read the statement to the House of Commons in December 1942.
62  M. Gilbert, *Churchill: A Life*, London, 1991, p. 836.
63  Gilbert, *Road to Victory*, p. 1305. A number of American delegations did visit the camps: see Chamberlain and Feldman, *The Liberation*, pp. 75–7.
64  *Daily Herald*, 20 April 1945.
65  Tom Wickham, MP, a member of the delegation, in *Picture Post*, 12 May 1945.
66  *Hansard*, 411, col. 714, 5 June 1945: Driberg to Peake.

67 See the editorial in *The Times*, 20 April 1945; *Hansard*, 410, col. 1377, 2 May 1945: Sir R. Glyn; MO: D 5337, 21 April 1945.
68 *The Times*, 21 April 1945: Galbraith, letter to the editor.
69 Laqueur, *Terrible Secret*, pp. 8–9; see M. Balfour, *Propaganda in War, 1939–1945*, London, 1979, p. 300 for a more apologetic view of First World War 'atrocity stories'.
70 Churchill to Eden and Bedell-Smith to Lord Ismay, both cited in Gilbert, *Road to Victory*, p. 1305.
71 See MO: D 5270, 4 May 1945 and D 5231, 21 April 1945 who conversed with British soldiers on leave. See also IWM (Docs) DS/MISC/49: N.F. Ellison, letters from a neighbour's husband.
72 *The Times*, 18 June 1945: 'the full horror and chaos took us unawares'.
73 Laqueur, *Terrible Secret*, pp. 3, 198.
74 MO: FR 2228, 'Pre-Peace News Questionnaire', 18 April 1945.
75 *Evening Standard*, 21 April 1945: K. Battsek, letter to the editor.
76 *The Times*, 28 April 1945; see also the *Manchester Guardian*, 23, 24, 25 May which printed three articles by F.A. Voigt, the *Guardian* German correspondent in the 1930s. The articles – 'How the Terror Began', 'The Brown Houses' and 'Prisoners and Gaolers' – all concentrated on the Nazi regime before the war and made no mention of Jewish persecution.
77 *Daily Telegraph*, 1 May 1945.
78 *The Times*, 19 April; *Daily Mail*, 19 April; *Evening Standard*, 20 April 1945.
79 *The Times*, 14 April 1945.
80 MO: D 5358, 20 April 1945.
81 Reported in the *Manchester Guardian*, 18 May 1945.
82 MO: D 5445, 20 April 1945.
83 MO: D 5358, 20 April 1945.
84 MO: TC Politics, Box 15, File C: see comments by a middle-aged woman in Hampstead, 4 May 1945.
85 Bevin, *Hansard*, 410, col. 391, 19 April 1945. See also Kirby to Henderson, *Hansard*, 410, col. 1003, 26 April 1945.
86 *Illustrated London News*, 28 April 1945.
87 *Evening Standard*, 18 April 1945; see also Hawkins, *War Report*, pp. 398–400 for a BBC interview with Burney. Christopher Burney was the leader of a prisoner organisation in Buchenwald representing non-communists. Because of the limited cache of arms available he endorsed a policy of delivering 6,000 Jewish people into the hands of the SS – they were not thought worth fighting over. On this, see Reitlinger, *Final Solution*, p. 505n. See also C. Burney, *The Dungeon Democracy*, New York, 1948.
88 MO: D 5110, 27 April 1945.
89 I. McLaine, *Ministry of Morale: Homefront Morale and the Ministry of Information in World War II*, London, 1979, ch. 5.
90 PRO FO 898/294, PWE Central Directive, 21 Oct. 1943 cited in Balfour, *Propaganda in War*, p. 302.
91 *Hansard*, 410, cols. 819–20, 25 April 1945.
92 N. Pronay, 'Defeated Germany in British Newsreels: 1944–45', in R.M.K. Short and S. Dolezel, *Hitler's Fall: the Newsreel Witness*, London and New York, 1988, p. 29.
93 ibid., p. 30.
94 MO: TC Victory Box 1, File A: comments by F/60/D and F/35/B.
95 *Sunday Express*, 22 April 1945: J. Gordon, letter to the editor.
96 MO: D 5132, 19 April; D 5270, 21 April 1945.
97 MO: FR 2228; *The Times*, 21 April: H.C. Burton, letter to the editor.

98  PRO INF 1/292, HI Weekly Report 25 Nov.–4 Dec. 1940, cited in McLaine, *Ministry of Morale*, p. 156.
99  MO: D 5098, 22 May; *The Times*, 21 May 1945: L. Wood, letter to the editor.
100 MO: TC Politics, Box 15, File C: comment by M/50/C.
101 *The Times*, 28 April 1945: D. Agnew, letter to the editor.
102 *The Times*, 27 April 1945.
103 MO: D 5375, 22 April 1945.
104 MO: TC Politics, Box 15, File C.
105 S. Orwell and I. Angus (eds), *The Collected Essays, Journalism and Letters of George Orwell*, vol. III, London, 1968, pp. 89–93. See also G. Orwell, 'Anti-semitism in Britain', *Contemporary Jewish Record*, April 1945, pp. 163–71 and for some 'serious investigation', Kushner, *Persistence of Prejudice*.
106 MO: D 5270, April 1945. Schleunes, *Twisted Road* provides an account of the ruinous and humiliating legislation applied to the Jews in Germany in the 1930s.
107 MO: D 5303, 29 Sept. 1945.
108 MO: D 5443, 28 April 1945.
109 MO: D 5338, 16 April 1945.
110 ibid., 25 April 1945.
111 MO: D 5358, 20 April 1945.
112 For example, see MO: D 5132. Also *Hansard*, 410, col. 214, 18 April 1945: Petherick; col. 831, 25 April 1945: Martin; col. 1863, 8 May 1945: Keeling; col. 1831, 8 May 1945: Smithers.
113 Caiger-Smith, *Face of the Enemy*, p. 77; *Illustrated London News*, 16 June 1945.
114 MO: D 5239, 21 April 1945; MO: D 5344, 20 April 1945.
115 PRO FO 898/300: PWE Central Directive, 26 June 1945 cited in Balfour, *Propaganda in War*, p. 302.
116 *Evening Standard*, 19 April 1945. See D. Low, *Years of Wrath: A Cartoon History 1932–1945*, London, 1986 for his other wartime cartoons and also C. Seymour-Ure and J. Schaff, *David Low*, London, 1985.
117 For Russell, see 'Whose Guilt?' in *Picture Post*, 16 June 1945; V. Gollancz, *What Buchenwald Really Means*, London, 1945.
118 MO: D 5378, 28 April 1945.
119 *Manchester Guardian*, 22 May 1945.
120 MO: FR 2228.
121 The exhibition is described by George Orwell in *Tribune*, 12 Jan. 1945.
122 *The Times*, 28 April 1945.
123 *Manchester Guardian*, letter to the editor, 25 April 1945.
124 *Hansard*, 410, cols. 213–14, 18 April 1945; for Silverman on the film of the Buchenwald delegation see cols. 1912–13, 9 May 1945.
125 *Reynolds News*, 22 April 1945.
126 *Tribune*, 20 April 1945.
127 *Manchester Guardian*, 16 April 1945.
128 ibid., 21 April 1945; *Daily Herald*, 23 April 1945.
129 *News of the World*, 22 April 1945.
130 *Daily Mail*, 24 April 1945; see also Gordon Walker's book on the war years, *The Lid Lifts*. A small number of other journalists noted the presence of Jewish people in the camps: Colin Wills in the *News Chronicle*, 19 April 1945 makes reference to Hungarian Jews in Belsen and the readers of the *Illustrated London News* were informed that the children there had suffered 'because they were Jewish-born' (28 April 1945). The point is that one has to look quite hard to find any reference to Jews in the newspapers, not to mention refer-ences which truly represented the suffering of the Jewish people.

131 *The Times*, 8 May 1945; *Manchester Guardian*, 26 April 1945.
132 MO: D 5390, 20 April 1945.
133 *The Times*, 20 April 1945.
134 MO: D 5390, 23 April 1945.
135 *Daily Herald*, 18 Sept. 1945; *Jewish Chronicle*, 12 Aug. 1945; Phillips, *Trial*, *passim*.
136 The original footage (which was never shown in 1945 for political reasons) is held by the Imperial War Museum and was incorporated into a Granada Television documentary, *A Painful Reminder*, broadcast on 8 Sept. 1985. On the making of the film and the decision not to show it, see: PRO INF 1/636; C. Moorehead, *Sidney Bernstein, A Biography*, London, 1984, pp. 164–9.
137 See Kushner, *Liberal Imagination, passim*.

## 3 BELSEN DISPLACED PERSONS' CAMP: BRITISH STATE RESPONSES

1 The designation of displaced person was given to an individual of Allied nationality who, at the end of hostilities and as a result of the war, found himself or herself living outside the boundaries of their own country.
2 Lord Strang, *Home and Abroad*, London, 1956, pp. 199–225, in particular pp. 218–19.
3 M. Pasley (ed.), *Germany: a Companion to German Studies*, London, 2nd edn, 1982, pp. 370–1.
4 ibid., pp. 373–5.
5 *Hansard*, 422 HC DEB 5s, cols. 1352–3, 10 May 1946; Strang, *Home and Abroad*, p. 231.
6 B. Horrocks, *A Full Life*, London, 1974, p. 268.
7 M.J. Proudfoot, *European Refugees, 1939–1952*, London, 1957, p. 159; see M. Wyman, *The D.P.s: Europe's Displaced Persons, 1945–1951*, Philadelphia, 1989 for a general overview of the DP problem.
8 See *Hansard*, 422, col. 1353, 10 May 1946.
9 Wyman, *The D.P.s*, p. 17.
10 F.S.V. Donnison, *Civil Affairs and Military Government in North West Europe, 1944–46*, London, 1961, p. 345.
11 *The Times*, 6 July 1945.
12 Wyman, *The D.P.s*, p. 64.
13 See *Hansard*, 422, col. 1360 for Hynd's statement.
14 Donnison, *Civil Affairs*, p. 344; PRO FO 1010/1: Report, week ending 19 May 1945, App. F; Report, 26 May, App. L.
15 PRO FO 1010/1: Report, 12 May 1945. Scholars working on contemporary documents, however, have shown that the Allied repatriation policy was often quite brutal. In June/July 1945 the British forcibly returned to the Eastern zone, from Austria, 22,500 Cossacks and Caucasians who had fought on the German side and were unwilling to return for fear of their lives. On this see: N. Tolstoy, *Victims of Yalta*, London, 1979; Wyman, *The D.P.s*, pp. 61–85; M.R. Marrus, *The Unwanted: European Refugees in the Twentieth Century*, Oxford, 1985, pp. 313–17; Proudfoot, *European Refugees*, pp. 189–229.
16 Y. Bauer, *Flight and Rescue*, New York, 1970, p. 51.
17 Proudfoot, *European Refugees*, p. 306.
18 Bauer, 'Death Marches', p. 2.
19 Bridgman, *End of the Holocaust*, quotes 32,000 while Lavsky in 'Day After' estimates 30,000.
20 PRO WO 171/4031: War Diary, 8 Corps.

21 PRO FO 1010/1/229: MG 2nd Army Weekly Summary, week ending 19 May, App. F.
22 PRO WO 171/8035: War Diary, 618 MGD; Sington, *Belsen Uncovered*, p. 204.
23 The figure of 17,000 is quoted in *British Zone Review*, 13 Oct. 1945; IWM (Docs) P78: Barker papers.
24 H. Leivick *et al.*, *Belsen*, Tel Aviv, 1957, p. 27.
25 ibid., pp. 89–90.
26 SUA Schonfeld 47: short biography of camp leaders.
27 Those with relatives abroad often chose to try for a visa to a relative's country rather than Palestine. In terms of perceived opportunities, many others would have chosen America over Palestine given a free choice: see A.L. Sacher, *The Redemption of the Unwanted*, New York, 1983, p. 171.
28 PRO FO 1010/1: week ending 26 May.
29 Leivick *et al.*, *Belsen*, p. 27; for the poor conditions in the Polish transit camp in Celle see IWM (Docs) 91/21/1(R): Horwell papers: report by J. Leverson, 23 May 1945.
30 Leivick, *Belsen*, pp. 27–9; see IWM (Docs) 91/21/1(R): Horwell papers.
31 Hardman, *Survivors*, pp. 85–6.
32 ibid., pp. 86–9.
33 IWM (Docs) 91/21/1(R): Horwell: letter from Lingen, Leverson to Horwell, 11 June 1945; report from Lingen, 6 June 1945.
34 *Jewish Chronicle*, 15 June 1945; indeed, some of the DPs actually enjoyed their stay at Lingen through the summer and thought of it as a vacation away from Belsen: see MJM (Sound Archive), C410/005: Bernstein.
35 Leivick *et al.*, *Belsen*, p. 29; S.J. Goldsmith, *Twenty Twentieth-Century Jews*, New York, 1962, p. 89.
36 L. Dinnerstein, *America and the Survivors of the Holocaust*, Columbia, NY, 1982, p. 28; Wyman, *The D.P.s*, p. 134.
37 Leivick *et al.*, *Belsen*, p. 35.
38 Sacher, *Redemption*, is an example of a work which concentrates on the American zone. An example of a more specific study is A. Grobman, *Rekindling the Flame: American Jewish Chaplains and the Survivors of European Jewry, 1944–1948*, Detroit, MI, 1993. Israeli historian Hagit Lavsky has recognised this imbalance and is currently researching a project on the British zone. See also U. Büttner, *Not nach der Befreiung: Die Situation der deutschen Juden in der britischen Besatzungszone 1945 bis 1948*, Hamburg, 1986, cited in J. Tydor Baumel, 'The Politics of Spiritual Rehabilitation in the D.P. Camps', *Simon Wiesenthal Centre Annual*, 1989, vol. 6, p. 57.
39 See R.W. Zweig, *Britain and Palestine During the Second World War*, London, 1986; M.J. Cohen, *Palestine: Retreat from the Mandate. The Making of British Policy, 1936–1945*, London, 1978.
40 J. Gorny, *The British Labour Movement and Zionism, 1917–1948*, London, 1983, pp. 188, 195.
41 PRO FO 1030/300: letter, Dewing (CCG) to WO, 18 Aug. 1945.
42 ibid.: letter, Weeks (CCG) to Marquess of Reading, London, 26 July 1945.
43 PRO FO 1049/81/177: Steel to Britten, 24 July 1945; see R. Crossman, *The Palestine Mission*, London, 1947, p. 27 for a similar expression of feeling.
44 SUA Schonfeld 130/2: Greenbaum to Cohen, 5 August 1945. See also CZA C/2527: Goldstoff, chairman, Committee of the Jewish community in Luneburg to Easterman, 5 Nov. 1945.
45 *Jewish Chronicle*, 4 May 1945.

46 IWM (Docs) 91/21/1(R): Horwell: letter, Levy to T.T. Scott (UNRRA), 16 May 1945.

47 *Jewish Chronicle*, 15 June 1945; *Jewish Standard*, 29 June 1945; *Jewish Chronicle*, 20 July 1945.

48 *The Times*, 21 July 1945.

49 See Dinnerstein, *America*, pp. 34–8 for the events leading up to Harrison's departure, and chap. 2, pp. 39–71 for the ramifications of the report. Dinnerstein also cites the report in full: App. B, 291–305; Sacher, *Redemption*, pp. 162–4.

50 ibid., Dinnerstein.

51 Bauer, *Out of the Ashes*, pp. 47–51; *Manchester Guardian*, 27 Aug., 13 Sept. 1945.

52 PRO FO 1030/300: telegram, Joint Staff Mission (Washington) to WO (London), 3 Aug. 1945; also PRO FO 1049/195/107.

53 PRO FO 1030/300: Directorate Civil Affairs, WO to Chief of Staff, CCG, 11 Aug. 1945.

54 PRO FO 1049/195/107: CCG to WO, 6 Sept. 1945.

55 *News Chronicle*, 31 July 1945; PRO FO 1030/301: letter, Randel, FO to Chief of Staff, 5 Sept. 1945.

56 ibid.: Britten to WO, Sept. 1945.

57 ibid.: Templar to Reading, 26 Oct. 1945.

58 PRO FO 1030/369: telegram, Exfor to 1 Brit. Corps, 19 June 1945.

59 PRO FO 1010/1/229: Weekly summary, 19 May 1945, App. A.

60 PRO FO 1049/81/177: telegram, FO to Washington, 5 Oct. 1945.

61 See Panikos article. C. Shindler, *Exit Visa: Detente, Human Rights and the Jewish Emigration Movement in the USSR*, London, 1978.

62 PRO FO 1010/1/229: Weekly summary, week ending 26 May 1945.

63 YV 0-70/4/1: minutes, 8 July 1945.

64 YV 0-70/4/2: minutes, 16 July 1945.

65 YV 0-70/25/4/11: programme and /17: resolutions; PRO FO 1049/195/107: report by Pickford, Sept. 1945; *Jewish Chronicle*, 21 Sept. 1945; *Jewish Standard*, 5 Oct. 1945.

66 PRO FO 1049/195/107: letter, Robertson to Sir Eric Speed, 6 Oct. 1945.

67 PRO FO 1049/195/107: Bovenschen (WO) to Sargent (FO), 10 Oct. 1945 and reply: Sargent to Cash, 24 Oct. 1945 (marginal notes by Robertson).

68 PRO FO 371/55705/410: Parliamentary question, Hynd to Orbach, 18 March 1946.

69 It is worth noting that at this stage many Zionists actually feared that the 100,000 certificates would be issued; such a gesture would take the sting from the tail of the claim for a Jewish state in Palestine: Marrus, *The Unwanted*, p. 335.

70 Gorny, *Labour Movement*, p. 188; Hebrew University [herafter HU], Institute of Contemporary History [hereafter ICH], Oral History Department [hereafter OHD]: Levenburg interview.

71 Bauer, *Out of the Ashes*, p. 49.

72 A. Bullock, *Ernest Bevin: Foreign Secretary*, London, 1983, p. 175.

73 *Hansard*, 415, cols. 1927–35, 13 Nov. 1945: statement by Bevin announcing the Anglo-American Committee of Enquiry; Crossman, *Palestine Mission*, *passim.*, is a participant's view of the enquiry.

74 Bullock, *Bevin*, p. 180; contrast the five recommendations put forward by the political sub-committee of the Zionist Federation of Great Britain: YV M-2/496, Jan. 1946.

75 ibid., p. 181.

76 PRO FO 1049/81/177: MG report, Nov. 1945.
77 ibid.
78 The author has been unable to trace any documentation on this incident from the Jewish side, therefore the account may not be a balanced one. It is not clear why Grande did not co-operate or what was the exact reaction of Lipka. Nevertheless, Lipka, after a trial, was given six months' imprisonment, the others one month to three months' or an acquittal. A lighter sentence was passed than usual in view of the fact they were ex-concentration camp prisoners: PRO FO 1049/81/177: Pink to King, 24 Dec. 1945.
79 PRO FO 1049/81/177: text reproduced in a telegram, King to Pink, no date (No. 08422).
80 Grande was German but he was also an Auschwitz survivor. Moreover, he had not been appointed to his post by the British authorities: PRO FO 1049/81/177: King to Pink, 29 Dec. 1945.
81 PRO FO 1049/195/107: Pink (Pol. Div., Berlin) to PW and DP Div., 24 Oct. 1945.
82 See PRO 1049/368: King to Pink, 20 Nov. 1946.
83 *New York Times*, 20 Nov. 1945; PRO FO 1049/195/107: CONCOMB to BERCOMB, Dec. 1945.
84 PRO FO 1049/81/177: draft telegram (secret), CONCOMB to FO, Dec. 1945.
85 *Hansard*, 417, cols. 1525–29, 20 Dec. 1945; PRO FO 1049/81/177, telegram, FO to Washington, 20 Dec. 1945.
86 See *Jewish Standard*, for example: 12 Oct. 1945; 30 Nov. 1945; 4 Jan. 1946; 18 Jan. 1946; 15 March 1946; 22 March 1946; 12 April 1946.
87 PRO FO 1049/195/107: telegram, FO to Lübbecke, 7 Dec. 1945 and Pol. Div. to Refugees Dept, 24 Dec. 1945; PRO FO 1049/81/177: draft telegram, CONCOMB to FO, Dec. 1945. Goldsmith also worked for the Jewish Telegraphic Agency.
88 The Belsen Committee consisted of the Belsen contingent of the Central Jewish Committee until March 1947 when a separate committee was elected.
89 PRO FO 1049/81/177: Kenchington (PW and DP) to HQ, 30 Corps District, 10 Dec. 1945 (see appended handwritten note for comments on Rosensaft's return); PRO 1049/195/107: Lübbecke to FO, 13 Dec. 1945.
90 PRO FO 1049/81/177: telegram, FO to Washington, 18 Dec. 1945; PRO FO 1049/367.
91 PRO FO 371/46959/4162: FO to WO, 6 Nov. 1945.
92 PRO FO 1049/195/107: Bovenschen (WO) to Sargent (FO), 10 Oct. 1945; this visit did take place and had a rousing effect on the political leaders in Belsen: see Leivick *et al.*, *Belsen*, p. 38.
93 PRO FO 1049/81/177: telegram, Pink to King, 21 Feb. 1946.
94 See Dinnerstein, *America*, *passim*, for a full account of the discussions and the other recommendations. See also Crossman, *Palestine Mission*, pp. 181–4. The Jewish Standard followed events closely, see most issues between 11 Jan. and 3 May 1946.
95 See Z. Warhaftig, *Uprooted: Jewish Refugees and Displaced Persons after Liberation*, New York, 1946, pp. 72–85 for the movement from Poland and British attempts to halt it.
96 PRO FO 1005/834 and /835: PW and DP Directorate, minutes, Dec. 1945; and see also /838 for the final meeting. By the end of 1945, 60 per cent of the DPs receiving aid from UNRRA in Europe were Poles; Wyman, *The D.P.s*, pp. 59–60.
97 Bauer, *Flight and Rescue*; Crossman, *Palestine Mission*, pp. 93–4.

98 Bauer, *Flight and Rescue*, introduction; Sacher, *Redemption*, pp. 149–51. It is estimated that, by 1946, 18,000 had reached Palestine, perhaps half of them illegally: M. Joyce Haron, 'Note: United States–British collaboration on Illegal Immigration to Palestine, 1945–1947', *Jewish Social Studies*, 1980–1, vol. 42–3, p. 177.

99 PRO FO 371/51525/3582: Friends Ambulance Unit, report on Berlin, Sept. 1945.

100 PRO FO 1049/81/177: Pink to King, 12 Dec. 1945.

101 See Bauer, *Flight and Rescue*, pp. 194–6 for the related Morgan affair. The head of UNRRA caused a storm with his statement on the organised nature of the Jewish migration; *Jewish Chronicle*, 4 Jan. 1946.

102 PRO FO 1049/367: Steel to FO (repeated to Warsaw and Lübbecke), 1 Feb. 1946.

103 Wyman, *The D.P.s*, pp. 143–4; Bauer, *Flight and Rescue*, p. 211.

104 HU, ICH, OHD: Swartz interview.

105 Wyman, *The D.P.s*, p. 154.

106 PRO FO 1049/417/95: top secret telegram, CONCOMB to BERCOMB, 30 July 1946 and reply, 2 Aug. 1946. See also in same file, report on interview with McAllen by Jones, 20 Aug. 1946.

107 VY: 0-70/6: Technical Instruction No. 6: Status and Treatment of DPs Living Outside Assembly Centres.

108 PRO FO 1049/417/95: top secret telegram, CONCOMB to BERCOMB, 1 Aug. 1946.

109 PRO FO 4049/417/95: report by Jones, 20 Aug. 1946.

110 See PRO FO 1049/417: top secret telegram, BERCOMB to CONFOLK, 2 Aug. 1946.

111 PRO FO 1071/39: CONFOLK to BERCOMB, 8, 13 Aug. 1946; for quote see PRO FO 1049/417 or 1071/39: BERCOMB to CONFOLK, 15 Aug. 1946. See also PRO FO 1005/1668: Niedersachen monthly reports, 1–31 Aug. 1946.

112 PRO FO 1049/417: BERCOMB to CONCOMB, 31 July 1946.

113 See PRO FO 1049/417: comment by Pink to King (secret), 31 Aug. 1946.

114 See also PRO FO 1049/417: top secret telegram, CONCOMB to BERCOMB, 30 July 1946 and BERCOMB to CONFOLK, 2 Aug. 1946; PRO FO 1049/799: FO to BERCOMB, 10 May 1947: MI5 had been asked to supply information on AJDC activities.

115 HU, ICH, OHD: Levinthal interview.

116 Britain held the same fears for Palestine, claiming that the illegal immigrants who reached Haifa were part of a communist plot: see Sacher, *Redemption*, pp. 186–7.

117 HU, OHD, ICH: L.E. Levinthal.

118 PRO FO 1049/417: Pink to King, 31 Aug. 1946.

119 PRO FO 1049/626: CONFOLK to BERCOMB, 31 Oct. 1946.

120 PRO FO 1049/626: telegram, Strang to FO, 14 Sept. 1946.

121 PRO FO 1049/147: PW and DP Div. (Belsen) to Chief, PW and DP Div., 23 April 1946. See also PRO FO 1049/626: BERCOMB to CONFOLK, 12 Nov. 1946: the incident was later remembered and held against Wollheim when he requested a visa to travel to London.

122 PRO FO 1049/417: Kenchington to DCOS (Policy), 30 June 1946; see handwritten note dated 4 May 1946.

123 Acceding to British pressure, American policy officially changed on 6 August 1946 when a statement was issued stating that all organised movements of

refugees entering the American zones would be turned back: Joyce Haron, 'United States–British Collaboration', p. 177.

124  PRO FO 1049/417: BERCOMB to CONFOLK, 15 Aug. 1946.
125  PRO FO 1070/39: HQ Intell. Div. to Entries and Exits Branch, 17 Aug. 1946.
126  PRO FO 1049/417: telegram, FO to San Jose, 28 July 1946 and Steel to FO, 29 July 1946.
127  PRO FO 1049/417: Holman in Bucharest to FO, 28 July 1946; see *The Times*, 9 Aug. 1946 for further diplomatic approaches designed to stop the illegal immigration and also PRO FO 1071/39: telegram, FO to various British embassies, 2 May 1947.
128  PRO FO 1049/417: Secretariat, Berlin to PW & DP Div., 9 Aug. 1946. NB: some pieces that have been withheld from this PRO file might be connected with the matter in hand or with the issue of the illegal immigration into the British zone.
129  See PRO FO 1049/417: Secretariat, Berlin to PW & DP, Berlin, 18 July 1946 for an example of the way British officials viewed the situation: following the announcement of the recommendations of the Anglo-American Committee of Enquiry, the Control Commission was asked to give 'the problem of [the] selection and movement of the Jewish Displaced Persons . . . urgent consideration'. A handwritten comment on the request reads: 'Isn't this a bit unrealistic viewed from the ruins of the King David Hotel?' See W.M. Louis, *The British Empire in the Middle East, 1945–1951*, Oxford, 1984 on this period.
130  PRO FO 1049/417: FO to Paris (Peace Conference Delegation), 11 Aug. 1946. The telegram, which included the whole statement on 'illegal immigration' to Palestine, stated that the announcement would be issued on 13 Aug.
131  ibid.: Secretariat, Lübbecke to PW & DP Div., 20 Aug. 1946.
132  PRO FO 1049/367: Chief, PW & DP Div. to Deputy Chief of Staff, 2 May 1946.
133  YV: 0-70/6: AJDC Survey, March 1946.
134  ibid.: King to IA & C Div., 9 May 1946.
135  PRO FO 1049/626: Steel to Dean, 8 Oct. 1946.
136  PRO FO 371/55705/410: Control Office to FO, Oct. 1946.
137  PRO FO 1049/626: Steel to Dean, personal and confidential, 8 Oct. 1946.
138  See *The Times*, 1 Aug. 1947 and the following day for comment on the murder of two British sergeants.
139  Gorny, *British Labour Movement*, pp. 197–200.
140  PRO FO 1049/798 or YV 0-70/9: Rosensaft to Solomon, 31 Jan. 1947.
141  PRO FO 1049/798: Ivimy to Kenchington, 11 Feb. 1947 and Dean to Robertson, 26 Feb. 1947. The documents are repeated in PRO FO 1049/2106.
142  PRO FO 1049/798: Brownjohn to PW & DP Div., 11 March 1947.
143  PRO FO 1049/799: PW & DP Div. to CONFOLK, 9 May 1947.
144  YV 0-70/8; Franshaw to Rosensaft, 12 Dec. 1947.
145  PRO FO 1071/41: Entries and Exit Branch, Bocholt to E and E Branch, Berlin, monthly report, 16 April 1947. In same file: CCG, PW & DP Div., Technical Instruction No. 13: Emigration of Jewish DPs to Palestine.
146  PRO FO 1049/2106: FO to BERCOMB, 16 May 1947.
147  PRO FO 1049/798: Ivimy, CONFOLK to Secretariat, Berlin, 21 March 1947.
148  ibid.: Com. Services Div. to CONCOMB, 12 Feb. 1947.
149  PRO FO 1049/799: Bishop to FO, 12 June 1947.
150  PRO FO 1049/800: Pol. Div., Berlin to Eastern Dept, FO, 12 Aug. 1947; Warhaftig, *Uprooted*, p. 80.
151  PRO FO 1049/800: Thickenesse, PW & DP Div. to Political Div., Berlin, 8 Aug. 1947.

152 PRO FO 1049/799: FO to Berlin, 5 June 1947.
153 PRO FO 1049/800: Intelligence, British Consulate, Frankfurt to London, 28 July 1947.
154 See T. Kushner, 'Anti-Semitism and Austerity: the August 1947 Riots in Britain', in P. Panayi (ed.), *Racial Violence in Britain, 1840–1950*, Leicester, 1993, pp. 149–68.
155 PRO FO 1049/800: British Consulate, Frankfurt to FO, 11 Aug. 1947.
156 YV 0-70/8: Easterman to Rosensaft; see PRO FO 1049/800: Rosensaft and Wollheim to Kenchington, undated for the text of the statement.
157 PRO FO 1049/2106: PW & DP, LEMGO to PW & DP, Berlin, 10 July 1947; Brownjohn to Bishop, 12 July; FO to BERCOMB, 16 July; BERCOMB to CONFOLK, 19 July.
158 YV 0-70/17: Dallob to Katzlin, 3 March 1948; PRO FO 1005/1670: Niedersachen monthly report, Feb. 1948.
159 See Kushner, *Persistence of Prejudice*, pp. 119–22 on this type of stereotypical accusation.
160 YV 0-70/9: Rosensaft to Solomon, 31 March 1948; *The Star*, 22 March 1948.
161 YV 0-70/9: Solomon to Rosensaft, 17 March 1948.
162 YV 0-70/7: Rosensaft to Kenchington, 16 July 1948.
163 ibid.
164 ibid.: Rosensaft to Kenchington, 10 Aug. 1948.
165 *Manchester Guardian*, 30 July 1947.
166 YV 0-70/6: Clarke to Relief Detach., Celle, no date.
167 ibid.: Public Safety, Niedersachen to PW & DP Div., 8 July 1948.
168 PRO FO 1071/39: 2 May 1947.
169 Goldsmith, *Twenty Jews*, pp. 89–90. See Y. Gelber, 'The Historical Role of the Central European Immigration to Israel', *Leo Baeck Institute Yearbook*, 1993, vol. 38, p. 339.
170 See SUA A793, the papers of A.C. Barclay who commanded the military escort on the *Runnymede Park*, one of the three British ships used to return the Jews to Europe; see coverage of the incident in *The Times*, 22 July 1947 to 11 Sept. 1947. Most major newspapers reported regularly on the story: see the Barclay file for various press clippings.
171 See Bullock, *Bevin*, p. 449.
172 SUA Barclay: report, 3 Sept. 1947.
173 On American protest see Joyce Haron, 'United States–British Collaboration', pp. 178–9.
174 CZA C2/510: Barou to Brotman, 25 August 1947; PRO FO 1010/30: report by Fowler, 7 Sept. 1947.
175 Marrus, *The Unwanted*, p. 339.
176 *The Times*, 29 Sept. 1947 and 6 Oct. 1947.
177 YV 0-70/17: Dallob and Bloomberg to Central Committee, 4 Sept. 1947.
178 PRO FO 1005/1669: Niedersachen monthly reports, Oct. 1947.
179 Sacher, *Redemption*, p. 185.
180 YV 0-70/9: FO to Solomon, 24 Feb. 1948; CZA C2/524: Rosensaft to Barou, WJC, 24 March 1948; SUA Schonfeld 130/1: JCRA Bulletin, 8 March 1948.
181 PRO FO 1071/41: Report, 28 Jan. 1949.
182 ibid.: BERCOMB to FO, 8 Dec. 1948; CCG PW & DP Div., Technical Instruction No. 33, 4 Jan. 1949.
183 PRO FO 1005/1672: Monthly reports, July and Sept. 1950.
184 YV 0-70/10: Br. Sect. WJC, Executive to Rosensaft, 12 Dec. 1951.
185 PRO FO 1005/1700: Intelligence Reviews, nos. 14, 15 and 17.

## 4 ANGLO-JEWISH RESPONSES

1 V.D. Lipman, *Social History of the Jews in England 1850–1950*, London, 1954; Alderman, *Modern British Jewry*.
2 M. Raven, 'British Jewry in Heavy Weather', *Commentary*, 1947, vol. 3, no. 5, p. 448.
3 SUA Hertz 94/3: letter to the community in his role as the patron of the Chief Rabbi's Religious Emergency Council, 2 July 1943; SUA AJA 37/16/34: Annual General Meeting, 2 July 1942.
4 ibid., Stein.
5 SUA CCJ 2/3: council meeting, 26 Sept. 1949, comments by Landman.
6 See S. Gewirtz, 'Anglo-Jewish Responses to Nazi Germany 1933–39: the Anti-Nazi Boycott and the Board of Deputies of British Jews', *Journal of Contemporary History*, 1991, vol. 26, no. 2, pp. 268–9; Alderman, *Modern British Jewry*, p. 231.
7 See Alderman, *Modern British Jewry*, pp. 202–3.
8 N. Bentwich, *They Found Refuge: An Account of British Jewry's Work for Victims of Nazi Oppression*, London, 1956, p. 121.
9 SUA AJA 37/6/6/17: refugee pamphlets.
10 SUA Hertz 94/3: appeal for volunteers, Sept. 1943; SUA Schonfeld 130/2, file 2: *passim*.
11 SUA Hertz 94/3: 18 Jan. 1944.
12 SUA Hertz 94/3: letter to the community, 2 July 1943; SUA Schonfeld 123, file 3: letter to Greenberg, 1 Jan. 1945; SUA Schonfeld 196: leaflet, undated.
13 Bentwich, *Refuge*, p. 74.
14 ibid., p. 130. See the testimony of Alice Fink, 'My Lifestory' in the Wiener Library (4110): born in Berlin in 1920, she emigrated to Britain in 1938 and during the war trained as a nurse. She was one of the first to join the JCRA training scheme and went to Belsen in 1945. She herself had lost many relatives in the Holocaust.
15 SUA Schonfeld 197: WO to Schonfeld, 27 June 1945; SUA Schonfeld 222.
16 *Jewish Monthly*, Sept. 1947, no. 6, p. 20.
17 United Synagogue, file 1931, concentration camps, 1945, quoted in Bolchover, *British Jewry*, pp. 72–3.
18 SUA Schonfeld 130/1: Carlebach to Henriques, 4 Dec. 1947 and reply, 5 Dec.
19 SUA Hertz 79/3: Sternberg to Hertz, 1 June 1945.
20 See SUA Schonfeld 287: Greenberg to REC, 12 Sept. 1945; Schonfeld 196: Greenberg to Pels, 26 April 1945.
21 Central British Fund papers [hereafter CBF], SUA, 26/144: Zarbac to Burnett, Sept. 1945.
22 SUA Schonfeld 287: Mozes to Greenberg, 15 July 1945.
23 See SUA Schonfeld 286 or 288 for an idea of the level of correspondence the CCREC had to deal with.
24 SUA Schonfeld 286: Gold to Schonfeld, 28 Sept. 1945.
25 SUA Schonfeld 292: CCREC to Silberstein, 5 July 1947.
26 SUA Schonfeld 297: CCREC to Reinman, 14 Jan. 1947.
27 SUA Schonfeld 436: Moses to Orbach, 6 May 1946.
28 SUA Schonfeld 195/2: meetings 18 Oct. 1945, 8 April 1946, 2 April 1946.
29 ibid.: Grunfeld to Schonfeld, 2 April 1946.
30 SUA Schonfeld 288: Munk to Schonfeld, 10 July 1945. There were other orphaned children in Belsen but the Central Jewish Committee made the decision that they should remain in Germany and await transfer to Palestine rather than travel to Britain. They were cared for and schooled in the superb surround-

ings of the Warburg family estate at Blankenese: Leivick, *Belsen*, p. 31; *Zionist Review*, letter from the CJC defending its decision, 14 Dec. 1945.

31 CBF 37/198: Care of Children, M. Gilbert, *The Boys*.
32 Bentwich, *Refuge*, pp. 123–4.
33 CBF 26/144: Stiebels to Wood, 11 Sept. 1946.
34 CBF 26/144: Zarbac to Burnett, Sept. 1945.
35 SUA Schonfeld 196: Kibel to Schonfeld, 24 March 1945.
36 See, for example, MO D 5376: 14–21 Sept. 1945 and MO D 5401: 26 Sept. 1945; also N. Bentwich, *My 77 Years: An Account of my Life and Times, 1883–1960*, Philadelphia, PA, 1961, p. 226.
37 SUA Schonfeld 123, file 3; letters to *Jewish Chronicle*, 5 March and 8 June 1945.
38 SUA Hertz 55/3: Jewish Weekly, 27 July 1945.
39 For example, see the half-page advertisement in *Zionist Review*, 30 March, p. 4 and their call for readers to support it, 13 April, p. 1. Prominent advertisements were also placed in the *Jewish Chronicle* and other journals including *Gates of Zion*: see issues during 1947.
40 CBF 5/34: Annual Report 1945; see *Jewish Chronicle*, 21 Sept. 1945 for criticisms of the clothing that was donated for the camps; some of it was hardly 'fit for rags'.
41 CBF 8/46: minutes, 16 Oct. 1947, 18 Nov. 1948.
42 On the lack of donations and general interest in the issue of DPs in Germany see *Jewish Chronicle*, 9 Sept. 1945, 5 July 1946, 10 Jan. 1947, 14 Nov. 1947.
43 SUA Schonfeld 130/1: Most to Pels, 22 Nov. 1946.
44 The organisers behind the United Palestine Apppeal for 1945 agreed to postpone their launch until later in the year to give the CBF a free run: CZA C2/60: Reading to Easterman, 27 Dec. 1944; but in 1946 and 1947 the CBF struggled.
45 SUA Schonfeld 440/4: report of conference, 30 Oct. 1947.
46 CBF 21/111: Montefiore fund raising appeal.
47 CBF 23/122: Functions organiser to Capt. Bulkely-Johnson, 12 April 1950.
48 SUA Schonfeld 297: report on CCREC Executive meeting, 8 Dec. 1947.
49 SUA Schonfeld 292: Schonfeld to Rabbinate in Belsen, 3 Feb. 1947; see Schonfeld 144: the CCREC had sent regular cigarette consignments, a useful currency in Germany, to pay the salaries of religious officials.
50 SUA Schonfeld 833: Schonfeld to brother, 14 Sept. 1945.
51 SUA Schonfeld 82/1, file 1: Schonfeld to Brodie, 29 June 1948.
52 SUA Schonfeld 416, file 2: 16 May 1947.
53 SUA Schonfeld 196: Pels to Skrek, 11 Oct. 1944.
54 CBF 26/144: Steibels to Wood, 11 Sept. 1946.
55 SUA Schonfeld 302: Eppel to Schonfeld, 28 Dec. 1946.
56 CZA C2/670: Easterman to Hayes, 8 Oct. 1945.
57 Cited in Alderman, *Modern British Jewry*, p. 303.
58 Gates of Zion, Jan. 1947, vol. 1, no. 2, pp. 25–6.
59 CBF 21/111: Montefiore fund raising appeal.
60 Bolchover, *British Jewry*, p. 73.
61 See T. Kushner, 'Sex and Semitism: Jewish Women in Britain in War and Peace', in P. Panayi, *Minorities in Wartime*, pp. 118–49.
62 SUA Schonfeld 142: Moss to Schonfeld, 31 July 1945; see also Schonfeld 186/3: Major Leon to Schonfeld, 19 April 1947, feeling that there were 'too many individual efforts all designed to help the same object'.
63 SUA Hertz 116/2: Hertz to Rothschild, 19 Oct. 1945.
64 CBF 23/123: 'Picture of Relief – An Outline' by L. Cohen for the *Jewish Chronicle*, 19 Jan. 1945; although see also C2/60: Reading to Bentwich,

24 May 1945, on his belief that there was too much duplicity within JCRA itself and that more co-ordination was needed.
65 See HU, ICH, OHD: interviews with Lipman, Swartz and Schwartz.
66 SUA Schonfeld 130/2, file 2: minutes, JCRA Executive meeting, 25 Jan. 1945.
67 SUA Schonfeld 123, file 3: Schonfeld to Greenberg, 12 July 1945.
68 SUA AJA 37/6/6/14: comments by Brodetsky, London conference of Jewish organisations 1946, 26 Feb.
69 CZA C2/60: Reading to Bentwich, 24 May 1945.
70 SUA AJA 37/4/7: General Purposes and Foreign Committee, 17 May 1945: consideration of Brodetsky's approach.
71 CZA C2/516: Rubenstein to BOD, 29 May 1945, 1 June 1945, 4 June 1945.
72 Quoted in *Zionist Review*, 6 July 1945, p. 7.
73 CZA C2/2516: minutes, 13 June 1945; also in CBF 12/64.
74 *Zionist Review*, 6 July 1945, p. 2.
75 CBF 12/64: memorandum, 25 June 1945.
76 ibid.: report on the meeting of the CJG, 25 July 1945.
77 PRO FO 1049/195: Office of the Chief of Staff to WO, 18 Aug. 1945 and Britten, MG HQ to WO, 27 July 1945.
78 See also: CBF 12/64 or SUA Schonfeld 151: Mason to CJG, 20 Sept. 1945; SUA AJA 37/1/5: council meeting, 17 Oct. 1945.
79 CBF 12/64: BOD to Mason, 9 Oct. 1945.
80 ibid.: Brodetsky to Hynd, Jan. 1946.
81 See, for example, SUA Schonfeld 151: minutes, Cohen report, 15 Aug. 1945 and Henriques report, 12 Dec. 1945.
82 SUA Schonfeld 151: minutes, 19 Feb. 1946.
83 SUA AJA 37/4/7: European Committee, 25 Nov. 1946.
84 ibid.: General Purpose and Foreign Committee, 24 June 1947.
85 Bentwich, *They Found Refuge*, p. 14.
86 See, for example, Gewirtz, 'Anglo-Jewish Responses' and Alderman, *Modern British Jewry*, ch. 6.
87 CZA C2/516: Zelmanovitz to Brotman, 20 June 1945.
88 SUA AJA 37/4/7: General Purposes and Foreign Committee, 8 Oct. 1947.
89 There is not the space here to discuss Anglo-Jewish political life. See my doctoral thesis, 'Britain and Belsen', University of Southampton, 1994, pp. 226–45 for a limited examination of communal politics in this period.
90 SUA Hertz 116/2: Hertz to Rothschild, 19 Oct. 1945.
91 SUA Schonfeld 130/2: minutes, JCRA Executive meeting, 6 Sept. 1945.
92 ibid.
93 HU, ICH, OHD: Schwartz interview.
94 For general observations on the work of the JRU see: N. Bentwich, 'The Relief Units in Germany', *Jewish Monthly*, Feb. 1948, no. 11, pp. 30–6 and *They Found Refuge, passim*.
95 SUA Hertz 94/3.
96 SUA Schonfeld 50: Kritzler to Pels, 17 Nov. 1945.
97 ibid.: Schonfeld to Baumgarten, 27 Aug. 1945.
98 SUA Schonfeld 615/7, file 1: Schonfeld to *Jewish Chronicle*, 7 Oct. 1945.
99 SUA Schonfeld 366: Stephany to Schonfeld, 12 July 1945 and reply, 27 July 1945.
100 SUA Hertz 118/2, file 2: Brodetsky to Hertz, 17 Oct. 1945.
101 ibid.: Hertz to Brodetsky, 24 Oct. 1945.
102 CBF 25/127: report by Cohen and Pollitzer on Germany, 25 Nov. 1946.
103 SUA Schonfeld 222: Kahan to Rabbi Rosen, 2 Sept. 1946.

104 SUA Schonfeld 227/1: Lunzer to Schonfeld, 16 May 1946 and reply, 19 May 1946.
105 SUA Schonfeld 130/1: Schonfeld to Joseph, 2 Jan. 1947 and reply 30 Jan. 1947.
106 SUA Schonfeld 130/2: Cohen to Hertz, 18 July 1945.
107 ibid.: Cohen to Schonfeld, 20 July 1945.
108 ibid.: Salaman to Cohen, 24 July 1945.
109 ibid.: Schonfeld to Cohen, 26 July 1945.
110 SUA Schonfeld 123, file 4: Schonfeld to Greenberg, 12 Dec. 1945; see also file 3 for Greenberg's letter, 16 Aug. where Vilenski is described as a 'good man' as opposed to 'our assimilated specimens'.
111 SUA Schonfeld 440/2: Lunzer to CBF, 20 Jan. 1947; see also more public letter to the *Jewish Chronicle*, 17 Jan. 1947 and reply by Rothschild in the issue of 24 Jan. 1947.
112 CZA WJC C2/528: Barou to Easterman, 24 Dec. 1946.
113 SUA Schonfeld 440/2: Lunzer's letter.
114 SUA Schonfeld 123, file 4: Schonfeld to Greenberg, 17 Aug. 1945.
115 SUA Schonfeld 130/2: Schonfeld to Salaman, 20 Aug. 1945; see also Schonfeld 50: Salaman to Baumgarten, 17 Aug. 1945.
116 SUA Schonfeld 123: Schonfeld to Greenberg, 26 Sept. 1945.
117 SUA Schonfeld 130/2: Salaman to Hertz, 21 Sept. 1945.
118 ibid.: Hertz to Salaman, 25 Sept. 1945.
119 SUA Schonfeld 50, file 3: Schonfeld to Handler, 26 Sept. 1945; see also Schonfeld 123, file 4: CCREC Executive meeting, 16 Sept. 1945.
120 SUA Schonfeld 227/1: proposal for a Jewish reserve in the Azores, 15 Feb. 1946.
121 SUA Schonfeld 771/2: Schonfeld to Colonial Office, West Indies Dept, 12 Feb. 1947.
122 ibid. The small island of 240 acres near Abaco was to cost £7,000 0s 0d to buy.
123 SUA Schonfeld 416, file 2: letter to Schonfeld, 3 July 1947; for the Zionist reaction to the earliest version of the plan in 1945, see *Zionist Review*, 6 July 1945, p. 6.
124 SUA AJA 37/6/1a/1: Henriques, 1945.
125 See R. Webster, 'American Relief and Jews in Germany, 1945–1960: Diverging Perspectives', *Leo Baeck Institute Yearbook*, 1993, vol. 38, pp. 306–10, 312–15; also R. Webster, 'Why They Returned. How They Fared. Jews in Germany after 1945', *YIVO Annual of Jewish Social Science*, 1993.
126 SUA AJA 37/1/6: report of the Foreign Affairs Committee, Council meeting, 14 Nov. 1950.
127 SUA AJA 37/6/4/16: Brotman to Defence Committee, 1950.
128 SUA AJA 37/4/7: General Purpose Committee minutes, 15 June, 19 Nov. 1949.
129 CBF 12/64: Henriques to Wollheim, 19 Dec. 1950.

# 5 THE SURVIVORS

1 See Z. Mankowitz, 'The Affirmation of Life in She'erith Hapleita', in *Holocaust and Genocide Studies*, 1990, vol. 5, no. 1, pp. 13–21; NB: the term *She'erith Hapleita* (used with a variety of spellings) can be translated as 'The Saved Remnant'. There is some disagreement about to whom exactly the term applies, whether to the entire Jewish people remaining after the Holocaust or, more specifically, to those Jewish survivors who, between 1945 and 1952, converged on the occupied zones of Germany, Austria and Italy (the author uses the latter

definition). See the review essay by D. Michman, 'She'erit Hapletah, 1944–1948: Rehabilitation and Political Struggle', in *Holocaust and Genocide Studies*, Spring 1993, vol. 7, no. 1, pp. 107–9 for this debate concerning definition; for a critique of the role of the Holocaust in the creation of the Israeli state, see E. Friesel, 'The Holocaust and the Birth of Israel', *Wiener Library Bulletin*, 1979, vol. 32, nos. 49–50, pp. 51–60.

2 Mankowitz, 'Affirmation of Life', p. 20.
3 Levi committed suicide in 1987.
4 P. Levi, *The Drowned and the Saved*, London, 1989, pp. 11–12.
5 On Belsen see: Laqueur, *Bergen-Belsen – Tagebuch 1944/1945*; H. Lévy-Hass, *Vielleicht war das alles erst der Anfang. Tagebuch aus dem KZ Bergen-Belsen 1944–1945*, ed. E. Geisel, Berlin, 1979 and the English edition *Inside Belsen*, Brighton, 1982; Trepman used original diary notes in his book, *Among Men and Beasts*. Not only was it illegal to keep a diary in the camps but writing materials were difficult to come by: H. Langbein, *Against All Hope: Resistance in the Nazi Concentration Camps 1939–1945*, London, 1994, p. 64 suggests that prisoners in Belsen were aided in their endeavours to keep a diary by the disorganisation of the camp. Indeed Lévy-Hass wrote that in the last months of the war, SS personnel were 'very careful not to get too close to the inmates', *Vielleicht*, p. 61.
6 Ferderber-Salz, *And the Sun*, p. 152.
7 H. Fried, *Fragments of a Life: The Road to Auschwitz*, London, 1990, pp. 132, 139.
8 IWM (S), Knoller, 9092/13, r. 13.
9 Trepman, *Men and Beasts*, p. 221.
10 See the chapter on J. Brandes-Brilleslijper in Lindwer, *Last Seven Months*, p. 76.
11 Perl, *Doctor in Auschwitz*, p. 172.
12 Weinberg, *Self Portrait*, p. 85.
13 MJM Sound Archive, C410/005, Bernstein, r. 7B (transcript p. 79) and IWM (S), Abisch, 9181/11, r. 8; YV, 033/6, Survivor Testimony (German), p. 80.
14 Perl, *Doctor in Auschwitz*, p. 173.
15 IWM (S) 9092/13, r. 13.
16 IWM (S) 9181/11, r. 8.
17 IWM (S) 9092/13, r. 12; MJM C410/005, r. 7B (trans. p. 82); YV, 033/6, p. 81.
18 YV, 033/6, p. 81.
19 S. Feder, 'The Yiddish Theatre of Belsen' in Leivick *et al.*, *Belsen*, p. 135.
20 Trepman, *Men and Beasts*, p. 221.
21 See the chapter on B. Evers-Emden in Lindwer, *Last Seven Months*, pp. 131–32.
22 Fried, *Fragments*, p. 161; IWM (S) 9092/13, r. 12.
23 Fried, *Fragments*, p. 160.
24 IWM (S), Tribich, 9121/4, r. 3.
25 IWM (S), Dessau, 9236/4, r. 4; for a witness to this varied reaction see Bick-Berkowitz, *Where Are My Brothers?*, p. 111.
26 A. Sassoon, *Agnes: How My Spirit Survived*, Edgware, Mx, 1985, p. 50.
27 IWM (S), Brunstein, 9122/5, r. 4.
28 Sassoon, *Agnes*, p. 50. See ch. 1 for some of the difficulties faced by patients and nursing staff in the early days of liberation.
29 Levi, *Drowned and Saved*, p. 52.
30 For example, see Hart, *Return to Auschwitz*, p. 14. In Gill, *Journey Back*, p. 154, Hart states: 'In some ways the suffering I endured in the early post-war years was worse than it had been in the KZ'; Josef Rosensaft notes a similar feeling, this time with regard to the DP situation, in Leivick *et al.*, *Belsen*, p. 25:

'From a psychological viewpoint the years 1945 and 1946 . . . were more oppressive to our souls than the years in the hell of *Auschwitz and Belsen*' (his italics).

31 IWM (S) 9181/11, r. 9. See also Trepman, *Men and Beasts*, pp. 227–8; he walked all day with a friend as far as Follingbostel POW camp (approximately 20 km from Belsen). The ex-prisoners there had plenty of Red Cross parcels and Trepman returned to Belsen loaded with supplies.

32 IWM (S) 9092/13, r. 12; see also IWM (S) 9181/11, r. 9 on prisoner reprisals. In fact, in the testimonies one finds very few references to the need for personal revenge on behalf of the Jewish survivors.

33 IWM (S) 9092/13, r. 12.

34 This is commonly mentioned in the testimonies; see, for example, the interview with 'K' in Gill, *Journey Back*, p. 194.

35 IWM (S) 9122/5, r. 4.

36 Trepman, *Men and Beasts*, p. 225.

37 MJM C410/005, r. 8A (trans. p. 90).

38 ibid., r. 7B–8A, (trans. pp. 87–91).

39 Ferderber-Salz, *And the Sun*, p. 165.

40 ibid.

41 ibid., pp. 15–17.

42 Bick-Berkowitz, *Where Are My Brothers?*, p. 110; see the comments by E. Tanay, 'On Being a Survivor' in A. Berger (ed.), *Bearing Witness to the Holocaust 1939– 1989*, New York, 1991, pp. 21–2 and *passim*.

43 Trepman, *Men and Beasts*, p. 223.

44 N. Wollheim, 'Belsen's Place in the Process of "Death-and-Rebirth" of the Jewish People' in Leivick *et al.*, *Belsen*, p. 53; the title and the final words of the memoir of Sarah Bick-Berkowitz, also sum up this feeling: 'I was on my way to a new life. But where are my brothers?' (*Where Are My Brothers?*, p. 121).

45 Perl, *Doctor in Auschwitz*, pp. 183–4.

46 For the difficulties in trying to trace individuals in the chaos of Europe, see, for example, SUA Schonfeld 366: CBF draft annual report, 1945, p. 14.

47 Hardman, *Survivors*, p. 53.

48 Fried, *Fragments*, p. 162.

49 Trepman, *Men and Beasts*, pp. 223–7.

50 Ferderber-Salz, *And the Sun*, p. 166.

51 ibid., p. 167.

52 IWM (S) 9181/11, r. 9; see also Trepman, *Men and Beasts*, p. 228; IWM (S) 9236/4, r. 4.

53 Sington, *Belsen Uncovered*, p. 154; see also interview with 'A' in Gill, *Journey Back*, p. 404 and Lasker-Wallfisch, *Inherit the Truth*.

54 Perl, *Doctor in Auschwitz*, pp. 173–4.

55 ibid., p. 82.

56 Hardman, *Survivors*, p. 61; see ibid., ch. 8 as a whole for Hardman's account of his meeting with Perl (who is given the pseudonym Marta).

57 Perl, *Doctor in Auschwitz*, pp. 187–9.

58 Bick-Berkowitz, *Where Are My Brothers?*, pp. 114–18.

59 Fried, *Fragments*, p. 165.

60 MJM C410/005, r. 8A (trans. pp. 96–9).

61 Fried, *Fragments*, p. 168; this attitude towards post-liberation life, especially in the case of the younger survivors, often gave onlookers the impression that they were fully rehabilitated after their camp experience. More often, however, the individual had simply managed to bury the hurt temporarily and it would emerge in one form or another later in life.

62 Sassoon, *Agnes*, p. 53.
63 See, for example, Turgel *I Light a Candle*, who married a British Intelligence officer.
64 MJM C410/005, r. 8A (trans. p. 99).
65 Perl, *Doctor in Auschwitz*, p. 182.
66 ibid., p. 183; see also Hardman, *Survivors*, p. 64.
67 Perl, *Doctor in Auschwitz*, p. 178.
68 MJM C410/005, r. 8A (trans. pp. 101–2).
69 Hardman, *Survivors*, pp. 33–5.
70 ibid., p. 93.
71 ibid., pp. 77, 109–10.
72 Fried, *Fragments*, p. 175.
73 See Gill, *Journey Back*, ch. 5.
74 IWM (S) 9236/4, r. 4.
75 See SUA Schonfeld 130/2: Henriques to JCRA, 3 Aug. 1945 for the small Jewish quarter that was established in Celle around the old synagogue (the latter still exists today as a museum).
76 IWM (S) 9181/11, r. 10–11.
77 This was made clear in the *Report of the Anglo-American Committee of Enquiry regarding the problems of European Jewry and Palestine*, Miscellaneous paper, no. 8, London, 1946; see letter by Leslie Hardman in *Jewish Chronicle*, 24 Jan. 1947.
78 Bernstein in Gill, *Journey Back*, p. 141.
79 See, for example, MJM C410/005, r. 8B (trans. p. 104), Palestine was not a consideration for the 18-year-old Bernstein. See also Hart in Gill, *Journey Back*, p. 155: she notes that she wanted to distance herself from Jewish life, 'all Judaism has ever done for me is destroy my life'; see YV, Rosensaft 070/43–60 for a card catalogue of the names of those people who left Belsen, 1947–9: although Palestine/Israel attracted more Jewish DPs from Belsen than any other single country, nevertheless, thousands of people preferred to settle in numerous other countries including the United States, Canada, Australia and New Zealand, various states in South America and other European countries.
80 The CBF agreed with the British Government to provide a home for 1,000 concentration camp children on a temporary basis. In addition, other groups of Jewish children were brought from Poland by Rabbi Solomon Schonfeld under the auspices of the Chief Rabbi's Religious Emergency Council; for example, see SUA Schonfeld 82/1, file 1 and 302.
81 See interview with Margareta Burkill who worked with the Cambridge Refugee Committee: IWM (S) 004588/08, r. 8 (trans. p. 58). Also C. Blackstock, *Wednesday's Children*, London, 1967, pp. 26, 28: Blackstock became the secretary of the Jewish Children's Scheme in 1948; she did not expect then that the post would last for five years.
82 See Gill, *Journey Back*, pp. 7-8, 58.
83 For example, *The Living Memory of the Jewish Community* is an oral history archive within the National Life Story Collection at the British Library National Sound Archive in London. In-depth interviews have been conducted with Holocaust survivors and the second generation. In the USA an important collection of video testimonies is held at the Fortunoff Video Archive for Holocaust Testimonies at Yale University. See L.L. Langer, *Holocaust Testimonies: The Ruins of Memory*, New Haven, CT and London, 1991, as the result of a project based on this latter collection. The Shoah Foundation, funded by Steven Spielberg is involved in an extensive video-testimony project with Holo-

caust eye-witnesses all over the world. The medical profession has also taken an interest in the second generation, see, for example, S. Davidson, 'Transgenerational Transmission in the Families of Holocaust Survivors', *International Journal of Family Psychiatry*, 1980, vol. 1, no. 1, pp. 95–111.

84  On this see Y. Zerubavel, 'The Death of Memory and the Memory of Death: Masada and the Holocaust as Historical Metaphors', *Reflections*, 1994, no. 45, p. 80.
85  K. Hart, *I Am Alive*, London and New York, 1962 and *Return to Auschwitz*.
86  Hart, *Return to Auschwitz*, p. 17; see also her testimony in Gill, *Journey Back*, p. 152.
87  ibid., pp. 11–12.
88  The journalist was Gill; see *Journey Back*, pp. 137–43 for the interview with Bernstein.
89  MJM C410/005, r. 8B (trans. p. 115).
90  ibid., r. 9A (trans. pp. 124–6).
91  Quoted in Gill, *Journey Back*, p. 74.
92  ibid., p. 424.
93  ibid., p. 154.
94  ibid., p. 281.
95  See the chapter on van Amerongen-Frankfoorder in Lindwer, *Last Seven Months*, p. 89.
96  D. Rabinowitz, *New Lives: Survivors of the Holocaust Living in America*, New York, 1976, p. 93.
97  Testimony of 'A' in Gill, *Journey Back*, p. 405.
98  Rabinowitz, *New Lives*, p. 93.
99  Fried, *Fragments*, p. 179 (these questions she faced in Sweden).
100  See *Jewish Socialist*, 1991, no. 24, p. 23.
101  MJM C410/005, r. 8B (trans. pp. 106–15); Josephs, *Survivors*, pp. 177–9.
102  MJM C410/005, r. 9A (trans. pp. 121–2); see also Gill, *Journey Back*, p. 143, here Bernstein does not mention the matron but only the fact that she could not cope with being continually surrounded by death once again.
103  IWM (S) 9181/11, r. 11; the interview does not make clear at what time of year the incident took place. In 1947, however, we should bear in mind that the background of the violence between the British and the Jewish community in Palestine caused considerable tensions in Britain. On this see Kushner, 'Anti-Semitism and Austerity', pp. 149–68. See M. Banton, *The Coloured Quarter*, London, 1955 – an early postwar study of the Black community in Stepney – for the insult meant by placing him 'with the Africans'.
104  For example, see IWM (S) 9122/5, r. 5.
105  IWM (S) 004588/08, r. 6 (trans. p. 44).
106  Cited by Brunstein: see *Jewish Socialist*, 1991, no. 24, p. 24 (the Yiddish newspaper was *Di Tzeit*).
107  IWM 9236/4, r. 4.
108  IWM (S) 004588/08, r. 6 (trans. p. 44); IWM 9181/11, r. 11.
109  Gill, *Journey Back*, p. 180.
110  See *Jewish Socialist*, 1991, no. 24, p. 23; these feelings have been echoed by Birkin, talking of England, and Unger on Israel: see Gill, *Journey Back*, pp. 423, 281 respectively.
111  Blackstock, *Wednesday's Children*, pp. 166–7.
112  IWM (S) 004588/08, r. 6 (trans. p. 45).
113  *Jewish Socialist*, 1991, no. 24, p. 23.
114  Comments by IWM (S) 004588/08, r. 8 (trans. p. 58) and Blackstock, *Wednesday's Children*, p. 27 respectively; see Kahn-Minden, *The Road Back*, for

observations on a small group of ex-camp children with TB who were still in care in Britain in 1949.

115  Blackstock, *Wednesday's Children*, p. 27.

116  ibid.

117  ibid., p. 54.

118  See Rabinowitz, *New Lives*, pp. 94–5: Emil Wolf, a camp survivor, became depressed when diagnosed as having TB a few years after liberation. The loss of his hard-won independence and the thought of being institutionalised were difficult to come to terms with.

119  ibid., p. 102.

120  See Sington, *Belsen Uncovered*, pp. 193–200 for the administration involved in organising these transports.

121  For example, see Fried, *Fragments*, p. 185.

122  For example, see Sassoon, *Agnes*, p. 53; on returning to Hungary she became involved in the *Brichah* movement and eventually reached Israel herself.

123  On some of the difficulties in estimating the Jewish population in Belsen see Lavsky, 'The Day After'. There are few official figures on the number of DPs, and specifically Jewish DPs, in the Belsen camp. Indeed, the role of the camp as a centre for directing prospective illegal immigrants to Palestine, relied on there being ambiguity about the actual number of DPs. The Central Committee resisted calls from the British authorities to hold a census: see Ch. 3.

124  Ferderber-Salz, *And the Sun*, p. 220; see YV070/115–19, Rosensaft Papers, for a photographic record of everyday life in the Displaced Persons camp.

125  Z. Zamarion, 'A Shaliach in Belsen' in Leivick, *Belsen*, p. 178.

126  Wollheim in Leivick, *Belsen*, p. 60.

127  ibid., p. 66.

128  S.E. Bloch (ed.), *Holocaust and Rebirth: Bergen-Belsen 1945–1965*, New York, 1965, p. liii.

129  J. Rosensaft, 'Our Belsen' in Leivick *et al.*, *Belsen*, p. 42.

130  SUA Schonfeld 146/3: Bloomberg, director UNRRA Team 806 to Central Jewish Committee, 18 Nov. 1946. Elections were due in Sept. 1946, a year after the Belsen Congress, and the Central Committee promised UNRRA that an election would be called on 15 Nov. 1946. When no action was taken, Bloomberg gave notice of the election himself and, to ensure fair play, ruled that it would be held under the auspices of the UNRRA team and the voluntary organisations in Belsen. In fact, the election did not take place until March 1947.

131  YV 070/32, Rosensaft; candidates in the election stood for several parties including Agudat Yisrael, Eretz Israel Labour Party, Hashomer Hatzair, General Zionists, Mizrachi Torah V'avoda, Poalei Zion and Revisionists.

132  Leivick *et al*, *Belsen* (it was published by Irgun Sheerit Hapleita Me'haezor Habriti).

133  SUA Schonfeld 146/3: Rabbi Meisels to CCREC, 21 Nov. 1946.

134  Kehillah (Hebrew) describes an organised Jewish community or congregation, particularly such as were common in pre-war eastern Europe.

135  SUA Schonfeld 222, file 2: Breuer, Jewish Agency to Committee for Jews in Germany, 10 Dec. 1946. To follow up some of the issues affecting the religious communities see Tydor Baumel, 'Politics of Spiritual Rehabilitation', pp. 57–79.

136  SUA Schonfeld 233: Schonfeld to 'whom it may concern', 5 Dec. 1945.

137  SUA Schonfeld 151: CJG meeting minutes, 12 Dec. 1946.

138  SUA Schonfeld 146/3: Bloomberg to CCREC, 10 Oct. 1946 and reply 16 Oct. 1946.

139 SUA Schonfeld 151: report from (unnamed) rabbi in Belsen, 13 Nov. 1945.
140 SUA Schonfeld 222, file 2: Breuer to CCREC, 23 Oct. 1946.
141 SUA Schonfeld 151: Hertz to Brodetsky, 24 Oct. 1945.
142 SUA Schonfeld 222: minutes, special meeting CJG with Schonfeld and Rosensaft present, 20 June 1947.
143 SUA Schonfeld 151: minutes, CJG, 9 March 1946.
144 SUA Schonfeld 146/3: MacPhersons, 711/618/R Det. Military Government to Adath Sheerith Yisrael, 11 Nov. 1946.
145 SUA Schonfeld 222, file 1: Major Murray, 711/618/R Det. Military Government to Bloomberg, Oct 1946.
146 YV 070/27 and 30, Rosensaft.
147 The relationship, after a few initial hiccups, was generally good.
148 SUA Schonfeld 151: minutes, CJG, 1 Oct. 1945.
149 ibid.: minutes, CJG, 9 March 1946.
150 This latter figure, compared with other reports, seems like an under-estimate, particularly if we consider that during this period there was a large influx of infiltrees from Eastern Europe. The Anglo-American Committee of Enquiry Report, published in April 1947, quotes a figure of 9,000 for the Jewish population of Belsen; see note 123 on the problems involved in establishing the correct figure.
151 SUA Schonfeld 366: minutes, CBF Council meeting, 24 April 1946.
152 SUA Schonfeld 440/2: JCRA Volunteers' Newsletter, Oct./Nov. 1946, no. 20.
153 SUA CBF 24/129: JRU Monthly Report, April 1947.
154 SUA CBF 24/129: JRU (Team 110), report, 13 Nov. 1946.
155 SUA Schonfeld 366: JCRA Volunteers' Newsletter, March/April 1946, no. 16; on the hospital generally see YV 070/35, Rosensaft.
156 Leivick *et al.*, *Belsen*, p. 155.
157 Rosensaft in Bloch, *Holocaust and Rebirth*, p. 1.
158 SUA CBF 24/129: Survey of Educational Work in Bergen-Belsen, 30 July–10 Sept. 1946 by J. Weingreen; see YV 070/28, Rosensaft on education generally and /29 for the Yeshiva.
159 M. Lubliner, 'Jewish Education in Belsen' in Leivick *et al.*, *Belsen*, pp. 156–61.
160 SUA CBF 24/129: Survey of Educational Work.
161 SUA Schonfeld 440/2: minutes, CBF Council meeting, 19 Feb. 1947.
162 Not least because such enterprises gave a cover to the activities of those involved in organising illegal immigration to Israel: see Ch. 3.
163 ORT, meaning *Obszczestwo Rasprastranieniji Truda*, was originally founded as a response to the discrimination of the Tsarist regime: by giving training in skilled crafts and providing access to tools and equipment, ORT gave invaluable support to the Jewish communities in western Russia, providing effective means with which to help themselves. After the First World War the headquarters of the organisation moved to Berlin and focused on the training of pioneers for Palestine. See J. Olejski and L. Walinsky, *ORT in the US-Zone of Germany*, Munich, 1948 for a contemporary account of the work of the World ORT Union with the DPs in Germany. Also L. Shapiro, *The History of ORT: A Jewish Movement for Social Change*, New York, 1980.
164 SUA CBF 24/129: JCRA Bulletin, 28 Feb. 1949.
165 Quotation is from Weingreen's Report on Education; SUA Schonfeld 366: JCRA Volunteers' Newsletter, June/July 1946; SUA CBF 24/129: JRU Monthly Report, Jan.1949 and JCRA Bulletin, 6 Jan. 1949 – a number of hospital patients managed to attain ORT diplomas.
166 Sington, *Belsen Uncovered*, pp. 161–6.

167 See YV 070/31, /31A and /31B, Rosensaft, for information compiled on the theatre by Feder (Yiddish).
168 Feder in Leivick *et al.*, *Belsen*, p. 139.
169 YV 033/1306, Butnik; a tour to the USA was cancelled when the *Exodus* affair erupted in 1947.
170 Rosensaft in Leivick *et al.*, *Belsen*, p. 33; Perl, *Doctor in Auschwitz*, p. 186; SUA CBF 24/129: JRU (81 HQ) Monthly Report, Jan. 1949.
171 SUA CBF 24/129: JRU Monthly Report, Feb. 1949.
172 Wollheim in Leivick *et al.*, *Belsen*, p. 58.
173 Bloch, *Holocaust and Rebirth*, p. li.
174 Rosensaft in Leivick *et al.*, *Belsen*, p. 25.
175 SUA Schonfeld 222, file 2: minutes, CJG, 22 May 1946.
176 Bloch, *Holocaust and Rebirth*, p. liv.
177 SUA Schonfeld 366: Bentwich, report, undated.
178 Such an avenue of enquiry is outside the scope of this book. It is, however, crucial that such work is carried out before the witnesses are lost to us and it is too late to collect testimonies.
179 Sington, *Belsen Uncovered*, pp. 189–90.
180 See YV070/38–42, Rosensaft for miscellaneous copies of the publications produced in the camp. Copies of *Unzer Sztyme* are also held at the Wiener Library.
181 For example, see R. Olevski, D. Rosenthal and P. Trepman, *Our Destruction in Pictures*, Bergen-Belsen, 1946 and B. Friedler, *Back from Hell: Collected Sketches*, Bergen-Belsen, 1947. Both can be found in the Wiener Library, London, together with a microfilmed copy of the first List of Names of Survivors in Belsen, produced by the Jewish Committee in Sept. 1945.
182 Levi Eshkol, former Prime Minister of Israel in Bloch, *Holocaust and Rebirth*, p. 315.
183 Rosensaft in Leivick *et al.*, *Belsen*, p. 33.
184 SUA CBF 24/129: précis of Belsen reports, undated.
185 SUA CBF 24/129: JRU (81 HQ) report, Jan. 1950.

## CONCLUSION

1 Bauer, 'Death Marches'; see also the comments by Bridgman, *End of the Holocaust*, pp. 137–41.
2 See D.J. Goldhagen, *Hitler's Willing Executioners: Ordinary Germans and the Holocaust*, New York, 1996 for an important exception.
3 For example, Corgi books produced a series of paperbacks following on the success of Lord Russell of Liverpool's *The Scourge of the Swastika: A Short History of Nazi War Crimes*, London, 1954.
4 The quote is from the *Daily Telegraph*, 2 May 1995.
5 Bridgman, *End of the Holocaust*, p. 33.
6 Chamberlain and Feldman, *Liberation*, *passim*.
7 In April 1995 survivors, liberators and historians gathered in London on two occasions to mark the anniversary of the liberation of Belsen camp; first at the Imperial War Museum on 12 April and again at an international conference, 'The Liberation of Belsen', which took place on 9/10 April and was organised jointly by the Institute of Contemporary History and Wiener Library, London and the Parkes Library, Southampton. The proceedings from this conference formed an edited collection: J. Reilly, *et. al.*, (eds) *Belsen in History and Memory*, London, 1997, forthcoming; also published as a special issue of the *Journal of Holocaust Education*, vol. 5, nos. 2–3, Winter 1996.

8 Chamberlain and Feldman, *Liberation*, p. 174.
9 R. Barton, 'Belsen', *History of the Second World War*, 1979, no. 109, p. 3085.
10 D. Laurence, *Bernard Shaw: Collected Letters, 1926–1950*, Oxford, 1983, p. 752.
11 For articles printed on and around the actual anniversary of the liberation of Belsen see: the *Guardian*, 13 April 1995, section II, pp. 1–3, including the testimony of Tom Stretch and also 15 April, where Belsen is described as having given the 'most graphic and disturbing contemporary glimpse of the Holocaust'; the *Independent*, 13 April 1995 for an interview with Mr and Mrs Turgel, liberator and survivor who met in Belsen and later married; *Jewish Chronicle*, 14 April; the *Observer*, 16 April. The official German ceremony took place on 27 April 1995, after Passover. See: the *Guardian*, the *Independent*, *Daily Telegraph* and *Jewish Chronicle*, 28 April 1995, which attempted to incorporate the history of the Belsen camp with survivor testimony; also *The Times*, 28 April. The *Daily Telegraph*, 2 May 1995, in a fifty-year retrospective article, selects the liberation of Belsen as an important event but chooses in 1995, as in 1945, the testimony of an unusual *British* prisoner only.
12 Esther Brunstein interviewed by Monica Porter in the *Jewish Chronicle*, 14 April 1995, p. 28.

# Bibliography

## MANUSCRIPT SOURCES

### 1 Public archives

*Central Zionist Archive*, Jerusalem
  Papers of the British Section of the World Jewish Congress
*Greater London Record Office*
  Papers of the Chief Rabbi
*Hebrew University*, Jerusalem
  Institute of Contemporary History: oral history records
*Imperial War Museum*, London
  (a) *Department of Documents*
     Papers of various Belsen liberators
  (b) *Department of Sound Records*
     Sound recordings of interviews with liberators (including medical students) and survivors
*Manchester Jewish Museum*
  Papers of Sgt F. Kirby
  Sound recording: F. Bernstein
*Public Record Office*, London
  FO 371; FO 1005; FO 1010; FO 1030; FO 1049; FO 1060; WO 171; WO 177
*Southampton University Archive*, Southampton
  Papers of: Anglo-Jewish Association; Capt. A.C. Barclay; Central British Fund (microfilm); Council of Christians and Jews; Chief Rabbi Hertz; Dr Solomon Schonfeld
*Sussex University Library*, Falmer, Sussex
  Mass-Observation archive
*Wellcome Institute Archive*, London
  Papers of Brig. Glyn Hughes, DDMS, 2nd Army
  Papers of the RAMC
*Wiener Library*, London
  Central Jewish Committee, Bergen-Belsen: lists of survivors, September 1945
  Press cuttings, 1945
*Yad Vashem*, Jerusalem
  Papers of Josef Rosensaft
  Survivor memoirs and testimonies

## 2 Theses

R. Bolchover, 'Anglo-Jewish Responses to the Holocaust 1942–46', MPhil, University of London, 1992.
L. London, 'British Immigration Control Procedures and Jewish Refugees, 1933–1942', PhD, University of London, 1992.
J. Reilly, 'Britain and Belsen', PhD, University of Southampton, 1994.

## 3 Unpublished memoirs

L. Brilleman, 'This Is the Story of my Life and that of Others', Wiener Library, London.
A. Fink, 'My Lifestory', Wiener Library, London.
H. Kruskal, 'Two Years behind Barbed Wire: Factual Report of a Dutchman Describing his Experience under the German Oppression', Wiener Library, London.
A. Lasker-Wallfisch, 'Memoirs 1925–1946', Wiener Library, London.
A. Laurence, 'Dachau Overcome', Parkes Library, Southampton University.
A. Oppenheim, 'The Chosen People: the Story of the 222 Transport', Wiener Library, London.
I. Taubes, 'The Persecution of the Jews in the Netherlands 1940–1944', Jewish Central Information Office, London, 1945, Parkes Library, Southampton University.
[No author] Untitled memoir on Buchenwald, Lindsay Papers, Keele University Archive.

## 4 Interviews with the author

Eric Freedman, London, Summer 1993.
Rev. Leslie Hardman, London, Summer 1993.

## PRINTED SOURCES

## 1 Official and Press reports

*Hansard.*
*Jewish Telegraphic Agency Daily News Bulletin.*
Newspapers: *British Zone Review, Daily Herald, Illustrated London News, Jewish Chronicle, Jewish Standard, Manchester Guardian, Picture Post, The Times.*

## 2 Diaries, testimony, autobiographies, biographies

S. Baumgarten, 'A Belsen Diary', *Jewish Spectator*, Oct. 1945, vol. 10, no. 11.
N. Bentwich, 'The Relief Units in Germany', *Jewish Monthly*, Feb. 1948, no. 11, pp. 30–6.
N. Bentwich, *My 77 Years: An Account of my Life and Times, 1883–1960*, Philadelphia, PA, The Jewish Publication Society of America, 1961.
D. Bernstein, 'Europe's Jews, Summer 1947', *Commentary*, Aug. 1947, vol. 4, no. 2, pp. 101–9.
S. Bick-Berkowitz, *Where Are My Brothers?*, New York, Helies Books, 1965.
C. Blackstock, *Wednesday's Children*, London, Hutchinson, 1967.
M. Bourke-White, *Deutschland, April 1945*, Munich, Schimmer/Mosel, 1979.

S. Brodetsky, *Memoirs: From Ghetto to Israel*, London, Weidenfeld & Nicolson, 1960.

A. Bullock, *The Life and Times of Ernest Bevin: Vol. 3, Foreign Secretary, 1945–1951*, London, Heinemann, 1983.

M. Caiger-Smith, *The Face of the Enemy: British Photographers in Germany 1944–52*, Berlin, Nishen, no date.

B.M. Casper, *With the Jewish Brigade*, London, Golston, 1947.

R. Collis, *To Be A Pilgrim*, London, Secker & Warburg, 1975.

R. Collis and H. Hogerzeil, *Straight On (Journey to Belsen and the Road Home)*, London, Methuen, 1947.

W.R.F. Collis, 'Belsen Camp: A Preliminary Report', *British Medical Journal*, 9 June 1945, no. 21, p. 100.

R. du Cros, *ATA Girl*, London, Muller, 1983.

R. Crossman, *The Palestine Mission: A Personal Record*, London, Hamish Hamilton, 1947.

J. Dimbleby, *Richard Dimbleby, a Biography*, London, Hodder & Stoughton, 1975.

T. Driberg, *Ruling Passions*, London, Cape, 1977.

B. Ferderber-Salz, *And the Sun Kept Shining . . .* , New York, Holocaust Library, 1980.

T. Fitzgeorge-Parker, *Roscoe: the Bright Shiner: the Biography of Brigadier Roscoe Harvey DSO*, London, Severn House, 1987.

H. Fried, *Fragments of a Life: The Road to Auschwitz*, ed. and trans. (from Swedish) Michael Meyer, London, Hale, 1990.

B. Friedler, *Back from Hell: Collected Sketches*, Bergen-Belsen, privately printed, 1947.

M. Gilbert (ed., trans. J. Michalowicz), *Survivors of the Holocaust: The Kovno Ghetto Diary*, London, Pimlico, 1991.

M. Gilbert, *Churchill: A Life*, London, Heinemann, 1991.

C. Goodman, see L. Hardman.

P. Gordon Walker, *The Lid Lifts*, London, Victor Gollancz, 1945.

E. Hall Williams, *A Page of History in Relief*, York, Sessions Book Trust, 1993.

J. Hankinson, 'Belsen', *St Mary's Hospital Gazette*, 1945, no. 51.

L. Hardman, *The Survivors: The Story of the Belsen Remnant*, written by Cecily Goodman, London, Vallentine, Mitchell, 1958.

K. Hart, *I Am Alive*, London and New York, Abelard-Shuman, 1962.

K. Hart, *Return to Auschwitz*, London, Granada, 1983.

S.H. Herrmann, *Austauschlager Bergen-Belsen. (Geschichte eines Austausch-transportes)*, Tel Aviv, Irgun Olej Merkaz Europa, 1944.

A.J. Herzberg, *Amor Fati. Zeven opstellen over Bergen-Belsen*, Amsterdam, Mousault, 1947 (trans. J. Santcross, *Between Two Streams: a diary from Bergen-Belsen*, London, IB Tauris in assoc. with the European Jewish Publication Society, 1997).

R. Hewins, *Count Folke Bernadotte: His Life and Work*, London, Hutchinson, 1948.

R. Hilberg *et al.*, *The Warsaw Diary of Adam Czerniakow: Prelude to Doom*, New York, Stein and Day, 1979.

B. Horrocks, *A Full Life*, London, Lee Cooper, 1974.

E. Kahn-Minden, *The Road Back: Quare Mead*, New York, Gefen Books, 1991.

P. Kemp (ed.), *The Relief of Belsen, April 1945: Eyewitness Accounts*, London, Imperial War Museum, 1991.

F. Kersten, *The Kersten Memoirs 1940–1945*, London, Hutchinson, 1956.

Y. Kleiman and N. Springer-Aharoni (eds), *The Anguish of Liberation: Testimonies from 1945*, Jerusalem, Yad Vashem, 1995.

R. Laqueur, *Dagboek uit Bergen-Belsen maart 1944–april 1945*, Amsterdam, 1965; also published as *Bergen-Belsen – Tagebuch 1944/1945*, Hannover, Fackeltraeger, 1983.

A. Lasker-Wallfisch, *Inherit the Truth 1939–1945: the documented experiences of a survivor of Auschwitz and Belsen*, London, Giles de la Mare, 1996.

J. Lees-Milne, *Prophesying Peace*, London, Chatto & Windus, 1977.

P. Levi, *Survival in Auschwitz*, New York, Collier Books, 1960.

P. Levi, *If This Is A Man*, London, Sphere Books, 1987.

P. Levi, *The Drowned and the Saved*, London, Sphere Books, 1989.

I. Levy, *Witness to Evil*, London, Peter Halban, 1995.

H. Lévy-Hass, *Inside Belsen*, Brighton, Sx, The Harvester Press, 1982.

R.G. Lewin, *Witnesses to the Holocaust: An Oral History*, Boston, MA, Twayne, 1990.

W. Lindwer, *The Last Seven Months of Anne Frank*, trans. (from Dutch) Alison Mearsschaert, New York, Pantheon Books, 1991.

J. Maclaren-Ross, *Memoirs of the 40's*, London, Alan Ross, 1984.

L. Miall (ed.), *Richard Dimbleby, Broadcaster*, London, BBC, 1966.

C. Moorehead, *Sidney Bernstein, A Biography*, London, Jonathan Cape, 1984.

I. Morris, 'Belsen – a Letter', in *Aspects of Jewish Life and Education*, London, Joint Emergency Committee for Jewish Religious Education in Great Britain, 1945.

[no author] see end of section.

R. Olevski, D. Rosenthal and P. Trepman, *Our Destruction in Pictures*, Bergen-Belsen, privately printed, 1946.

P. Padfield, *Himmler*, London, Macmillan, 1990.

A. Paton, 'Mission to Belsen 1945', *British Medical Journal*, Dec. 1981, vol. 283, pp. 1656–9.

M. Peake, *Writings and Drawings*, London, Academy Editions, 1974.

R. Pearce (ed.), *Patrick Gordon Walker: Political Diaries 1932–1971*, London, Historian's Press, 1991.

G. Perl, *I Was a Doctor in Auschwitz*, Salem, NH, Ayer, 1992; reprint of work published New York, International University Press, 1948.

R. Phillips (ed.), *The Trial of Joseph Kramer and Forty-four Others*, London, William Hodge, 1949.

S. Ryder, *And the Morrow Is Theirs*, Bristol, Burleigh Press, 1975.

A. Sassoon, *Agnes: How My Spirit Survived*, Edgware, Mx, Today's Woman Publications, 1985.

M. Seizer, *The Last Hours at Dachau*, London, Sphere Books, 1980.

C. Seymour-Ure and J. Schaff, *David Low*, London, 1985.

D. Sington, *Belsen Uncovered*, London, Duckworth, 1946.

B.F. Skinner, *Beyond Freedom and Dignity*, London, Cape, 1972.

J. Sloan (ed. and trans.), *Notes from the Warsaw Ghetto: The Journal of Emmanuel Ringelblum*, New York, Schocken, 1974.

Sir J. Smyth, *The Will to Live: The Story of Dame Margot Turner*, London, Cassell, 1970.

B. Spanjaard, *Don't Fence Me In!*, Los Angeles, CA, B & B Publishing, 1985.

Lord W. Strang, *Home and Abroad*, London, Andre Deutsch, 1956.

S. Teveth, *Ben-Gurion: The Burning Ground 1886–1985*, Boston, MA, Houghton Mifflin Co., 1987.

*The Story of Belsen*, London, 113th Light Anti-Aircraft Regiment, Royal Artillery, 1945.

P. Trepman, *Among Men and Beasts*, trans. (from Yiddish) S. Perla and G. Hirschler, New York, A.S. Barnes, 1978.

M. Tribich, 'I Owe It to All Who Died to Tell My Story', *Woman's Own*, 27 April 1992.

G. Turgel, *I Light a Candle*, London, Grafton, 1987.

B. Urquhart, *A Life in Peace and War*, London, Weidenfeld & Nicolson, 1987.

J. Watney, *Mervyn Peake*, London, Michael Joseph, 1976.

W. Weinberg, *Self Portrait of a Holocaust Survivor*, Jefferson, NC, McFarland, 1985.

P. Wyand, *Useless if Delayed: Adventures in Putting History on Film*, London, Harrap, 1959.

[no author] 'The Medical Students at Belsen', *British Medical Journal*, 23 June 1945.

[no author] *The War Years, 1939–1945: Eyewitness Accounts*, London, 1994.


## 3 Articles

H. Arendt, 'The Stateless People', *Contemporary Jewish Record*, April 1945, vol. 8, no. 2, pp. 137–53.

Dr R. Barton, 'Belsen', *History of the Second World War*, 1979, no. 109, pp. 3080–5.

Y. Bauer, 'When Did They Know?', *Midstream*, April 1968, no. 14, pp. 51–8.

Y. Bauer, 'The Death Marches, January–May 1945', *Modern Judaism*, Feb. 1983, vol. 3, pt 1, pp. 1–21.

R. Breitman, 'The Allied War Effort and the Jews', *Journal of Contemporary History*, 1985, vol. 20, pp. 135–56.

S. Davidson, 'Transgenerational Transmission in the Families of Holocaust Survivors', *International Journal of Family Psychiatry*, 1980, vol. 1, no. 1, pp. 95–111.

L. Dawidowicz, 'Belsen Remembered', *Commentary*, 1966, vol. 41, no. 3, pp. 82–5.

N. Eck, 'The Rescue of Jews with the Aid of Passports and Citizenship Papers of Latin American States', *Yad Vashem Studies*, 1957, vol. 1, pp. 136–41.

J. Fine, 'American Radio Coverage of the Holocaust', *Simon Wiesenthal Centre Annual*, 1988, vol. 5, pp. 145–65.

F. Friesel, 'The Holocaust and the Birth of Israel', *Wiener Library Bulletin*, 1979, vol. 32, nos. 49–50, pp. 51–60.

M. Gara, comments, in 'Angels of D-Day', *Outlook*, April/May, 1994, pp. 22–5 (published by South West Trains).

L.P. Gartner, 'A Quarter Century of Anglo-Jewish Historiography', *Jewish Social Studies*, 1986, vol. 48, no. 2, pp. 105–26.

Y. Gelber, 'The Historical Role of the Central European Immigration to Israel', *Leo Baeck Institute Yearbook*, 1993, vol. 38, pp. 323–39.

S. Gewirtz, 'Anglo-Jewish Responses to Nazi Germany 1933–39: the Anti-Nazi Boycott and the Board of Deputies of British Jews', *Journal of Contemporary History*, April 1991, vol. 26, no. 2, pp. 255–76.

G. Gringanz, 'Jewish Destiny as the D.P.'s See It', *Commentary*, Dec. 1947, vol. 4, no. 6, pp. 501–9.

J. Harris, 'An Elegy for Myself: British Poetry and the Holocaust', *English*, Autumn 1992, vol. 41, no. 171, pp. 213–33.

E. Hearst, 'The British and the Slaughter of the Jews', *Wiener Library Bulletin*, 1967, vol. 21, no. 1, pp. 32–8 and vol. 22, no. 2, pp. 30–40.

M. Joyce Haron, 'Note: United States – British Collaboration on Illegal Immigration to Palestine, 1945–1947', *Jewish Social Studies*, 1980–1, vol. 42–3, pp. 177–82.

P. Kemp, 'The Liberation of Bergen-Belsen Concentration Camp in April 1945: the Testimony of those Involved', *Imperial War Museum Review*, 1990, no. 5, pp. 28–41.

A.J. Kochavi, 'British Policy on Non-Repatriable Displaced Persons in Germany and Austria, 1945–47', *European History Quarterly*, July 1991, vol. 21, no. 3, pp. 365–82.

M. Korzak, 'Women at War – a Celebration', *History Workshop*, Autumn 1977, no. 4, pp. 239–40.

T. Kushner, 'The British and the Shoah', *Patterns of Prejudice*, 1989, vol. 23, no. 3, pp. 3–16.

T. Kushner, 'The Impact of the Holocaust on British Society and Culture', *Contemporary Record*, 1991, no. 5, pp. 349–75.

H. Lavsky, 'The Day After: Bergen-Belsen from Concentration Camp to the Centre of the Jewish Survivors in Germany', *German History*, 1993, vol. 11, no. 1, pp. 36–59.

Z. Mankowitz, 'The Affirmation of Life in She'erith Hapleita', *Holocaust and Genocide Studies*, Spring, 1990, vol. 5, no. 1, pp. 13–21.

D. Michman, 'She'erit Hapletah, 1944–1948: Rehabilitation and Political Struggle', *Holocaust and Genocide Studies*, Spring 1993, vol. 7, no. 1, pp. 107-9.

P.L. Mollison, 'Observations on Cases of Starvation at Belsen' *British Medical Journal*, 5 Jan. 1946, pp. 4–8.

[no author] see end of section and prev. section.

J. Noakes, 'Social Outcasts in Nazi Germany', *History Today*, Dec. 1985, pp. 15–19.

J. Oppenheimer, 'Reflections on a Visit to Bergen-Belsen' *The Edinburgh Star*, Sept. 1990, no. 7, pp. 25–6.

G. Orwell, 'Anti-semitism in Britain', *Contemporary Jewish Record*, April 1945, pp. 163-71.

N. Pronay, 'British Newsreels in the 1930s', *History*, 1971, no. 56, pp. 411–18, and no. 57, pp. 63–72.

D. Prowe, 'Prospects for the New Germany: Reading the Historical Evidence 1945–60, 1989–91', *The Historian*, Autumn 1991, vol. 54, no. 1, pp. 19–34.

M. Raven, 'British Jewry in Heavy Weather', *Commentary*, May 1947, vol. 3, no. 5, pp. 447–55.

J. Reilly *et al.*, 'Belsen in History and Memory', special issue, *Journal of Holocaust Education*, vol. 5, nos. 2–3, Winter 1996.

J. Rosensaft, 'The Nameless Dead of Belsen', *World Jewry*, Nov. 1958, vol. 1, no. 9.

M. Rosensaft, 'The Mass Graves of Bergen-Belsen: Focus for Confrontation', *Jewish Social Studies*, 1978–9, vols 40–1, pp. 155–86.

L. Rothkirchen, 'The "Final Solution" in its Last Stages', *Yad Vashem Studies*, 1970, vol. 8, pp. 7–28.

G. Shimoni, 'Selig Brodetsky and the Ascendancy of Zionism in Anglo-Jewry (1939–1945)', *Jewish Social Studies*, 1980, vol. 22, pp. 117–48.

G. Shimoni, 'The Non-Zionists in Anglo-Jewry, 1937–1948', *Jewish Journal of Sociology*, 1986, vol. 28, no. 2, pp. 89–115.

A. Straeter, 'Denazification', *Annals of the American Academy of Political and Social Science*, Nov. 1948, issue on 'Postwar Reconstruction in Western Germany', pp. 43–52.

J. Tydor Baumel, 'The Politics of Spiritual Rehabilitation in the D.P. camps', *Simon Wiesenthal Centre Annual*, 1989, vol. 6, pp. 57–79.

E.E. Vella, 'Belsen: Medical Aspects of a World War II Concentration Camp', *Journal of the Royal Army Medical Corps*, 1984, no. 130, pp. 34–59.

R. Webster, 'American Relief and Jews in Germany, 1945–1960: Diverging Perspectives', *Leo Baeck Institute Yearbook*, 1993, vol. 38, pp. 293–321.

R. Webster, 'Why They Returned. How They Fared. Jews in Germany after 1945', *YIVO Annual of Jewish Social Science*, 1993.

R. Weltch, 'Ten Years after the War. A Changed Jewish World', *Association of Jewish Refugees Information*, May 1955, vol. X, no. 5, pp. 1, 5.

Y. Zerubavel, 'The Death of Memory and the Memory of Death: Masada and the Holocaust as Historical Metaphors', *Reflections*, 1994, no. 45, pp. 72–100.

R. Zimmerman-Wolf, 'Cain and Abel: a Belsen Camp Diary', *Wiener Library Bulletin*, Sept./Nov. 1951, vol. 5, nos. 5/6, p. 28.

[no author], 'President Heuss at the Belsen Memorial', *Association of Jewish Refugees Information*, Jan. 1953, vol. VIII, no. 1, p. 1.

[no author] 'Belsen Anniversary' *Association of Jewish Refugees Information*, May 1955, vol. X, no. 5, p. 4.

[no author] 'The Belsen Memorial' *Association of Jewish Refugees Information*, Aug. 1956, vol. XI, no. 8, p. 5.

[no author] 'Belsen Liberation Anniversary' *Association of Jewish Refugees Information*, Sept. 1965, vol. XX, no. 9, p. 16.


## 4 Books

R.H. Abzug, *Inside the Vicious Heart: Americans and the Liberation of Nazi Concentration Camps*, New York, Oxford University Press, 1985.

G. Alderman, *Modern British Jewry*, Oxford, Oxford University Press, 1992.

Y. Arad, *Ghetto in Flames: The Struggle and Destruction of the Jews in Vilna in the Holocaust*, New York, Holocaust Library, 1982.

Y. Arad, *Belzec, Sobibor, Treblinka: The Operation Reinhard Death Camps*, Bloomington, IN, Indiana University Press, 1987.

Y. Arad *et al.* (eds), *The Einsatzgruppen Reports: Selections from the Dispatches of the Nazi Death Squads' Campaign Against the Jews, July 1941–January 1943*, New York, 1989.

M. Balfour, *Propaganda in War, 1939–1945*, London, Routledge & Kegan Paul, 1979.

M. Banton, *The Coloured Quarter*, London, Cape, 1955.

Y. Bauer, *Flight and Rescue*, New York, Random House, 1970.

Y. Bauer, *American Jewry and the Holocaust: The American Jewish Joint Distribution Committee, 1939–1945*, Detroit, MI, Wayne State University Press, 1981.

Y. Bauer, *A History of the Holocaust*, London, Franklin Watts, 1982.

Y. Bauer, *Out of the Ashes: The Impact of the American Jews on Post-Holocaust European Jewry*, Oxford, Pergamon Press, 1989.

S. de Beauvoir, *The Second Sex*, London, Pan Books, 1988.

N. Bentwich, *They Found Refuge: An Account of British Jewry's Work for Victims of Nazi Oppression*, London, Cresset Press, 1956.

A. Berger (ed.), *Bearing Witness to the Holocaust 1939–1989*, New York, Edwin Mellor, 1991.

M. Berghahn, *Continental Britons: German-Jewish Refugees from Nazi Germany*, Oxford, 1988, a reprint of *German-Jewish Refugees in England: The Ambiguities of Assimilation*, Basingstoke, Berg, 1984.

C. Bermant, *The Cousinhood*, London, Eyre & Spottiswoode, 1971.

S.E. Bloch (ed.), *Holocaust and Rebirth: Bergen-Belsen 1945–1965*, intro. J. Rosensaft, New York, Bergen-Belsen Memorial Press, 1965.

R. Bolchover, *British Jewry and the Holocaust*, Cambridge, Cambridge University Press, 1993.

G. Brayburn, *Women Workers in the First World War: The British Experience*, London, Croom Helm, 1981.

J. Bridgman, *The End of the Holocaust: The Liberation of the Camps*, London, Batsford, 1990.

A. Briggs, *The History of Broadcasting in the U.K.*, Volume IV, *Sound and Vision*, Oxford, Oxford University Press, 1979.

M. Broszat, *The Hitler State: The Foundation and Development of the Internal Structure of the Third Reich*, trans. J.W. Hiden, Longman, London, 1981.

C.R. Browning, *The Final Solution and the German Foreign Office*, London, Holmes & Meier, 1978.

C.R. Browning, *Fateful Months: Essays on the Emergence of the Final Solution*, New York, Holmes & Meier, 2nd edn, 1991.

C.R. Browning, *The Path to Genocide: Essays on Launching the Final Solution*, Cambridge, Cambridge University Press, 1992.

M. Burleigh and W. Wipperman, *The Racial State: Germany 1933–45*, Cambridge, Cambridge University Press, 1991.

C. Burney, *The Dungeon Democracy*, London, Toronto, Heinemann, 1945.

P.G. Cambray and G.G.B. Briggs, *The Official Record of the Humanitarian Services of the War Organisation of the British Red Cross Society, 1939–47*, British Red Cross, 1949.

D. Cesarani (ed.), *The Making of Modern Anglo-Jewry*, London, Basil Blackwell, 1990.

D. Cesarani, *Justice Delayed: How Britain Became a Refuge for Nazi War Criminals*, London, Heinemann, 1992.

D. Cesarani (ed.), *The Final Solution: Origins and Implementation*, London, Routledge, 1994.

B. Chamberlain and M. Feldman (eds), *The Liberation of the Nazi Concentration Camps, 1945: Eyewitness Accounts of the Liberators*, Washington, DC, US Memorial Council, 1987.

M.J. Cohen, *Palestine: Retreat from the Mandate. The Making of British Policy, 1936–1945*, London, Elek, 1978.

C. Connolly (ed.), *The Golden Horizon*, London, Weidenfeld & Nicolson, 1953.

F.A.E. Crew, *Medical History of the Second World War. Army Medical Services Campaigns*, Vol. 4, *N. W. Europe*, London, HMSO, 1962.

D. Czech, *The Auschwitz Chronicle 1939–45*, London, Tauris, 1990.

L. Dawidowcz, *The War Against the Jews, 1939–1945*, Harmondsworth, Penguin, 1975.

L. Dawidowicz, *The Holocaust and the Historians*, Cambridge, MA, Harvard University Press, 1981.

L. Dinnerstein, *America and the Survivors of the Holocaust*, New York, Columbia University Press, 1982.

L. Dobroszycki (ed.), *The Chronicle of the Lodz Ghetto 1941–1944*, New Haven, CT, Yale University Press, 1984.

A. Donat (ed.), *The Death Camp Treblinka*, New York, Holocaust Library, 1979.

F.S.V. Donnison, *Civil Affairs and Military Government in North West Europe 1944–46*, London, HMSO, 1961.

D. Dwork, *Children with a Star*, New Haven, CT and London, Yale University Press, 1991.

A. Eisenberg, *Witness to the Holocaust*, New York, Pilgrim, 1981.

S.D. Ezrahi, *By Words Alone: The Holocaust in Literature*, Chicago, University of Chicago Press, 1980.

K. Feig, *Hitler's Death Camps: The Sanity of Madness*, New York, Holmes & Meier, 1979.

P. Fussell, *The Great War and Modern Memory*, New York and London, Oxford University Press, 1975.

P. Fussell, *Wartime: Understanding and Behavior in the Second World War*, New York, Oxford, Oxford University Press, 1989.

H. Genizi, *America's Fair Share: The Admission and Resettlement of Displaced Persons, 1945-1952*, Detroit, MI, Wayne State University Press, 1993.

M. Gilbert, *Auschwitz and the Allies*, London, Michael Joseph, 1981.

M. Gilbert, *Atlas of the Holocaust*, London, Michael Joseph, 1982.

M. Gilbert, *The Holocaust: The Jewish Tragedy*, London, Fontana, 1986.

M. Gilbert, *Road to Victory*, London, Minerva, 1988.

M. Gilbert, *The Second World War*, London, Weidenfeld & Nicolson, 1989.

M. Gilbert, *The Boys, Triumph over Adversity*, London, Weidenfeld & Nicolson, 1996.

A. Gill, *The Journey back from Hell: Conversations with Concentration Camp Survivors*, London, Grafton Books, 1988.

L. Gilliam, *BBC Features*, London, Evans, 1950.

M. Godecke *et al.*, *Bergen-Belsen: Explanatory Notes on the Exhibition*, Hanover, Niedersächsische Landeszentrale für politische Bildung, 1991.

D.J. Goldhagen, *Hitler's Willing Executioners: Ordinary Germans and the Holocaust*, New York, Knopf, 1996.

S.J. Goldsmith, *Twenty Twentieth-Century Jews*, New York, Shengold, 1962.

V. Gollancz, *What Buchenwald **Really** Means*, London, Gollancz, 1945.

J. Gorny, *The British Labour Movement and Zionism, 1917–1948*, London, Frank Cass & Co., 1983.

H. Graml, *Antisemitism in the Third Reich*, Oxford, Blackwell, 1992.

J. Greenwood, *Quaker Encounters*, York, William Sessions, 1975.

R. Griffiths, *Fellow Travellers of the Right: British Enthusiasts for Nazi Germany 1933–1939*, Oxford, Oxford University Press, 1983.

A. Grobman, *Rekindling the Flame: American Jewish Chaplains and the Survivors of European Jewry, 1944–1948*, Detroit, MI, Wayne State University Press, 1993.

R. Grunberger, *A Social History of the Third Reich*, Harmondsworth, Mx, Penguin, 1971.

W. Günther, *'Ach Schwester, ich kann nicht mehr tanzen . . . ' Sinti und Roma im KZ Bergen-Belsen*, Hanover, Niedersächsische Verband deutscher Sinti e.V., 1990.

Y. Gutman, *The Nazi Concentration Camps: Proceedings of the Fourth Yad Vashem International Historical Conference in Jerusalem, January 1984*, Jerusalem, Yad Vashem, 1984.

Y. Gutman, *The Jews of Warsaw, 1939–43: Ghetto, Underground, Revolt*, trans. I. Friedman, Brighton, Sx, Harvester, 1982.

Y. Gutman and C.J. Haft (eds), *Patterns of Jewish Leadership in Nazi Europe, 1933–45: Proceedings of the Third Yad Vashem International Historical Conference*, Jerusalem, Yad Vashem, 1979.

A. Hass, *In the Shadow of the Holocaust. The Second Generation*, London, I.B. Tauris, 1991.

D. Hawkins (ed.), *War Report: A Record of Dispatches Broadcast by the BBC War Correspondents with the Allied Expeditionary Force, 6 June 1944–5 May 1945*, London, Oxford University Press, 1946.

R. Hilberg, *The Destruction of the European Jews*, New York, Holmes & Meier, rev. edn, 1985.

G. Hirschfeld (ed.), *The Policies of Genocide: Jews and Soviet Prisoners of War in Nazi Germany*, London, Allen & Unwin, 1986.

A. Jefferson and D. Robey, *Modern Literary Theory*, London, Batsford, 2nd rev. edn, 1988.

Z. Josephs, *Survivors: Jewish Refugees in Birmingham 1933–1945*, Oldbury, Meridian, 1988.

J. Keegan (ed.), *Encylopedia of the Second World War*, London, Bison Books, 1990.

I. Kershaw, *The Nazi Dictatorship: Problems and Perspectives of Interpretation*, London, Edward Arnold, 2nd edn, 1989.

P. Knauth, *Germany in Defeat*, New York, 1946.

E. Kogon, *The Theory and Practice of Hell*, New York, Octagon Books, 1979.

E. Kolb, *Bergen-Belsen: From 'Detention Camp' to Concentration Camp, 1943–1945*, Göttingen, Vandenhoeck & Ruprecht, 2nd rev. edn, 1986.

H. Krausnick *et al.*, *Anatomy of the SS State*, London, Collins, 1968.

T. Kushner, *The Persistence of Prejudice: Anti-semitism in British Society during the Second World War*, Manchester, Manchester University Press, 1989.

T. Kushner, *The Holocaust and the Liberal Imagination*, Oxford, Blackwell, 1994.

H. Langbein, *Against All Hope. Resistance in the Nazi Concentration Camps 1939–1945*, London, Constable, 1994.

L.L. Langer, *The Holocaust and the Literary Imagination*, New Haven, CT, Yale University Press, 1975.

L.L. Langer, *Versions of Survival: The Holocaust and the Human Spirit*, Albany, NY, SUNY Press, 1982.

L.L. Langer, *Holocaust Testimonies: The Ruins of Memory*, New Haven, CT, Yale University Press, 1991.

W. Laqueur, *The Terrible Secret*, London, Weidenfeld & Nicolson, 1980.

D. Laurence, *Bernard Shaw: Collected Letters, 1926–1950*, Oxford, Clarendon Press, 1983.

H. Leivick *et al.*, *Belsen*, Tel Aviv, Irgun Sheerit Hapeita Mehaezor Habriti, 1957.

H. Letherby-Tidy (hon. ed.), *Inter-Allied Conferences on War Medicine 1942–1945*, London, Staple Press, 1947.

N. Levin, *The Holocaust: The Destruction of European Jewry, 1933–1945*, New York, Schocken Books, 1973.

V.D. Lipman, *Social History of the Jews in England 1850–1950*, London, Watts, 1954.

I. Litten, *'All the Germans' – Are They Really Guilty?*, London, Gollancz, 1945.

W.M. Louis, *The British Empire in the Middle East, 1945–1951*, Oxford, Clarendon Press, 1984.

D. Low, *Years of Wrath: A Cartoon History 1932–1945*, London, Gollancz, 1986.

J. Lucas, *Last Days of the Reich*, London, Arms and Armour Press, 1986.

R.C. Lukas, *The Forgotten Holocaust: The Jews under German Occupation 1939–1944*, Lexington, Ky, University Press of Kentucky, 1986.

B. McBryde, *Quiet Heroines: Nurses of the Second World War*, London, Chatto & Windus, 1985.

I. McLaine, *Ministry of Morale: Homefront Morale and the Ministry of Information in the Second World War*, London, Allen & Unwin, 1979.

M.R. Marrus, *The Unwanted: European Refugees in the Twentieth Century*, Oxford, Oxford University Press, 1985.

M.R. Marrus, *The Holocaust in History*, London, Weidenfeld & Nicolson, 1988.

M.R. Marrus (ed.), *The Nazi Holocaust*, Vols. 1–9, Westport, CT and London, Meckler, 1989.

A. Marwick, *Britain in the Century of Total War*, London, Bodley Head, 1968.

J. Mendelsohn, *The Holocaust*, Vols. 12 and 14, New York, Garland, 1982.

K. Millett, *Sexual Politics*, London, Virago, 1989.

G. Mosse, *Toward the Final Solution: A History of European Racism*, Madison, WI, University of Wisconsin Press, 1985.

[no author] see end of this section.

J. Olejski and L. Walinsky, *ORT in the US-Zone of Germany*, Munich, World ORT Union, 1948.

Dame B. Oliver, *The British Red Cross in Action*, London, Faber, 1966.

S. Orwell and I. Angus (eds), *The Collected Essays, Journalism and Letters of George Orwell*, Vol. III, *'As I Please' 1943–45*, London, Secker & Warburg, 1968.

P. Panayi (ed.) *Racial Violence in Britain, 1840–1950*, Leicester, Leicester University Press, 1993.

P. Panayi, *Minorities in Wartime*, Oxford, Berg, 1993.

J. Parkes, *Antisemitism*, London, Vallentine, Mitchell, 1963.

M. Pasley (ed.), *Germany: A Companion to German Studies*, London, Methuen, 2nd edn, 1982.

M. Peake, *Titus Alone*, Harmondsworth, Mx, Penguin, 1970.

W.H. Pehle (ed.), *November 1938: From 'Reichskristallnacht' to Genocide*, New York, Oxford, Berg, 1991.

L. Poliakov, *Harvest of Hate*, Oxford, Oxford University Press (for the Littman Library), 1956.

L. Poliakov, *The History of Anti-Semitism*, Vol. 4, Oxford, Oxford University Press, 1985.

L. Poliakov, *The Aryan Myth: A History of Racist and Nationalist Ideas in Europe*, New York, Basic Books, 1974.

T. des Pres, *The Survivor: An Anatomy of Life in the Death Camps*, New York, Oxford University Press, 1976.

M.J. Proudfoot, *European Refugees: 1939–1952*, London, Faber, 1957.

D. Rabinowitz, *New Lives: Survivors of the Holocaust Living in America*, New York, Knopf, 1976.

A. Read and D. Fisher, *Kristallnacht: Unleashing the Holocaust*, London, Michael Joseph, 1989.

J. Reilly *et al.* (eds), *Belsen in History and Memory*, London, Frank Cass, 1997.

G. Reitlinger, *The Final Solution: The Attempt to Exterminate the Jews of Europe 1939–1945*, London, Vallentine, Mitchell, 2nd edn, 1968.

A. Rosenberg and G. Myers (eds), *Echoes from the Holocaust*, Philadelphia, PA, Temple University Press, 1988.

A.H. Rosenfeld and I. Greenburg (eds), *Confronting the Holocaust: The Impact of Elie Wiesel*, Bloomington, IN and London, Indiana University Press, 1978.

Lord Russell of Liverpool, *The Scourge of the Swastika: A Short History of Nazi War Crimes*, London, Cassell, 1954.

A.L. Sacher, *The Redemption of the Unwanted: From the Liberation of the Nazi Death Camps to the Founding of Israel*, New York, 1983.

K.A. Schleunes, *The Twisted Road to Auschwitz*, Urbana, IL, Illinois University Press, 1970.

L. Schwartz, *The Redeemers: The Saga of the Years 1945–1952*, New York, Farrer, Strauss and Young, 1953.

R. Schwertfeger, *Women of Theresienstadt: Voices from a Concentration Camp*, Oxford, Berg, 1989.

T. Segev, *The Seventh Million: The Israelis and the Holocaust*, trans. Haim Watzman, New York, Hill & Wang, 1993.

V. Selwyn (ed.), *More Poems of the Second World War: The Oasis Selection*, London, Dent & Sons, 1989.

C. Seymour-Ure, *The British Press and Broadcasting Since 1945*, Oxford, Blackwell, 1991.

L. Shapiro, *The History of ORT: A Jewish Movement for Social Change*, New York, Schocken Books, 1980.

A. Sharf, *The British Press and Jews under Nazi Rule*, London, Institute of Race Relations, 1964.

A.J. Sherman, *Island Refuge: British Refugees from the Third Reich, 1933–1939*, 2nd edn, Ilford, Essex, Frank Cass, 1994.

C. Shindler, *Exit Visa: Detente, Human Rights and the Jewish Emigration Movement in the USSR*, London, Bachman & Turner, 1978.

K.R.M. Short and S. Dolezel, *Hitler's Fall: The Newsreel Witness*, London and New York, Croom Helm, 1988.

G. Steiner, *In Bluebeard's Castle: or, Some Notes Towards a Redefinition of Culture*, London, Faber & Faber, 1971.

P. Summerfield, *Women Workers in the Second World War*, London, Croom Helm, 1984.

C. Supple, *From Prejudice to Genocide: Learning about the Holocaust*, Stoke-on-Trent, Staffs, Trentham Books, 1993.

E. Taylor, *Women Who Went To War*, London, Robert Hale, 1988.

R. Thurlow, *Fascism in Britain: a History 1918–1985*, Oxford, Blackwell, 1987.

N. Tolstoy, *Victims of Yalta*, London, Hodder and Stoughton, 1977.

H. Trevor-Roper, *The Last Days of Hitler*, London, Macmillan, 1947.

N.E. Tutorow (ed.), *War Crimes, War Criminals and War Crime Trials – An Annotated Bibliography and Source Book*, New York, Greenwood Press, 1987.

W. Warhaftig, *Uprooted: Jewish Refugees and Displaced Persons after Liberation*, New York, Institute of Jewish Affairs of the American Congress and the WJC, 1946.

B. Wasserstein, *Britain and the Jews of Europe 1939–1945*, Oxford, Clarendon Press for the Institute of Jewish Affairs, 1979.

R. Wilson, *Quaker Relief: An Account of the Relief Work of the Society of Friends 1940–48*, London, George Allen & Unwin, 1952.

T. Wilson, *The Myriad Faces of War*, Cambridge, Polity Press, 1987.

G. Woodbridge, *U.N.R.R.A.*, 3 vols., New York, Columbia University Press, 1950.

D.S. Wyman, *The Abandonment of the Jews: America and the Holocaust, 1941–1945*, Toronto, Associated University Presses, 1984.

M. Wyman, *The D.P.'s: Europe's Displaced Persons 1945–1951*, Philadelphia, PA, Balch Institute Press, 1989.

L. Yahil, *The Holocaust: The Fate of European Jewry 1932–1945*, New York, Oxford University Press, 1990.

J.E. Young, *Writing and Rewriting the Holocaust: Narrative and the Consequences of Interpretation*, Bloomington, Indiana University Press, 1988.

R.W. Zweig, *Britain and Palestine during the Second World War*, London, Boydell Press (for the Royal Historical Society), 1986.

# Index